WJEC/EDUQAS

Religious Studies for A Level & AS

Religion and Ethics

Revised Edition

Richard Gray
Peter Cole
Nick Heap

Edited by Richard Gray

hachette LEARNING

The Publishers would like to thank the following for permission to reproduce copyright material.

Bible quotes are from THE HOLY BIBLE, NEW INTERNATIONAL VERSION®, NIV® Copyright © 1973, 1978, 1984, 2011 by Biblica, Inc.® Used by permission. All rights reserved worldwide.

Qur'an quotations are from The Holy Qur'an translated by Abdullah Yusuf Ali.

Although every effort has been made to ensure that website addresses are correct at time of going to press, Hachette Learning cannot be held responsible for the content of any website mentioned in this book. It is sometimes possible to find a relocated web page by typing in the address of the home page for a website in the URL window of your browser.

Hachette UK's policy is to use papers that are natural, renewable and recyclable products and made from wood grown in well-managed forests and other controlled sources. The logging and manufacturing processes are expected to conform to the environmental regulations of the country of origin.

To order, please visit www.HachetteLearning.com or contact Customer Service at education@hachette.co.uk / +44 (0)1235 827827.

ISBN: 978 1 0360 0493 4

First published in 2020

This edition published in 2026 by

Hachette Learning (a trading division of Hodder & Stoughton Limited),

An Hachette UK Company

Carmelite House

50 Victoria Embankment

London EC4Y 0DZ

www.HachetteLearning.com

The authorised representative in the EEA is Hachette Ireland, 8 Castlecourt Centre, Dublin 15, D15 XTP3, Ireland (email: info@hbgi.ie)

Impression number 10 9 8 7 6 5 4 3 2 1

Year 2030 2029 2028 2027 2026

Illustrations by Integra Software Services Pvt. Ltd., Pondicherry, India.

Typeset in India by Integra Software Services Pvt. Ltd., Pondicherry, India.

Printed and bound in Great Britain by Bell and Bain Ltd, Glasgow.

A catalogue record for this title is available from the British Library.

Contents

About this book

With the A Level in Religious Studies, there is a lot to cover in preparation for the examinations at the end of the course. The aim of these books is to provide enough support for you to achieve success at A Level, whether as a teacher or a learner.

This series of books is skills-based in its approach to learning, which means it aims to combine covering the content of the specification with examination preparation from the start. In other words, it aims to help you get through the course while at the same time developing some important skills needed for the examinations.

To help you study, there are clearly defined sections for each of the AO1 and AO2 areas of the specification. These are arranged according to the specification themes and use, as far as is possible, specification headings to help you see that the content has been covered.

The AO1 content is detailed but precise, with the benefit of providing you with references to both religious/philosophical works and to the views of scholars. The AO2 responds to the issues raised in the specification and provides you with ideas for further debate, to help you develop your own evaluation skills.

Ways to use this book

In considering the different ways in which you may teach or learn, it was decided that the books needed to have an inbuilt flexibility to adapt. As a result, they can be used for classroom learning, for independent work by individuals, as homework, and they are even suitable for the purposes of 'flip learning' if your school or college does this.

You may be well aware that learning time is valuable at A Level and so we have also taken this into consideration by creating flexible features and activities, again to save you the time of painstaking research and preparation, either as teacher or learner.

Features of the books

The books all contain the following features that appear in the margins, or are highlighted in the main body of the text, in order to support teaching and learning.

Key term boxes define technical, religious and philosophical words or phrases.

Key term

casuistry: the art of applying key principles to an ethical case

Key quote boxes provide quotations from religious and philosophical works and/or the works of scholars.

Key quote

I … decided, after investigating everything carefully from the very first, to write an orderly account.

(Luke 1:3)

Key person boxes summarise essential figures.

Key person

St Augustine (354–430 CE): Bishop of Hippo in North Africa; his response to the Pelagian controversy shaped Christian teaching on original sin, grace and predestination; his key works were *Confessions* and *City of God*.

AO1 activities serve the purpose of focusing on identification, presentation and explanation, and developing the skills of knowledge and understanding required for the examination. This helps with presenting a thorough and extensive knowledge and understanding of the topic area.

AO1 Activity

Using bullet points, outline the key ideas in both the classical and modern forms of the problem of evil.

AO2 activities serve the purpose of focusing on conclusions, as a basis for thinking about the issues, developing critical analysis and the evaluation skills required for the examination.

AO2 Activity

Listed below are some conclusions that could be drawn from the AO2 reasoning in the accompanying text:

Specification content boxes highlight exactly what is being covered in each section and how it connects to the specification.

Specification content

The extent to which the classical form of the problem of evil is a problem.

A **glossary** of all the key terms is provided for quick reference.

AO2 skills: critical analysis and evaluation

A good way to prepare yourself for an AO2 part (b) evaluation answer is to consider the different ways to approach this. Sometimes writing frames or anacronyms may be suggested. While these are useful, they are meant as 'scaffolding' or support for an answer, but the danger is that they end up restricting more natural and personal evaluation.

One useful approach is to think about some different styles of writing and relate these to 'characters' that are easily remembered.

Strong evaluative characters

We can look at what are considered **strong evaluative character styles** that display all the qualities that avoid the pitfalls above. By this we mean different aspects, elements or ingredients of an effective critical analysis and evaluation.

If we look at the table that follows, we can see seven characters, each of which has a specific strength and quality that display skills of critical analysis and/or evaluation. The strength of each character forms a **part** of a strong evaluation. In a full AO2 answer it may be useful to vary the characters in terms of depth and breadth.

The characters can be used as a checklist not a structured plan or rigid writing frame. The best way to use them is to consider the different styles and skills **before** writing an answer and then measure your answer by checking that the critical analysis and evaluation elements are there.

Examples of this can be seen in the sample answers we provide. In these sample answers you may notice that not all the character styles have been used in the same order, detail or combination; however, generally, most are often covered.

In the table below, we have attempted to demonstrate how each character may fulfil the criteria for a band 5 evaluation using the descriptors it presents. These are in bold text in the third column.

Character	Strength	Application and AO2 band descriptor link
Tennis player	• The tennis player deals with specific lines of arguments (often from either named scholars or schools of thought) and returns counter arguments. • The tennis player manages arguments and counter arguments, making sure there is consideration of several lines of argument in response to the statement in the question. • This is sometimes understood as 'for' or in support of an argument and 'against'; however, this does not necessarily always have to be done in an even or balanced way since some answers may wish to argue effectively towards a conclusion that is supported by several lines of reasoning, evidence and argument that support each other.	• The tennis player ensures that **thorough, sustained and clear views are given** in an answer. • The tennis player also ensures that the **views of scholars/ schools of thought are used extensively**.
Detective	• The detective has a forensic ability to examine, collate and clarify evidence and provide examples. The detective makes sure that the argument presented is substantial in that it is based in evidence and examples to support the reasoning presented. • The detective selects details that are accurate and relevant in a thorough way. They make sure that there is correct reference to specialist language in the correct context.	• The **views of scholars/schools of thought are used appropriately and in context**. • There is a **thorough and accurate use of specialist language and vocabulary in context**.
Philosopher	• The philosopher likes to raise and ask interesting and relevant questions. • The philosopher often indicates that there may be problems or challenges to a specific approach and likes to suggest a solution. • When an argument or analysis is in 'full flow' we may think of questions that we would like to raise in response to views analysed. The philosopher loves to do this.	• The philosopher character is typical of **perceptive evaluation**. • The philosopher successfully **identifies the issues raised by the question set**.

Character	Strength	Application and AO2 band descriptor link
News reporter	• The news reporter provides perspective, clarity, an overview of the debate. Commentary is vital in an AO2 answer as it demonstrates that the student is engaging with the debate that the statement presents. It is an easy way to demonstrate that you are thinking about the issues. • The best way to provide yourself with an opportunity to develop a more personalised approach is to practise pausing and reflecting upon points made, developing them with evidence and examples and commenting on the qualities a line of argument possesses.	• Using a news reporter style ensures that a response **thoroughly addresses the issues raised by the question set.**
Explorer	• The explorer likes to suggest some alternative ways of answering a question. Sometimes it feels as though a debate needs a different angle, approach or perspective. The explorer often suggests new ways of attempting to arrive at a solution to the debate. • This can often be your own response in considering a given statement including a new suggestion or perhaps a question you would like to raise. • You can even try to bring in other strands and evidence beyond the immediate topic from other areas of the course.	• This ensures that there is **confident and perceptive analysis of the nature of connections between the various elements of the approaches studied.**
Critical thinker	• The critical thinker points out more technical aspects of an argument. The critical thinker is often concerned with how an argument 'works' and 'flows'. • The critical thinker sometimes challenges more forensic aspects of an argument. • The critical thinker checks for coherence and consistency. Does the evidence support the conclusion? Is there a counter argument?	• The critical thinker ensures that there is **extensive, detailed reasoning** in an answer.
Judge	• The judge makes an overall ruling and concludes matters. The judge in some ways is the most vital character. They cannot stand alone and rely upon others and their contributions to make a final decision. This can be in favour or against the statement, or, it may be that the statement itself is questionable. • Often an overall judgement ends an answer; however, sometimes an overall conclusion may start the answer and then discuss, analyse and reason why this may be the case. • Strong evaluative answers often have several judgements or mini-conclusions throughout the answer.	• The judge is the final voice of an answer. They may appear anywhere in an answer but usually summarises at the end. The judge should be clear evidence of **confident critical analysis**.

Summary of a strong evaluative answer

- Offers clear, sustained and varied lines of argument (view) like the exchanges of a tennis player.
- The varied evidence of scholarly views and schools of thought are precisely examined and coherently presented like the report of a detective.
- Issues are identified to focus on, and questions may be raised like a philosopher.
- Engages with a debate by offering commentary and reflection upon the points presented like a news reporter.
- May explore some new ways of answering the question and possibly refer to other elements of the course like an explorer.
- Contains reasoning that is detailed, ordered, coherent and effective like a critical thinker.
- Ensures there is an overall judgement made that clearly links to the reasoning and evidence contained in the answer like a judge.

Introduction to ethical thought

Ethics is the study of the guiding principles and systems of **moral** values that direct human action. It involves analysing how these values lead to moral goodness and identifying the obligations underlying the choice to do right rather than wrong.

A framework of guiding principles is known as an ethical theory. For a 'moral agent', acting consistently within such a framework constitutes moral behaviour. Choosing to act against these principles is defined as acting immorally. In this academic context, immoral actions are more than simple errors; they indicate a failure to meet a required standard or a specific moral obligation.

Key terms

ethics: from the Greek *ethike*, meaning habit or behaviour, and closely related to the word *ethos*; a study of the framework of guiding principles that direct an action

moral: a term used to describe ethical behaviour

Ethics provides frameworks to help us find our way through complex moral decisions

Meta-ethics, normative and applied ethics

In the study of ethics, there are three separate fields:

- **Meta-ethics** is the study of the nature of ethical thinking. It involves considering why we act as we do and whether 'right' and 'wrong' are dependent upon self-interest, subjective views or objective standards.
- **Normative ethics** is the study of the content of, or the principles that underlie, ethical theories.
- **Applied ethics** is the study of the debates that arise when normative ethical theories are used to address practical issues in the real world.

Ethics, then, considers the meaning behind terms such as 'moral' and 'right', studies proposed theories that outline 'moral' behaviour, and considers how such theories work in practice.

Key terms

meta-ethics: the debates that arise when the *nature* of ethics is considered

normative ethics: the debates that arise when ethical *theories* are considered (normative refers to norms of behaviour – how we should behave)

applied ethics: the debates that arise when ethical *issues* are considered

Categories of ethical theories

Philosophers have identified common links between various ethical theories and have categorised them into groups.

Absolutism

Absolutists believe that there is a standard of right and wrong that is fully and totally binding on all human beings. This standard is objective and unchanging, regardless of culture or individual opinion. For the absolutist, a wrong action is something they are under a binding obligation never to do. An absolutist would maintain: 'This is wrong for me, for you and for everyone.' There are two forms of absolutism:

- **Religious absolutism**: the standard proceeds from the mind and will of a supreme being
- **Non-religious absolutism**: the standard simply exists as a factual part of the universe

Key terms

absolutist: someone who believes in absolutism, a standard of right and wrong that is fully and totally binding on all human beings; describes something connected with absolutism

relativist: someone who believes in relativism, an ethical system in which there is no absolute right or wrong; describes something connected with relativism

subjective: describes something that is dependent on a personal view

objective: describes something that is independent of personal views

Relativism

Relativists believe there is no absolute right or wrong. They do not view morality as a binding obligation but as a response of human communities to social issues. While there are no absolute rules, there are norms of behaviour that promote desirable objectives, such as goodwill and happiness.

A relativist might find an action morally wrong but would find it difficult to conclude that everyone else should feel the same. They would maintain: 'This is wrong for me, but it may be right for you.'

Key quote

At the descriptive level, certainly, you would expect different cultures to develop different sorts of ethics and obviously they have; that doesn't mean that you can't think of overarching ethical principles you would want people to follow in all kinds of places.

(Singer)

Subjectivism

An ethical theory is **subjective** if its truth is dependent on the view or feelings of the individual. As the modern philosopher J.L. Mackie observed: 'What is often called moral subjectivism is the doctrine that, for example, "This action is right" means "I approve of this action."'

Distinction between subjectivism and relativism

While it is common to link subjectivism with relativism, these terms are distinct. One might conclude that values originate from personal feelings (subjectivism) but believe those feelings are universal to all humans. This results in an ethical theory that is subjectively grounded but holds to absolute values.

Objectivism

An ethical theory is **objective** if its truth is independent of a person's view. This is often referred to as moral realism – the idea that moral values exist as facts, similar to mathematical numbers. As the modern philosopher Julia Driver commented: 'I can't see 2 + 2 = 4; I know it to be true nevertheless [...] Am I justified in believing in moral facts? If I am justified believing in numbers [...] then yes.'

Key terms

teleological: concerned with the end purpose or goal of an action

***telos*:** a Greek word meaning 'end', 'goal' or 'purpose'; in ethics, it refers to the ultimate aim or outcome that an action is directed towards

Teleological (consequentialist)

Philosophers often categorise ethical systems based on whether the morality of an action lies in its result or in the nature of the act itself.

The term **teleological** comes from the Greek ***telos***, meaning 'end' or 'purpose'. Teleological theories focus on the goal, result or consequences of an action to determine its morality.

If a theory holds that 'the good of the majority' is the criterion for right action, then the right behaviour is whatever produces that specific result. In this approach, it is the outcome, not the act itself, that is decisive. This means that an action which might usually be considered wrong could be justified if it leads to a better end result. Because of this emphasis on results, teleological theories are also known as **consequentialist** theories.

Deontological

The term **deontological** comes from the Greek *deon*, meaning 'obligation' or 'duty'. Deontological theories focus on the acts themselves, irrespective of the consequences produced by those acts.

If a theory holds that certain actions are inherently right or wrong, then it is each person's duty to do the inherently right thing, regardless of the consequences in the situation. In this approach, it is the act, not the outcome, that is decisive. This means that a 'good' consequence cannot justify an action that is fundamentally wrong, such as murder or lying.

Applied ethics is the point at which these principles are tested. It often involves an ethical dilemma – a conflict between set principles – which challenges a person to re-examine and re-interpret their moral framework.

Key terms

consequentialist: refers to the theory that the morality of an action is based on the outcomes it produces

deontological: concerned with obligation or duty

T1

Ethical thought

A: Divine command theory

Specification content

Divine command theory

Divine command theory

According to divine command theory (DCT), God has established eternal, objective principles of morality. Moral values are not discovered through human reason or social consensus but have been revealed through the commands of a supreme being. As the modern philosopher William Frankena put it: 'The standard of right and wrong is the will or law of God.'

Specification content

God as the origin and regulator of morality

God as the origin and regulator of morality

Followers of DCT accept that an objective standard for ethics exists, but they maintain that this standard is not external to God. Instead, it originated entirely with God. In simple terms, that which God has said is good is good. Consequently, God acts as the sole regulator of the moral universe.

Specification content

Right or wrong as objective truths based on God's will/command

Right or wrong as objective truths based on God's will/command

Right and wrong are objective truths because they are grounded in God's specific will and command, rather than being human inventions or based on subjective feelings.

For DCT to function, there must be a method by which God's objective principles are communicated to humanity. This is achieved through revelation. Rather than relying on human intuition or logical deduction, the moral agent looks to sacred texts, such as the **Decalogue** (Ten Commandments), or direct divine communications.

Key term

Decalogue: a term for the Ten Commandments

In this framework, moral knowledge is not something humans invent or discover through science or philosophy; it is a gift granted by God. Consequently, the study of ethics becomes an act of interpreting and applying revealed law.

Specification content

Moral goodness is achieved by complying with divine command

Moral goodness is achieved by complying with divine command

Under this framework, moral goodness is achieved solely by complying with divine command. J.A.T. Robinson clarified this position in *Honest to God*: 'They are the commandments which God gives, the laws which he lays down [...] They come down direct from Heaven, and are eternally valid for human conduct.'

For the believer, an action is right 'if and only if and because' it is commanded by God. This creates a duty-based system where certain actions are always 'sins', regardless of whether human societies judge them to be crimes. St Augustine reinforced this by noting that even the general law against killing can have exceptions if the authority comes from God's 'express command'.

In this system, the motivation for being good is rooted in the relationship between the Creator and the created. Because God is the source of all life and the sustainer of existence, the obligation to obey is absolute. Obedience is not merely about avoiding punishment or seeking reward, but about acknowledging God's total **sovereignty**. This is why the theory is often linked to the concept of piety – the idea that the highest moral act is the humble submission of one's own will to the superior will of the Divine.

Divine command a requirement of God's omnipotence

DCT is often seen as a necessary consequence of God's **omnipotence**. If God were to command certain actions because they were already good in their own right, it would imply a standard of goodness that exists independently of God. If such an external standard existed, God would no longer be the creator of everything, as there would be a set of values outside of divine control. To protect the doctrine of omnipotence, it must be the case that the ethical template originates with God alone.

DCT stands in contrast to systems that promote **ethical autonomy** (the idea that humans can decide for themselves what is right) as an ethical approach whereby morality is based on the will of God. The Latin word for will is *voluntas*, which is why another name for DCT is **theological voluntarism**.

Under DCT, human reason is viewed as limited or even fallen. While reason might help a person understand how to follow a command, it is not considered a valid tool for deciding what the command should be. As William of Ockham suggested, the authority of the command does not depend on whether it seems logical to a human mind, but solely on the fact that it was issued by God. He supports this radical view of divine power, suggesting that even actions we consider 'evil' (such as theft or adultery) could be rendered meritorious if God were to command them, as God is not bound by any law higher than his own will.

Key quotes

I reply that hatred, theft, adultery, and the like may involve evil according to the common law, in so far as they are done by someone who is obligated by a Divine Command to perform the opposite act. As far as everything absolute in these actions is concerned, however, God can perform them without involving any evil. And they can even be performed meritoriously by someone on earth if they should fall under a Divine Command, just as now the opposite of these, in fact, fall under a Divine Command.

(William of Ockham)

There are, however, certain exceptions to the law against killing, made by the authority of God himself. There are some whose killing God orders, either by law, or by an express command to a particular person at a particular time.

(St Augustine)

Key term

sovereignty: supreme and absolute power

Specification content

Divine command a requirement of God's omnipotence

Key terms

omnipotence: the attribute of being all-powerful; in DCT, this implies God is not limited by any external moral law

ethical autonomy: the view that human reason is capable of discovering or creating moral laws independently

theological voluntarism: an ethical approach whereby morality is based on the will of God

Divine command as an objective metaphysical foundation for morality

DCT is an objective metaphysical foundation for morality. This means that right and wrong are not just biological accidents or social labels but are woven into the very fabric of reality by the Creator. Because God sets the rules, they are universal and apply to all people across all time and in all places.

When describing this foundation, it can be argued that morality is treated as a 'brute fact' of the universe. Just as laws of physics (like gravity) dictate the movement of physical bodies, divine commands dictate the movement of the moral agent. This makes morality a permanent feature of existence. For the proponent of DCT, rightness is a property bestowed upon an action by God's word, making that action fundamentally different from an un-commanded one.

Specification content

Divine command as an objective metaphysical foundation for morality

Robert Adams' modified DCT

Specification content

Robert Adams' 'modified divine command theory' (divine command based on God's omnibenevolence)

Key person

Robert Adams (1937–): An American philosopher and theologian; his best-known contribution to the philosophy of religion is his modified DCT, in which he explains that moral conduct is based not merely on God's power, but on God's essentially loving and omnibenevolent character

Key term

omnibenevolence: being all-loving

Robert Adams developed modified DCT to address specific logical difficulties found in the traditional version of the theory. Adams refined the theory to ensure that morality remains objective while being consistent with the **omnibenevolence** attributed to God.

Adams proposes that morality is not based solely on the power or will of God, but specifically on the character of God. Adams argues that because morality is grounded in the character of God, who is perfectly good, then God's commands are necessarily rooted in that character. Since a characteristic of God is his omnibenevolence (all-loving nature), then whatever God commands will inevitably reflect this.

For Adams, the statement '*x* is wrong' is equivalent to '*x* is contrary to the commands of a loving God'. Morality cannot be arbitrary because it is grounded in the unchanging, omnibenevolent nature of God. An action is ethically wrong if and only if it is contrary to the commands of a loving God.

Adams argued that goodness is an essential characteristic of God; it is in God's nature. Therefore, goodness is a matter of being like God. Since God is the ultimate standard of excellence and love, things are good in so far as they resemble God.

In this framework, an action is only a moral command if it is commanded by a God who is loving. Morality, therefore, always reflects the omnibenevolent character of God. This ensures that God is not subject to a moral law that exists external to him, but neither are his commands random.

Since God is essentially loving, it is 'morally unthinkable' that he would command cruelty. If such a command were ever issued, it would mean that the being issuing the command was not the loving God of Adams' theory. Therefore, the command would lack the objective metaphysical foundation required to make an action 'right'.

Adams also emphasises that morality exists within a social relationship between humans and God. He suggests that moral commands are a form of social requirement within this relationship. Just as a child might follow a parent's guidance because of the loving relationship they share, humans follow divine commands as a response to the love God has shown for humanity. This shifts the focus from a legalistic form of DCT to a morality based on relationship and character.

Challenges to DCT

Proponents of DCT argue that the theory provides a clear, objective and universal foundation for morality that bypasses the uncertainties of human opinion or cultural relativism. By grounding right and wrong in the commands of an omnipotent and omnibenevolent creator, it offers the moral agent an absolute sense of duty and a definite purpose for ethical behaviour.

The Euthyphro dilemma (inspired by Plato)

Plato wrote a dialogue entitled *Euthyphro*, in which a character named Euthyphro takes his father to court, charging him with murder. His father failed in care and attention and allowed a worker to die. Socrates is at the court awaiting his own trial, and so he engages Euthyphro in a dialogue about moral goodness. In the dialogue Socrates poses the question that has become known as the Euthyphro dilemma. Euthyphro states:

> Well, I should certainly say that what's holy is whatever all the gods approve of, and that its opposite, what all the gods disapprove of, is unholy [...]

Socrates then raises the question:

> Consider the following point: is the holy approved by the gods because it's holy, or is it holy because it's approved?

As generally applied in a philosophical and monotheistic context, Socrates is asking whether God commands things because they are good in themselves or things are good because God commands and approves them. Put simply, does good exist independently, and separate from approval, or does good exist as a consequence of it being approved?

Key quote

The idea that God could just decree that all that we thought evil was in fact good and vice versa seems to make a mockery of the seriousness of ethics. It makes right and wrong ultimately arbitrary.

(Baggini)

The challenge from the Euthyphro dilemma is traditionally seen to have two aspects to it, often referred to as the 'two horns' of the dilemma.

1 Is morality arbitrary if it is down to the command of a divine being?

If an action is good simply because God commands it, then morality is dependent on divine whim; if God were to command something typically viewed as harmful, it would, by definition, become good.

2 If God decides upon what is good because it is already right and good independent of God, is morality a standard external to God?

In this case, God is no longer the origin of morality but is instead subject to an independent moral law. Consequently, the dilemma may be suggesting that morality is indeed a matter external to God, which challenges the concept of divine omnipotence and the idea of God as the ultimate creator of all values.

Key quote

Morality, for the modified divine command theorist, is ultimately grounded in the perfect nature of God.

(Austin)

Specification content

Challenges: the Euthyphro dilemma (inspired by Plato); arbitrariness problem (DCT renders morality as purely arbitrary); pluralism objection (different religions claim different divine commands)

Socrates

Key quote

If there are reasons why God deems an action to be 'right' or 'wrong', then it is really those reasons that provide the account of 'right' and 'wrong' and not God's will.

(Driver)

Arbitrariness problem (DCT renders morality as purely arbitrary)

The problems raised by the Euthyphro dilemma are numerous, but a significant one is: if something is good solely because God wills it, then could God will what is generally considered evil to be good? As Frankena put it:

> If God were to order the exact opposite of what we generally take him to have ordered or of what we take to be right, then, by the hypothesis in question, this would be what we ought to do.

Key quote

God sets the moral rules and God's rules apply to all, irrespective of time and place. The problem here is that, actually, there are reasons to believe that God, if he exists, is the greatest relativist of them all.

(Baggini)

This is often referred to as the arbitrariness problem: that morality is not based on reason or justice, but on the shifting whims of a divine being.

Certainly, some have argued that this arbitrary nature is in keeping with depictions of God and his followers in the Bible. As the modern philosopher Julian Baggini points out: 'Christian texts seem to provide evidence that this is precisely what their God has done.'

This was justified further in the writings of William of Ockham, an English friar and scholastic philosopher born in the thirteenth century, who argued that God can perform acts that, according to common law, are evil, but without involving any evil. Baggini further notes that if God sets the rules and can change them at will, it implies a lack of fixed moral stability.

Robert Adams, in his modified DCT, has addressed this matter by pointing out that both the arbitrariness and external objectivity issues are resolved when one considers divine command as an expression of God's omnibenevolence. By grounding commands in an unchanging, loving character, Adams attempted to move morality away from 'whim'.

However, not all philosophers are convinced by this move. For some, this just extends the problem rather than solving it. For example, Baggini perceptively observes: 'This doesn't seem to work, however, because the dilemma can just be restated: is God's nature good because it is good or good because it is God's?'

If God's nature is good because it aligns with a standard of goodness, then that standard is independent of God. If it is good simply because it is God's nature, we have returned to the original problem of arbitrariness. The debate about whether Robert Adams' modified DCT provides a successful escape from this dilemma continues.

Pluralism objection (different religions claim different divine commands)

A significant challenge to DCT arises from the fact that there are numerous religious traditions worldwide, each proposing different ethical systems and principles. This is known as the pluralism objection. If morality is grounded solely in the command of God, the existence of contradictory commands from different religions raises the question of which system, if any, is the correct one. While some common moral ideas can be identified across various religions, the differences are often fundamental and seemingly incompatible.

The problem of pluralism is twofold:

- There is the issue of identifying which religion holds the true divine command. For instance, the absolute principle of *ahimsa* (non-violence) found in some Eastern traditions may stand in direct conflict with the concept of 'just war' found in some Western monotheistic traditions.
- There is the problem of variety and interpretation within any single religion. Even if one accepts a specific religion, there is rarely a consensus on what the 'divine command' actually is.

Within Islam, different law schools offer varying interpretations of *shari'a*; within Buddhism, there are different applications of the precepts; and within Christianity, there is significant debate over the application of the law of the Old Testament. Even central virtues can conflict; for example, the command 'Thou shalt not kill' is often challenged by the principle of ***agape*** (selfless love) when applied to complex ethical issues such as abortion or euthanasia.

Pluralism also manifests through minority groups within a religion proposing specific interpretations of texts that the majority may reject. This often involves reading historical religious texts as containing absolute divine commands for the modern world. Issues ranging from women's rights to social punishments highlight this internal conflict.

For example, certain interpretations of biblical texts have been used to condemn homosexuality, referencing passages like Leviticus 20:13:

> If a man has sexual relations with a man as one does with a woman, both of them have done what is detestable. They are to be put to death; their blood will be on their own heads.

This creates a dilemma for DCT: if a command is viewed as a direct decree from God, it would logically require strict adherence, such as the application of the death penalty. However, such an application is contrary to contemporary law and the wider teachings of tolerance and forgiveness found elsewhere in the tradition, as taught by Jesus.

This raises the question of whether a divine command can be relative to a particular historical and social context. If commands like those concerning the use of clothing made of mixed fibres (Leviticus 19:19) are now seen by Christians as irrelevant or superseded, it appears that human moral understanding has evolved independently of the original 'command'. The pluralism objection highlights that DCT often lacks the flexibility to adapt to changing moral landscapes. If different religions and different eras produce different commands, it becomes difficult to maintain that morality is based on an eternal, objective metaphysical foundation.

Summary

- DCT asserts that morality is objective and originates solely from the commands of God.
- As an expression of God's omnipotence, DCT maintains that there is no moral standard external to God; right and wrong are facts established by divine will.
- Moral goodness is achieved through obedience to these commands, creating a duty-based system where actions are right 'if and only if and because' God decrees them.
- Adams' modified DCT addresses the problem of arbitrariness by grounding divine commands in God's unchanging, omnibenevolent character rather than mere power.
- The Euthyphro dilemma challenges the theory by asking whether an action is good because God commands it or God commands it because it is already good.
- The arbitrariness problem suggests that if morality is based solely on divine whim then even actions typically considered evil could theoretically be commanded as good.
- The pluralism objection highlights the difficulty of identifying a single divine moral code, given the contradictory commands found across different religions and the varied interpretations within them.

Key term

***agape*:** Greek word for pure, unconditional love

AO1 Activity

a Outline the key points of DCT and modified DCT.

This will demonstrate your ability to select and present the key relevant features of God as the origin and regulator of morality.

b On small revision cards, summarise the three challenges to DCT. Support the summary with evidence, such as short quotations.

When you have completed the task, refer to the band descriptors for AS (WJEC) or A Level (Eduqas). In particular, look at the demands described in the higher band descriptors, towards which you should be aspiring. Band 5 requires that your answer demonstrates a 'thorough, accurate and relevant' response that 'addresses the question fully' using 'extensive use of evidence and examples' and 'specialist language and vocabulary' that is 'thorough and accurate.'

This section covers AO2 content and skills

Specification content

Whether morality is what God commands

Issues for analysis and evaluation

Whether morality is what God commands

Possible line of argument	Critical analysis and evaluation
The central claim of DCT is that morality originates solely with the will of God. This provides an objective, universal template for human behaviour, grounding right and wrong in a secure metaphysical foundation rather than subjective human opinion.	The Euthyphro dilemma challenges this by asking if God commands what is good because it is already good or if it is good because God commands it. This suggests morality might be either arbitrary or independent of God.
Adams defends DCT through his modified version. He argues that because morality is grounded in God's unchanging, omnibenevolent character, his commands cannot be arbitrary. In this view, goodness is not external to God but is a reflection of his nature.	Baggini rejects Adams' response, noting that it merely moves the problem back a step. He asks whether God's nature is good because it aligns with a standard of goodness, or good simply because it is God's, which leaves the dilemma unresolved.
Supporters of DCT, such as William of Ockham, emphasise divine sovereignty. They argue that as an omnipotent creator, God is not subject to any higher law, and his commands must be obeyed regardless of whether they align with human logic.	This raises the 'arbitrariness problem'. If God can command anything, then actions typically viewed as evil could theoretically be good. This conflicts with the concept of omnibenevolence and makes morality appear to be based on divine whim rather than reason.
A strength of DCT is its consistency with religious belief, offering a clear sense of duty and absolute moral truths. By following revealed law, moral agents avoid the risks of cultural relativism and the burden of creating their own ethical systems.	The pluralism objection highlights the lack of a single, consistent divine message. Conflicting commands between different religions – and varying interpretations within them – suggest that 'divine' morality is often relative to social and historical contexts.
DCT provides a strong framework for believers, because – especially in its modified form – there is no contradiction of, or issue with, any commands since they are always made by an omnibenevolent God.	For believers, it is difficult to reconcile historical and outdated 'commands' with the idea of an all-loving, objective moral regulator; for non-believers the whole concept of DCT is superfluous as there is no God.

AO2 Activity

a Evaluate three possible conclusions that could be drawn from the critical analysis and evaluation of the view that morality is what God commands.

b Try to evaluate the strengths and weaknesses of each conclusion and determine what challenges could be used against each.

When you have completed the task, refer to the band descriptors for AS (WJEC) or A Level (Eduqas). In particular, look at the demands described in the higher band descriptors, towards which you should be aspiring. Band 5 requires that your answer demonstrates 'a confident critical analysis and perceptive evaluation' of the issue and is 'a response that successfully identifies and thoroughly addresses the issues raised by the question set'.

Specification content

Whether one of DCT, virtue theory or ethical egoism is superior to the other theories

Exam practice

Note: This question draws on material from sub-themes 1A, 1B and 1C. You may wish to return to this exercise after completing all three sub-themes.

Below is an example of part of an evaluation of the extent to which one of DCT, virtue theory or ethical egoism is superior to the other theories.

Sample answer

Evaluating the superiority of DCT, virtue theory and ethical egoism requires assessing whether morality should be grounded in external commands, internal character or self-interest.

Tennis player The match is set with a clear opening and a balanced field of play.

DCT is often considered superior due to its consistency. As an absolutist and universal system, it provides clear moral boundaries sourced from religious texts. This offers certainty, removing the burden of subjective decision-making from the individual.

Judge This paragraph establishes a strong case for the importance of clarity and tradition.

However, DCT is frequently viewed as inferior due to its inflexibility. Critics argue it lacks the internal depth of virtue theory. Even within Christianity, the teachings of Jesus suggest that developing a virtuous character is more significant than simply adhering to rigid codes.

Philosopher The tension between external rules and internal character is captured effectively here.

DCT also struggles with modern dilemmas like embryology or euthanasia, which are not in ancient texts. In contrast, virtue theory and ethical egoism offer adaptable frameworks that promote individual reasoning and tolerate diverse personal outcomes in private matters.

Explorer

News reporter Navigating modern ethical terrain requires the flexibility found in these alternative systems.

A significant weakness of DCT is that it may hinder moral growth. By demanding obedience, it can ignore the importance of intention and reflection. Virtue theory and ethical egoism, however, require the agent to take responsibility for their choices.

Critical thinker Evaluating the role of human agency is vital when comparing these three theories.

Philosopher

This highlights a sophisticated shift from *doing* the right thing to *being* a good person.

Detective

Uncovering the true motives of the individual reveals a pragmatic side to this ethical debate.

Critical thinker

Explorer

This radical focus on *eigenheit* challenges the very foundations of traditional moral authority.

Judge

The final verdict acknowledges that the 'best' theory depends on the foundational values of the individual.

Virtue theory excels by focusing on the agent's long-term flourishing – *eudaimonia*. It suggests that morality is a habit-based skill, making it more holistic and practical than the command-based structure of DCT.

Ethical egoism provides a unique alternative by prioritising the agent's self-interest. It recognises the psychological reality of human motivation, arguing that a system based on personal flourishing is more realistic than perceived religious self-sacrifice.

Max Stirner develops egoism by rejecting *gespenster* – fixed ideas like the state or religion – which enslave the individual. He argues that true superiority lies in achieving *eigenheit*, where the individual is no longer a servant to external frameworks.

Ultimately, superiority is a matter of perspective. For those seeking objective authority, DCT remains a strong model. However, for those valuing autonomy and character, virtue theory and ethical egoism offer more relevant frameworks for the modern world.

Over to you

For this first task, try using the writing frame provided below to help you practise the AO2 skills to answer the question. Keep in mind what is required by the higher band descriptors – particularly the need for 'confident, critical analysis and perceptive evaluation'. When you have completed the task, check whether your response 'successfully identifies and thoroughly addresses the issues raised by the question set'.

Question

'The challenges to DCT clearly show it is not a good ethical theory.' Evaluate this view. (Eduqas AS Level 2024)

Writing frame

1. The issue for debate here is about the challenges to DCT. The theory asserts that …
2. Critics often point to the Euthyphro dilemma and the problem of arbitrariness to show that …
3. Furthermore, the pluralism objection suggests that DCT is difficult to apply in the modern world because …
4. On the other hand, proponents of the theory, such as Robert Adams, would reject the statement on the grounds that …
5. It is my view that … and this argument is based on the following reasons …

B: Virtue theory

An ethical system based on personal qualities

While DCT establishes morality through external obedience to a higher authority, other ethical systems look inward to the individual. Virtue theory represents a shift from following specific rules or commands to focusing on the development of a person's underlying character and moral disposition.

Virtue theory locates morality in the internal qualities and nature of a human person. Right and wrong are not determined by an objective list of laws, but by the personal qualities that an individual exhibits through their daily behaviour. This approach suggests that being moral is a matter of possessing the right characteristics which then direct how a person lives and interacts with others.

The focus of this theory is the development of a person's character rather than the analysis of specific, individual actions. This makes virtue theory neither deontological nor teleological.

The analogy of a fruit tree is useful here. While other ethical systems judge a person by the fruit they produce – asking whether a specific act was good, bad, right or wrong, or if it led to a good result – virtue theory is concerned with the health of the person's roots – their character. Just as a tree produces good fruit because it is healthy (it does not become healthy simply by producing a single piece of good fruit), so does a person, by focusing on cultivating the virtuousness of their own character, ensure that their behaviour will naturally be morally correct. In this sense, the theory is more concerned with the state of being (the roots) than the specific act of doing (the fruit).

Specification content

Ethical system based on defining the personal qualities that make a person moral; the focus on a person's character rather than their specific actions

Aristotle's moral virtues

Key person

Aristotle (384–22 BCE): An ancient Greek philosopher who studied under Plato and tutored Alexander the Great; he founded the Lyceum in Athens and wrote on many topics of philosophy, science and ethics; in *The Nicomachean Ethics*, he put forward his moral theory of virtue and the concept of *eudaimonia* on which modern virtue ethics is based

Virtue theory is grounded in **Aristotle**'s book *The Nicomachean Ethics*. The origins of virtue theory tie in with Aristotle's wider view of the universe, specifically the four causes and the concept of teleology, which is the idea that everything has an ultimate goal or purpose. For humans, this purpose is found in the development of character.

Key quote

Every art and every inquiry, and similarly every action and pursuit, is thought to aim at some good; and for this reason the good has rightly been declared to be that at which all things aim.

(Aristotle)

Specification content

Aristotle's moral virtues (based on the deficiency; the excess and the mean)

Aristotle

Key terms

hexis: a Greek word meaning a person's manner of behaviour
ethos: a Greek word meaning the character of a person, as expressed in habits and behaviour
eudaimonia: a Greek word used by Aristotle to define the end purpose of human life as happiness, flourishing or fulfillment
arete (plural, ***aretai***): a Greek word meaning virtue
aretaic ethics: another term for virtue theory

Key quote

Happiness, then, is something final and self-sufficient, and is the end of action.

(Aristotle)

Key quote

People have recognisable reasons for doing what is right because doing what is right, it is argued, is likely to lead to their happiness. Morality and personal happiness are entwined.

(Cave)

Key quote

Virtue, then, being of two kinds, intellectual and moral, intellectual virtue in the main owes both its birth and its growth to teaching (for which reason it requires experience and time), while moral virtue comes about as a result of habit, whence also its name (*ethike*) is one that is formed by a slight variation from the word *ethos* (habit).

(Aristotle)

The focus of virtue theory is on the quality, manner or disposition (***hexis***) of a human being. Right or wrong are therefore not a matter of rules, but of the personal character (***ethos***) and qualities that an individual exhibits in their behaviour. Virtue theory is concerned with how an individual can develop the correct character to behave virtuously and, accordingly, act in a way that is morally correct.

The concept of ***eudaimonia*** is key to understanding virtue theory. For Aristotle, this meant 'well-being' or flourishing in the sense of being successful or fulfilled. It is not a static quality but rather an activity of the virtuous person; it is the end product or outcome generated by being virtuous. In one sense it might be argued that this makes virtue theory teleological as it has the overall goal of *eudaimonia*.

It is through cultivating virtues (***arete***) that a person creates the good life. The Greek term *arete* means virtue, but it also conveys the meaning of moral excellence, intellectual excellence and also physical excellence. Virtue is the idea of being how we are meant to be or being 'fit for purpose'. This is why virtue theory is also known as **aretaic ethics**. Creating such a life cannot be done in isolation – it requires a social context enabling people to live together successfully.

Aristotle devotes a significant section of his work to the virtue of justice. He argues that justice is unique because it is not just one individual quality, but the collective outcome of all virtuous behaviour. For Aristotle, justice is 'virtue entire' because it represents a person using their moral excellence in relation to their neighbour and the community. In this sense, being a just person is the ultimate expression of a virtuous character.

When an individual achieves this state of virtuous character and social justice, they reach the ultimate goal of human life. However, this sense of fulfillment is not identical for everyone, as it depends on the focus of one's life. To explain this, Aristotle identified three aspects of happiness:

- a life of enjoyment
- a life with freedom
- a life of reflection and contemplation (lived by the philosopher).

The overall characteristic that maintains all three is wisdom. Such a state is not easily gained; as Aristotle noted, seeing 'one swallow does not make a summer nor does one day; and so too one day, or a short time, does not make a man blessed and happy.' Thus, the good life is developed over a complete lifetime.

Moral and intellectual virtues

According to Aristotle, there are two kinds of virtue: moral and intellectual. Such virtues are not easily learned; they must be cultivated carefully. Aristotle compares the development of such virtues to a sketch that gradually develops into a picture.

Moral virtues are acquired through habit and developed through practice:

courage	proper pride	wittiness
temperance	proper ambition	friendliness
liberality	patience	modesty
generosity	truthfulness	righteous indignation

Intellectual virtues are developed through education and the guidance of reason:

Virtue	Description
intelligence	insight and understanding
scientific knowledge	knowledge gained by demonstration and conclusion
wisdom	the highest form of reflection and contemplation
artistic endeavour	creating or making through the guidance of reason
prudence	common sense to make the right choice in practical matters

For Aristotle, cultivating virtues involves balancing the two extremes of excess and deficiency. Each extreme brings with it an associated vice. Balancing the virtues and achieving the **mean** is no easy feat: 'Hence also it is no easy task to be good. For in everything it is no easy task to find the middle.'

Aristotle's doctrine of the mean suggests that individuals differ in their ability to maintain the balance between extremes. The virtue is the mean: the specific balance found between two extremes of behaviour. However, this balance is not the same for everyone; for example, the mean amount of food can vary considerably between people based on factors such as their activity levels and genetics. In ethics, **courage** for a soldier in battle looks different from courage for a person standing up to a bully.

Finding the mean requires the use of practical wisdom to determine the appropriate response at the right time, towards the right people and for the right reason.

Aristotle categorises people into three types based on their relationship with temptation and the mean:

- **The *sophron* (the virtuous)**: They live within the mean without effort. Their desires are perfectly aligned with reason – they do not feel the temptation to fall into excess or deficiency.
- **The *enkrates* (the continent)**: They feel the temptation of the vices but possess the strength of will to overcome them – they ultimately choose to live within the mean.
- **The *akrates* (the incontinent)**: They lack the self-control to overcome temptation. Even if they know what the mean requires, they are governed by their emotions or desires and fail to act virtuously. This state of being overcome by temptation is known as ***akrasia***.

Key terms

mean: the rationally determined balance between the two extremes of excess and deficiency; also known as the 'golden' mean.

courage: a cardinal virtue involving physical, moral or spiritual endurance and strength of character

***sophron*:** one who effortlessly lives according to the mean

***enkrates*:** one who is tempted, but strong, and lives in the mean

***akrates*:** one who is weak-willed and overcome by vices

***akrasia*:** incontinent – lacking self-restraint and uncontrolled

Aristotle's account of the mean can be summarised as follows:

Vice of excess	Mean (virtue)	Vice of deficiency
rashness	courage	cowardice
licentiousness	temperance	insensibility
prodigality	liberality	illiberality
vulgarity	generosity	pettiness
vanity	proper pride	humility
over-ambition	proper ambition	lack of ambition
boastfulness	patience	understatement
irascibility	truthfulness	lack of spirit
buffoonery	wittiness	boorishness
obsequiousness	friendliness	cantankerousness
shyness/bashfulness	modesty	shamelessness
envy/spitefulness	righteous indignation	malicious enjoyment/ callousness

Pythagoras

Four cardinal virtues

Many commentators on Aristotle highlight four key (cardinal) virtues as the most significant:

- temperance
- courage
- justice
- wisdom.

These are seen as essential for the development of character, with wisdom acting as the 'driver' that manages the other virtues to produce a morally virtuous and just outcome. The greatest advocate of virtue, according to Aristotle, is the philosopher, who is the one who pursues the 'loving' (*philos*) and 'wise' (*sophos*). This phrase was first used by Pythagoras, the ancient Greek philosopher and mathematician, to describe himself.

Specification content

Jesus' teachings on virtues (the Beatitudes)

Jesus' teachings on virtues

There is a long history of encouraging virtues in the Christian tradition, much of which can be traced back to the Old Testament. In the first section of the Sermon on the Mount (Matthew 5:3–12) Jesus teaches the importance of specific virtues. Each virtue is considered 'blessed' and has a spiritual reward. By calling them blessed, Jesus is giving praise and affirmation in recognition of the virtuous quality demonstrated. Together, these virtues are called the Beatitudes. The text reads:

> Blessed are the poor in spirit,
> for theirs is the kingdom of Heaven.
> Blessed are those who mourn,
> for they will be comforted.
> Blessed are the meek,

for they will inherit the earth.
Blessed are those who hunger and thirst for righteousness,
for they will be filled.
Blessed are the merciful,
for they will be shown mercy.
Blessed are the pure in heart,
for they will see God.
Blessed are the peacemakers,
for they will be called children of God.
Blessed are those who are persecuted because of righteousness,
for theirs is the kingdom of Heaven.

Some scholars suggest that the **Beatitudes** echo the prophecy in Isaiah 61:1–3. This Old Testament passage promises freedom from poverty, heartbreak and imprisonment, while offering hope to the righteous in despair and comfort to those who mourn.

> The Spirit of the Sovereign Lord is on me, because the Lord has anointed me to proclaim good news to the poor. He has sent me to bind up the broken-hearted, to proclaim freedom for the captive and release from darkness for the prisoners [...] to comfort all who mourn, and provide for those who grieve [...]

Other scholars suggest that the Beatitudes can be viewed as the antithesis of Proverbs 6:16–19. This Old Testament passage describes people who have an unrighteous character.

> There are six things the Lord hates, seven that are detestable to him: haughty eyes, a lying tongue, hands that shed innocent blood, a heart that devises wicked schemes, feet that are quick to rush into evil, a false witness who pours out lies and a person who stirs up conflict in the community.

A general summary of views about each of the Beatitudes would include the following:

Virtue	Meaning
poor in spirit	This is often interpreted as an understanding of poverty in relation to the whole person; that is, physical, mental and spiritual. It can be understood as an internal state of humility. It includes those who are oppressed or enslaved and have had their rights taken from them. Such people are viewed as humble before God. This also includes those who are poor in spirit through an awareness of their insignificance and helplessness before God.
mourning	This extends beyond the immediate concern for loss of a loved one to the loss of possessions, status or even health. It is the state of recognising concern and regret for the current situation of being separated from God. It is also mourning for the state of the whole world in general.

Jesus taught the importance of specific virtues in the Sermon on the Mount

Key term

Beatitude: blessing given by Jesus for certain personal virtues

Key quote

Even more striking, when seen against the background of Greek ethics, is the positive value which Christianity attaches to qualities such as meekness and humility, in contrast to self-assertion and world success. This is a central theme of Jesus' Sermon on the Mount, which begins with the Beatitudes. (Norman)

Virtue	Meaning
meekness	Meekness is not weakness but strength under control. It is a state of self-discipline. A meek person displays a gentle disposition towards other people.
hunger and thirst for righteousness	This is a desire for the virtuous outcome of justice in life in relation to the kingdom of God. It is the virtue of seeking righteousness or justice in a personal, spiritual, social and global sense.
mercy	Through humility and an awareness of God's mercy, Christians are encouraged to display mercy towards others, not because it brings the reward of God's mercy, but because it is a virtuous disposition in itself.
purity of heart	This is often understood as sincerity of character that wills and determines the correct choices and decisions in life without the contamination of selfish drives.
peacemaking	This is traditionally ascribed to the role of the Messiah. Those who follow suit and work for peace in a world of conflict truly appreciate the nature of God's kingdom.
persecuted for the sake of righteousness	Those who are persecuted are willing to suffer for religious and moral principles. They have an underlying determination to survive and stand up for what is right, despite the obstacles.

Key quotes

We value virtue but do not discuss it. The honest bookkeeper, the faithful wife, the earnest scholar get little of our attention compared to the embezzler, the tramp, the cheat.

(Steinbeck)

Our current task is, thereby, to do what we can to develop those virtues in ourselves and our children [...] in the hope that we may bequeath to them a world that is not irrevocably spoiled.

(Hursthouse)

The virtues of virtue theory

Virtue theory offers a practical alternative to rule-based ethics by focusing on the development of a character that is naturally 'other-regarding'. While the process of development begins with the individual, its ultimate goal is the creation of an ideal community in which virtuous behaviour fosters social justice rather than subjective whim. It is important to note that virtue theory was not designed to provide answers to individual acts of moral behaviour – instead, the application of virtue theory is a lifelong reflective task focused on the holistic development of an individual's character and their overall flourishing.

By providing clear role models, such as the philosopher, the theory offers guiding principles, through the example of moral excellence, rather than rigid commands. Furthermore, it prioritises character and relationships over what might be seen as the traditional masculine focus on abstract rules and duties that has historically dominated ethical discourse. For some, this makes it a much more adaptable and relevant ethical approach.

In recent years, a number of female philosophers have emerged as virtue ethicists. One example is Rosalind Hursthouse (1943–), who wrote about environmental virtue ethics. She discusses the vice of cruelty involved in intensive factory farming of animals and the need for the virtue of compassion.

Challenges to virtue theory

Virtue theory is often criticised for not providing a practical guide to moral behaviour. It is imprecise as it does not focus on specific behaviours in complex situations. Unlike deontological or teleological systems, it provides no clear formula for action. This is problematic when virtues conflict; for instance, receiving an unwanted gift creates a clash between truthfulness and friendliness.

Furthermore, the theory is arguably circular: a virtuous act is defined by what a virtuous person does, while a virtuous person is defined by their acts. One could ask: 'How can we tell a virtuous person from one who is not virtuous?' This reliance on individual judgement, as well as the uncertainty of each person's potential virtue, makes the system appear impractical for consistent application in communities. We saw earlier how Aristotle argued that some individuals, such as the *akrates*, are unable to apply wisdom effectively.

Virtue theory also faces the problem of cultural relativism, since ideas on the good virtues are not universal. History shows that one society's virtue is frequently another's vice, suggesting there is no universal set of good characteristics. For example, courage might be exemplified by enduring persecution in one culture, but by fighting against tyranny in another. Similarly, Aristotelian pride is viewed as a vice in many Christian traditions.

Since virtue theory relies on community standards to define excellence, it lacks the objective authority required for a universal ethical system. If virtues change according to the ethos of one community, the theory remains highly subjective. Furthermore, this might even raise the question of whether there are actually such things as *virtues* in the first place. A modern writer on virtue theory, Alasdair MacIntyre, argued in *After Virtue* (1981) that virtues need to be understood within their specific cultural and social context:

> At least some of the items in a Homeric list of the *aretai* would clearly not be counted by most of us nowadays as virtues at all, physical strength being the most obvious example.

Finally, virtues can be used for immoral acts. By prioritising internal dispositions over specific actions, the theory fails to account for virtuous traits being directed towards evil ends. An individual might display courage and intelligence while planning and carrying out a bank robbery; in this instance, virtue makes the criminal more effective rather than more moral. Critics argue the theory is naive, trusting individual goodness without imposing rules to prevent the misuse of effective character traits. This undermines the claim that a virtuous character naturally ensures morally correct behaviour.

Summary

- Virtue theory is an aretaic (virtue-based) approach to morality, focusing on the development of a person's character rather than specific rules or consequences.
- The system is grounded in the work of Aristotle: that the ultimate human goal is *eudaimonia* (flourishing) and this is achieved through developing intellectual virtues (through education) and moral virtues (through habit and practice).
- The doctrine of the mean is central: virtue is the 'golden' balance between the two extremes of excess and deficiency.

Specification content

Challenges: virtues are not a practical guide to moral behaviour; issue of cultural relativism (ideas on the good virtues are not universal); virtues can be used for immoral acts

Key quote

He has all the virtues I dislike and none of the vices I admire.

(Churchill)

Does a soldier's courage depend on the cause they fight for, or is courage a virtue regardless of the outcome?

- ★ The Beatitudes in the Sermon on the Mount provide a Christian context for virtue theory. Jesus affirms specific qualities, such as mercy, as 'blessed'.
- ★ Modern virtue ethicists, such as Rosalind Hursthouse, make the theory a relevant and adaptable approach that prioritises compassion and character over duties and consequences.
- ★ Challenges to the theory include its lack of practical guidance in moral dilemmas, the issue of cultural relativism where virtues are not universal and the fact that virtuous traits can be used to facilitate immoral acts.

AO1 Activity

a Outline three challenges that have been raised against virtue theory as an ethical system.

b From the list of ten key points below, choose six that you feel are the most important in presenting the weaknesses of virtue theory. Put your points in order of priority, explaining why you have selected those six and placed them in that order. This skill of selecting and prioritising material will help you structure strong examination answers.

Key points

- It does not fall within the deontological or teleological categories.
- It is teleological, in that it focuses on achieving *eudaimonia*.
- It is arbitrary, imprecise and vague.
- It has little practical guidance for real life circumstances.
- It does not provide a clear method for determining which behaviours are good and which are bad.
- It is too dependent on the goodness of people.
- It places too much focus on the individual and is self-centred.
- It is too complex a system for all people; it is only relevant for the philosopher.
- It presents a circular argument – a virtuous person has virtues; but how do we know they are virtues? Because the person is virtuous.
- It provides no method for deciding what to do when two virtues conflict, such as when being honest might also be unkind.

Refer to the band descriptors for AS (WJEC) or A Level (Eduqas) and, in particular, look at the demands described in the band 5 descriptors, which you should be aspiring towards. A band 5 AO1 response will be 'an excellent demonstration of knowledge and understanding [...] thorough, accurate and relevant [...] presented clearly and coherently.'

Issues for analysis and evaluation

Whether being a good person is better than just doing good deeds

Possible line of argument	Critical analysis and evaluation
Being a good person is better because it means focusing on the internal character and motives of the person rather than simple rule-following.	Internal states are secondary to external impact; character is hidden and unverifiable, whereas a good deed provides a measurable, objective benefit to society.
Developing virtues (*arete*) creates an intrinsic change in the individual, ensuring they consistently perform good deeds.	If a person claims virtue but never acts, that character is redundant. Deeds must be the outward proof of internal goodness.
A good virtuous person acts naturally and independently without the need for external rules.	Virtue theory promotes independence and personal responsibility. But without external rules, there is nothing to govern each person's moral compass. Rules provide a safety net for those lacking moral maturity.
The presence of moral exemplars and role models of goodness provides a more effective guide for behaviour than abstract ethical theories.	Guiding principles arise from internal character, inspired by role models rather than commands. However, this risks being elitist; Aristotle argued that some people (such as the *akrates*) do not possess the natural capacity to resist vice or apply wisdom.
Focusing on being rather than doing allows for a more adaptable and holistic approach to the moral life.	This argument avoids the rigidity of traditional rules and appeals to modern thinkers. However, virtues can be directed towards immoral outcomes; a person can exhibit courage and intelligence while committing a crime.

AO2 Activity

a Analyse three possible conclusions that could be drawn from the critical analysis and evaluation on whether being a good person is better than just doing good deeds. Select evidence and examples to support each of the three conclusions. Select one conclusion that you think is the **most convincing** and explain why it is so.

b Now contrast this with the **weakest** conclusion of the three. Justify your argument with clear reasoning and evidence.

Refer to the band descriptors for AS (WJEC) or A Level (Eduqas). In particular, look at the demands described in the band 5 descriptors, which you should be aspiring towards. A band 5 AO2 response will demonstrate 'a confident critical analysis and perceptive evaluation of the issue [and] a well-structured, sustained argument with a clear conclusion.'

This section covers AO1 content and skills

Specification content

Whether being a good person is better than just doing good deeds

Specification content

Whether virtue theory is useful when faced with a moral dilemma

News reporter

The essay clearly defines the scope of the debate and introduces the central conflict regarding the practical application of the theory.

Critical thinker

This paragraph effectively highlights the ambiguity of virtue definitions and the difficulty of applying them to concrete dilemmas.

Philosopher

The analysis correctly identifies that the theory's utility lies in long-term character development rather than immediate, rule-based decision-making.

Judge

This section weighs the need for structure against the flexibility of the theory, reaching a balanced assessment of its perceived deficiency in not providing a clear method for evaluating behaviour.

Critical thinker

The argument identifies why the theory may be rejected by those seeking a more traditional, legalistic framework for morality.

Explorer

The analysis investigates how the theory adapts to modern issues, showing its relevance beyond its original ancient Greek context.

Detective

The analysis uncovers the social depth of the theory, showing how internal character leads to practical, outward social benefits.

Tennis player

The argument maintains strong momentum here by focusing on the practical utility of role models in moral education.

Exam practice

Below is an example of part of an evaluation of whether virtue theory is useful when faced with a moral dilemma.

Sample answer

A moral dilemma arises when multiple justifiable actions lead to opposing outcomes. For virtue theory, the challenge is whether a character-based system provides meaningful guidance during specific crises, such as persecution.

In a Christian context, the Beatitudes might suggest accepting injustice: 'blessed are those who are persecuted'. Conversely, Aristotelian courage is ambiguous; it could imply patient endurance or active resistance against tyranny.

Virtue theory was not designed as an instruction manual for solving immediate moral dilemmas. Aristotle viewed ethics as a lifelong reflective task, where the goal is the gradual cultivation of character rather than the quick resolution of isolated incidents.

Since the virtues are not moral absolutes, their application remains contextual. This lack of rigid rules may suggest an 'anything goes' approach, but this contradicts the intentions of both Aristotle and the Beatitudes.

Consequently, those preferring absolute moral boundaries, like those found in deontological ethics, may find virtue theory lacks the certainty required for a stable society or structured ethics.

However, the flexibility of the theory is a strength. Modern thinkers like Rosalind Hursthouse have applied it to new dilemmas, such as environmental ethics, by discussing how the virtue of compassion should replace the vice of cruelty towards animals.

Another strength of virtue theory is its focus on the well-being of others. Although the virtues are self-focused, they develop a character that seeks to build an ideal community.

Furthermore, the virtuous person acts as an exemplar, providing a clear guide for others facing similar dilemmas. And Aristotle argued that the application of wisdom and the delivery of justice ensure the system is not merely subjective.

In conclusion, while virtue theory may not suit those seeking absolutist solutions, it remains a useful tool for navigating dilemmas through its adaptability. Its value lies in its insistence that moral wisdom is developed through habit and the observation of excellence.

Philosopher

The conclusion provides a sophisticated synthesis, acknowledging the limitations of the theory while affirming its unique value in moral development

Over to you

Below is a table of points answering a question about virtue theory. Your task is to select, develop and expand the points you think work best, first into an essay plan and then into an essay. When you have completed the exercise, provide your own considered conclusion in response to the question.

Question

'Virtue theory offers little guidance when making moral decisions.' Evaluate this view.

Points

Agree (offers little guidance)	Disagree (offers useful guidance)	Analysis and evaluation
It does not provide clear rules for action.	It avoids the pitfalls of rigid absolutism.	Flexibility prevents just following deontological rules.
It is subjective and open to interpretation.	It encourages a flexible internal compass.	Motives matter more than rules.
Virtues may be culturally biased.	Virtues are universal because they encourage moral growth.	Character outlives changing social laws.
DCT provides more certain, objective commands.	The system is teleological, aiming for *eudaimonia*.	The purpose of virtue theory is not merely obedience, but flourishing.
It is not designed for individual dilemmas.	MacIntyre argues that virtues and dilemmas evolve with society.	It focuses on life, not particular incidents.
Hursthouse argues that virtue theory can be updated for modern times.	It can only be used for general guidance.	Wisdom gained through experience in life solves the conflict.

Refer to the band descriptors for A2 (WJEC) or A Level (Eduqas). In particular, look at the demands described in the higher band descriptors, which you should be aspiring towards. Ask yourself the following questions:

- Is my answer a confident critical analysis and perceptive evaluation of the issue?
- Is my answer a response that successfully identifies and thoroughly addresses the issues the question raises?

Key term

ethical egoism: the normative view that holds that all action ought to be motivated by self-interest

Specification content

Agent-focused ethic based on self-interest as opposed to altruism; ethical theory that matches the moral agent's psychological state (psychological egoism); concentration on long-term self-interests rather than short-term interests

Key terms

altruism: selfless concern for the well-being of others

psychological egoism: the descriptive view that all human action is motivated by self-interest

descriptive: term used as a criticism of naturalism that it can only describe and not be prescriptive

C: Ethical egoism

Ethical egoism is a meta-ethical investigation that focuses on the agent (individual character) to give an understanding of 'norms' (behaviour). In looking at the individual character, and the motives behind an individual's actions, there is a very important question that emerges: do we behave in a manner that is purely driven by our self-interest?

Ethical egoism: a normative agent-focused ethic based upon self-interest as opposed to altruism

In the study of ethical egoism, morality is viewed through the lens of the individual agent rather than external laws. To understand this system, it is necessary to distinguish between human nature and moral duty, and to explore the tension between **altruism** and self-interest.

The distinction between ethical egoism and psychological egoism

Key quotes

Sometimes people act simply for the sake of others. Parents help children for the children's sake. Environmentalists save the beached whale for the sake of that whale beached.

(Cave)

Within our own moral culture [...] an altruistic concern for others is widely held to be a, or even the, supreme value. If, however, in caring for other people, I do so because I think that it will make my own life happier, then it would seem that it is not really a concern for others which motivates me, but a concern for myself.

(Norman)

Altruism refers to the tendency to perform actions purely for the sake of others, without any expectation of personal gain.

Self-interest is the prioritisation of one's own well-being and advantage. This can be understood as either short-term or long-term.

- Short-term interests are often based on immediate gratification or impulsive selfishness, which can ultimately be harmful.
- Long-term interests involve calculated decisions that lead to a more flourishing life.

For an ethical egoist, long-term interests are preferred over short-term impulses. For instance, being honest and contributing to a community helps to build a stable and trusting environment, which serves an individual's own long-term self-interests over a complete lifetime.

There is a distinction between **psychological egoism** and ethical egoism:

- Psychological egoism: This is a **descriptive** claim regarding human nature: that all actions are motivated by self-interest, meaning that genuine altruism is a psychological impossibility. This describes what is perceived to be an unchangeable fact of how humans behave.
- Ethical egoism: This is a *normative moral directive*. It maintains that an individual should act in their own self-interest as their primary moral duty. This prescribes what ought to be done to ensure personal flourishing and success.

This distinction lies in the gap between what is (psychological egoism) and what ought to be (ethical egoism). It is possible to believe that humans are capable of altruism yet still argue that they should prioritise their own interests as a rational choice.

Key quotes

Psychological egoism is the descriptive view that all human action is motivated by self-interest. Ethical egoism, on the other hand, is the normative view that holds that all action ought to be motivated by self-interest.

(Driver)

an ethical egoist need not be an egotist or even an egoistic and selfish man in the everyday sense of these terms. Ethical egoism is an ethical theory, not a pattern of action or trait of character, and is compatible with being self-effacing and unselfish in practice.

(Frankena)

The motivation behind an action is rarely one of pure altruism. Acting out of self-interest is frequently linked to serving long-term goals.

The eighteenth-century economist Adam Smith recognised this in a commercial context, noting: 'It is not from the benevolence of the butcher, the brewer, or the baker, that we expect our dinner, but from their regard to their own interest.'

Today, when supermarkets use slogans such as 'the customer is always right', the reality is that they care about the customer because it is in their own long-term self-interest to do so. Even a parent helping their child has long-term interests of family stability and support in mind.

Julia Driver writes: 'Altruistic actions are those that are performed purely for the sake of others. The psychological egoist denies that there are such acts.'

The response of the psychological egoist to donating money to charity would suggest that the motive could be:

- to look good in front of others
- to support a moral system to which they are dutybound
- to avoid shame and personal anguish if they decide not to give.

In every case, behind the apparent altruism of donating money to charity the motives always have the root intention of self-interest.

Max Stirner

Specification content

Max Stirner, self-interest as the root cause of every human action even if it appears altruistic; rejection of egoism for material gain; union of egoists

Key person

Max Stirner (1806–56): Born Johann Caspar Schmidt, was a German philosopher; best known for his controversial work *The Ego and Its Own* (1844), Stirner promoted extreme individualism, arguing that the self (ego) was unique and couldn't be categorised by external labels; influenced by the philosophy of Hegel while attending his lectures, Stirner believed that in order to own oneself (German: *eigenheit*) one must be free of everything external to oneself, such as religion, state and morality; he influenced much anarchist thought as well as existentialism and impacted many philosophers, such as Jean-Paul Sartre and Karl Marx; he also introduced the concept of a union of egoists (*verein von egoisten*), a voluntary non-repressive association; he lived most of his later life in poverty and died in 1856 aged just 49

Stirner's ideas are difficult to interpret as his writing is often repetitive, provocative and deliberately chaotic – a style intended to mirror his belief that language itself can be a tool of constraint.

To understand Stirner's complex thought, it is important to keep in mind some important concepts:

- ***Gespenst*** (plural *gespenster* and translated as 'ghost(s)'): These are fixed ideas, such as religion, nationalism and traditional morality, which individuals mistakenly treat as objective authorities. Stirner argues these are illusions that haunt and enslave the ego.
- ***Eigenheit*** (translated as 'ownness'): This describes the internal state of being one's own **master**. It is the realisation that the individual is not subservient to any external law or moral system, but instead possesses the autonomy to act according to their own will.
- ***Einzig*** (translated as 'uniqueness'): This refers to the absolute individuality of the person. It is the recognition that the self is an unrepeatable being that cannot be categorised by external labels, ideologies, or even concepts like humanity.
- ***Verein von egoisten*** (translated as 'union of egoists'): This is a voluntary, non-binding, and impermanent association between unique individuals. It is a form of co-operation that serves the participants' interests without requiring them to sacrifice their autonomy to a collective.

Key term

master: the state of being a self-governing moral agent

Key quotes

Thousands of years of civilisation have obscured to you what you are, have made you believe you are not egoists but are called to be idealists ('good men'). Shake that off! [...] just recognise yourselves again, just recognise what you really are, and let go your hypocritical endeavours, your foolish mania to be something else than you are.

(Stirner)

I decide whether it is the right thing in me; there is no right outside me.

(Stirner)

Every higher essence above me, be it God, be it man, weakens the feeling of my uniqueness, and pales only before the sun of this consciousness.

(Stirner)

The delusion of the past and the true nature of self-interest: the ego

The **first issue** is whether self-interest is the root cause of every human action, even if it appears altruistic. While Stirner acknowledges the role of self-interest in decision-making, he rejects psychological egoism because it relies on a deluded understanding of the self. He argues that self-interest is often enslaved to external frameworks or *gespenster*. In this sense, even psychological egoism is a *gespenst*. To develop *einzig* it is necessary for a person to act entirely out of self-interest and to reject acting in the interests of others as has to happen during childhood. The *gespenster* of childhood have to be shed.

Stirner uses the analogy of a *libertinus* who, in Roman history, was an enslaved person who had been given legal freedom:

> The man who is set free is nothing but a freed man, a *libertinus*, [...] dragging a piece of chain with him: he is an unfree man in the garment of freedom, like the donkey in the lion's skin.

Here, the person thinks of themself as free, but their freedom is not internal to them; it is defined and granted by *gespenster* – it is dependent on something else. A person is only truly free when they drop the 'chain' of duty and act solely because they will it, not because a system allows it.

True self-interest only occurs through *eigenheit*, when one is a master of oneself rather than being mastered by God, the state, one's own **conscience** or ethical theories. Here, the donkey in the lion's skin refers to Aesop's fable in which the donkey wears the lion's skin to look powerful, but it remains a donkey. Stirner is suggesting that a person might adopt the language and 'garment' of a free thinker, but, if they are still following a fixed moral code, they are merely pretending to be autonomous.

Stirner is not advocating for **amoralism** (the outright rejection of all values). Instead, he rejects the way morality posits obligations to behave in fixed ways. As Professor David Leopold, writing in the *Stanford Encyclopedia of Philosophy*, suggests, Stirner's rejection of moral claims is not a denial of all normative judgement, but an affirmation of 'non-moral goods' – values chosen by the unique individual rather than imposed by a system.

The **second issue** is Stirner's rejection of egoism for material gain. Stirner's egoism does not advocate greed; in fact, he rejects material gain if that pursuit becomes another *gespenst* that enslaves the individual. Just as one can be enslaved by religion, one can be enslaved by a hunger for money.

True egoism requires emotional detachment from both external ideologies and internal appetites. Stirner suggests that the egoist should not be controlled by their senses. Instead, the individual must remain the 'owner' of their desires. This is not a call for narrow materialism or equality – which Stirner views as just another conceptual framework for humanity to 'kneel to' – but a call for total autonomy where the individual is the central point of their own existence.

Consider the different motives for giving money to a person in need:

- 'I give money because it makes me feel good.' Stirner argues this person is still not free; their happiness is tied to a *gespenst* – the internalised duty to be a good person.
- 'I give money because I feel I must.' This is clear enslavement to an external moral obligation or fear of being judged.
- 'I do not give, but I spend time justifying my decision.' The need to justify proves they are still controlled by the moral framework they seek to avoid.
- 'I give (or do not give) simply because I please.' There is no regard for whether the act is 'good' or 'bad'. The individual is the master of the action, driven by *eigenheit*.

For Stirner, once an individual recognises they are not accountable to any obligation, they become aware of their true unique self. They can then judge accurately what serves their own nature, acting because they *will* it, rather than being driven by a sense of duty or a greed for materialistic gain.

Key term

conscience: traditionally an internal, intuitive guide to good or bad; Joseph Fletcher reinterpreted this notion as a description of ethical action

Key quote

It would also be a mistake to think of Stirner as advocating a normative proposition about the value of self-interested action as ordinarily understood. Stirnerian egoism needs to be distinguished from the individual pursuit of conventional self-interest.

(David Leopold)

Key quote

Away, then, with every concern that is not altogether my concern! You think at least the 'good cause' must be my concern? What's good, what's bad? Why, I myself am my concern, and I am neither good nor bad. Neither has meaning for me.

(Stirner)

Specification content

Challenges: destruction of a community ethos; social injustices could occur as individuals put their own interests first; a form of bigotry (why is one moral agent more important than any other?)

Key term

community ethos: the character or spirit of a community

Union of egoists

The **third issue** is the union of egoists (*verein von egoisten*). For Stirner, egoism is not antisocial. He proposes the union as a voluntary association in which unique individuals co-operate without sacrificing their autonomy. Unlike the state, which demands loyalty to a 'fixed idea' of society, the union is:

- **voluntary**: individuals join and leave based on their own will
- **non-binding**: it does not impose moral or legal obligations
- **temporary**: it consists of impermanent relationships of 'uniting' between self-determining individuals.

This union supports individuals in their unique goals without requiring shared 'final ends'. It is a practical way for the unique ego to engage with the world while remaining independent.

Challenges to ethical egoism

Erosion of community ethos

The first challenge to ethical egoism is that it can destroy a **community ethos**. It can do this by promoting the will of the individual over the collective. Traditionally, the state and its laws exist for the benefit of the majority and serve as a guard against exploitation. If every individual prioritises their own interests, the shared values that bind a society together – such as sacrifice, duty and the common good – are viewed as obstacles.

Critics argue that if psychological egoism is true then a genuine community ethos is actually impossible. If every individual is biologically or psychologically driven to seek only their own benefit, then social bonds are merely a mask for self-interest. This reduces society to a collection of competing agents rather than a cohesive group with shared moral values.

Stirner would argue that this very aim to free people through community is a formula that enslaves them to a collective fixed idea. While some interpret this as advocating anarchy or an active fight to eliminate the state, Stirner's position is more nuanced. For Stirner, the state is illegitimate because it causes a conflict between the individual's uniqueness and an obligation to serve the law.

However, this does not necessarily mean an active challenge to the state, opposing the systems imposed by the state; rather, it is up to each unique individual to decide whether to agree with the state's demands. This co-operation is best understood through the *verein von egoisten* – a voluntary, non-binding, and impermanent association between unique individuals. It is a form of co-operation that serves the participants' interests without requiring them to sacrifice their autonomy to a collective. According to David Leopold: 'While individuals have no duty to overthrow the state, Stirner does think that the state will eventually collapse as a result of the spread of egoism.'

Consequently, the destruction of community is not an accidental side effect but a necessary result of individuals achieving *eigenheit*. *Eigenheit* is the ownness or internal state of being one's own master, involving the realisation that the individual is not subservient to any external law or moral system, but instead possesses the autonomy to act according to their own will.

Risk of social injustice

The second challenge is that social injustices could occur as individuals put their own interests first. In pursuing one's own interests, there will inevitably be a conflict of interests with others. Standard ethical theories provide a framework to resolve these conflicts fairly, but egoism suggests that the individual should simply seek to prevail. This could lead to social injustices, particularly where power imbalances exist.

This challenge is also evident in the claims of psychological egoism. If human nature is fundamentally self-serving, then 'justice' and 'fairness' are merely tools used by people without power to restrain those who have it. In this view, there is no psychological incentive to act justly unless it happens to coincide with personal gain.

Stirner's own words provoke accusations of inequality in social and political life:

> Now am I, who am competent for much [...] to have no advantage over the less competent? We are all in the midst of abundance; now shall I not help myself as well as I can, but only wait and see how much is left me in an equal division?

This suggests that those with the might or competence to take what they want should do so, rather than adhering to concepts of fair distribution. In this framework, social injustice is not a moral failing because justice itself is regarded as an external conceptual theory and a *gespenst*. A *gespenst* is a fixed idea, such as religion, nationalism or traditional morality, which individuals mistakenly treat as an objective authority. Stirner argues these are illusions that haunt and enslave the ego. This raises the question of how a society can function if individuals feel no obligation to protect vulnerable people or act with fairness towards others.

Problem of moral bigotry

The third challenge is that egoism might be seen as a form of **bigotry** as it raises the question of why one moral agent is more important than any other. Bigotry involves dividing people into groups and treating one group's interests as more important than another's based on an arbitrary difference. Critics like James Rachels argue that the egoist does exactly this by dividing the world into 'myself' and 'everyone else'. If there is no fundamental, objective difference between the egoist and another person, then there is no rational reason to prioritise the egoist's interests.

> **Key term**
>
> **bigotry:** intolerance and narrow-mindedness

From the perspective of psychological egoism, however, this prioritisation is not a moral choice but a psychological necessity. If a moral agent cannot help but prefer their own interests, then the accusation of bigotry is directed at a fixed aspect of human nature rather than a chosen ethical position.

Stirner's response to this is radical; he denies the premise of equality entirely. To Stirner, equality is just another conceptual framework for humanity to kneel to. He writes: 'But I am not an ego along with other egos, but the sole ego: I am unique.'

By asserting that every person is *einzig*, Stirner avoids the standard claim that everyone is an egoist and therefore equal. *Einzig* refers to the absolute individuality of the person; it is the recognition that the self is an unrepeatable being that cannot be categorised by external labels, ideologies, or even concepts like humanity. Instead, he suggests that because no two individuals can be equated there is no requirement to treat their interests with equal weight. This undermines ethical egoism as it contradicts the requirement of universal consistency for ethics. This is the principle that a moral rule must be capable of being applied to all people (universal) and be free from contradiction (consistency). From this perspective, ethical egoism can be seen as discriminatory and as supporting a form of moral bigotry.

The challenges to ethical egoism highlight a fundamental tension between absolute individual autonomy and the requirements of a stable society. If psychological egoism is accepted as an accurate description of human nature, then the normative claims of Stirner and other ethical egoists appear to be a logical extension of innate drives.

Summary

- Ethical egoism is a normative, agent-focused approach to morality that maintains an individual's primary moral duty is to act in their own long-term self-interest.
- The system is often distinguished from psychological egoism, the descriptive claim that all human actions are inevitably motivated by self-interest, making genuine altruism a psychological impossibility.
- Max Stirner provides a radical development of egoism, arguing that individuals must reject *gespenster* (ghosts) – fixed ideas like religion or the state – to achieve *eigenheit* (ownness) and self-mastery.
- Central to Stirner's thought is the *einzig* (uniqueness), the recognition of the individual as an unrepeatable being who must remain the owner of their desires rather than being enslaved by material greed.
- The *verein von egoisten* (union of egoists) offers a model for social interaction, consisting of voluntary, impermanent, and non-binding associations that serve the interests of unique individuals without a loss of autonomy.
- Challenges to the theory include the potential destruction of a community ethos, the occurrence of social injustices through power imbalances, and the charge that egoism is a form of bigotry.

AO1 Activity

a Explain the key principles of ethical egoism, including the distinction between ethical egoism and psychological egoism, and the contribution of Max Stirner.

b Read the response below to a question about what is meant by ethical egoism. Check the relevant band descriptors for AO1 and decide where you might place it. It is not in the top bands.

Now rewrite the response, aiming for band 5. In particular, make sure you demonstrate excellent use of evidence and examples, thorough and accurate use of specialist language in context, and reference to sources of wisdom.

Response

Ethical egoism says people should do what is best for themselves. It is a moral rule that tells us our duty is to look after our own interests. This is different from when you do things for other people.

The theory is based on the idea that humans look after themselves anyway, which is called egoism. However, being another type of egoist does not mean being greedy or doing whatever you want right now. It is better to look at the interests involved. For example, being nice to others might be good for you in the future because they will be nice back.

Max Stirner thought people should be free from rules made by the government or *gespenster*. He believed that everyone is special and should not have to follow what society wants. He said that people could still work together in like-minded groups, but only if they wanted to and if it helped them.

Issues for analysis and evaluation

The extent to which ethical egoism inevitably leads to moral evil

Possible line of argument	Critical analysis and evaluation
Ethical egoism rejects external moral absolutes, allowing the individual to define right and wrong based on their own internal will.	This risks justifying harmful actions by removing objective restraints. However, Stirner argued most wills are not truly autonomous but are 'unfree in the garment of freedom' – like a donkey in a lion's skin – still enslaved by internalised social frameworks or *gespenster*.
Prioritising self-interest provides a path to personal liberation, avoiding the constraints of collective fixed ideas and state control.	Such prioritisation can lead to bigotry and conflict between agents. The rejection of objective laws carries the risk of social anarchy, which may have problematic consequences for society.
Social co-operation is valid when based on personal pleasure rather than a moral commandment. Therefore social good is not ruled out but can be achieved through the union of egoists (*verein von egoisten*).	Psychological and ethical egoism suggest self-interest often results in moral good. However, if benevolence is purely for the benefit of the egoist's happiness, it lacks the objective status required for a consistent justice system.
The union of egoists allows for co-operation through mutual self-interest without sacrificing individual uniqueness.	Maintaining a balance between an individual's calculated will and the needs of others is practically impossible. This makes the union an idealistic concept rather than a functional solution for a complex society. This is because the union of egoists is only voluntary, non-binding, and impermanent.
The pursuit of *eigenheit* and *einzig* must lead to moral evil because unchained human nature will follow decision-making contrary to individual well-being and to the common good.	Stirner argues that evil is merely another external label used to control the individual. While this grants total freedom, it offers no protection for vulnerable people, as the only restraint on an individual's will is their own power or competence.

AO2 Activity

a Analyse three possible conclusions that could be drawn from the critical analysis and evaluation on the extent to which ethical egoism inevitably leads to moral evil. Select evidence and examples to support each of the three conclusions. Select one conclusion that you think is the **most convincing** and explain why it is so.

This section covers AO2 content and skills

Specification content

The extent to which ethical egoism inevitably leads to moral evil

b Using your analysis from part a, evaluate which conclusion is most convincing. Write a concluding paragraph that presents your own justified viewpoint. Refer to the AO2 band descriptors and ensure your conclusion demonstrates a 'confident and justified conclusion' (band 5).

When you have completed the task, refer to the band descriptors for AS (WJEC) or AS Level (Eduqas). In particular, look at the demands described in the higher band descriptors, which you should be aspiring towards.

Specification content

The extent to which all moral actions are motivated by self-interest

Exam practice

Below is an example of part of an evaluation of the extent to which all moral actions are motivated by self-interest.

Sample answer

Whether all moral actions are motivated by self-interest depends on whether one views human nature as inherently selfish or capable of altruism. This issue involves a tension between psychological egoism, which claims we always act for ourselves, and ethical egoism, which suggests we have a duty to do so.

Tennis player: The argument is served with excellent precision and a clear sustained line of logic.

Psychological egoism asserts that all actions are driven by self-interest. Richard Norman notes: 'if, in caring for other people, I do so because I think that it will make my own life happier, then it would seem that it is not really a concern for others which motivates me, but a concern for myself.'

Detective: The evidence presented here points towards a hidden motive beneath every human action.

Critics such as Cave challenge this descriptive claim, arguing that people sometimes act simply for others, such as parents helping children for the children's sake. This suggests that genuine altruistic motivation remains possible.

Critical thinker: This provides a necessary counter-balance to ensure the debate is not one-sided.

Ethical egoism moves from a descriptive claim to a normative one. Driver explains that while the former describes motivation, ethical egoism 'is normative. It purports to tell us how people ought to act,' making self-interest a moral duty.

Philosopher: The shift from a descriptive *is* to a normative *ought* is a significant step in the reasoning.

Frankena clarifies that an ethical egoist is not necessarily a selfish person. The theory is an ethical framework compatible with being modest and unpretentious in practice, focusing on long-term flourishing rather than immediate, impulsive greed.

Judge: This clarification effectively distinguishes between a character trait and a formal ethical system.

Stirner redefined the self by identifying the individual as unique. He wrote: 'I am owner of my might, and I am so when I know myself as *einzig*.' This suggests self-interest is only valid when the true self is realised.

Explorer: Navigating Stirner's work requires a deep dive into the absolute nature of the self.

For Stirner, most people are unfree because they are enslaved by external *gespenster* like religion or the state. True self-interest requires *eigenheit*, where the individual becomes their own master.

News reporter: Identifying these external 'ghosts' exposes the complexity of achieving true individual autonomy.

Co-operation remains possible through the *verein von egoisten*, a voluntary association serving mutual interests. Here, moral actions are still motivated by the self through a framework of non-binding and impermanent social interaction.

In conclusion, while some actions appear altruistic, a deeper understanding of the self often reveals long-term interests. Ultimately, whether all moral actions are self-interested depends on how one interprets the self and its motivations.

Explorer

This concept maps out a new way for independent agents to navigate social territory.

Judge – **Philosopher**

The final verdict depends entirely on how the initial premises of *self* and *interest* are interpreted.

Over to you

Below is a writing frame for an essay on moral actions and selfishness. Your task is to complete the sentence prompts and so complete the essay. The sentence starters can be followed, or you may create your own.

Question

'All so-called moral actions are ultimately selfish.' Evaluate this view.

Writing frame

Introduction:

- The claim that all moral actions are ultimately selfish rests on the assumption that …
- This view is primarily supported by psychological egoism, which maintains that no action is truly …

First line of argument (the case for psychological egoism):

- Proponents of this view, such as Richard Norman, suggest that even when we help others, the ultimate motive is …
- This implies that what we call altruism is actually a hidden form of …

Critical counter-point (the problem of universal consistency):

- One can question the word 'all' by pointing to thinkers like Peter Cave, who argue that …
- If even a single action, such as a parent's sacrifice, is done purely for another, then the claim that all actions are selfish …

Second line of argument (Max Stirner's redefinition of selfishness):

- Stirner challenges the question by arguing that most 'so-called moral actions' are not selfish enough, because they are …
- He suggests that true self-interest is not narrow greed, but the realisation of *eigenheit*, meaning that …

Critical counter-point (the distinction between self-interest and selfishness):

- A flaw in the statement in the question is that using the word 'selfish' is not straightforward regarding ethical egoism …
- While Stirner's 'unique' (*einzig*) person acts out of their own will, this does not ultimately mean the action is selfish if it includes …

Conclusion:

- In conclusion, the claim that all moral actions are ultimately selfish is plausible because behind all moral actions there could still be long-term self-interests. For example …
- While the self is necessarily involved in every action a person takes, the word 'all' ignores the possibility of …

- Ultimately, the most persuasive view is that …

Refer to the band descriptors for A2 (WJEC) or A Level (Eduqas) and, in particular, look at the demands described in the higher band descriptors, which you should be aspiring towards. Ask yourself the following questions:

- Is my answer a confident critical analysis and perceptive evaluation of the issue?
- Is my answer a response that successfully identifies and thoroughly addresses the issues the question raises?

D: Meta-ethical approaches – naturalism

This section covers AO1 content and skills

Objective moral laws exist independently of human beings, moral terms can be understood by analysing the natural world

Naturalism is closely tied to **empiricism**, a philosophical view that all knowledge comes from our senses. This idea, central to the study of knowledge known as **epistemology**, states that we are born with a 'clean slate' (***tabula rasa***). Our minds are initially empty, and everything we learn and know is derived from what we see, hear, touch, smell and feel.

This concept, that 'Nothing is in the intellect that was not first in the senses', was developed by the philosopher David Hume but has roots in ancient philosophy.

According to empiricism, we first understand a statement by using our past experiences of the world around us. We then use our senses and observations to check if the statement is true. Thus, meaning comes from our knowledge and **cognition**, while truth is determined by what we observe in the world.

Cognitivism and realism

In philosophy, **cognitivism** is the idea that a statement, or **proposition**, is meaningful if and only if it can be verified through our experience. This concept is a linguistic extension of empiricism, focusing on how our mental processes handle information. This was central to a group of twentieth-century philosophers known as **logical positivists**; a famous group of logical positivists discussed these ideas in the 1920s and 1930s at the University of Vienna, so they are referred to as the Vienna Circle.

Specification content

Objective moral laws exist independently of human beings; moral terms can be understood by analysing the natural world; ethical statements are cognitivist and can be verified or falsified; verified moral statements are objective truths and universal

Key terms

empiricism: the idea that we gain knowledge through our senses

epistemology: philosophy of knowledge, derived from the Greek *episteme* (knowledge) and *logos* (words or discussion)

***tabula rasa*:** Latin for 'a clean slate' and refers to the peripatetic axiom – the idea that we are born with no built-in knowledge and learn everything through experience

cognition: the mental action or process of acquiring knowledge and understanding through thought, experience and the senses

cognitivism: the philosophical view that sentences express meaningful propositions

proposition: statement

logical positivists: philosophers who believe that a statement's truth and meaning must be testable in the real world

Key terms

logical positivism: school of Western philosophy that sought to legitimise philosophical discussion by arguing philosophical language should be based on scientific language

verification principle: the claim, made by logical positivists such as A.J. Ayer, that a statement is only meaningful if it is either analytically true (true by definition) or empirically verifiable through sense experience

empirical: based on observation or experience rather than theory or pure logic

realism: the view that an object exists in reality independently of our minds

Logical positivism holds that a statement's truth and meaning must be testable in the real world. This is known as the **verification principle**: that for a statement to be considered meaningful, it must be either a mathematical/logical tautology or capable of being proved true or false through sensory experience and **empirical** evidence.

Realism is the idea that the world exists independently of our minds and perceptions. This means that what we see and experience is not just a figment of our imagination.

An assumption of cognitivism is that we can gain objective knowledge about the world because it is real and exists independently of our thoughts. This makes realism the foundation for judging the truth of statements and for understanding moral behaviours as objective facts.

For example, take the statement 'My kind neighbour takes out my bins to the road every Monday morning.' In cognitive terms this makes sense as it concurs with our world of experience and what we know – our minds recognise the notions of kindness, neighbour, taking and the rest. A cognitive realist would acknowledge the truth of this statement (that it is not merely the product of imagination) only in the light of experience, such as seeing the neighbour taking out the bins. And the judgement about the neighbour's kindness can be reasonably derived from experience too: it is a generous, helpful, pleasing act. The language is meaningful and the moral judgement relates directly to the consequences of the physical act. A cognitive realist understands a moral or ethical proposition as being related directly to the empirical world.

An act as simple as taking out another's bin for collection can be seen in ethical terms

Naturalism and analysis of the natural world

Key quotes

Naturalism was supposed to explain away ethics altogether by associating ethical concepts such as goodness or duty with non-ethical concepts such as pleasure or utility or the desire that society should be preserved.
(Warnock)

Naturalism is a philosophical approach rooted in empiricism, cognitivism and realism. The central idea is that we can find answers to philosophical questions, including those about ethics, by observing the natural world through our senses. **Ethical naturalism** is the philosophical view that all human behaviour and ethical knowledge – including how to determine what is good, bad, right and wrong – can be explained by referring only to natural causes and observable phenomena (without involving abstract ideas). This approach suggests that moral truths are not abstract; they are grounded in the facts of the natural world.

Ethical naturalism can be further explained as follows:

- **Moral terms can be understood by analysing the natural world**: For example, we recognise kindness as a good experience and cruelty as a bad experience.
- **Ethical statements can be verified or falsified**: For example, the statement that 'kind acts are good and cruel acts are bad' can be verified by observing the happiness and suffering caused by the acts.
- **Verified moral statements are objective truths and universal**: Given that the world exists independently of our minds, it can be relied upon to establish objective truths, including ethical truths. These objective ethical truths, such as 'kindness is good' are universally understood and accepted. With universally shared facts it is much easier to conduct ethical discussions and determine which behaviours are good and which are bad.
- **Objective features of the world make propositions true or false**: If these experiences are mind-independent, uniform and universal, then the statements 'kindness is an ethically good act' and 'cruelty is an ethically bad act' are true. This is because these ethical truths are grounded in the objective features of the world we can all observe and agree upon. We can see how kindness works in the world, and this verifies its goodness for everyone. By observing such natural properties, we can verify moral claims in the same way we verify scientific ones.

Key terms

ethical naturalism: the view that ethical propositions can be understood by analysing the natural world

utilitarianism: theory first outlined by Bentham and then developed by Mill, stating that we ought to aim to produce the greatest amount of pleasure/happiness for the greatest number of people and the least amount of pain

Utilitarianism: an example of ethical naturalism

The key example of ethical naturalism is **utilitarianism**, as proposed by the philosopher Jeremy Bentham and developed by J.S. Mill (see sub-themes D–F in theme 3 (pages 183–207)). This theory is naturalistic because it bases ethical reasoning on the experience of happiness. The most 'useful' ethical action is one that produces the maximum amount of happiness or pleasure. Utilitarians argue that in any situation we should all perform the action that results in the most happiness.

> **Key term**
>
> **universalisability:** Mill's utilitarian principle that everyone ought to aim at the happiness of everyone, as increasing the general happiness will increase individual happiness

Mill was particularly interested in creating an ethical society, not just giving individual guidance. His most important contribution was the concept of **universalisability**, which proposed that everyone should aim for the happiness of all, as increasing the general happiness ultimately increases individual happiness. This supports the idea that the interests of the group should be prioritised over individual interests.

Mill's theory of utilitarianism mirrors the progressive statements on page 45:

- Moral terms can be understood by analysing the natural world in relation to the effects of our actions.
- Ethical statements are cognitive, meaning they can be verified or falsified. This is done by examining actions and their consequences, specifically the amount of happiness or pain they produce, in the empirical world.
- Verified moral statements are objective truths and universal, so we can establish that everyone ought to aim at the happiness of everyone, as increasing the general happiness will increase individual happiness.
- These objective features of the world, namely the impact of acts that create happiness and acts that create suffering, make our ethical propositions about the nature of such action true or false.

Mill's argument that the interests of the group should come before the interests of the individual is the underlying feature of democracy

Ethical naturalism supports the view that objective moral laws exist independently of human beings and are grounded in the empirical world. By linking an objective external reality with a cognitivist approach that verifies our experiences, naturalism concludes that our ethical statements are objective. We can, therefore, recognise objective moral laws that are located in the world around us.

F.H. Bradley's *Ethical Studies* and idealist moral philosophy

F.H. Bradley

> **Key person**
>
> **F.H. Bradley (1846–1924):** An Oxford philosopher who transformed British thought by arguing that morality is found in our social roles; in *Ethical Studies* (1876), he introduced the essay 'My Station and its Duties', suggesting we find purpose by serving our community; he became the dominant philosopher of his era

> **Key person**
>
> **Georg Wilhelm Friedrich Hegel (1770–1831):** A German philosopher who tried to overcome the problems of dualistic ideas and contrasting ideologies by considering one view (thesis), then the contrary view (antithesis) and then combining what he thought were the unifying truth factors (synthesis) – this method was known as dialectical synthesis

For our purposes, ethical naturalism should be understood as empirical, cognitive and realist. We should also understand it in relation to the philosophy of **F.H. Bradley**.

F.H. Bradley, a nineteenth-century British philosopher, was heavily influenced by the German philosopher **Hegel**. His essay 'My Station and its Duties' from his work *Ethical Studies* presents a unique form of ethical naturalism which, in its day, was highly influential.

In this essay, Bradley tries to reconcile two opposing ethical theories – utilitarianism and Kantian ethics – by using Hegel's **dialectical synthesis** method. He used this to try to formulate a new ethical theory. Bradley was unsuccessful with the new ethical theory because he did not believe it could successfully achieve the proposed goal of **self-realisation**. Towards the end of *Ethical Studies*, Bradley reverted to a metaphysical position, having decided that the best explanation for morality was religion.

Hegel

Key terms

dialectical synthesis: Hegel's view that two opposite views (hypothesis and antithesis) can be united (synthesis) through philosophical analysis, for example: hypothesis 'the universe began with the Big Bang'; antithesis 'God created the world'; synthesis 'God was the first cause and is compatible with the Big Bang'

self-realisation: Bradley's view that, through a philosophical course of discovery, the self interacts with society and nature, and ends with a realisation of its identity and ethical role within the world

Bradley's unique form of naturalism advances upon utilitarianism, while also improving on Emmanuel Kant's **transcendental idealism**.

Bradley was drawn to the empirical basis of utilitarianism but was also interested in Kant's concept of universal **duty**. Using the Hegelian method, he aimed to combine naturalism's empirical foundation with the idea of universal obligation from Kant's idealist ethics.

He aimed at an ethical theory that was not just naturalistic but also incorporated the idea of a metaphysical self. In a complex way he wanted the self to be apart from the world and at the same time be fully engaged by the existence of others in the world.

The philosopher Emmanuel Kant (1724–1804)

Station and duty through self-realisation

For Bradley, ethics is about the self-realisation of a person within the physical world, not in abstract isolation. He argues that the self can only be fully understood in relation to the whole society, which he terms 'a social organism'. He sees the social organism as a community where individuals are members or organs of the larger whole; the individuals have no true identity or purpose outside of the social organism. A person discovers their purpose and duty by finding their '**station**' or place within the social organism:

> To know what a man is [...] you must not take him in isolation. He is one of a people, he was born in a family, he lives in a certain society, in a certain state. What he has to do depends on what his place is, what his function is, and that all comes from his station in the organism.

This process involves identifying one's role and function in society. Through interaction with the world, the self discovers its ethical sense of duty, thereby overcoming the delusion of self-isolation. Bradley concludes that the true self is integral to the society it inhabits.

Key terms

transcendental idealism: Emmanuel Kant's complex philosophy found in the *Critique of Pure Reason* (1781, 1787) that rejects the notion of objective empiricism and argues that our experiences of things are only 'sensible forms of our intuition'

duty: Bradley's view that ethical awareness develops through self-realisation as we interact with society and nature and recognise our station (our role and function within it)

station: Bradley's term to acknowledge the location, role and function of a human being in the social and natural world

Specification content

F.H. Bradley – ethical sentences express propositions; objective features of the world make propositions true or false; meta-ethical statements can be seen in scientific terms

Key term

concrete universal: Bradley's view that the self is not isolated but is derived from dialectical relations with the world

Key quotes

The initial movement is from the hedonistic utilitarianism of 'pleasure for pleasure's sake' to the Kantian morality of 'duty for duty's sake', and from that to the social morality of 'My Station and its Duties'.

(Norman)

The difficulty is: being limited and so not a whole, how to extend myself so as to be a whole? The answer is be a member in a whole. Here your private self, your finitude, ceases as such to exist; it becomes the function of an organism.

(Bradley)

The nature of ethical statements as part of the concrete universal

For Bradley, true ethical statements describe interactions within the world, recognising that we are part of a greater whole. A person's station and duty are found within the empirical world, making ethical statements both verifiable and factual. We achieve our goal of self-realisation by observing and adopting the values of our community and other societies. This is referred to as the '**concrete universal**'.

According to the philosopher Mary Warnock, Bradley's ethical starting point is the 'moral consciousness' we all share, as seen in our sense of obligation and feelings of moral failure. Self-realisation is a long-term process, a 'system of interconnected actions', in which a person's moral acts are judged as part of their life's overall actions. Morality becomes an act of self-expression.

Bradley's view was that any moral act shatters the illusion of being separate from the world. The ultimate goal of morality is to end a person's sense of isolation entirely. Through self-realisation, Bradley's naturalistic ethics not only identifies what a person *is* but also what they *ought to be*. He claimed that the conflict between our private, selfish will and our desire for good disappears when we align ourselves with the good we will realise in the world. By performing our individual duties, we contribute to a universal work, and, through self-sacrifice, the self is restored. By fulfilling our role within the social organism, we understand both who we are and what it means to be ethical.

Bradley believed that by understanding our role in society and fulfilling its responsibilities, we discover both who we are and how to act morally

Bradley's conclusions about 'My Station and its Duties'

According to Bradley, his ethical theory improves on utilitarianism and Kant's idea of duty:

- It is objective. It brings together subject (individual) and object (the world around us). The 'whole' works and functions as it should do when everyone discovers and works within their particular station.

- It combines objectivity (empirical fact) with the **non-sensuous moral ideal** (duty or moral obligation). Bradley's theory is that all sense of conflict between duty and individual sensuality is resolved as all these elements become part of the wider external world that is the concrete universal.
- It is also to do with the 'concrete' and considers actual empirical ethical facts that derive from, and are prescribed from, the whole. Ethical statements are therefore empirically verified and seen in scientific terms as true or false in relation to objective features of the world.

Key terms

non-sensuous moral ideal: Bradley's term for Kant's general theory of duty

despotism: Bradley's understanding of absolute power or the ultimate controlling all

categorical imperative: Kant's view of an unconditional moral obligation which is binding in all circumstances and is not dependent on a person's inclination or purpose

Key quotes

This is the Hegelian morality which stresses the social character of the individual, and finds the content of moral life in the actions which derive from particular social relations and functions.

(Norman)

I and everyone else must have some station with duties pertaining to it, and those duties do not depend on our opinion or liking.

(Bradley)

There is nothing better than my station and its duties, nor anything higher or more truly beautiful.

(Bradley)

Bradley and normative ethics

Although Bradley's exploration is meta-ethical, he doesn't provide normative guidance; he simply explains the origins of our ethical sense. He argues that philosophers can find verification for ethical statements in the empirical world (the concrete universal).

Despite this, he believed that moral philosophy cannot and should not tell us what specific actions to take. To him, this idea was 'simply ludicrous'.

Bradley's moral naturalism resolves the conflict between **despotism** and individualism. It denies each in isolation while preserving the truth of both: a person's individuality is understood through their relationship with the social whole, and in turn, the whole shapes the individual. His ultimate moral command is to be aware of this all-encompassing morality, which he describes as a '**categorical imperative**' that also surrounds us with an 'atmosphere of love'.

As for how we know our duty, Bradley's solution is that this knowledge has a physical and scientific basis. We find our duty by accepting the social and moral norms of our station. He supports this with a quote from Hegel, stating that wisdom and virtue consist of 'living agreeably to the ethos of one's people'.

The Scottish philosopher David Hume (1711–76)

Challenges to naturalism

Naturalism faces several challenges, including those from alternative theories like intuitionism and emotivism. Here are three immediate challenges.

Specification content

Challenges: Hume's law (the is-ought problem); Moore's naturalistic fallacy (moral language is indefinable); the open question argument (moral facts cannot be reduced to natural properties)

Hume's law (the is-ought problem)

The first objection to naturalism is that it reduces ethical statements to factual observations. For example, while we can observe that giving money to someone in need brings comfort, the ethical conclusion that 'it is good to give' is a separate layer of knowledge not present in the original observation.

Key terms

Hume's law: that an *ought* cannot be derived from an *is*

Hume's fork: the principles of *a priori* knowledge (conceptual and prior to experience) and *a posteriori* knowledge (relating to experience) are completely separate types of knowledge

***a priori*:** from Latin, meaning 'from what comes before' and refers to knowledge or reasoning that is gained without needing experience or observation

Critics argue that one cannot logically introduce a new element, like the concept of 'good', into a conclusion when it was not part of the initial observation. This is known as **Hume's law** or Hume's guillotine: the idea that you cannot logically derive an *ought* from an *is*. Hume writes:

> For as this *ought*, or *ought not*, expresses some new relation or affirmation, it is necessary that it should be observed and explained; and at the same time that a reason should be given, for what seems altogether inconceivable, how this new relation can be a deduction from others, which are entirely different from it.

Hume's view on moral propositions is linked to his principle known as **Hume's fork** (see the diagram) which separates knowledge into two distinct categories: ***a priori*** (conceptual, prior to experience) and *a posteriori* (empirical, relating to experience).

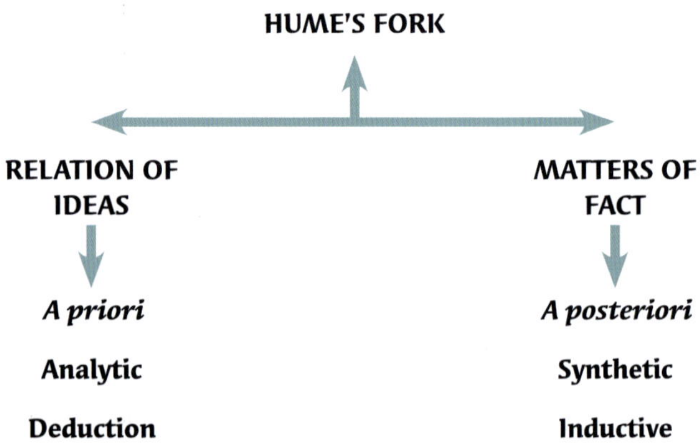

Hume's fork

Hume argued that a moral proposition is neither a factual *a posteriori* statement nor an *a priori* truth. It is a statement of value or judgement that cannot be logically deduced or empirically proven. Philosophers such as Bertrand Russell (1872–1970) and A.J. Ayer (1910–89) used Hume's Fork as a foundation for their own philosophies.

Here is an example to illustrate Hume's law:

1. A person gives money freely to another who is less fortunate.
2. They can see that it has brought more comfort to the life of the less fortunate person.
3. The action did not come with any real material detriment to the giver.
4. A conclusion is drawn that 'if it causes no material detriment and brings comfort, therefore we *ought* to give money to a less fortunate person'.

Following Hume's analysis, the conclusion that 'we *ought* to give money' is a separate judgement, not an inherent part of the action itself. The first three statements simply show 'facts of the matter'; the conclusion using the word ought is not logically valid as it does not follow from the preceding statements.

To reach a conclusion like 'we ought to do this' we would need a hidden premise, such as 'comfort and financial health are good'. However, even if we reveal this premise, it is flawed. It equates good with comfort and financial health without defining what good actually is or demonstrating that this equation is valid. Without a proper premise, the argument fails.

Key quote

> Naturalism provides a view from the outside, and from that perspective, it provides all sorts of interesting information. But it misses something that can be experienced only from the inside, namely the normative force of the reasoning.
>
> (Rachels)

Moore's naturalistic fallacy

G.E. Moore's critique of naturalism was fundamental to his own ethical theory, intuitionism – which will be examined in the next section. He began by asking a simple but crucial question: 'What is good?' Moore writes:

> [...] this question, how good is to be defined, is the most fundamental question in all Ethics [...] Its definition is, therefore, the most essential point in the definition of Ethics.

By this, Moore is concerned with what he calls the 'intrinsic value' of good as an end in itself – he is *not* concerned with what makes a good action or what brings about a good end.

Moore writes:

> My point is that **good is a simple notion**, just as yellow is a simple notion; that, just as you cannot, by any manner of means, explain to anyone who does not already know it, what yellow is, so you cannot explain what good is. Definitions of the kind that I was asking for, definitions which describe the real nature of the object or notion denoted by a word, and which do not merely tell us what the word is used to mean, are only possible when the object or notion in question is something complex.

Moore is not saying that things cannot be 'good'; indeed, there are many things that can be identified by their 'goodness', such as pleasure, love, happiness and health. What Moore was pointing out was that a particular quality that is described as good cannot be used to define good; in other words, we cannot identify a single property or quality that explains what goodness in itself is. We can say a door is yellow so that it is a yellow door, but the door does not define what yellow is. In the same way with good, we can identify pleasure *as* good but to answer that goodness *is* pleasure does not satisfy our quest for a definition as there are many other things that are also good or a means to goodness. There is no shortage of possible definitions: naturalness, virtue, wisdom, love, peace, duty, and so on.

For Moore, good is not a natural property and cannot be defined by one. He called the idea that it could be defined as a natural property the **naturalistic fallacy**. Just as Hume argued against deriving an ought from an is, Moore argued you cannot define goodness through nature or experience. Good is a simple concept which cannot be broken down into parts. While complex things like a horse can be defined by their constituent parts (such as the head, legs and tail), good has no constituent parts; it is a simple notion. He wrote that good is indefinable because it is an 'ultimate term of reference'.

Moore specifically targeted utilitarianism for equating good with pleasure. He argued that ethics seeks to identify a property of goodness that might be common to other properties, such as pleasure or happiness. However, since we cannot find this shared element, it is incorrect to say they are the same thing.

Moore concluded that:

- good is a simple concept or notion that cannot be broken down
- good, in itself, is not dependent upon any other constituent part and neither is it a constituent part itself
- the term good is indefinable.

Moore also addressed the question, 'What ought we to do?' While Hume's law focused on the logical flaw of deriving an ought from an is, Moore concentrated on the linguistic mistake of defining good as a natural quality.

He argued that Mill's utilitarianism, by equating good with pleasure, commits a linguistic tautology. When you try to discover what you ought to do based on this definition, you simply conclude with what people already do, which is to seek pleasure. You do not arrive at a new ethical duty or moral obligation.

The door cannot define yellow in the same way an action cannot reveal what good means

Key term

naturalistic fallacy: Moore's view that it is a logical error to explain that which is good reductively in terms of natural properties such as 'pleasant' or 'desirable'

Key quotes

If I am asked, 'What is good?' my answer is that good is good, and that is the end of the matter. Or if I am asked 'How is good to be defined?' my answer is that it cannot be defined, and that is all I have to say about it.

(Moore)

Moore makes it perfectly clear that what he thinks you cannot legitimately do to 'good' is to analyse it. It is impossible to name its parts because it has no parts.

(Warnock)

Moore's reasoning is as follows:

- If we think that we can define good by a natural quality such as 'what is desired' we are mistaken. Then to argue that we 'ought to pursue desire because it is good' is another fallacy.
- We are mistaken because it creates a **tautology**. That is, if desire is good then we ought to seek desire. Unfortunately, this then means that we ought to seek what we do in fact seek.

Key term

tautology: saying the same thing twice over in different words

Moore's argument is that since good is indefinable we cannot identify it as a natural quality. When we consider what this implies ethically in terms of duty all we are doing is describing what we are already doing.

A closed question always invites a definitive answer

The open question argument

The open question argument demonstrates that defining good using natural properties is futile because it always leaves an unanswered question. If we could define good precisely, we would be able to state what good is in terms of psychological, biological or sociological truths, creating a closed question with a definitive yes or no answer. For example, 'Is 2 + 2 equal to 4?' has a straightforward answer of 'yes'.

However, this does not work for good. When we attempt to define good as a natural property, such as pleasure, we create an open question because it is still a legitimate and meaningful question to ask, 'Is pleasure good?' If we had truly succeeded in defining good, this follow-up question would be illogical, but it is not. This proves the definition is incomplete.

- If 'pleasure is the same as good' then saying 'whatever promotes pleasure is good' would be a tautology equivalent to saying 'whatever promotes pleasure promotes pleasure'. This reduces a moral claim to a circular statement that conveys no meaningful information about value.
- It is never absurd to ask of natural properties 'Is this good?'; we know that we can logically ask the question 'Is the promotion of pleasure good?' and, in fact, it is *not nonsense* because pleasure is a complex notion.
- Good cannot be identified as, or defined by, natural properties which are by their very nature complex notions.
- For any natural property *x* (like pleasure or survival), the question 'Is *x* good?' remains an open question. We can always meaningfully doubt whether *x* is actually good.

Summary

- ★ Naturalism is linked to empiricism, realism and cognitivism and includes the idea that a person's past experiences of the world help them to verify whether a proposition is true or false.
- ★ Naturalism is linked to the scholar F.H. Bradley, who argued that true ethical statements describe interactions within the world, where the self is part of a wider whole.
- ★ Bradley linked Kantian ethics and utilitarianism to argue that a person can understand their world and find fulfillment in knowing their duties and station.

- Hume's law/guillotine stated that you cannot derive an ought from an is and that a moral proposition is neither a factual *a posteriori* statement nor an *a priori* truth – it is nothing more than a statement of value or judgement.
- Moore used the naturalistic fallacy to argue that a person could not define goodness through nature or experience – good cannot be equated with other properties.
- The open question argument, according to Moore, states that 'good can never be truly defined as there always remains the question "Is *x* good?"'.

AO1 Activity

a In a few short notes, outline the key features of ethical naturalism as presented in the following summary.

b Use your outline to write your own summary of approximately 140 words. When you have completed the task, refer to the band descriptors for A2 (WJEC) or A Level (Eduqas) and check your summary is both accurate and relevant.

Summary

The most important point about ethical naturalism is that it supports the view that objective moral laws exist independently of human beings and are grounded in the empirical world. Having established the link between an objective external existence (realism) and the idea that a cognitivist approach can establish the truth or falsity (objective knowledge) of what we experience (empiricism), then it logically follows that what we know about what we experience makes our ethical statements objective. Therefore, we can recognise objective moral laws that exist independently of human beings and that are located firmly in the world around us.

In other words, ethical language can be understood by referring to, and carefully analysing, what we experience in the natural world around us. For example, we all understand that to experience the kindness of another is a good experience and that to experience cruelty from another is a bad experience. Taken further, this means that our ethical statements have meaning because we can verify with others that kind acts are good and cruel acts are bad by observing the happiness or suffering that these experiences contain. We can all recognise this and this means the same to everyone.

If the ethical descriptions and statements have meaning for everyone then it follows that they are objective truths and universal. We can discuss ethics meaningfully and establish certain propositions about good and bad ethical behaviour. If these experiences are uniform and universal, then this also means that the statements 'kindness is an ethically good act' and 'cruelty is an ethically bad act' are true because these experiences are grounded in the objective features of the world around us.

This section covers AO2 content and skills

Specification content

Whether ethical and non-ethical statements are the same

Issues for analysis and evaluation

Whether ethical and non-ethical statements are the same

Possible line of argument	Critical analysis and evaluation
Ethical naturalism argues that ethical and non-ethical statements are the same. Ethical terms like good are reducible to natural properties (such as pleasure, biology and social utility). For naturalists, moral claims are objective facts that can be verified empirically through science or observation.	Moore's naturalistic fallacy challenges this by arguing that good is a simple, indefinable property like yellow. He uses the open question argument: even if good is defined as pleasure, it can still be meaningfully asked, 'Is pleasure good?' This suggests good is not a natural property.
Evolutionary ethics suggests morality is embedded in biology. Altruistic behaviour is explained by 'selfish genes' and the 'handicap principle'. Just as human beings avoid fire because it is hot (fact), they avoid violence because it causes pain (fact). Thus, moral statements are just biological descriptions.	Hume's law (the is-ought problem) states that you cannot derive a value from a fact. Just because nature *is* a certain way (e.g. humans have a survival instinct) does not mean humans *ought* to act that way. This logical problem implies ethical statements belong to a different category than non-ethical ones.
Ethical statements appear to be objective and real in practice. Parables like that of the Good Samaritan teach goodness through concrete actions. For naturalists like Bradley, finding one's duty is a matter of realising one's station in a concrete, social reality, making morality as observable as any social science.	Intuitionists argue that ethical statements are *sui generis* (unique). While we use the word good for non-ethical objects (a 'good door' based on purpose), a phrase like 'good person' refers to a non-natural moral quality. This quality is known via *a priori* intuition, similarly to how we recognise mathematical truths.
Naturalists argue that moral disagreements are simply part of social adaptation and learning. As science (biology and psychology) advances, we are moving towards a purely empirical explanation for ethics, treating moral data the same way we treat physical data.	Critics argue this is too reductionist. If morality is just biology or psychology, it loses its normative force – the sense of obligation a person feels. If ethical statements were just facts, there would be no reason for the deep evaluative debates that define human morality.
The convergence of the two views suggests that while ethical language is distinct, it must relate to the empirical world to be practical. Bradley attempted to unite the conceptual with the empirical, suggesting that moral statements are the bridge between a person's inner ideals and their social duties.	The debate remains unresolved because of Hume's fork. If ethical statements are not 'matters of fact' (naturalism) or 'relations of ideas' (intuitionism/mathematics), then emotivists might argue they are merely emotional expressions, further distancing them from non-ethical statements.

AO2 Activity

a Using the table on page 54, analyse three possible conclusions that could be drawn from the view that ethical and non-ethical statements are the same. Select evidence and examples to support each conclusion. Select the one that you think is **most convincing** and explain why.

b Using your analysis from part a, write a concluding paragraph that presents your own justified viewpoint. Refer to the AO2 band descriptors and ensure your conclusion demonstrates 'a confident and justified conclusion' (band 5).

Specification content

The extent to which ethical statements are not objective

Exam practice

Below is an example of part of an evaluation of the extent to which ethical statements are not objective.

Sample answer

The debate over whether ethical statements are objective often starts with ethical naturalism. Naturalists argue that moral claims are objective because they can be tested empirically. For example, some argue that goodness is linked to happiness or fulfilling one's duty in society. If morality is based on facts about the world, then moral statements are as objective as scientific ones.

News reporter: The essay clearly defines the starting point of the debate by linking morality to observable facts.

However, many philosophers disagree. David Hume argued that ethical statements are fundamentally different from empirical facts. He suggested that when we say something is wrong, we are not describing a fact in the world, but expressing our own feeling of disapproval. This move from is (a fact) to ought (a value) suggests that morality is subjective and rooted in human emotion.

Philosopher / **Detective**: This paragraph successfully identifies the logical gap between facts and values that challenges the idea of objectivity.

The 'argument from relativity' adds weight to the idea that ethics are not objective. Different cultures across history have held wildly different moral codes. If moral values were objective and 'out there' to be discovered, we would expect more agreement. The variety of theories – from divine command theory to emotivism – presents a fundamental challenge to the claim that ethical statements are objective.

Explorer / **Critical thinker**: By looking at the global variety of moral codes, the essay effectively questions why an objective truth would be so hard to find.

A major problem for objective theories like intuitionism is the 'I just know' defence. If two people have a different intuition about a moral issue, there is no way to prove who is right. If morality is purely objective, there should be a way to distinguish between something actually being right and it merely seeming right to a specific person.

Judge: The argument highlights a significant procedural weakness in theories that claim objectivity without empirical proof.

Despite these challenges, naturalism remains popular because it raises morality above mere personal opinion. It allows us to form moral absolutes, such as 'murder is wrong', which matches our common-sense view of the world. This approach aligns with a scientific worldview in which we prefer to test claims rather than accepting them blindly.

Tennis player: The essay maintains a strong, balanced volley here by presenting the common-sense appeal of the naturalist position.

Critical thinker

This section correctly pauses to analyse the language being used, which is helpful for a high-level meta-ethics response.

We must also consider what objective actually means. Does it mean a moral rule is as consistent as a mathematical formula? Or does it mean it is simply recognised by all people across different cultures? Depending on your definition, you might reach a very different conclusion about whether a statement like 'stealing is wrong' is an objective fact or a social tool.

Detective **Explorer**

A nuanced point is made here, searching for a middle-ground between total objectivity and total subjectivity.

Some suggest that while the foundations of morality might be objective, the application is subjective. For instance, we might all agree that justice is an objective good, but we disagree subjectively on how to achieve it. This suggests that morality might be a mix of absolute truths and human interpretation.

Philosopher

This paragraph synthesises the complex arguments into a clear final thought on the nature of moral language.

While deontological systems often claim that moral truths are objective and *a priori*, more empirical systems accept a level of subjectivity. The is-ought problem and the diversity of global cultures make a strong case that ethical statements are not purely objective.

Judge

The final ruling finds that the tension between absolute rules and cultural variety suggests morality is rarely a simple case of binary choice.

Overall, it seems that while we may desire morality to be objective to give it authority, it often functions as a product of human culture. Many people accept a hybrid view: some core principles may be objective, while others are contingent on the needs of a specific society at a specific time.

Over to you

For this task, select six key points from the following list, which are relevant to the evaluation question. Put your selection into the order that you would use to address the question and explain your selections. When explaining why you have chosen your six to answer the question, you will find that you are developing a process of reasoning. This helps you to develop an argument to decide whether or not ethical statements are objective.

Question

'Ethical statements are not objective.' Discuss.

Points

1 F.H. Bradley argued that we can observe a person's station and duties in society to find objective moral facts.
2 If we say 'murder is wrong', we are describing a fact about the world that can be true or false.
3 A.J. Ayer argued that moral statements are just expressions of emotion and cannot be proven true.
4 People in different cultures have different moral rules – some argue that morality is just a human invention.
5 Naturalists believe that we can use our senses to observe moral properties in the same way we observe properties of natural phenomena.
6 Some philosophers argue that if morality is not objective then there is no real reason to behave well.
7 Hume argued that you cannot move from a factual is (how the world is) to a moral ought (how we should act).
8 If ethical statements were objective, we would expect everyone to agree on them, yet moral disagreements are common.
9 Divine command theory suggests that morality is objective because it is based on the unchanging commands of God.

E: Meta-ethical approaches – intuitionism

Intuitionism: objective moral laws exist independently of human beings and moral truths can be discovered by using our minds in an intuitive way

This section covers AO1 content and skills

Specification content

Objective moral laws exist independently of human beings; moral truths can be discovered by using our minds in an intuitive way

Key person

G.E. Moore (1873–1958): A British philosopher and professor at the University of Cambridge; his most influential work, *Principia Ethica* (1903), established the foundation of ethical intuitionism; he argued that good is a simple, indefinable property known through intuition, and that attempts to define it in natural terms commit the naturalistic fallacy; he is regarded as one of the founders of analytic philosophy

Moore proposed that good was a simple and indefinable concept. Then, just as with mathematics, the principles of ethics are *a priori* and exist independently of human beings. In addition, these are **self-evident** truths and therefore truths that do not need to be established and known through some kind of rationalism.

Moore did not explain how a recognition of good was to be implemented, processed or caused; it just *is*. Just as good is indefinable, or at best defined as good (as itself), in the same way we just recognise goodness through **intuition**, and it does not need any working out. He wrote:

> I would wish it observed that, when I call such propositions intuitions, I mean merely to assert that they are incapable of proof; I imply nothing whatever as to the manner or origin of our cognition of them.

According to Moore, once we begin to apply reason or suggest something is worked out through reason with regard to good, error becomes likely.

In his book *Principia Ethica*, Moore posed two fundamental questions for moral philosophy:

- What kind of things ought to exist for their own sake? His answer: these things are intrinsically good and are known through intuition rather than empirical evidence.
- What kind of actions ought we to perform? His answer: we should perform actions that bring about this intrinsic goodness, and this can be supported by empirical evidence.

Moore's ethical intuitionism is also known as **ethical non-naturalism** because it rejects the idea that objective moral laws can be derived from the empirical world. However, it is not a metaphysical theory in the traditional sense, as it asserts that moral principles exist in the same way concepts like numbers do. It is therefore referred to as **non-metaphysical moral realism**.

Moore sees no connection between meta-ethics and metaphysics since meta-ethics is concerned with the very first question about ethics, namely the nature of goodness. As we have seen from the naturalistic fallacy, neither exploration, examination nor enquiry into the innate properties of the empirical and physical world could provide insight into what goodness *is*.

G.E. Moore

Key terms

self-evident: describes something (e.g. a proposition) that needs no verification and remains true independently of whether or not we perceive it to be so

intuition: immediate knowledge or understanding without conscious reasoning or proof

ethical non-naturalism: an alternative term for intuitionism

non-metaphysical moral realism: an alternative term for intuitionism

Key quote

G.E. Moore's *Principia Ethica* was first published in 1903. It has become the custom to regard it as the source from which the subsequent moral philosophy of the century has flowed.

(Warnock)

Specification content

Intuitive ability is innate and the same for all moral agents

Key terms

***sui generis*:** a Latin phrase meaning 'of its own kind'

innate: part of, integral to

Intuitive ability is innate and the same for all moral agents

While the word good cannot be defined, it is not meaningless. For intuitionists, good is ***sui generis*** (from the Latin 'of its own kind'), which means it is unique and cannot be compared to anything else. The ability to recognise good is an **innate** and universal truth for all people. This perceived goodness is an objective and self-evident truth, not a relative one based on empirical perception.

Moore explains that everyone understands the question 'Is this good?' This is because our state of mind is different when we ask this question compared to asking 'Is this pleasant?' Good refers to a unique property that we are all constantly aware of. For sound ethical reasoning, it is crucial to understand this distinction, which Moore believes is straightforward once the problem is properly analysed.

Moore distinguishes between the act of intuition and the nature of self-evident truths. Intuition is the mental faculty that allows us to recognise self-evident truths. Unlike common sense, which can be subjective, a self-evident truth exists independently of our perception. For instance, the mathematical proposition '2 + 2 = 4' is a self-evident truth; its validity does not depend on whether a person understands it. Intuition does not provide the proof for such a claim; it is simply the tool we use to access it.

According to Richard Norman, Moore's intuitionism is distinct in two ways:

- Intuition is about identifying things that are intrinsically good, not about what actions are right.
- Moore does not suggest a special way of knowing these truths. He means we can know they are true, but we cannot give any further reasons for why they are true. It is a belief you know to be true, without being able to explain why.

Specification content

Intuition allows for objective moral values

Intuition allows for objective moral values

The last two chapters of Moore's *Principia Ethica* are concerned with two questions:

- What should we do?
- What things are good?

Moore's answer to the first question is very simple: any moral obligation has inherent within it the obligation to do good and produce the greatest amount of good. Moore states that our duty can only be defined as the action that will create more good in the universe than any possible alternative. Therefore, an action is right or morally permissible only if it results in the maximum possible sum of good. An action is a duty if it is the most effective means of increasing the sum of good.

Key quote

All moral laws, I wish to shew, are merely statements that certain kinds of actions will have good effects.

(Moore)

This sounds like a very utilitarian approach. As Mary Warnock observes, Moore is more aligned with utilitarians on the issue of conduct than with any other moral philosophers. They only differ on how to assess the value of consequences. For this reason, Moore's theory has been labelled a form of consequentialist intuitionism.

At the end of *Principia Ethica,* Moore identifies some intrinsic moral goodness. His method for identification of such goods is to propose such things that if they were to exist independently and abstractly, they would still be considered good. Moore writes:

> Indeed, once the meaning of the question is clearly understood, the answer to it, in its main outlines, appears to be

> so obvious, that it runs the risk of seeming to be a **platitude**. By far the most valuable things, which we know or can imagine, are certain states of consciousness, which may be roughly described as the pleasures of human intercourse and the enjoyment of beautiful objects.

For Moore, human friendship and aesthetic beauty are **intrinsic goods** because we can perceive them as good even in isolation. He acknowledged that other goods might be 'mixed' due to the complexity of the natural world.

> **Key terms**
>
> **platitude:** a moral comment that has been used too often to be meaningful; cliché
>
> **intrinsic goods:** acts that are always good no matter what the circumstances

Moore's method was to consider what things, if they existed alone, would still be judged as good. To determine their comparative value, he would similarly consider the value of each thing in isolation. Moore's list of goods is similar to Aristotle's virtues, and his recognition of their mixed nature aligns with his analysis of simple and complex concepts.

Moore believed that friendship is good in itself, even when considered in isolation

Moore's evils are divided into three groups:

- Evils which involve the enjoyment or admiring contemplation of things which are themselves evil or ugly.
- Mixed evils, which involve a combination of misplaced emotions, such as the love of what is evil or the hatred of what is good.
- Great positive evils, which involve the consciousness of intense pain, which is considered an evil in itself regardless of whether it is accompanied by other thoughts or feelings.

Intuition needs a mature mind so not infallible

> **Specification content**
>
> Intuition needs a mature mind so not infallible

The foundation of knowledge must have a starting point or anchor. As Aristotle argued in *Metaphysics*, it is impossible to prove everything, as this would lead to an infinite regress of proofs. Therefore, knowledge must rest on a fundamental basis. This concept is similar to the cosmological argument's idea of a first cause. The key question for intuitionists is whether this starting point for knowledge is innate and *a priori*, or if it is acquired through education. Moore suggests that our intuition, which provides access to self-evident knowledge, is *a priori*.

For intuitionists, the knowledge of good is innate and *a priori*, meaning it is independent of sensory experience. The implication of this is that moral knowledge is viewed as objectively certain; once the mind recognises a self-evident truth, such as 'friendship is good', it requires no further external proof. This suggests a sense of **infallibility** regarding the core properties of goodness itself. Moore, however, focused on what could be intuitively recognised as good in itself – the ideal goods – rather than on how these might apply in every circumstance. In complex, everyday decisions, mistakes may be made in application, but this does not contradict the fact that the fundamental knowledge of good exists.

> **Key term**
>
> **infallibility:** without error

Moore's answer to his secondary question, 'What ought I do?', was to pursue actions that produce the most good, identified through our awareness of self-evident intrinsic goods like beauty and friendship. Other intuitionists, however, disagree with this.

H.A. Prichard believed the basis of moral thinking was not the intrinsic good but the innate obligation or duty to act, which he saw as *sui generis*.

> **Key term**
>
> ***prima facie*:** first impression; accepted as correct until proved otherwise

Similarly, W.D. Ross rejected Moore's focus on consequences. In his *The Right and the Good*, Ross argued that some actions are right or wrong regardless of their consequences. He proposed that intuition helps us establish ***prima facie*** duties, such as fidelity and justice. These duties are only *prima facie* because they are conditional and can be prioritised over one another; in a conflict situation, intuition allows us to discern which duty carries the most weight.

Intuition recognises the good, but its application requires maturity and can be mistaken

According to Ross, these self-evident insights require a gradual awakening and mental maturity. He states that they are 'evident without any need of proof, or of evidence beyond itself', but only once a person has developed sufficiently. Prichard also believed that this intuitive awareness was not evenly distributed, and some people possessed a more developed sense of intuition than others.

For Ross, moral intuition is not an immediate, magical insight available to everyone at birth. Instead, it is more like mathematical reasoning. A child may not immediately understand '2 + 2 = 4', but as their mind matures and they engage with the world, the truth of the statement becomes self-evident. Therefore, if someone fails to recognise a moral truth, it is not because the truth is subjective, but because their moral reason has not yet reached the necessary level of maturity. The need for a mature mind explains why some people might disagree on ethics but it does not take away from the view that there are objective moral laws.

> **Key quotes**
>
> A self-evident proposition is one of which a clear intuition is sufficient justification for believing it, and for believing it on the basis of that intuition.
>
> **(Moore)**
>
> Ross maintains that 'both in mathematics and in ethics we have certain crystal-clear intuitions from which we build up all that we can know about the nature of numbers and the nature of duty'.
>
> **(Skelton)**
>
> But despite what has been said above, critics of intuitionism can claim that the fact that there is disagreement between moral philosophers and even intuitionists themselves undermine the view that certain propositions are self-evident
>
> **(Stratton-Lake)**

> **Specification content**
>
> H.A. Prichard, 'ought to do' has no definition; recognise what we 'ought to do' by intuition

Ought is indefinable but can be recognised by intuition

Like Moore, **H.A. Prichard** believed moral knowledge was indefinable, but he saw the basis of intuitive moral insight as duty or 'rightness', not Moore's concept of goodness.

Key person

H.A. Prichard (1871–1947): A British moral philosopher who taught at the University of Oxford; his essay 'Does Moral Philosophy Rest on a Mistake?' (1912) was foundational to the intuitionist school of thought; he believed that moral obligation (the feeling that we ought to do something) is *sui generis*, self-evident and apprehended intuitively rather than through reason or empirical knowledge; he opposed 'general reasoning' with 'moral reasoning' to explain that our duty is perceived directly via our unreflective consciousness

Moore viewed rightness as a *consequence* of understanding what is good, while Prichard and Ross saw it as the *core*, intuitive element of moral thinking. Their approach was more deontological. They argued that in moral conflicts, we learn to decide based on the greater obligation, thereby developing a more advanced sense of right and wrong, independent of a goal to create the most good.

Prichard asserted that moral knowledge is *sui generis*, separate from both reason and empirical influence. He rejected Moore's consequentialism – that we ought to act to produce the most good. For Prichard, since we intuitively feel a sense of obligation, the answer to 'What should we do?' is already contained within that feeling. This moral truth is not subject to rational debate; we just *know* what we ought to do.

Prichard considered duty to be an **underivative**, indefinable and **irreducible** concept, similar to how Moore viewed good. He believed this for three reasons:

- **Normative truths of duty are sui generis**: They are self-evident and cannot be reduced to or derived from empirical investigation.
- **They do not come from non-moral origins**: Duties are not extracted from non-moral judgements or values.
- **Duties are specific and not consequentialist**: Duties like keeping promises or not harming others are self-standing; as Thomas Hurka stated, the 'main reason we ought to keep our promises or not harm others is just that we ought to'.

While specific duties can conflict, they are not reducible to one single duty as in consequentialism. When duties conflict, we must make a direct intuitive judgement to determine which one is stronger, as there are no rules for deciding between them.

Key terms

underivative: not dependent on or derived from something else; a simple concept

irreducible: cannot be broken down into further parts

Specification content

H.A. Prichard: two ways of thinking (general and moral)

Two ways of thinking (general and moral)

It may seem illogical that duties conflict when there is only one right action. Prichard would argue that this is a flaw of **general reasoning**, which relies on empirical evidence to make logical arguments. He refers to the facts of a situation as **preliminaries**; they inform a decision but do not create an obligation. While general reasoning may present different **claims**, the ultimate moral duty can only be identified through intuition, not logical deduction.

Moral reasoning, for Prichard, is the intuitive recognition of one's duty. It exists in our **unreflective consciousness**. Moral reasoning is a higher form of thought that should supersede general reasoning. The danger is when general reasoning, which focuses on the complexities and consequences of a moral issue, takes precedence over our inherent moral intuition.

Prichard was wary of this consequentialist general reasoning, arguing that it can distort our sense of duty. For example, trying to justify the duty to keep a promise by saying it promotes a greater good (like honesty or trust) fundamentally changes the nature of the original obligation. This is similar to the open question argument, as it allows us to legitimately ask, 'but is

Key terms

general reasoning: using the empirical evidence around us to present logical argument

preliminaries: gathering of claims

claims: Prichard's term for arguments put together from general reasoning

moral reasoning: application of intuition

unreflective consciousness: Prichard's explanation that intuition is not determined by philosophical reflection

> **Key term**
>
> **other-regarding:** actions, duties or considerations that concern the welfare, interests or rights of other people rather than oneself

honesty good?' Consequentialism, in trying to explain the duty, essentially turns it into something else, thereby 'destroying' the original duty.

For example, why do we have a duty to relieve another person's pain? A consequentialist might say it is because it contributes to our own well-being. However, Prichard argues this is the wrong explanation. The true and obvious reason is that relieving someone's pain is a good in itself for that person. Therefore, the duty is fundamentally **other-regarding** – it is an immediate recognition of what is required, not a conclusion reached through a calculation of our own well-being.

However, if general reasoning can be dangerous if it is given too much emphasis, the question remains, 'How can we ensure that moral duty succeeds?'

For Prichard, moral duty succeeds because its methodology is epistemological and uses **Descartes' principle of scepticism** to confirm its validity. He argues that we use general reasoning to support and double-check what we already intuitively know. Just as we might check a mathematical calculation even when we are confident in the method, we can use reason to confirm our moral intuitions.

> **Key term**
>
> **Descartes' principle of scepticism:** that doubt can be resolved through challenge

Key quotes

The sense that we ought to do certain things arises in our unreflective consciousness, being an activity of moral thinking occasioned by the various situations in which we find ourselves.

(Prichard)

Descartes was the famous philosopher who coined the term 'I think, therefore I am' (French: *je pense, donc je suis*/Latin: *cogito ergo sum*) and introduced the principle of doubt to confirm a truth

Prichard explains that when our duty conflicts with our desires, we may doubt our initial moral sense. This is similar to Descartes' philosophical scepticism. We then use a process of reflection (general reasoning) to confirm that our original intuition was correct. In this way, reason is not used to build an argument or evaluate what is right but to deflect doubt about our initial, intuitive judgement.

The purpose of this reflective process is to strengthen our initial intuition, not to distort it. According to Thomas Hurka, this stage of scepticism is an essential part of philosophical reflection, but its ultimate purpose is a return to our original moral convictions.

General reasoning should not be used independently to reach a moral conclusion. Instead, it is used to support the knowledge already gained through intuition about our obligation. Prichard calls these independently derived arguments 'illegitimate claims'. The purpose of general reasoning is to provide a 'second glance' to confirm our intuitive understanding of duty, not to build a case for what is right. Prichard writes in his 'Does Moral Philosophy Rest on a Mistake' (1912):

> The sense that we ought to do certain things arises in our unreflective consciousness, being an activity of moral thinking occasioned by the various situations in which we find ourselves. At this stage our attitude to these obligations is one of unquestioning confidence. But inevitably the appreciation of the degree to which the execution of these obligations is contrary to our interest raises the doubt whether after all these obligations are really obligatory, i.e., whether our sense that we ought not to do certain things is not illusion. We then want to have it proved to us that we ought to do so, i.e., to be convinced of this by a process which, as an argument, is different in kind from our original and unreflective appreciation of it.

Challenges to intuitionism

No proof that moral intuition exists: the argument from queerness

J.L. Mackie's **argument from queerness**, presented in his *Ethics: Inventing Right and Wrong*, is a challenge to intuitionism. He argues that no objective ethical values exist.

Mackie's argument has two parts:

- **Metaphysical** queerness: If objective values existed, they would be incredibly strange – 'utterly different from anything else in the universe'. Mackie, a strong empiricist, objects that such unique, non-natural properties are metaphysically implausible because they are unlike anything we experience in the world. He compares this to Kant's objection to the cosmological argument: a 'first cause' would be so different from anything we know that we could not even recognise it.
- **Epistemological queerness**: If we could be aware of these strange ethical properties, it would require a 'special faculty of moral perception or intuition', which is 'utterly different from our normal ways of knowing everything else'. Mackie believes this idea of a unique, intuitive ability to perceive moral truths is also highly implausible.

Mackie also references Hume, stating that ethical terms add a queerness by influencing our will. In the natural world, facts do not tell us how to act; for example, knowing that the sun is hot does not compel us to do anything. Intuitionists claim that moral facts have a built-in command that automatically motivates us to behave in a certain way, but Mackie argues it is queer (strange) to suggest that an objective fact could have this power to change our desires. Ultimately, he dismisses intuition as a 'travesty of actual moral thinking', arguing that we are simply projecting our own feelings onto the world and mistaking them for objective laws.

Specification content

Challenges: no proof that moral intuition exists; intuitive 'truths' can differ widely; no obvious way to resolve conflicting intuitions

Key term

argument from queerness: J.L. Mackie's view that intuitionism is too odd to accept

Knowledge that cannot be verified by empirical means has the same queerness as metaphysical entities that exist beyond all that we know of existence within our physical universe, according to J.L. Mackie

Intuitive 'truths' can differ widely and there is no way to resolve conflicting intuitions

The main problem with intuitionism, as identified by many philosophers, is the lack of a universal, established list of duties or obligations. This leads to wide disagreements on what people should do and what they believe is right. The problem of these disagreements and responses to them can be set out as below.

The problem of disagreement:

- **Differing intuitions**: Intuitionists like Ross and Prichard suggested some duties, but the fact that duties vary from person to person and situation to situation makes widespread differences unavoidable. If two people face the same dilemma but have different intuitions about the right course of action, the theory offers no clear way to resolve the conflict.
- **Conflict among intuitionists**: Even intuitionist philosophers themselves disagree on which duties are universal. For example, Moore's consequentialist approach to intuitionism conflicts with the deontological views of Prichard and Ross. As Richard Norman points out, what is 'self-evidently true' for one may be 'self-evidently false' for the other.
- **Lack of logical resolution**: Critics argue that because intuitive truths are not based on logical reasoning and cannot be proven, there is no way to resolve disagreements. Norman highlights that since no reasons can be given for these self-evident truths, it is impossible to determine which view is correct.

The intuitionist response:

- **Distinguishing true intuition**: Deontological intuitionists would argue that moral disagreements do not mean that the truths themselves are conflicting. They suggest that in any given situation, there is a single intuitive truth. The conflict arises from distinguishing between a true intuition and one that has been distorted by consequentialist or empirical thinking.
- **Suppressed intuitions**: As Stratton-Lake notes, moral disagreement does not necessarily mean people have different intuitions. He suggests that some people might have an intuition (for example, that it is wrong to harvest one healthy person's organs to save five others), but they reject this intuition because they have 'persuaded themselves of the truth of act consequentialism'.

However, the argument that moral duties and obligations are universal makes many philosophers sceptical. They argue that if moral propositions were truly self-evident and known, everyone would accept and agree on them. The existence of widespread moral disagreement casts doubt on the core claim of intuitionism that moral truths are self-evident.

Key quotes

J.L. Mackie maintained that moral properties, understood broadly along intuitionist lines, are queer because they are inherently motivational, in the sense that when we come to see that some act is good, we are motivated to do it.

(Stratton-Lake)

Philosophers who claim that fundamental value-judgements are self-evident are not necessarily committed to claiming that their truth is always apparent to everyone [...] other philosophers have concluded that these fundamental value-judgements are really not the expression of self-evident truths at all; they are merely the expressions of personal preferences, of feelings and emotions, of individual likes and dislikes.

(Norman)

Summary

- Intuitionism is a form of ethical non-naturalism and non-metaphysical moral realism which asserts that objective moral laws exist independently of human beings and are discovered via the mind, not the senses.
- G.E. Moore argued that good is a simple, indefinable concept, similar to the colour yellow; it is *sui generis* and cannot be broken down into or defined by natural properties without committing the naturalistic fallacy.

* Moral truths are *a priori* and self-evident, meaning they are known through innate intuition rather than empirical evidence or rational proof; Moore specifically identified human friendship and aesthetic beauty as intrinsic goods.
* H.A. Prichard argued that duty is underivative and known through our unreflective consciousness, distinguishing between general reasoning (using empirical facts) and moral reasoning (the intuition of duty) and asserting that reason simply confirms what we already know.
* J.L. Mackie rejected the theory using the argument from queerness, claiming that objective moral values are too strange to exist and that a special faculty like intuition is epistemologically implausible.
* Other critics argue that the existence of widespread moral disagreement proves that intuitions are not self-evident; if they were, moral truths would be universal rather than differing between individuals and cultures.

AO1 Activity

a Examine the following summary of the challenges to intuitionism. In writing the passage, **eight key errors** have been made. Identify and correct the errors.

b Using the technical terms provided in the knowledge bank below, write a summary of intuitionism that is exactly 150 words (give or take 10 per cent). Your summary must explain what the theory is, how we know 'the good', and the difference between Moore and Prichard.

Summary

J.L. Mackie challenged intuitionism using the argument from logic. He argued that objective moral values do not exist. He proposed metaphysical queerness, which suggests that if moral values existed, they would be exactly the same as everything else we experience in the world. He also argued for epistemological queerness, which claims we access these truths through normal general reasoning. Mackie famously dismissed the idea of intuition as a 'triumph of moral thinking'.

Furthermore, the theory is weakened because intuitive truths are the same for everyone. Richard Norman points out that what is self-evidently true for one person must be self-evidently true for another, which explains why there is so much agreement between Moore and Prichard. While Moore is a deontologist, Prichard is a consequentialist, yet they agree on every duty. Finally, Stratton-Lake suggests that moral disagreement happens because some people have suppressed their intuitions by persuading themselves that naturalism is the only truth. This proves that there is a universal, established list of duties that everyone can easily follow without conflict.

Knowledge bank

1. ethical non-naturalism: the rejection of empirical definitions of good; intuitionism
2. *sui generis*: unique; of its own kind
3. *a priori*: known by the mind independently of experience
4. self-evident: truths that need no further proof or verification
5. underivative: a duty that is not based on or derived from anything else
6. unreflective consciousness: Prichard's term for the immediate awareness of duty

When you have completed the task, refer to the band descriptors for A2 (WJEC) or A Level (Eduqas). In particular, have a look at the demands described in the higher band descriptors towards which you should be aspiring. Check that you have met the demands.

This section covers AO2 content and skills

Specification content

Whether moral terms are intuitive

Issues for analysis and evaluation

Whether moral terms are intuitive

Possible line of argument	Critical analysis and evaluation
Common experience: Many people report an instinctive sense of right and wrong, taking moral truths for granted as objective features of the world. For believers, this mimics religious revelation; for others, it aligns with an ordered universe that conforms to laws similar to the laws of mathematics.	**Lack of verification**: Critics argue there is no way to verify intuitionism. Unlike empirical facts, there is neither evidence for the existence of intuition, nor agreement on its origin. Without a method of testing these claims, the theory remains a subjective assertion.
Prichard's duty: H.A. Prichard argued that moral knowledge is *sui generis* (unique) and separate from reason. He claimed we just know our obligations. By locating intuition in duty rather than consequences, he protected the theory from empirical challenges, as duty is not subject to rational debate.	**The problem of disagreement**: If moral terms were intuitive and self-evident, we would expect global uniformity. However, anthropologists, psychologists and sociologists demonstrate that intuition is often just social conditioning from one's culture, family or tribe.
Avoidance of fallacy: Approaching moral terms as intuitive avoids the naturalistic fallacy. By treating good as an underived, simple concept, intuitionists argue that we prevent the error of reducing complex moral values to limited empirical definitions like pleasure or utility.	**Internal conflict**: Intuitionists themselves cannot agree on what morality consists of. Moore (consequentialist) focuses on goodness, while Prichard and Ross (deontologists) focus on duty. If experts disagree on what is self-evident, the core claim of the theory is undermined.
Mathematical realism: According to intuitionism, moral laws exist independently, much like numbers. In this view, morality is not a human invention but a discovery of objective truths that exist apart from analysis or the physical world of space and time.	**Mackie's argument from queerness**: J.L. Mackie argues that objective values would be entities of a very strange sort and utterly different from anything else in the universe. He claims the special faculty required to perceive them is an implausible 'travesty of actual moral thinking'.
Self-evidence as a defence: The ultimate strength of the theory is that intuition is self-evident. If a critic demonstrates that ethical terms are not intuitive, an intuitionist simply argues the critic has not used their intuition correctly or lacks the necessary mental maturity.	**Circular logic**: Critics, following Hume, argue that knowledge alone cannot motivate the will. By claiming that disagreement is simply a failure of the agent's intuition, the theory becomes circular and impossible to disprove, effectively 'hiding' behind the label of self-evidence.

AO2 Activity

a Using the table on page 66, analyse three possible conclusions that could be drawn from the view that moral terms are intuitive.

b Using your analysis, write a concluding paragraph presenting your justified viewpoint. Refer to the AO2 band descriptors and ensure your conclusion demonstrates a confident and justified conclusion (band 5).

Exam practice

Below is an answer that a student has written in response to a question on whether or not intuitionism is the most convincing meta-ethical theory.

Sample question

'Intuitionism is the most convincing meta-ethical theory.' Evaluate this view.

Sample answer

Intuitionism is a meta-ethical theory which suggests that good is a property that can be defined by using scientific observations of the natural world. Instead, it is a complex, natural quality that we recognise through our moral intuition. G.E. Moore is the most significant supporter of this view. He argued that good is like the colour yellow: you know what it is when you see it, but you can break it down into smaller parts to explain it to someone else.

One reason this might be convincing is that it matches our experience of making quick moral choices without needing a logical calculation. However, a major weakness is that people's intuitions often conflict. For example, two people might have different 'gut feelings' about the morality of war. Furthermore, because intuition cannot be measured or proven by a test, critics argue it is just a way of disguising personal opinions as facts. This makes the theory appear less convincing to those who prefer empirical evidence.

Over to you

This is a below-average answer and so would be band 2. It will be useful, initially, to consider what is missing from the answer and what is inaccurate. The list of observations is provided to assist you. When analysing the answer's weaknesses, in a group, consider ways in which you would improve the answer to make it stronger. Then write out your additions, with each addition as a clear paragraph. Remember: it is how you use the points that is the most important factor. Apply the principles of evaluation by making sure that you:

- identify issues clearly
- present accurate views of others and comment on the views presented
- reach an overall personal judgement.

You may add more of your own suggestions but try to negotiate as a group and prioritise the most important things to add. One approach to the question would be to compare intuitionism with naturalism, which you have covered in 1D, and with emotivism, which you will cover in 1F, and then evaluate which of the three is the most convincing. However, it is important to remember that the focus of the question is first and foremost on intuitionism.

Observations

1. The first paragraph contains two significant factual errors regarding how Moore defines good. Can you find and correct them?
2. Moore's analogy of the colour yellow is used to show that good is a simple property. What mistake has the passage made in the description of this analogy?
3. What is the title of G.E. Moore's book in which he introduces this theory?
4. What is the technical term Moore uses for the error of defining good through natural things like pleasure or desire?
5. The passage mentions that intuitions conflict. How do W.D. Ross's *prima facie* duties address this specific problem in an essay?
6. Are there other arguments against intuitionism, such as those of A.J. Ayer and the logical positivist view that intuition is unverifiable and therefore meaningless?
7. The conclusion is quite brief. How could it be rewritten to provide a more balanced evaluation of whether intuitionism is the most convincing theory?

F: Meta-ethical approaches – emotivism

This section covers AO1 content and skills

Specification content

Theory that believes objective moral laws do not exist; a non-cognitivist theory; moral terms express personal emotional attitudes and not propositions

Emotivism as an ethical theory

The theory of **emotivism** is associated with **A.J. Ayer** and Charles L. Stevenson. Ayer was influenced by logical positivism and the verification principle, while Stevenson was influenced by Ludwig Wittgenstein. However, the idea that moral language is emotive was previously raised by empiricists such as David Hume and Bertrand Russell.

In his 1935 book *Religion and Science*, Russell argued that moral judgements of right and wrong, while justified if they promote good, are ultimately based on emotions. He claimed that when we say something has 'value', we are simply expressing our own feelings, not stating an objective fact. For example, the goodness of beauty is subjective, as shown by the phrase 'Beauty is in the eye of the beholder.'

Russell's conclusion was the opposite of G.E. Moore's: he argued that **intrinsic value** is a matter of pure subjectivity, not objectivity. For Russell, if something is self-evident it cannot be judged as true or false. Therefore, as Richard Norman states, such ethical claims 'make no statements and they convey no knowledge'.

Key terms

emotivism: theory that ethical propositions are simply expressions of approval or disapproval

intrinsic value: the worth something has in itself, for its own sake, rather than as a means to an end

Key quotes

Moore would agree that moral judgements are neither analytic nor empirically verifiable. But he believed that they are nevertheless true or false, because they are about non-natural properties. But Ayer responds that our 'intuitions' are simply our feelings of approval or disapproval.

(Lacewing)

Questions as to 'value' lie wholly outside the domain of knowledge. That is to say, when we assert that this or that has 'value', we are giving expression to our own emotions, not to a fact which would still be true if our personal feelings were different.

(Russell)

It was the philosopher Bertrand Russell who first really challenged Moore's views and suggested that ethical language was emotive

Ayer, influenced by the logical positivists and Hume's fork, argued that for a statement to be meaningful, it must fit into one of two categories. It should be noted that following this approach there are no other categories of knowledge and language than these:

- It can be an analytic statement, which is necessarily true by definition (like a logical or mathematical proposition).
- It can be a synthetic statement, which is an empirical hypothesis verified by sense experience.

The problem for ethical propositions is that they do not fit into either category of Hume's fork, which divides knowledge into 'relations of ideas' (analytic) and 'matters of fact' (synthetic)' (see 'Hume's law (the is-ought problem)' in T1D for a diagram and explanation). They are neither analytic, as they are not matters of logic or mathematics, nor synthetic, as they cannot be verified by empirical observation.

Hume, Russell and Ayer all concluded that ethical propositions do not fit into the categories of analytic or synthetic knowledge. Hume argued that when we call an action such as murder 'vicious' we are simply expressing our own feeling of dislike and horror, not describing a quality of the action itself. He stated that these feelings are 'perceptions in the mind', not objective qualities.

Key quote

Even the most enthusiastic intuitionist would never maintain that one literally saw or heard the goodness of an action.

(Warnock)

While Hume linked these feelings to naturalistic causes like biology and social conditioning, Russell and Ayer reached a different conclusion. Ayer, in particular, argued that ethical propositions, while not factual or verifiable, still have a purpose. He presented his argument in his book *Language, Truth and Logic*. He made it clear that ethical language is not meaningless, but it should not be the subject of meta-ethical philosophical enquiry, which attempts to verify its factual basis. In short, the verification principle does not render ethical language meaningless; it simply identifies that it is different and that its purpose lies outside of making factual claims or of meta-ethical philosophical enquiry.

Key quote

On Hume's account, our ethical nature is characterised by the capacity for sympathy, or the ability to feel with (empathise with) others. On such an account any variation in moral codes must be a consequence of differing social conditions, while ultimately all such codes must express some fundamentals which humanity shares.

(Hayward)

For Ayer, ethical language does not communicate specific meanings or definitions. Instead, his interest was limited to understanding the function of ethical language. As he suggests in *Language, Truth and Logic*, moral terms do not describe facts but serve to express the speaker's feelings.

Specification content

A.J. Ayer – ethical statements are neither verifiable nor analytic; made to express joy or pain (emotion); expressed to be persuasive; emotivism is not subjectivism

A.J. Ayer: ethical statements are neither verifiable nor analytic

Key person

A.J. Ayer (1910–89): A British philosopher who, after studying at the University of Oxford, became a leading promoter of logical positivism after a visit to the Vienna Circle in the 1930s; members of this movement were scientists and philosophers who collectively believed that the only statements that were meaningful were those that could be verified empirically; published when he was 26, Ayer's book *Language, Truth and Logic* caused immediate controversy for its dismissal of metaphysics, theology and ethics as factually meaningless; he later served as Wykeham Chair of Logic at Oxford; he moderated some of his earlier views but his emotivist approach to ethical language remained highly influential on the creation of meta-ethics

A.J. Ayer was influenced by Hume's empiricism and also the scientific approach of the logical positivists. His 1936 book *Language, Truth & Logic* generated much debate among moral philosophers at the time of publication.

Ayer argued that for a sentence to be literally significant, it must be an 'ordinary "scientific" statement' that can be verified through empirical observation. Since ethical judgements cannot be tested in this way, he concluded they are 'simply expressions of emotion which can be neither true nor false.' In this view, moral terms are not scientific descriptions of the world, but are instead used to express the speaker's feelings.

Ayer identifies four categories within ethical philosophy:

- **Definitions of ethical terms**: This is the only category that he believed constitutes true ethical philosophy, as it deals with **meta-ethics**.
- **Descriptions of moral phenomena and their causes**: Ayer assigned these to the scientific fields of psychology and sociology.
- **Exhortations to moral virtue**: He saw these as mere commands meant to provoke action, which do not belong to philosophy or science.

- **Ethical judgements that ascribe value**: These are expressions of personal approval or disapproval and are not part of moral philosophy.

Ayer points out that philosophers often fail to distinguish between these categories, making their work unclear. He asks if it is possible for value judgements to be translated into 'ethical fact', but his focus remains on what people are doing when they make moral judgements, rather than on proving them to be true or false.

Emotivism is not subjectivism

The position of subjectivism is that values stem from the emotions or attitudes of an individual or society. For example, a feeling that capital punishment is bad is what makes the action bad (for that individual or society). However, according to Ayer, these emotions do not affect the moral value of an action itself.

Ayer's point is that ethical statements in our language are not equivalent to psychological or empirical propositions. He rejects theories like utilitarianism and subjectivism, not as proposals for a new language, but as incorrect analyses of the ethical language we already use. Our current language, he argues, does not equate normative ethical statements with psychological or other empirical claims.

Rejection of intuitionism

Ayer explicitly rejects intuitionism due to its lack of verifiability, which he sees as a core problem. While Russell rejected intuition because it was subjective, Ayer's argument is that since there is no way to resolve conflicts between different intuitions, appealing to them is pointless. He argues that this makes moral statements unverifiable. He wrote: 'it is notorious that what seems intuitively certain to one person may seem doubtful, or even false, to another'.

Ayer points out that adding an ethical term like 'wrong' to a factual statement adds nothing to its factual content. For example, saying 'You acted wrongly in stealing that money,' is no different from simply saying 'You stole that money.' The ethical term *wrong* does not provide a verifiable fact; it is merely an expression of disapproval.

Ethical statements can be persuasive

Ayer's one concession to ethical statements was that they can serve as a means of persuasion. He argued that ethical terms not only express feelings but also are 'calculated to arouse feeling, and so to stimulate action'. For example, the statement, 'It is your duty to tell the truth,' can be seen as both an expression of a certain feeling and a command to 'Tell the truth.'

According to Ayer, there is no way to verify the validity of ethical judgements. Ethical statements have no objective validity; they are simply **pseudo-concepts** and are unanalysable. The ethical element of a statement adds nothing factual to it, making it illogical to ask whether that element is true or false. Ayer viewed ethical statements as 'pure expressions of feeling' that, like a cry of pain, cannot be verified. He believed the study of these expressions and moral habits falls under the disciplines of psychology, sociology and anthropology, but not philosophy. He stated that there is no procedure to examine the 'value of the facts, as distinct from examining the facts themselves'.

Key quote

We are not now concerned to discover which term, within the sphere of ethical terms, is to be taken as fundamental [...] We are inquiring whether statements of ethical value can be translated into statements of empirical fact.

(Ayer)

Ayer felt that ethical language and its use and meaning belonged to the subject area of psychology rather than philosophy

Key quote

For in saying that a certain type of action is right or wrong, I am not making any factual statement, not even a statement about my own state of mind. I am merely expressing certain moral sentiments. And the man who is ostensibly contradicting me is merely expressing his moral sentiments. So that there is plainly no sense in asking which of us is in the right. For neither of us is asserting a genuine proposition.

(Ayer)

Key term

pseudo-concepts: things that are treated as concepts but can only be mentally apprehended, not empirically verified

For Ayer, ethical language consisted of nothing more than personal approval or disapproval

Key quote

When I say that moral judgements are emotive rather than descriptive, that they are persuasive expressions of attitudes and not statements of fact [...] I am not saying that nothing is good or bad, right or wrong, or that it does not matter what we do.

(Ayer)

Specification content

Ethical terms are just expressions of personal approval (hurrah) or disapproval (boo); explains why people disagree about morality

Key term

'hurrah-boo!' theory: another term for the theory of emotivism

Key quotes

in every case in which one would commonly be said to be making an ethical judgement, the function of the relevant ethical word is purely 'emotive'. It is used to express feeling about certain objects, but not to make any assertion about them.

(Ayer)

The sentence 'You ought to tell the truth' also involves the command 'Tell the truth', but here the tone of the command is less emphatic. In the sentence 'It is good to tell the truth' the command has become little more than a suggestion [...] In fact we may define the meaning of the various ethical words in terms both of the different feelings they are ordinarily taken to express, and also the different responses which they are calculated to provoke.

(Ayer)

Ayer concluded by reaffirming his position that moral philosophy is purely analytical. He stated that he was not claiming that morals are unimportant, as this would be an unverifiable value judgement. His theory, like all moral theories, operates on a meta-ethical level, seeking to understand what people are doing when they make moral judgements, rather than prescribing what moral judgements they should make. Therefore, all philosophical moral theories are 'neutral as regards actual conduct' because they are concerned with analysis, not guidance. This is why people who seek moral direction from philosophers often find the subject unsatisfying.

Ethical terms are just expressions of personal approval (hurrah) or disapproval (boo)

Key person

Charles L. Stevenson (1908–79): An American philosopher; after studying at Yale, he spent time at Cambridge, where he encountered the ideas of Moore and Wittgenstein on the nature of language; he completed his doctorate at Harvard and went on to teach at Yale and the University of Michigan; in 1937, he published the influential article 'The Emotive Meaning of Ethical Terms' in the journal *Mind*, followed by his major work *Ethics and Language* in 1944; where Ayer had argued that moral statements were simply expressions of emotion, Stevenson developed emotivism into a fuller systematic theory, emphasising the persuasive and dynamic power of ethical language; his concept of 'interest theory' remains a key reference point in meta-ethics

There emerged in response to Ayer's ideas a nickname for his theory of emotivism. This was because Ayer insisted that ethical propositions were simply emotive and feelings of either approval or disapproval. Emotivism therefore became known as the **'hurrah-boo!' theory** as it was felt that Ayer proposed that ethical terms are just expressions of personal approval (hurrah) or disapproval (boo).

The 'hurrah-boo!' theory also became associated with the writings of **C.L. Stevenson** – an American philosopher noted for his work on emotivism who developed it into a systematic theory.

Stevenson's interest was not in verifying ethical language, but he agreed that if viewed scientifically, emotivism is unhelpful. He argued that a proper definition of good must:

- allow for disagreement
- have a 'magnetism' to inspire action
- not be subject to scientific verification.

Stevenson preferred the term **interest theory** for his view of emotivism. He focused on how ethical propositions are used, specifically how they gain power and how that **dynamic power** influences their meaning. He identified that words have a 'causal or dispositional property' to achieve various goals, such as arousing sympathy or persuading.

He defined the **emotive meaning** of a word as 'the tendency of a word, arising through the history of its usage, to produce [...] affective responses in people'. Words like good have a **dynamic use**, and to ignore their emotive element would be to misunderstand their true meaning. He argued that good is indefinable because any attempt to define it would distort its emotive power. The best that could be said was that good has a pleasing emotive quality.

Key terms

interest theory: Stevenson's theory of emotivism

dynamic power: the way in which a word can express or arouse feelings; according to Stevenson, language is best understood by looking at this power to move the listener rather than just its literal definition

emotive meaning: the tendency of a word to produce or express feelings and attitudes rather than to describe facts

dynamic use: Stevenson's view that ethical language is used actively to influence attitudes and behaviour, not just to describe

Key quote

> While Stevenson granted that moral language didn't have factual or cognitive content, he argued that it had emotive meaning. Moral propositions aren't true or false, but they aren't meaningless either – moral language allows us to express emotions.
>
> (Messerly)

Stevenson believed the emotive aspects of ethical propositions were used in a variety of ways, particularly as persuasive definitions. While his research in *Ethics and Language* is extensive, his initial observations show that ethical propositions are more than just simple expressions of personal approval or disapproval.

Emotivism explains why people disagree about morality

According to emotivism, since ethical propositions are expressions of approval or disapproval, moral disagreements are inevitable. This might suggest that ethical debate is pointless, as it is just a clash of emotions without any basis in verifiable facts.

However, for Stevenson, ethical debate is meaningful because he distinguished between **propositions about belief** and **propositions about attitude**:

- Beliefs are more to do with factual statements that can be verified, such as 'War is the last resort.' These are not ethical convictions.
- Attitudes are more to do with statements that express feelings and reveal a person's emotions about an issue, such as 'War is always wrong.'

In ethical debate, people are not trying to change each other's beliefs, but rather their attitudes. The disagreement is not about which attitude is better, as emotivism provides no objective basis to determine superiority; rather, it is a 'disagreement in attitude' where two individuals simply hold conflicting emotional responses towards the same issue. This is what makes the debate meaningful. We use emotive language to try to influence and affect the feelings of others. Therefore, emotivism can account for moral disagreement without making ethical debate meaningless.

Key terms

propositions about belief: statements of fact or verifiable by empirical means

propositions about attitude: views or value judgements about statements of belief

Stevenson saw persuasion as a key purpose of ethical discourse

Specification content

Challenges: no basic moral principles can be established; ethical debate becomes a pointless activity; there is no universal agreement that some actions are wrong

Key quote

"The minds of all men are similar in their feelings and operations; nor can anyone be actuated by any affection, of which all others are not, in some degree, susceptible.

(Hume)"

Challenges to emotivism

Mary Warnock argued that emotivism is too broad because it fails to distinguish between ethical and non-ethical uses of emotive language. In addition, many people view morality as both a rational and logical process, not just an emotional one. There are three more specific challenges.

No basic moral principles can be established

A general criticism of emotivism is that it is too limited in scope, as it only values meta-ethics and fails to provide a foundation for normative ethics.

Both Ayer and Stevenson focused on the meaning and use of ethical language, concluding that it expresses no factual information and is purely emotive:

- Ayer used meta-ethics to reduce ethical statements to mere sentiments, thereby preventing the establishment of any basic moral principles.
- Stevenson also confined his analysis to meta-ethics, studying the use of language without offering any real insight into meta-ethical definitions or normative principles for guiding behaviour.

This limitation means that emotivism, while offering a theory about the nature of ethical language, provides no concrete guidance on how people should act or what constitutes a good or bad action.

As Hume argued, value judgements are not rational – no rational agreement or knowledge is possible on ethical matters. This is a significant problem because emotivism offers no method for resolving differences in opinion; it can only observe that they occur. This seems to trivialise major ethical decisions throughout history by reducing them to mere emotional responses.

Furthermore, by reducing morality to emotions that lack a rational basis, the theory suggests that fundamental moral principles are unfounded or do not exist. Alternatively, if moral principles can be identified through emotions, their conflicting nature makes it impossible to find any sense of ethical coherence.

Ethical debate becomes a pointless activity

If, according to emotivism, there are no basic moral principles, then ethical debate seems pointless because there is nothing to debate besides subjective feelings. If we cannot rationally differentiate between good and bad, ethical arguments are reduced to mere exercises of emotional influence or propaganda.

However, this view fails to explain why many people still engage in ethical debate, using evidence and reasoning to support their arguments. Even if the conclusion of a debate is a personal opinion, the process of reasoning itself is considered valuable. This consideration suggests that ethical debate is not just about emotions.

It could be asked whether this is any different from Prichard's intuitionism, which holds that we use general reasoning to confirm our intuitive, self-evident moral truths. This highlights a key criticism of emotivism: it dismisses the rational component of ethical reasoning, which many people, including other philosophers, see as a crucial part of the reasoning process. The idea that ethical debate is entirely pointless or irrational is seen as an oversimplification.

There is no universal agreement that some actions are wrong

Although it could be argued that there is still some value in moral debate when it is reduced to being just an exercise in persuasion, it would never be able to establish a unanimous, universal agreement on which actions should be considered to be wrong. It lacks a sense of authority to appeal to.

J.L. Mackie has also pointed out that we are not clearly differentiating between the things we disapprove of when he writes:

> The emotivist is unable to distinguish between my dislike of curries and my dislike of genocide. But the difference between the two is profound. I dislike curry because I don't like its taste. I abhor genocide because it's immoral.

Emotivism reduces both of Mackie's examples of dislikes to mere emotional expressions, ignoring the profound difference between them.

Furthermore, emotivism seems unable to account for moral progress over time. History shows that ethical debate led to concrete decisions about what is wrong which resulted in definitive legal reforms. Significant advances in social justice and human rights – such as the expansion of women's rights since the mid-nineteenth century – illustrate this. These advances were not just the outcome of clashes of emotion, but of serious arguments that established basic principles. Emotivism does not accurately reflect this process of moral progress; ethical debates are more than just expressions of feeling – they are the pursuit of objective fairness and the rational extension of legal rights.

Summary

- Emotivism is a non-cognitivist theory which argues that objective moral laws do not exist; instead, moral terms are used to express personal emotional attitudes rather than factual propositions.
- Linked to A.J. Ayer and logical positivism, the theory uses the verification principle to argue that because ethical statements are neither analytic (true by definition) nor synthetic (testable by the senses), they are factually meaningless.
- Ayer argues that adding an ethical term like 'wrong' to a statement adds no factual content; it is merely an emotional 'exclamation' or 'pseudo-concept' used to show approval or disapproval (often called the 'hurrah-boo!' theory).
- C.L. Stevenson developed the theory into an 'interest theory', distinguishing between propositions about belief (facts) and about attitude (feelings), suggesting moral language has a dynamic power to persuade others.
- Emotivism explains the persistent nature of moral disagreement as a clash of attitudes rather than a debate over facts, acknowledging that while we use reason to support our feelings, we are ultimately trying to influence the emotions of others.
- Critics like J.L. Mackie argue that the theory fails to distinguish between different types of disapproval, such as a dislike of curry and an abhorrence of genocide, thereby trivialising major ethical decisions and ignoring moral progress.

Not liking the taste of a certain food is a very different expression of disapproval from abhorring genocide

Key quote

One advantage of this theory is that it easily explains how and why it is that moral judgements motivate us. If moral language were just descriptive, stating how things are, why would that get us to act in certain ways? We need to care. And what we care about is captured in our attitudes to the world.

(Lacewing)

AO1 Activity

a The summary below presents one challenge to emotivism. You want to use it as a basis for an essay, but it is too brief. Read it carefully and assess its accuracy.

b In order that you demonstrate more depth of understanding, develop this summary by providing examples that will help you explain it further. Aim for 200 words in total.

When you have completed the task, refer to the band descriptors for A2 (WJEC) or A Level (Eduqas) and in particular have a look at the demands described in the higher band descriptors towards which you should be aspiring. Ask yourself the following questions:

- Does my work demonstrate thorough, accurate and relevant knowledge and understanding of religion and belief?
- Is my work coherent (consistent or make logical sense), clear and well organised?
- Will my work, when developed, be an extensive and relevant response which is specific to the focus of the task?
- Does my work have extensive depth and/or suitable breadth and have excellent use of evidence and examples?
- If appropriate to the task, does my response have thorough and accurate references to sacred texts and sources of wisdom?
- Are there any insightful connections to be made with other elements of my course?
- Will my answer, when developed and extended to match what is expected in an examination answer, have an extensive range of views of scholars/schools of thought?
- When used, is specialist language and vocabulary both thorough and accurate?

Summary

Moral debate, even if it is just about persuasion, will never be able to establish a unanimous, universal agreement on those actions that are considered as wrong. There is no sense of authority to appeal to. In addition, what would happen in ethical debate? History has proven that minority interests and emotions (to use Ayer's perspective) have actually been the correct way forward. The outcome has shown that basic principles of what is wrong can be established through ethical argument. Emotivism does not seem to reflect what has actually happened through historical ethical debate.

Issues for analysis and evaluation

The extent to which moral terms are just expressions of our emotions

This section covers AO2 content and skills

Specification content

The extent to which moral terms are just expressions of our emotions

Possible line of argument	Critical analysis and evaluation
Emotivism explains global moral diversity as varying emotional responses. Unlike intuitionism, which relies on unprovable 'innate' abilities, emotivism aligns with a scientific worldview by recognising that emotions can be psychologically and biologically measured.	If moral terms are merely emotional, 'murder is wrong' is reduced to the level of a dislike of a particular food. Critics like Mary Warnock argue this trivialises serious ethics, which requires cautious deliberation and consistency rather than just seeking approval.
A.J. Ayer's verification principle provides a logical framework. By showing moral terms cannot be verified analytically or synthetically, emotivism correctly categorises them as factually meaningless expressions, avoiding the unprovable metaphysical claims of older theories.	Critics argue that if morality is purely emotional, debate becomes mere propaganda. While Stevenson focuses on persuasion, many feel rational ethical statements should be assessed on the quality of the argument and logic, not just emotional magnetism.
C.L. Stevenson argued emotivism makes debate meaningful. Speakers use the 'dynamic power' of language to influence attitudes. This 'interest theory' explains our passion: we are trying to create a social magnetism towards our values.	If emotivism were true, there would be no objective basis to challenge one's culture. The fact that individuals can 'stand outside' their society to challenge injustice suggests a moral basis beyond personal emotion or social conditioning.
By refusing to define good as a natural property, emotivism avoids Moore's naturalistic fallacy. It acknowledges moral terms are pseudo-concepts that don't add factual content but function as emotive exclamations or outcries.	Emotivism is criticised for ignoring 'ethics proper' (how to live). By reducing morality to the level of persuasive influence or emotional appeals, it ignores the deep-seated conscience that many feel drives moral action.
Stevenson's version allows for a hybrid understanding where we provide reasons for feelings. This reflects historical applied ethics, where moral progress often stems from shifting a society's collective emotional attitude.	If ethics were down to shifting emotions, obligations would be inconsistent. Naturalism and intuitionism argue that for morality to function it must be anchored in something more stable than individual 'boo/hurrah' sentiments.

AO2 Activity

a Analyse three possible conclusions that could be drawn from the critical analysis and evaluation of the view that moral terms are just expressions of our emotions. Select evidence and examples to support each of the three conclusions. Select one conclusion that you think is the **most convincing** and explain why it is so.

b Now contrast this with the **weakest** conclusion of the three. Justify your argument with clear reasoning and evidence. Refer to the AO2 band descriptors and ensure your conclusion demonstrates 'a confident and justified conclusion' (band 5).

Specification content

Whether one of naturalism, intuitionism or emotivism is superior to the other theories

Exam practice

Below is an example of part of an evaluation of whether one of naturalism, intuitionism or emotivism is superior to the other theories.

Sample answer

News reporter: The essay clearly defines the starting point of the debate by linking morality to observable facts.

Which theory is superior depends on whether you value scientific evidence, personal intuition or emotional honesty. Naturalism is often seen as superior because it treats morality as an objective fact. By linking goodness to observable things like happiness or social duty, it allows for moral debate based on evidence. This gives ethics a solid, factual foundation similar to science.

Detective: This paragraph successfully identifies the psychological foundations of moral claims.

However, emotivism offers a more robust scientific alternative. Unlike intuitionism, which relies on unprovable 'inner senses', emotivism views morality as a social and psychological creation. It appeals to the modern mind by acknowledging that while we cannot *see* goodness, we can certainly measure the emotional impact of our language.

Tennis player: The argument manages a clear, sustained line of argument here.

One major advantage of emotivism is its simplicity. It explains all ethical propositions, from 'Thou shalt not kill' as 'Boo to murder!' to 'Helping others is good' as 'Hurrah for kindness!' It suggests that all moral rules – even the most complex ones – are ultimately rooted in human sentiment and social approval.

Critical thinker / **Judge**: This section effectively weighs the danger of reducing morality to mere subjective persuasion.

Nevertheless, critics argue that emotivism trivialises morality. If moral terms are just emotions, a statement like 'genocide is wrong' is reduced to the same level as a dislike of a specific food or an advertising slogan. Intuitionism, by contrast, maintains that moral truths are unique and superior to mere personal preferences.

Explorer: The essay effectively searches for a more stable basis for morality beyond simple feelings.

Intuitionism corresponds with the common human experience that some things are *just right* or *just wrong*. For philosophers like Prichard, moral reasoning is a higher faculty that allows us to recognise objective duties. This gives morality an authority and stability that emotional responses simply lack.

Philosopher: This point raises the debate to a metaphysical level by questioning the origin of our values.

Furthermore, intuitionism explains how people can 'stand outside' their own culture to challenge injustice. If morality were only a product of social conditioning or emotion, it would be impossible to argue that a society's laws are objectively evil. This suggests there must be a moral basis beyond human feelings.

Despite this, naturalism remains popular because it encourages practical moral discussion. If we can verify moral claims through evidence – such as the utilitarian focus on the greatest happiness – we can use ethics to shape our laws and political systems in a way that is visible and accountable.

Ultimately, each theory addresses a different aspect of ethics. Emotivism focuses on how we use language to persuade (Stevenson), naturalism calculates decisions based on experience (Mill) and intuitionism explores our inner sense of obligation (Moore). Perhaps a superior theory would be a synthesis of all three.

In conclusion, it is difficult to judge one as superior because the source of morality remains unproven. If one requires empirical proof, naturalism or emotivism is the logical choice. However, if one believes in objective truths that transcend the physical world, intuitionism remains the most compelling.

News reporter **Explorer**

The essay highlights the practical, real-world applications of the naturalist position.

Critical thinker

A nuanced point is made here, looking for a middle ground between the three theories.

Judge

The final ruling provides a balanced summary that reflects the complexity of the debate.

Below is an example of part of an evaluation of the extent to which the different meta-ethical theories encourage moral debate.

Specification content

The extent to which the different meta-ethical theories encourage moral debate

Sample answer

Whether meta-ethical theories encourage moral debate depends on how they define moral language. Some argue emotivism discourages debate because it views disagreement as a mere clash of emotional stances. In this view, what looks like rational discussion is actually an exchange of feelings that cannot be proved true or false.

News reporter

The essay effectively outlines how a theory can appear to simplify complex interactions into emotional outcries.

Similarly, intuitionism might seem to discourage discussion by claiming morality is known through an innate inner sense. If we simply know our duty, there is little room for explanation. For Prichard, moral thinking determines the outcome rather than general reasoning, which technically reduces the need for external dialogue.

Explorer **Critical thinker**

This paragraph correctly identifies the tension between an inner compass and public justification.

However, Prichard concedes we must consider claims and preliminaries before confirming our intuition. By using a process similar to Descartes' sceptical doubt, we check our initial thoughts. Since intuitive ability requires a mature mind and careful reflection, intuitionism actually demands a high level of internal and external debate.

Detective

The essay successfully investigates the hidden layers of reasoning within a seemingly 'silent' theory.

Critics argue that absolutist theories, like divine command theory, have no need for dialogue because insights cannot change an objective stance. Yet, the history of religious ethics proves otherwise. Debates over the doctrine of double effect show that even within objective systems, rule application remains a constant area of discussion.

Philosopher **Judge**

This point highlights that even fixed rules require deep interpretation and analysis in practice.

Naturalism clearly encourages debate because it relies on observation. In utilitarianism, we can debate whether an action truly causes more pleasure than pain. This encourages engagement with social and political issues, using principles like the hedonic calculus to turn ethics into a public, evidence-based discussion.

News reporter

The essay highlights the practical, real-world transparency that naturalism brings to the table.

Tennis player

The argument manages a clear, sustained volley here by turning a potential weakness into a strength.

Furthermore, Stevenson's emotivism suggests the very purpose of moral language is debate. We use emotive terms to persuade others and seek affirmation. Emotivism has provoked significant debate because its reductive nature forces us to ask what the true essence of ethics really is.

Critical thinker

Judge

This section effectively weighs the value of the moral process against the final conclusion.

Ayer's emotivism is challenged for ignoring that most people use evidence and reasoning in arguments. Even if the final conclusion is a personal opinion, the process of debating is still vital. Suggesting ethical debate is pointless is often seen as 'throwing the baby out with the bathwater'.

Explorer

A developed point is made here, suggesting every theory provides a different map for the same journey.

Ultimately, the impact on debate depends on the theory's focus: persuasion, evidence-based calculations or the sense of obligation. While they offer different starting points, they all provide a framework within which moral conversation must take place.

Judge

The final paragraph returns to the overall question being discussed and provides a balanced viewpoint.

In conclusion, meta-ethical theories do not stop moral debate; they define what that debate is about. Whether discussing facts, intuitions or emotions, determining right and wrong through debate remains a central human activity. These theories outline the rules of the game rather than the final score.

Over to you

Evaluation skills can often involve weighing up the arguments, finding a counter-argument with a 'however' objection and then providing a personal perspective.

For each of the five arguments in the writing frame below, identify if it is a strength or weakness of emotivism. Then, write a 'however' objection to challenge it. At the completion of the exercise, write a conclusion as to where you stand with regard to emotivism.

Question

'Moral terms, like right and wrong, are no more than expressions of our emotions.' Evaluate this view.

Writing frame

Argument	Strength or weakness?	Counter-analysis ('However ...')
Moral terms are just emotions: saying 'murder is wrong' is logically the same as saying 'I love coffee,' 'euthanasia boo!' or 'I hate Mondays.'		
By viewing right and wrong as emotional expressions rather than facts, the theory avoids the mistake of trying to define morality through the natural world or physical properties.		

Argument	Strength or weakness?	Counter-analysis ('However …')
By arguing that moral terms are no more than expressions of our emotions, progressive social changes – such as equality for women – are not *right* but just reflections of public feelings.		
Moral terms act as a way to influence the attitudes of others. This explains the magnetic quality of language and why we use emotional appeals to gain social agreement.		
If right and wrong are just expressions of emotion, it is impossible to have a rational argument about anything. We are simply shouting, e.g. 'animal experimentation boo!' or 'nuclear deterrence hurrah!' at each other without any logical foundation.		

T2

Deontological ethics

A: Aquinas' natural law: a religious approach to ethics

St Thomas Aquinas

This section covers AO1 content and skills

Specification content

Aquinas' four levels of law (eternal, divine, natural and human); natural law derived from rational thought; based on a belief in a divine creator (the highest good as being the rational understanding of God's final purpose)

Laws and precepts as the basis of morality

Natural law is a theory built on the belief that the universe operates with a natural order towards a specific purpose or end (*telos*). This direction and purpose are determined by the divine Creator. Since human beings are part of this natural order, they also possess an inbuilt purpose or nature common to all. Therefore, natural law is about identifying and following those actions that consistently move humanity towards its ultimate intended *telos*.

Natural law has its roots in ancient Greek philosophy, most notably Aristotle:

- **Aristotle's teleology**: Aristotle believed the ultimate *telos* for human beings was *eudaimonia* – often translated as flourishing and living well in such a way that there is happiness. He argued that we pursue all other goals as a means to achieve *eudaimonia*.
- **The role of reason**: For Aristotle, achieving *eudaimonia* requires using reason to make sound, moral choices. When humans act morally and rationally, they are fulfilling their unique nature and moving in accordance with the natural order. It is in this requirement for reasoned moral action to achieve a natural *telos* that the seeds of natural law can be found.

This philosophical tradition was later systematised by the Roman lawyer Cicero, who provided one of the earliest definitions of natural law. He also stated that the author of this universal law was the divine eternal rational mind – God.

Key quote

True law is right reason in agreement with Nature; it is of universal application. Unchanging and everlasting; it summons to duty by its commands and averts from wrongdoing by its prohibitions.
(Cicero)

Key person

St Thomas Aquinas (1225–74 CE): A Dominican friar and philosopher; his influence on Western thought is considerable, owing to his writing on ethics, political morality and sexual morality; he integrated Aristotelian ethical ideas with Christian theology

It was the medieval theologian and philosopher **St Thomas Aquinas** (1225–74 CE) who took these pre-existing concepts – Aristotle's use of reason to achieve a *telos* and Cicero's link between natural law and the divine eternal rational mind – and developed them into the comprehensive ethical system known today as natural law.

Aquinas developed his natural law theory amid a period of intellectual revival during which the works of Aristotle were rediscovered. Aquinas was profoundly influenced by Aristotle, agreeing that reason is a fundamental part of human nature and key to living well.

Aquinas used reason to demonstrate that Christian teachings were consistent with natural law, thus defending the religion. Like Aristotle, he believed that everything has a final purpose and that cultivating virtues is essential. Aquinas used many of Aristotle's terms and arguments and combined them with the teachings of the Bible and Christianity. He saw his task as combining *fides et ratio* (faith and reason).

Aquinas diverged from Aristotle by asserting that the ultimate purpose in human life is given by the personal God, as revealed in the Bible and the teaching of the Church. This ultimate purpose or ***summum bonum*** (highest good) was to be perfect in the image of God and to gain perfect fellowship with God after death. For Aquinas, obeying natural law meant a person taking actions that develop their image to reflect as closely as possible the image of God; however, true perfection of this kind was not possible in a person's life on earth.

For Aquinas, natural law is God's design rooted in human reason. By applying reason to moral decisions, a person discovers the good acts that align with their true nature and moves towards their *summum bonum*. Therefore, good reasoning coincides with the natural law, which guides a person towards this eternal purpose. It is important to note, therefore, that for Aquinas the *telos* of human life was not achieved in the temporal life lived on earth but only in the eternal life after death in heaven.

Applying the understanding gained from the Bible, Christianity, Aristotle, *fides et ratio* and his observations of the world around him, Aquinas proposed that there were four levels of law, arranged in a hierarchy, which were ordered by God's rational plan:

- The eternal law is the mind of God – the rational plan by which God orders and governs the entire universe. It is complete, unchanging and known fully only by God. Humans can only know it in part through its effects and appearances in the world.
- The divine law is the law of God revealed directly to humanity, primarily through scripture (the Bible). Its purpose is to guide humans towards their ultimate, supernatural goal of perfection and fellowship with God, a goal which is not fully achievable during the temporal life on earth.
- Natural law is the part of the eternal law accessible to all human beings. It is the rational person's participation in God's eternal plan, and it is known through natural reason. By applying reason, humans can identify the fundamental moral requirements known as the **primary precepts**.
- Human law consists of specific, practical rules and customs established by governments or societies to promote the common good. It must be derived from the general principles of natural law. Aquinas cautioned that if human law deflects from the natural law, it loses its moral force, arguing, 'If in any point it deflects from the law of nature, it is no longer a law but a perversion of law.'

Key quote

The idea of Natural Law is sometimes described as the view that there is an unchanging, normative order that is part of the natural world.

(Buckle)

Key terms

fides et ratio: Latin for faith and reason

summum bonum: Latin for the highest good, which for Aquinas is perfect fellowship with God

Key quote

Natural law is the same for all [...] there is a single standard of truth and right for everyone [...] which is known by everyone.

(Aquinas)

Key term

primary precepts: Aquinas' five principles: preserve innocent life, orderly living in society, worship God, educate children, reproduce to continue the species

This idea that there is a universal natural standard of good needed to be clarified. Natural law is within all of us, but it is not like a physical law that has to be followed. It derives from reason and reason needs to be applied carefully and coherently in order to avoid a mistaken outcome.

Natural law as a form of moral absolutism with both deontological and teleological aspects

Specification content

Natural law as a form of moral absolutism and a theory which has both deontological and teleological aspects

Natural law ethics uses reason to determine the morally correct behaviour that aligns with humanity's divinely ordained *telos*. The theory is generally regarded as having three distinct yet interconnected features:

- **Teleological**: Natural law is fundamentally teleological because its moral framework is entirely directed towards a final, ultimate end or goal – the *summum bonum*. All good acts are defined as those that move a person closer to this predetermined final purpose.
- **Absolutist**: It is a form of moral absolutism because the fundamental moral requirements, known as the primary precepts, are derived from God's unchanging nature and are therefore universal, applying to all people in all situations without exception.
- **Deontological**: It is also strongly deontological because the moral rightness or wrongness of an action is determined by how closely it follows the absolute moral duties (*deon*), not by its consequences. The focus is on performing the *act* that aligns with a person's duty, regardless of the outcome.

Therefore, natural law represents a deontological approach to ethics because it follows predetermined absolute principles. It is also teleological because, in applying the predetermined absolute principles, the end result is considered. Applying these principles through reason to a particular context is called **casuistry** (from the Latin *casus*, meaning case). Even when considering a case, the act must first conform to the absolute principles (*deon*) that guide a person towards the ultimate good (*telos*).

Key term

casuistry: the art of applying key principles to an ethical case

The five primary precepts

Specification content

The five primary precepts (preservation of life, ordered society, worship of God, education and reproduction of the human species) as derived from rational thought and based on the premise of 'doing good and avoiding evil'

The primary precepts are the universal, absolute moral rules that apply to all people, leading them towards the final human *telos*.

The key precept, from which all others flow, is: 'Act in such a way as to achieve good and avoid evil.'

From this basic rational position, Aquinas identified five general precepts that correspond to the main human purposes. Fulfilling these precepts helps humanity re-establish a 'right' relationship with God and achieve the *summum bonum*.

These five universal precepts are:

- preservation of life (self-preservation; protecting the innocent)
- ordered society (living peacefully in a community)
- worship of God (recognising and seeking truth about God)
- education (caring for and educating children)
- reproduction (continuing the species).

The morality of any action is determined by whether it aligns with these God-given purposes. Actions that fulfil these primary precepts are deemed good because they move a person closer to their ultimate purpose.

The secondary precepts and the importance of keeping the precepts

From the universal primary precepts, **secondary precepts** can be deduced using human reason.

The key difference is that primary precepts are self-evident, absolute and always true without exception – for example, 'preserve innocent life' – whereas secondary precepts are practical, specific rules – for example, 'do not steal' and 'do not lie' – which are not strictly universal because they can be suspended in certain circumstances.

For example, the secondary precept 'do not steal' is derived from the primary precept of 'ordered society'. However, if stealing a loaf of bread is the only means to satisfy the primary precept of 'preservation of life' for a starving child, the higher primary precept takes precedence, and the action is justified. Natural law always demands following the primary precepts. Casuistry becomes essential, as the application of general principles to particular circumstances requires the careful use of reason.

Keeping the precepts, both primary and secondary, is vital because it ensures each person's acts align with their God-given nature and purpose. By acting correctly, a person establishes a right relationship with God in this life, thereby fulfilling the conditions necessary to attain eternal life with God in heaven – the *summum bonum*.

Specification content

The secondary precepts which derive from the primary precepts; the importance of keeping the precepts in order to establish a right relationship with God and gain eternal life with God in heaven

Key term

secondary precepts: deduced from the primary precepts, these apply to specific situations

Summary

- Natural law is based on the universe having a God-given order within which human beings live.
- Natural law has its foundations in the writings of Aristotle and Cicero and was fully developed by St Thomas Aquinas in the thirteenth century.
- The four levels of law are eternal, divine, natural and human.
- Natural law is absolutist, teleological – the goal is the *summum bonum* – and deontological – based on following absolute principles.
- The key precept is to do good and to avoid evil; from this the five primary precepts are derived and applied via casuistry using secondary precepts.
- The focus of natural law is on how human beings can live in this life so that they can achieve the *summum bonum*.

AO1 Activity

a Explain the meaning of each of the technical terms (in bold) as used in the context of natural law in the passage below. Copy out the passage on a large piece of paper. Draw lines or speech bubbles connected to the technical terms and write a definition for each one.

Natural law is **deontological**, **teleological** and **absolutist**. A person keeps the **primary precepts** and, using **casuistry**, applies the **secondary precepts**. Aristotle argued that a person can achieve ***eudaimonia*** in this life but Aquinas – through using ***fides et ratio*** – stated that a person achieved the ***summum bonum*** in their life after death.

b There a number of common mistakes often made about natural law. Some of these are listed below. Write out and complete the sentences to explain the mistakes.

i To say that natural law is about what happens in the natural world around us is inaccurate because …

ii To say that the primary precepts and secondary precepts are only relevant to how people live their daily lives is mistaken because …

iii To say that Aquinas' natural law is not religious and does not require belief in God is an error because …

iv To say that Aquinas understood natural law to be something that could only be understood by religious believers is wrong because …

In responding to examination questions on natural law, it is important to be familiar with the use and meaning of specialist language and vocabulary and to avoid common mistakes. This exercise helps to consolidate your AO1 knowledge and understanding in this area. Refer to the band descriptors for AS (WJEC) or AS/A Level (Eduqas) AO1 and, in particular, look at the demands described in the higher band descriptors, which you should be aspiring towards. Ask yourself the following questions:

- Does my work demonstrate thorough, accurate and relevant knowledge and understanding of religion and belief?
- Is my work coherent, clear and well organised?
- Will my work, when developed, be an extensive and relevant response which is specific to the focus of the task?
- Does my work have extensive depth and/or suitable breadth and have excellent use of evidence and examples?
- If appropriate to the task, does my response have thorough and accurate references to sacred texts and sources of wisdom?
- When used, is specialist language and vocabulary both thorough and accurate?

Issues for analysis and evaluation

The degree to which human law should be influenced by Aquinas' natural law

Possible line of argument	Critical analysis and evaluation
Natural law provides objective and universal guidance: it can positively influence human law, as through the primary precepts, giving clear definitions of right and wrong.	What is derived from natural law and the primary precepts is sometimes regarded as inflexible and unacceptable in much of modern human law. This is particularly true with regard to preservation of life, which has been used to challenge laws enabling abortion and euthanasia.
Aquinas' primary precept of ordered society can only be of benefit to human law. This precept is all about living peacefully in a community. Precepts such as education and preservation of life (e.g. do not harm or murder) are also essential.	Aquinas' natural law should not influence human law as it is based on deontological and absolutist principles from the time of Aristotle and Aquinas. With its focus on reproduction and continuing the species, it would not accept contraception, homosexuality, same-sex relationships or same-sex marriages.
Human law has developed over the centuries, but the concepts of natural law should continue to influence it; laws about private property are based, e.g. on one of the Ten Commandments, 'Do not steal,' because the commandment keeps the primary precept of an ordered society.	Human law should not be influenced by Aquinas' natural law since, in the end, his approach is a religious one, combining *fides et ratio*; the whole point of natural law is for human beings to reach the *summum bonum* in the afterlife – a belief which has no place in modern secular societies.
Human law should be influenced by Aquinas' natural law because natural law shows the vital importance of law in society and its place in terms of a rational understanding of the universe.	Human law should not be influenced by natural law because the hierarchical approach taken by Aquinas is outdated and lacks any evidence; in the modern view one cannot say that there are four layers of law (eternal, divine, natural and human).
Natural law should influence human law because it is based on a structured method which is still used today – general principles (primary precepts) are applied to particular situations (secondary precepts) through looking at decisions about similar situations (casuistry).	Aquinas' natural law might have some value but in the end it is too religious, absolutist and deontological for practical human law: in every situation human law has to be secular, flexible and teleological, always keeping the common good of society in mind.

This section covers AO2 content and skills

Specification content

The degree to which human law should be influenced by Aquinas' natural law

AO2 Activity

a Analyse three possible conclusions that could be drawn from the critical analysis and evaluation of the view that human law should be influenced by Aquinas' natural law. Select evidence and examples to support each of the three conclusions. Select one conclusion that you think is the **most convincing** and explain why it is so.

b Now contrast this with the **weakest** conclusion of the three. Justify your argument with clear reasoning and evidence.

Specification content

The extent to which the absolutist and/or deontological nature of Aquinas' natural law works in contemporary society

Exam practice

Below is an example of part of an evaluation of the extent to which the absolutist and/or deontological nature of Aquinas' natural law works in contemporary society.

Sample answer

News reporter – A clear overview of the issue is provided with clarity and coherence.

The main argument against natural law is that its absolutist nature makes it too restrictive and it does not allow people to follow their conscience. It sets fixed, universal standards, leaving no flexibility for individual circumstances or personal reasoning that might challenge the set precepts.

Explorer – Alternative angles are suggested for comparison showing knowledge of schools of thought.

Many people prefer moral systems based on love or happiness, leading them to favour more flexible teleological or person-based theories like situation ethics, utilitarianism or virtue theory. These approaches are seen as more applicable in a world of ethical complexity than natural law's simple, rigid rules.

Philosopher – A good challenge is identified here which is entirely relevant to what is being discussed.

The rejection of the deontological approach is driven by a desire for greater autonomy. Natural law's universal rules are centuries old, and while the precepts have not changed, society has, leading to clear conflicts.

Detective – More evidence is provided supporting the points already made and bringing substance to the essay.

Atheists and humanists object to the theory because they do not believe in a divine being as the source of morality. They will not follow a religious ethical system based on God's eternal plan because it is inappropriate as a universal moral guide for a secular society.

Tennis player – This paragraph presents a strong counter-argument fielding the points made earlier and providing flow in the essay.

However, those who favour a deontological approach argue that natural law's principles are eternal and unchanging. This means they can apply consistently to all people at all times, providing moral stability and clarity in ethical decision-making.

Critical thinker – Here another new angle is presented with supporting evidence for the cumulative discussion taking place.

They stress that natural law offers clear rules for life, eliminating complicated 'grey areas'. For instance, it provides an unambiguous ruling that any sexual act that cannot possibly lead to reproduction is wrong because it challenges a primary precept.

Philosopher – This paragraph identifies an interesting and relevant issue with natural law.

A key conflict is that natural law would condemn practices now accepted by law in many countries, such as divorce, homosexuality and abortion. For many, these prohibitions represent a regression, not progress, meaning the theory cannot fully function in modern legal or ethical discourse.

However, natural law remains the foundation of the moral teaching of the Roman Catholic Church and is adhered to by millions today. The long history and widespread religious support for natural law demonstrate its enduring relevance as an ethical guide.

Tennis player

Again, the overall discussion in the essay continues with multiple lines of argument going back and forth.

In conclusion, natural law only works partially in contemporary society. While its strict moral code remains valuable for condemning severe antisocial behaviour (like violence and murder), its absolutes clearly fail when applied to complex issues of family law, medical ethics and sexuality, making its influence limited in modern contexts.

Judge

The verdict is reached, bringing together a number of strands of argument from earlier in the essay with a clear evaluative judgement.

Over to you

Below is a table evaluating whether human law should be completely based on natural law. It includes arguments supporting the statement and some which disagree, but it is incomplete. Complete the table, develop all the points made and write your response to the question. Make sure that you put your conclusion at the end where you state what your considered opinion might be. Remember to respond to the phrase in the question: 'completely based'.

Question

'Human law should be completely based on natural law.' Evaluate this view.

Table

Natural law is a reflection of God's eternal law, providing a blueprint for how God intends humanity to live.	However, it could be argued that ...
Natural law is fixed (primary precepts do not change), whereas human law needs to evolve to reflect social changes, such as those regarding abortion.	A weakness of this argument is that ...
It treats everyone equally through universal principles, as seen in its influence on the United Nations Universal Declaration of Human Rights (1948).	On the other hand, universal principles are not enough because ...
Basing human law on natural law ensures that justice is not subject to the whims of contemporary politics but is grounded in objective truths.	This is questionable because ...
The phrase 'completely based' is used in the statement. On one hand this is true, given that natural law has four clear levels of law and it has been established over the centuries.	Yet, from a different perspective, the phrase 'completely based' is questionable because ...

Refer to the band descriptors for A2 (WJEC) or A Level (Eduqas) and, in particular, look at the demands described in the higher band descriptors, which you should be aspiring towards. Ask yourself the following questions:

- Is my answer a confident critical analysis and perceptive evaluation of the issue?
- Is my answer a response that successfully identifies and thoroughly addresses the issues the question raises?

This section covers AO1 content and skills

Specification content

The need for humans to be more godlike by developing the three revealed virtues (faith, hope and charity) and four cardinal virtues (fortitude, temperance, prudence and justice)

Key terms

God's grace: the love and mercy given to humanity by God because God desires humanity to have it, not because of anything humanity has done to deserve it

beatific vision: the teleological end of Natural Law according to Aquinas whereby one is united with God through Christ

St Paul the Apostle

B: Aquinas' natural law: the role of virtues and goods in supporting moral behaviour

The three revealed virtues

For Aquinas, correct moral reasoning can be achieved by developing specific virtues. He identified three special virtues, called the theological virtues, which are named by St Paul the Apostle in 1 Corinthians 13 concluding with the words: 'Now these three remain: faith, hope and love. But the greatest of these is love.':

- **Faith**, for Aquinas, is much more than simply agreeing with an idea in the mind. It is above all an act of the will – a deliberate, active choice. The intellect accepts the divine truth because the will commands it to, and behind this process is **God's grace**. Faith involves the whole person and means making a total, reasoned and active commitment to God.
- **Hope** is the constant and secure trust that the person will reach their *summum bonum* (highest good) through the **beatific vision** (seeing God in heaven). It is like an inner spiritual energy or pure desire that keeps the person focused only on this ultimate aim. It is a background virtue that consistently supports and encourages the person to actively practise all the other moral virtues in their life.
- **Charity** (love) is the *greatest* of the theological virtues and is the key to Aquinas' entire moral system. Charity towards God is shown through a person's love of their neighbour. It is the one virtue that actively guides all other virtues towards their proper goal, which is God. Without charity, every other good action or virtue is empty and meaningless. Charity also helps to heal fallen human nature.

One crucial aspect of charity for Aquinas is that it includes the special gift of wisdom, which means having an insight into the supernatural truths of creation, the goodness of God and the beatific vision. Those who have this wisdom can guide others towards a virtuous life. In this sense, charity is the greatest virtue because it is the essence of all others, actively directing them towards their proper end: God and the beatific vision.

Key quotes

'Love the Lord your God with all your heart and with all your soul and with all your mind.' This is the first and greatest commandment. And the second is like it: 'Love your neighbour as yourself.' All the Law and the Prophets hang on these two commandments.

(Matthew 22:37–40)

A new command I give you: Love one another. As I have loved you, so you must love one another. By this everyone will know that you are my disciples, if you love one another.

(John 13:34–35)

Faith has to do with things that are not seen and hope with things that are not at hand.

(Aquinas)

Four cardinal virtues

Besides the three revealed virtues, Aquinas also identified natural virtues. He believed that to develop correct moral reasoning, people need to cultivate these specific virtues. He considered four to be the most important, calling them the cardinal virtues.

Here the word cardinal comes from the Latin for 'hinge' (*cardo*), showing that all other natural virtues fall under and hinge upon these four. By applying these virtues as the basis for morality, Aquinas believed that human beings could then become more godlike:

- **Prudence** is the ability to make sound judgements by using correct reasoning in daily life. Aquinas defined it as 'right reason with respect to action'. Prudence requires a person to be aware of the general moral rules (like natural law) and understand how to apply them correctly to a specific situation. Prudence is the foundation of casuistry (case-based moral reasoning) and works through three steps:
    1. counsel: thinking through all the possible actions one could take
    2. judgement: deciding which course of action is the morally correct one
    3. command: putting that decision into practice

  Prudence is crucial because many other virtues rely on it, including memory, intelligence, foresight and caution, all of which help a person choose and command the good.
- **Temperance** is the virtue of moderation and self-control. We can see in it the influence of Aristotle's idea of finding the balance – the golden mean – in behaviour. It involves sobriety and restraint, and its purpose is to purify and guide our physical desires and pleasures (like eating and drinking). Aquinas taught that physical goods are not bad, but they must be controlled by reason and used as tools to help us achieve our moral goals. This virtue also includes related qualities like humility and meekness (gentleness), which help a person control vices such as vanity and anger. It ensures that our physical desires are kept in check by our rational mind.
- **Fortitude** is the ability to face challenging circumstances – whether they are physical, moral or spiritual – with strength and reason. A person with fortitude possesses qualities like discipline, patience and perseverance. They remain steady and will not be defeated by stress or sorrow. Fortitude helps a person develop a noble character by avoiding two extremes. On one side, they are not controlled by fear (cowardice); on the other side, they are not reckless or irresponsible, ensuring their actions are always guided by reason.
- **Justice** uniquely focuses on other people – specifically, how we act towards them. It is less about a person's individual character and more about governing our actions in the world. Justice applies to the law, covering the welfare of the entire community and dealing fairly with individual situations. It ensures that goods and responsibilities are correctly managed and fairly distributed among people in society, but always in 'due proportion'. It is important to note that Aquinas' concept of justice does not mean everyone receives strict equality; instead, it recognises that justice must account for individual needs and circumstances. For example, a person in poverty may justly require more assistance than a wealthy person.

Key terms

prudence: a cardinal virtue involving sound judgement
temperance: a cardinal virtue involving balance and restraint
fortitude: a cardinal virtue involving physical, moral or spiritual endurance, courage and strength of character
justice: a cardinal virtue involving guidance in how we act towards others

Specification content

Aquinas' definition of different types of acts and goods: internal acts (the intention of the moral agent when carrying out an action) and external acts (the actions of a moral agent); real goods (correctly reasoned goods that help the moral agent achieve their *telos*) and apparent goods (wrongly reasoned goods that do not help the moral agent achieve their God-given purpose)

Key terms

moral agent: an individual who possesses the rational capacity to distinguish between right and wrong and is, therefore, held accountable for their voluntary actions

internal act: the motive or choice of the will

external act: the physical action itself

doctrine of double effect (DDE): a term to describe an ethical method of interpretation first identified in Aquinas' treatment of killing in self-defence

Key quote

Actions are about singular matters: and so it is necessary for the prudent man to know both the universal principles of reason, and the singulars about which actions are concerned.

(Aquinas)

Aquinas' definition of different types of acts and goods

Aquinas made a fundamental distinction, regarding a **moral agent**, between the intention of the agent (the **internal act**) and the action they perform (the **external act**).

Internal acts (the intention of the moral agent when carrying out an action)

The internal act is the motive – the choice of the will, the intention – and, for Aquinas, it is the most important factor in deciding whether an external act is morally good or bad. For instance, if an external act appears good to an onlooker, but the agent's real underlying motive was selfish or evil, the external act is morally wrong. In natural law ethics, an external act is only truly right if both the internal act and the external act are good. One should never intentionally choose to do a bad external act, even if the ultimate aim is to bring about a good result. The internal act must always be good.

External acts (the actions of a moral agent)

The external act is the physical action itself. For an action to be entirely moral, both the internal act (intention) and the external act (the physical thing done) must be good. If the external act is wrong in itself – such as lying or murder – it cannot be justified by a good intention.

Application: the doctrine of double effect

Understanding the distinction between these two acts is vital when facing complex moral dilemmas in which one action can have two effects: one good and one bad. Aquinas' method for addressing such dilemmas is called the **doctrine of double effect (DDE)**.

The DDE states that if a person performs a good external act with a good internal act, the action is morally right, even if a known, unfortunate side effect (a 'bad consequence') occurs. The key is that the bad consequence must not be intended.

Classical DDE requires four conditions to be met for the action to be morally permissible:

- Good intention: The bad consequence must not be wished for, and all reasonable efforts must be made to avoid it.
- Immediate effect is good: The external act itself must be good or neutral.
- Means not evil: The bad consequence cannot be the means by which the good external act is achieved.
- Proportionate reason: The good external act must be at least as important as the bad consequence.

An example is treating a pregnant person for aggressive cancer to save their life. If the treatment tragically results in the loss of the unborn fetus, the external act may be permissible. This is because the internal act (intention) was solely to save the pregnant person (a good external act), and the death of the fetus was an unintended and unavoidable side effect. In this case, the external act that brought it about – the treatment for cancer – may be judged to be good and morally right, according to natural law ethics.

Different types of goods

As has been seen, natural law is built into human nature, but unlike a physical law, it is not followed automatically. It derives from reason, which can sometimes be incorrectly directed or applied. For Aquinas, the things that count as 'goods' are those objects or actions that fulfil the moral agent's natural, God-given inclinations. These fundamental inclinations correspond to the primary precepts of natural law, such as preserving life, seeking knowledge and living in an ordered society. This leads to the distinction between different types of goods.

Real goods (correctly reasoned goods that help the moral agent achieve their *telos*)

Real goods are those things that are correctly reasoned to help the moral agent achieve their ultimate purpose (*telos*), which is perfection in the image of God.

Reason should correctly identify what humans should desire, following natural inclinations towards the primary precepts. This path should lead to the moral agent's goal of perfection (likeness to God). An example of a real good is being generous and giving to charity (provided the intention is correct).

Apparent goods (wrongly reasoned goods that do not help the moral agent achieve their God-given purpose)

Apparent goods are things that are wrongly reasoned and do not help the moral agent achieve their God-given purpose. Aquinas recognised that people only ever desire something because they judge it to be good at that moment. However, this personal judgement does not automatically make the action morally good.

While Aquinas believed that humanity's reason was weakened by the Fall, he did not believe it was destroyed. He argued that humans still have a natural inclination towards the good, but this can be clouded by the passions or a lack of knowledge. This leads a person to choose an apparent good – something that seems desirable in the moment but does not actually lead to their ultimate perfection (the real good). Sin, therefore, is not a deliberate choice to be evil, but a mistake in reasoning when an individual pursues a perceived good that is actually contrary to their true nature.

Choosing an apparent good is following a desire for something that seems good at the time but is not in line with the moral agent's overall good in relation to natural law. For example, eating an excessive amount simply because the food tastes good. In this example, the person confuses an apparent good – the pleasure experienced by eating the good-tasting food – with a real good – eating to preserve their life.

This action shows a lack of the cardinal virtue of temperance and cultivates a greedy character. This in turn contradicts the primary precept of an ordered society, since a person dominated by greed is unable to focus on their social duties.

Aquinas did not believe that people choose to be genuinely 'evil'; instead, he believed they perform evil acts because they use their ability to reason incorrectly in pursuit of an apparent good.

Key terms

real goods: actions that the moral agent correctly reasons will fulfil a natural human inclination (primary precept) and help them move closer to their ultimate perfection in the image of God

apparent goods: actions or objects that the moral agent wrongly reasons are good – they satisfy desires but contradict one or more primary precepts – ultimately leading the agent away from their true purpose (*telos*)

Summary

- Developing virtues leads to correct moral reasoning.
- Three revealed virtues are faith, hope and charity: charity is the most important because, when it is combined with wisdom, it can be used to guide another person to their *telos*.
- Four natural virtues also help in developing correct moral reasoning: prudence, temperance, fortitude and justice; they are cardinal because all other virtues hinge on (depend on) them.
- Human actions have an internal side (the motive) and an external side (the physical act itself). When an action can have two effects, one good and one bad, the DDE can be useful. If applied correctly, the DDE can explain how an action with an unintended bad consequence can still be morally right.
- Aquinas distinguished two types of goods – real and apparent. Real goods help people draw closer to the ideal human nature and apparent goods do the opposite; in distinguishing the two, reasoning is essential.

AO1 Activity

a Explain how a moral agent might choose an apparent good over a real good with the example of a student cheating in an examination. In your explanation, incorporate as many key concepts as needed, such as primary precepts, the will, reason, fallen human nature, *telos*, real good and apparent good. This task will help you to develop the ability to select and explain the precise philosophical steps by which Aquinas accounts for human sin.

b Draw a flowchart showing the virtues described by Aquinas, and how they connect with each other. This task develops the skill of organising theological concepts hierarchically, which will help you structure clear and coherent AO1 answers that show the relationships between key ideas.

Refer to the higher band descriptors for A Level (Eduqas/WJEC), which you should be aspiring towards. Ask yourself the following questions:

- Does my response demonstrate thorough, accurate and relevant knowledge and understanding?
- Is my response coherent, clear and well organised?
- Does my response use evidence and examples with extensive depth and/or breadth?
- Is my use of specialist language and vocabulary both thorough and accurate?

Issues for analysis and evaluation

The strengths and weaknesses of Aquinas' natural law

Possible line of argument	Critical analysis and evaluation
Natural law is universal in application and recognises that throughout the world – regardless of time and place – there is a common constant and unchanging human nature. For example, it is natural for us to continue valuing and educating children.	The sheer diversity and variety of cultural practices and values in human society over the world and over time demonstrate that there is no constant human nature. For example, in many places today, children are exploited for work and mistreated.
Natural law is entirely rational and relies on basic common sense. Everyone accepts that the primary precepts, such as an orderly society, are fundamental.	Aquinas' formulation of natural law ultimately finds its meaning and purpose in the existence of God. One of the primary precepts is the worship of God. But there is no proof for God's existence and Western liberal democracies are secular.
Natural law is positive and optimistic as it recognises the good in people: love is a guiding virtue for everyone and, with the use of reason, people can uncover the other virtues. Ultimately everyone seeks the good of others and their *telos*, which is ultimate perfection in the image of God.	Too much weight is placed on the view that people are religious and rational in their attitude and approach to life. Reality shows that people are guided by emotions such as pleasure rather than virtues such as temperance. People have to be self-interested and selfish to flourish in today's secular society.
Natural law is a coherent, well-structured and hierarchical approach to morality: the key precept of doing good leads to recognising the primary precepts from which follow the secondary precepts; by reason and by developing virtues everyone can then accept and put natural law into practice.	Human life is full of complexity and cannot be moulded to follow rigid hierarchical precepts. There are conflicting human needs, desires, pleasures and wants. A consequentialist approach which promotes pleasure and avoids suffering is realistic and democratic – it does not rely on abstract concepts such as the cardinal virtues or four levels of law.
Natural law provides a clear pathway through moral dilemmas via the DDE, which makes it flexible and adaptable to changing times. For example, the good intention of ending war may require the use of force and collateral damage, but this is justified by the good effect of lasting peace.	The DDE is simply a way of justifying something wrong. For example, achieving peace through using force to end a war cannot justify collateral damage (injury, death and destruction to a country's infrastructure). Natural law makes religion's role in ethics too important and views compassion and love in a purely legalistic way.

This section covers AO2 content and skills

Specification content

The strengths and weaknesses of Aquinas' natural law

AO2 Activity

a Analyse three possible conclusions that could be drawn from the critical analysis and evaluation of the strengths and weaknesses of Aquinas' natural law. Select evidence and examples to support each of the three conclusions. Select one conclusion that you think is the **most convincing** and explain why it is so.

b Evaluate this by contrasting it with the **weakest** conclusion of the three. Justify your argument with clear reasoning and evidence.

Refer to the higher band descriptors for A Level (Eduqas/WJEC), which you should be aspiring towards. Ask yourself the following questions:

- Does my response demonstrate confident critical analysis and evaluation?
- Are my views sustained, clear and supported by reasoning and evidence?
- Do I refer to the views of scholars or schools of thought to support my argument?
- Is my use of specialist language and vocabulary both thorough and accurate?

Specification content

A consideration of whether natural law promotes injustice

Exam practice

Below is an example of part of an evaluation of whether natural law promotes injustice.

Sample answer

News reporter **Judge**

The topic under discussion is clearly identified and explained and a mini-conclusion is already suggested.

The claim that natural law promotes injustice is strong because the theory fails to acknowledge that many human actions, such as sex, can have more than one legitimate purpose. This inflexible approach leads to discrimination, such as the condemnation of homosexuality and pre-marital relationships, against those whose actions do not strictly fulfil their primary purposes.

Tennis player

A strong argument has been served in this paragraph which helps the further development of the essay.

Due to its inflexible nature, natural law fails to adapt to modern social progress, supporting what many view as outdated ideals. This is evident in its condemnation of divorce and abortion; both are legally accepted in most modern societies today.

Detective

Further evidence is uncovered to support the view already expressed in the introduction.

Unlike relativistic theories, natural law fails to consider personal context or specific individual situations. For instance, instead of being legalistic about love, some argue it could be more loving to allow non-married couples to express their commitment through sex.

Philosopher

One of the key problems of natural law is identified here which helps clarify the issues raised by the question.

This application of rigid, universal principles acts almost like a 'one-size-fits-all' theory. It does not reflect the spirit of modern justice, which always considers 'mitigating circumstances' when judging a crime. This lack of situational context is inconsistent with contemporary ethical practice.

However, many argue that natural law fundamentally promotes justice by providing all humans with a universally applicable set of moral rules. Because it fosters a shared ethical framework, the theory is vital for maintaining a strong sense of social justice and community.

Tennis player This paragraph presents a strong counter-argument fielding the points made earlier and providing flow in the essay.

Natural law also provides universal and eternal laws that are above mere human justice. This means that people, regardless of their time or culture, have the primary precepts as guidance, knowing definitively what actions are acceptable.

Critical thinker This presents a coherent set of points which focus on the technical aspects of the argument.

For religious believers, this moral framework promotes justice by recognising that God punishes those who deliberately choose to contravene the primary precepts and reject the virtues, thereby moving them further away from the goal of eternal life with God. Having God as the ultimate judge must promote justice, not injustice.

Philosopher This raises an interesting and relevant question as to religion, natural law and injustice.

The theory further promotes justice by calling for fundamental basic human rights derived from the precepts, such as the right to life, the right to education and the right to live in an ordered society. All of these always promote justice.

Tennis player Again the overall discussion in the essay continues with a strong line of argument countering previous points.

In conclusion, while natural law's rigid application in certain areas might create the potential for injustice, its entire basis is to promote the essential virtue, love, and the protection of the innocent through an ordered society. Therefore, having considered the issues, natural law does not promote injustice.

Judge The essay reaches a conclusion based on the evaluation and analysis given throughout.

Over to you

Below is a strong response to the question of whether or not natural law has a place in twenty-first-century moral decision-making. The response provides evidence and examples to support the analysis and evaluation.

a Read the essay carefully and make a note of evidence and examples which can be used in response to exam questions on natural law.

b Read through the numbered notes given after the essay and consider how they can be used in developing a strong approach to AO2 questions.

c Using the evidence in the essay, write a conclusion which presents the opposite point of view. Then evaluate both conclusions and explain which you find most convincing and why.

You may wish to return to this question after studying other themes in this book, as a strong answer may draw on knowledge of other ethical theories for comparison.

Question

'Absolutist theories such as natural law have no place in twenty-first-century moral decision-making.' Evaluate this view.

Response

For many believers worldwide, natural law provides a strong basis for making moral decisions, challenging the claim that it has no place in the twenty-first century. Its absolutist deontological approach determines that some actions are always right or wrong, offering moral stability through clear rules that echo biblical commandments like 'Do not kill.' [1]

As the foundation for the Roman Catholic Church, natural law remains a significant part of twenty-first-century decision-making for millions. The Pope has criticised modern relativist theories as a 'dictatorship of relativism' that prioritises individual desire. In contrast, natural law focuses on the common good and an ordered society, promoting justice through the cardinal virtues and the Golden Rule. [2]

However, critics argue that natural law's absolutist nature is ill-suited to modern pluralistic societies. While deontological theories provide certainty, twenty-first-century moral agents often prefer teleological approaches, such as situation ethics, that prioritise compassionate outcomes over fixed duties. Furthermore, the idea of a universal human nature is contested by philosophers who observe that moral values vary significantly across different cultures. [3]

Religious critics like Luther and Calvin also challenged the theory's heavy emphasis on human reason. They argued that the Bible, rather than reason, must be the highest form of authority. [4] This suggests that even within Christianity, a fixed, reason-based system may not be the most appropriate path for the modern believer.

Many also consider natural law's views on abortion and euthanasia to be outdated. In the twenty-first century, individual autonomy and quality of life are highly valued, yet natural law gives absolute priority to the primary precepts of reproduction and the preservation of life. This led the Pope to condemn contraception in poverty-stricken regions, where a situational approach might suggest that preventing such hardship is the more loving, ethical response. [5]

While natural law offers clear moral consistency, it appears fundamentally flawed in a globalised context. Because perceptions of what is rational vary according to cultural background, its claim to universality is undermined. Consequently, fixed absolutist theories struggle to accommodate the diversity and complexity of twenty-first-century moral life. [6]

Notes

[1] **Focus**: The answer addresses the benefits of an absolutist approach within a modern context.

[2] **Understanding**: This displays clear knowledge of natural law's core principles and its contrast with relativism.

[3] **Examples**: Here, the writer uses the tension between deontological duties and teleological priorities to highlight weaknesses.

[4] **Authority**: References to Luther and Calvin demonstrate understanding of the debate between reason and scriptural authority.

[5] **Development**: This explains how fixed primary precepts can clash with twenty-first-century values like autonomy and compassion.

[6] **Link**: The conclusion directly addresses the wording of the question regarding the theory's place in the modern world.

Refer to the higher band descriptors for A Level (Eduqas/WJEC), which you should be aspiring towards. Ask yourself the following questions:

- In what ways does this response show confident critical analysis and evaluation?
- Are the views sustained, clear and supported by reasoning and evidence?
- How are the views of scholars/schools of thought used?
- Is the specialist language used both thorough and accurate?

This section covers AO1 content and skills

Specification content

Aquinas' natural law: application of the theory; the application of Aquinas' natural law to the issue of abortion

Key terms

medical abortion: abortion by means of the abortion pill

surgical abortion: abortion by means of the suction method

potential: the possibility, at conception, of becoming a human person

zygote: a cell formed by the union of a male sex cell (a sperm) and a female sex cell (an ovum), which develops into an embryo according to information encoded in its genetic material

blastocyst: a group of multiplying cells

embryo: an animal in the early stage of development before birth; in humans, the embryo stage is the first two months after conception

fetus: the unborn baby; in humans, the fetus stage lasts from the end of the eighth week after conception (when the major structures have formed) until birth

C: Aquinas' natural law: application of the theory

The issues arising from abortion

Abortion is the termination of a pregnancy before 24 weeks' gestation. While available through the National Health Service (NHS), pregnant people must be referred for an abortion by a doctor, and it is generally easiest to obtain one before 12 weeks.

There are two main classifications:

- **Medical abortion**: Achieved without surgery, this uses the abortion pill (mifepristone), followed 36 to 48 hours later by a second tablet (prostaglandin) to complete the process.
- **Surgical abortion**: Most commonly achieved through vacuum aspiration (suction) up to approximately 13 weeks. In later stages, dilation and evacuation (D&E) is used, which involves a combination of surgery and suction.

A crucial issue in the abortion debate surrounds the beginning of 'humanness'. Biologically, development begins at conception (fertilisation). The development, or actualisation of the **potential** to become fully human, proceeds through these stages:

1. conception
2. **zygote**/pre-embryo (0–5 days)
3. **blastocyst**/pre-embryo (5–14 days)
4. **embryo** (14 days to 8 weeks)
5. **fetus** (8 weeks onwards)
6. newborn (birth, usually between 38 and 42 weeks)

Pregnancy is calculated from the first day of the pregnant person's last menstrual period. The specific timings are based on typical growth rates.

Key quotes

Personhood may be one thing and human life another; hence it is possible to argue that, while the zygote may not be a person, there is no logical alternative to regarding it as the first stage in human life.

(Mason and Laurie)

The basic argument against abortion, on which all others build, is that the unborn child is already a human being, a person, a bearer of rights, and that abortion is therefore murder.

(Mackie)

Up until the middle of the twentieth century, many doctors took the ancient form of the Hippocratic oath which had been used from ancient times by physicians. This included the line: 'I will not give to a woman an abortive remedy.' That approach of not allowing any form of medical abortion had been the norm for many centuries.

Changes in UK abortion law reflect shifting social attitudes, beginning with the Offences Against the Person Act (1861) which stated that procuring a miscarriage was a criminal offence. These are the key legal milestones:

1. **Infant Life (Preservation) Act (1929)**: This allowed termination only to preserve the pregnant person's life.

2 **Abortion Act (1967)**: This legalised abortion, provided that two doctors agreed termination was necessary to prevent greater risk of injury to the pregnant person's physical or mental health or to existing children in the family, or if there was a high risk the baby would develop a disability.

3 **Human Fertilisation and Embryology Act (1990)**: The legal limit on abortion was reduced from 28 to 24 weeks. Crucially, it removed time restrictions for abortions performed due to fetal abnormality.

The 1990 Act raises a significant legal and ethical challenge regarding where the line of personhood is drawn. Usually, the law protects a 'viable' fetus after 24 weeks, yet the 1990 Act allows for the abortion of a fetus with abnormalities up until birth. This creates a contradiction: it suggests that the legal protection of a fetus depends on its physical health rather than its stage of development. This uncertainty leads philosophers like Peter Singer to argue that any such 'line' is arbitrary, noting that 'there is no obvious sharp line dividing the zygote from the adult'.

The debate about abortion also involves the **sanctity of life** (the traditional belief that life is sacred/God-given). Some philosophers, including Singer, argue for shifting the focus away from a religious perspective by rejecting the concept of the sanctity of life and applying instead a non-religious, ethical perspective about the value of life. With that approach, the issue becomes whether an act can be classed as killing, or even murder, and at which point potential human life acquires such value as to make abortion an ethical injustice.

The **anti-abortion** and **pro-choice** division can also be understood as a clash of rights. For example, anti-abortion views often assert the right of the 'unborn child' to life in the same way that all human beings have the right to life. From the other perspective, pro-choice views often highlight the pregnant person and their reproductive rights – including the absolute right to freely choose whether or not to terminate the pregnancy.

A major problem is the blurred terminology used by opposing groups. Anti-abortion and pro-choice campaigners often interpret terms like 'life' and 'unborn' differently – disagreeing on whether the terms apply to the embryo and fetus stages or only to the stage after birth. It is essential to establish consistent definitions for 'person', 'baby' and 'life'. As Peter Vardy notes, many arguments are based on different interpretations of the same words – what he calls **relational factors** – and this prevents universal agreement on when personhood status is awarded.

While biological debates depend upon physical evidence, philosophical and religious debates about personhood are based on concepts beyond the physical. Since there is no empirical evidence to prove when personhood starts, the debate becomes more complex.

Development point	Definition
conception	when the potential for life begins
quickening	when the pregnant person first feels movement (varies individually)
viability	the point at which the fetus can survive (be kept alive outside the womb) without depending on the pregnant person
birth	separation from the pregnant person

Hippocrates (460–370 BCE)

Key quote

Whether or not abortion should be legal turns on the answer to the question of whether and at what point a foetus is a person. This is a question that cannot be answered logically or empirically. The concept of personhood is neither logical nor empirical: it is essentially a religious, or quasi-religious idea, based on one's fundamental (and therefore unverifiable) assumptions about the nature of the world.

(Campos)

Key terms

sanctity of life: the belief that life is sacred or holy, given by God
anti-abortion: against abortion
pro-choice: supporting pregnant people's reproductive rights (including the right to have an abortion)
relational factors: different interpretations of the same words or terms, depending on the viewpoint of the observer

Development point	Definition
consciousness	when the ability to think and feel becomes clear
ensoulment	when the soul is believed to enter the body (a point debated across different religious traditions but rejected by a secular approach)

One final consideration is the variation in individual development. For example, when exactly a person moves from childhood to adulthood varies from one individual to another. Why should the development milestones in the early stages of life (embryo and fetus) be any different?

Pope Pius XI (1857–1939)

Key quotes

Whether inflicted upon the mother or upon the child, [abortion] is against the precept of God and the law of nature: 'Thou shalt not kill.'

(Pope Pius XI)

The only absolute in the saga is that 'life' as it is generally understood begins with the formation of the zygote; on this view, the conservative Roman Catholic view represents the only tenable option – the difficulty is that it is also the least practical solution to the question.

(Mason and Laurie)

Specification content

Aquinas' natural law: application of the theory; the application of Aquinas' natural law to the issue of abortion

The application of natural law to the issue of abortion

Applying Aquinas' natural law to abortion, the act is considered inherently evil because it violates the primary precept of preserving life. It also directly violates the primary precept of reproduction. Within natural law, the *telos* of the reproductive system is procreation. By terminating a pregnancy, a moral agent deliberately thwarts this natural biological and teleological process. Consequently, abortion is viewed as a failure to fulfil the fundamental human requirement to continue the species and nurture the next generation. In this strict view, abortion is wrong in all situations, including cases of rape and incest.

Furthermore, abortion contravenes divine law – the revealed truths in scripture. For example, the commandment: 'Thou shalt not kill,' (Exodus 20:13) and the concept that human beings are created in the image of God (*imago dei*), reinforce the prohibition against ending life in the womb. For Aquinas, because God is the sole author of life and death, any human intervention to end life prematurely is a rebellion against God's will.

There is also the issue of real and apparent goods. A pregnant person seeking an abortion may believe they are pursuing good ends, such as the relief of suffering or the pursuit of career goals. However, under natural law, their choice violates a primary precept, so the goods cannot be real goods; they are only apparent goods. Reason (*recta ratio*) dictates that a real good must be consistent with the primary precepts. Therefore, the 'right to choose' is viewed as a misguided use of reason that prioritises a preference over a primary moral obligation.

The distinction between the internal act (the intention) and the external act (the physical act itself) also needs to be noted in relation to abortion. If the internal act is the termination of the pregnancy itself, the action is always wrong, regardless of the circumstances. In this sense, natural law remains deontological and focused on the nature of the act rather than the consequences.

Some would argue that natural law upholds human rights, such as the right to life, and that this should include the right of autonomy over one's body. This would support the view that abortion should be regarded as a pregnant person's right to choose. However, others would argue that abortion directly prevents the natural development of human life towards its *telos*, so it cannot be justified under natural law.

The immediate debate often centres on determining the moment the fetus acquires personhood, with religious and secular opinions ranging from conception to the appearance of certain features like neural activity. However, the Catholic Church teaches that personhood and ensoulment take place from the moment of conception.

It could be argued that the DDE permits the death of a fetus, but only as a by-product of another good action where the death of the fetus was not intended. For instance, the performance of a hysterectomy or the use of chemotherapy to remove cancer from the uterus is acceptable, even if it leads to the unintended death of the fetus, because the intention is solely the preservation of the pregnant person's life.

A Catholic professor of ethics, Howard Kainz, noted that those who defend abortion when the pregnant person's life is in danger, using the DDE, have already made an exception to the preservation of life precept due to a conflict of rights. He argues that this willingness to accept exceptions must logically extend to other precepts.

Kainz argued that a person has a right to voluntarily choose to procreate, and that rape and incest represent the most obvious infractions of this choice. If one admits the possibility of exceptions to the precepts in order to preserve life, one must admit the possibility of similar exceptions for preserving the right to choose to procreate. This reveals a potential conflict between primary precepts within natural law itself.

Despite this conflict, Kainz ultimately argues that a virtuous approach should supersede natural law conflicts. He claims that Christian principles may override considerations of conflicting rights. A person who chooses to nurture their child after rape, or who sacrifices their life for the child's survival during a problematic pregnancy, demonstrates 'heroic virtue' and 'going the extra mile'. From a natural law standpoint, these are 'sacrifices of personal rights that go beyond the normal call of parental responsibility'.

Kainz highlights that natural law includes an obligation to use reason, to apply it to cases and to incorporate Christian virtues. However, anti-abortion critics of Kainz would be reluctant to accept that *agape*, the greatest virtue, can be interpreted in such a way that it moves away from what is stated in the primary precepts, suggesting Kainz's interpretation of virtue is not a true application of natural law.

All of this suggests that in its application, natural law itself is not as straightforward as it might seem.

Specification content

Aquinas' natural law: application of the theory; the application of Aquinas' natural law to the issue of voluntary euthanasia

Key terms

euthanasia: literally meaning a gentle or easy death, it is the act of intentionally ending a person's life to relieve their suffering and help them to die with dignity

voluntary euthanasia: the intentional ending of a person's life when they have expressed a competent and conscious wish to die

non-voluntary euthanasia: the intentional ending of a person's life when they are unable to express a wish (e.g. in a persistent vegetative state), and the decision is made by others in their best interest

active euthanasia: a deliberate action taken to end life, such as administering a lethal dose of medication

passive euthanasia: withdrawing or withholding life-prolonging treatment (e.g. turning off a ventilator), allowing the patient to die from their underlying condition

The issues arising from euthanasia

The issue of **euthanasia** (concerning the end of life) and abortion (concerning the beginning of life) are equally complex and progress under similar ethical headings.

The term derives from the Greek *eu thanatos* (good death), suggesting a death that is beneficial for the person involved. **Voluntary euthanasia** (physician-assisted suicide) is the focus here. In this case, the request to die is made by a person who is mentally competent.

Historically, the Suicide Act (1961) decriminalised suicide but explicitly maintained that aiding or assisting suicide remains a crime in the UK. This legal position was placed under review by the UK Parliament in 2024 with the Terminally Ill Adults (End of Life) Bill (often referred to as 'assisted dying' legislation). This private member's bill came under scrutiny in the UK Parliament in 2024 with the introduction of the Terminally Ill Adults (End of Life) Bill. This proposed legislation sought to allow terminally ill adults with less than six months to live to request medical assistance to end their own life. To protect vulnerable people, the process required approval from two independent doctors and a review panel. Although the bill won early support in the House of Commons, it faced strong opposition and major delays when it reached the House of Lords. The legislation ultimately ran out of time and did not become law.

As with abortion, two central principles are at stake:

- whether killing should be allowed in any circumstances
- the value given to life (sanctity vs quality).

The difficulties that arise when determining the point at which a life begins are mirrored at the end of a life. While physical death can usually be determined, a person in a coma and kept artificially alive raises questions about the definition of life and whether a physical definition is sufficient. This links directly to philosophical questions about quality of life – at what point does life lose its value, and who decides?

Current law in the UK allows a competent patient to refuse medical treatment, even if that refusal leads to harm or death (they have the right not to prolong their own life). This choice is regarded as their human right. However, they do not have the right to hasten death by requesting and being administered specific medication. This presents an uncomfortable inconsistency: refusing treatment, knowing the consequence is death, is acceptable, but willingly receiving medication to achieve death sooner and with less pain is not.

This dilemma is at the heart of the debate: How far should a person's individual rights and autonomy extend over their own body and fate? Ethically, some argue that people have a duty to prevent prolonged and meaningless suffering, considering the impact on family and friends.

At present, it may be argued, medical practitioners have no clear legal guidelines on intervention or withholding treatment

Arguments against legalising euthanasia point to the very real risk of abuse and systemic problems:

- How could the administration of euthanasia be effectively monitored in practice?
- Would it be in the best interest of society as a whole (the 'slippery slope' argument)?
- Does it contravene the Hippocratic oath or interfere with the natural or divinely ordained course of events?

Currently, it may be argued, medical practitioners rely on vague professional guidelines regarding active intervention and the withholding of treatment, leaving doctors legally and ethically vulnerable.

Key quotes

When suffering is the result of following an ethical principle then we need to look very carefully at our ethical principle and ask whether we are applying it too inflexibly.

(Hope)

It is perverse to seek a sense of ethical purity when this is gained at the expense of the suffering of others.

(Hope)

The application of Aquinas' natural law to the issue of voluntary euthanasia

When applying Aquinas' natural law to euthanasia, the primary precept of preserving innocent life is the central principle, often expressed through the concept of the sanctity of life. Natural law teaches that human life is a gift from God and must be protected from conception until natural death. Therefore, taking one's own life or the life of another, even when requested, is considered a violation of the natural order and a failure to fulfil our human *telos*.

This position is reinforced by divine law, which provides revealed instructions such as the commandment 'Thou shalt not kill.' From this perspective, human beings do not have absolute autonomy over their bodies; instead, they are stewards of a life that belongs ultimately to God as the creator of life.

The precept of an ordered society is also fundamental to the natural law rejection of euthanasia. Proponents argue that the stability of society relies on an absolute prohibition against intentional killing. Legalising euthanasia would undermine the foundational trust between doctors and patients, potentially transforming the medical profession from one that preserves life to one that ends it.

Furthermore, it risks creating a slippery slope where vulnerable people – such as older and disabled people – feel a 'duty to die' to avoid being a burden to their families or the state. For Aquinas, any law that permits the killing of innocent people is a corruption of law rather than a true law, as it fails to serve the common good or maintain social stability.

The *Catechism of the Catholic Church* (or the ***Catechism***) defines euthanasia as 'an act or omission which, of itself or by intention, causes the death of handicapped, sick, or dying persons [...] sometimes with an attempt to justify the act as a means of eliminating suffering.' Proponents of natural law object to any approach that suggests casuistry or considering consequences is subordinate to the primary precepts. What appears to be a virtuous act of 'mercy' is classified as an apparent good rather than a real good. While the intention may be to end suffering, the external act (killing) is inherently wrong, and therefore the action cannot be justified.

Despite this rigidity, the DDE offers a significant nuance. Although administering drugs to deliberately end a life is unacceptable, it is morally permissible under natural law to provide high doses of pain relief, such as morphine, to a terminally ill patient, even if it is foreseen that this will shorten their life. In this instance, the internal act is the intention to relieve pain and the external act is the administration of medicine. The resulting death is a foreseen but unintended side effect.

Key term

Catechism: a formal summary of Christian beliefs and moral teachings, traditionally used for religious instruction

However, critics like Professor Ian Harriss argue that in making this concession to the DDE, natural law is 'compromised by a latent concession to utilitarianism'. He questions whether the DDE is truly an absolutist stance, noting that in countries with bodies of legislation that are strongly influenced by natural law, the use of heavy sedation can sometimes be an ambiguous 'best way out'.

The debate surrounding the UK Parliament's Terminally Ill Adults (End of Life) Bill has directly challenged natural law. Legalising voluntary assisted dying would potentially not only contravene the precept of preserving life but also threaten the precept of living in an ordered society by altering the legal and moral protections afforded to all citizens.

In conclusion, while natural law provides a definitive model based on the sanctity of life and the requirements of social order, the complexity of its application and the difficulties in balancing primary precepts mean its approach remains a point of intense philosophical and legal contention.

Summary

- Abortion (medical or surgical) is legal in the UK up to 24 weeks and there is no limit if there is fetal abnormality.
- Debates about abortion tend to focus on sanctity of life, and whether what is in the pregnant person's womb is a person and, if so, when personhood begins.
- Natural law opposes abortion as it violates the primary precept of preservation of life, although the DDE may allow for the death of the fetus to save the pregnant person's life in some circumstances.
- Euthanasia (voluntary) is under review by the UK Parliament.
- Debates about euthanasia tend to focus on sanctity of life, quality of life and whether a person should have the right to request that their life is ended and under what circumstances.
- Natural law opposes euthanasia as it violates the primary precept of preservation of life, although the DDE may allow for administering drugs which control pain and which will shorten the patient's life, provided that the intention is not to kill the patient.

AO1 Activity

a Outline the key issues surrounding abortion, using the letters ABORTION as an acrostic framework. (An acrostic is a form of writing in which the first letter of each line spells out a word. For example, A could be for 'autonomy'.)

b Choose either abortion or voluntary euthanasia. Create a flowchart or diagram that shows how Aquinas' natural law is applied to that issue, including the relevant primary precept(s), how the DDE applies and any conflicts between precepts. Use key terminology and at least two scholars or sources in your diagram. This will help you develop the skill of selecting and organising relevant knowledge into a clear, logical structure, which is a key feature of answers in the higher bands.

Refer to the higher band descriptors for A Level (Eduqas/WJEC), which you should be aspiring towards. Ask yourself the following questions:

- Does my response demonstrate thorough, accurate and relevant knowledge and understanding?
- Is my response coherent, clear and well organised?
- Does my response use evidence and examples with extensive depth and/or breadth?
- Is my use of specialist language and vocabulary both thorough and accurate?

Issues for analysis and evaluation

The effectiveness of natural law in dealing with ethical issues

This section covers AO2 content and skills

Specification content

The effectiveness of natural law in dealing with ethical issues

Possible line of argument	Critical analysis and evaluation
Natural law is effective because it can be applied universally and consistently: its rules apply to all people, at all times, providing a clear and coherent moral framework.	Natural law is outdated and ineffective; it fails to address the complexity of modern social and ethical issues, such as autonomy and the need for progressive human rights laws.
The theory has clear, rational rules and does not rely on weighing consequences: it is based purely on reason and provides clear, unambiguous rules (e.g. abortion is wrong) without relying on unpredictable consequences or emotions.	The theory is inflexible; it fails to consider the difficult situations individuals face, such as refusing to permit abortion even in cases of rape, leading to severe suffering or needlessly prolonging a life which is full of suffering.
Within natural law, the DDE allows for foreseen death (e.g. from high morphine doses for pain) provided the intention is pure (pain relief), which reduces the harshness of the primary precept about preservation of human life and makes it flexible.	As Kainz argued, the application of the DDE is often seen as internally inconsistent and contradictory: it compromises natural law's absolutist stance by referring to the consequences, making it no different to utilitarianism.
For believers, natural law links the creator, creation and human purpose, ensuring morality is anchored, rational and promotes justice and ordered society.	Natural law fails to align with modern human rights standards, particularly regarding sexual orientation, which is not allowed to be discriminated against in contemporary law. It also undermines the right of human autonomy in areas such as abortion and euthanasia.
Natural law's focus on cold, objective reason prevents emotional decision-making, which is key to ensuring justice and impartial application of the law.	Basing decisions on love and concern (*agape*) or on the consequences alone, can often guide ethical choices more effectively than the cold application of a single ruling, especially in deeply personal dilemmas.

AO2 Activity

a Analyse three possible conclusions that could be drawn from the critical analysis and evaluation of the effectiveness of natural law in dealing with ethical issues. Select evidence and examples to support each of the three conclusions. Select one conclusion that you think is the **most convincing** and explain why it is so.

b Now contrast this with the **weakest** conclusion of the three. Justify your argument with clear reasoning and evidence.

Refer to the higher band descriptors for A Level (Eduqas/WJEC), which you should be aspiring towards. Ask yourself the following questions:

- Does my response demonstrate confident critical analysis and evaluation?
- Are my views sustained, clear and supported by reasoning and evidence?
- Do I refer to the views of scholars or schools of thought to support my argument?
- Is my use of specialist language and vocabulary both thorough and accurate?

Specification content

The extent to which natural law is meaningless without a belief in a creator God

Exam practice

Below is an example of part of an evaluation of the extent to which natural law is meaningless without a belief in a creator God.

Sample answer

Aquinas adopted the principles established by Aristotle but asserted that natural law is fundamentally rooted in a creator God. For Aquinas, God established the order and purpose of the world, and natural law perfectly reflects God's eternal will. This creator belief is therefore central to his entire moral theory.

Critical thinker

The introduction states the core premise of Aquinas' argument: that natural law's coherence depends on the Creator.

This divine structure gives humanity its ultimate purpose: the beatific vision (returning to God for eternal life). All ethical behaviour and human laws are ultimately guided by God's eternal law, which is partially revealed through divine law.

Detective

This paragraph accurately brings together the evidence, correctly defining the relationship between ultimate purpose, eternal law and divine law.

Divine law includes the teachings found in religious scripture, including the commandments, such as the Ten Commandments. These revelations are used to shape acceptable ethical behaviour and human laws within society.

News reporter

This section provides clarity, summarising how the abstract concepts of divine law are made practical and applicable to human legislation.

The primary precepts (such as reproducing and living in an ordered society) mirror these fundamental religious purposes for humankind. Even the encouragement of virtuous behaviour is entirely consistent with the teachings of Jesus and the Church.

Explorer

This suggests a strong connection, bringing in Jesus and the Church.

Based on this theological foundation, Catholic theology and most religious adherents agree that natural law is fundamentally meaningless without a belief in a creator God who establishes the moral order and dictates human purpose.

However, this theological view is strongly challenged by many philosophical thinkers who argue that a system of objective morality does not necessarily require a deity to function.

The philosophical origins of natural law predate Christianity. Aristotle's Prime Mover, the original concept that inspired Aquinas, is a distant philosophical principle, not the active, interventionist, personal God found in Christian doctrine. This distinction undermines the idea in the statement that natural law is meaningless without God.

Furthermore, some modern natural law thinkers, who are Catholic, argue that a fully functioning ethical system can be developed without first needing to prove the existence of God. They argue that humans use their own reason to make decisions and that moral law is inherently autonomous.

In conclusion, whether natural law is truly meaningless depends entirely on one's philosophical starting perspective. While the system can operate independently through secular reason, for religious followers, its true, deeper meaning and ultimate purpose remain inextricably linked to the will of a creator God.

Judge

This is a confident interim judgement giving the 'for' side of the argument, stating the strongest conclusion drawn from the religious evidence presented.

Tennis player

This paragraph successfully presents the counter-argument, moving the essay towards the challenges to the issue.

Detective

Critical thinker

The use of Aristotle's Prime Mover is a highly relevant historical example that challenges the necessity of the Christian Creator concept.

Philosopher

This is a perceptive counter-argument: if Catholic thinkers can separate natural law from God, the dependence is philosophical, not absolute.

Judge

This paragraph provides the final, balanced ruling, confidently concluding that all depends on the philosophical lens which a person applies.

Over to you

Below is a reasonable answer that has been written in response to a question requiring an evaluation of the effectiveness of natural law in its application to abortion. It is a reasonable answer and so would be in the lower to middle bands.

a Read through the response carefully, taking notes on its contents.

b Refer to the lower to middle band descriptors for A2 (WJEC) or A Level (Eduqas) and compare these with the higher bands and the descriptions inside those bands.

c Consider what is both strong and weak about the answer and suggest at least three ways in which it could be developed.

Question

'Natural law is not an effective way to make decisions about abortion.' Evaluate this view.

Sample answer

On one hand, those who accept Aquinas' doctrine of natural law, and seek to apply this to the issue of abortion, believe that the primary precepts are prevented. Therefore, the act of abortion is seen as wrong because of the intentional killing of an innocent human being. For others, this is far too absolutist and simplistic an application and does not consider all circumstances.

Then there is the exception of the DDE in natural law. The DDE does permit the death of the fetus. This means that the intention was not to kill the fetus.

There is another approach; for example, a Catholic professor of ethics has argued that in the case of abortion, two other precepts are perhaps even more relevant to the issue of abortion: procreation and nurturing offspring. He argues if, for abortion, you defend the right of the woman if their life is in danger, then, in the same way, if every woman has a right to conceive and procreate, rape violates this right and so maybe abortion can be justified in the case of rape. In other words, if you use a principle of exception for the first precept then you have to be consistent in applying it to other precepts. Not all Catholics will accept this, but critics of natural law would agree with the apparent inconsistency.

Overall, I think there are problems in applying natural law to abortion, but this does not mean it is ineffective. It does, however, question how far natural law is consistent.

D: John Finnis' development of natural law

This section covers AO1 content and skills

John Finnis: *Natural Law and Natural Rights*

Key quote

Finnis argues that unless law is grounded in what it is to be human and relates to a moral code, then human beings will not see that following the law is morally right and will obey it only out of habit or fear whilst the tools of civic education and enforcement endure.

(Vardy)

Specification content

John Finnis' development of natural law; development of the seven basic human goods (life, knowledge, friendship, play, aesthetic experience, practical reasonableness and religion)

Statues of the great philosophers Aristotle and Aquinas, both of whom have made a significant contribution to the theory of natural law

John Finnis' *Natural Law and Natural Rights* (1980) presents a modern version of natural law focused on **jurisprudence** (the philosophy of law), moving away from the purely philosophical focus of Aristotle and the theological context of Aquinas.

The core of Finnis' system identifies seven basic goods (self-evident values like life, knowledge and play) and nine requirements of practical reasonableness (rational guidelines for pursuing those goods). Unlike Aquinas, whose system rests on God's eternal law and aims for the beatific vision, Finnis argues his system is accessible through secular reason and is independent of religious belief. His primary goal shifts from a divine *telos* to achieving human flourishing (*eudaimonia*) and securing the common good within society.

Key person

John Finnis (1940–): An Australian-born legal philosopher and Oxford and Notre Dame professor of law; his book, *Natural Law and Natural Rights* (1980) was a secular reinterpretation of natural law based on reason and revisiting Aristotle and Aquinas; he is considered one of the most significant natural law theorists of the twentieth century

Key term

jurisprudence: the philosophy of law as presented by a normative (rule-setting) legal system

The central purpose of Finnis' theory is to inform human law. Governments are justified only in so far as they use the requirements of practical reasonableness to create laws that secure these basic human goods for the common good.

While Finnis avoids relying on divine law for his foundation, he does not exclude religion. He suggests the existence and nature of God may ultimately explain *why* objective moral standards exist.

Key quotes

Finnis attempts to formulate a rational basis for moral action. His central thesis is that the act of making law is an act which can and should be guided by moral principles which are a matter of objective reasonableness.

(White)

The collapse of Christianity and other religious cultures, as the matrix for contemporary legal and political orders, has posed a challenge to those who wish to affirm that there is a Natural Law.

(Finnis)

Since Natural Law is part of the nature of things the knowledge of it is accessible to all [...] through reason apart from any supernatural revelation.

(Einwechter)

Although, Finnis indeed posits a place for morality in the law, the type of morality Finnis has in mind is questionable.

(White)

Finnis' presentation of natural law rests on three core methodological assumptions:

- **Basic goods are self-evident**: The basic goods are unchangeable, self-evident truths that are known through reason but are not derived from any other facts (like those found in history or through science), linking them to Aristotle's philosophical wisdom (***sophia***).
- **Moral reasoning is distinct**: Finnis argues that the process of discerning what people *ought to do* (ethics) is a separate, but equally rational, intellectual operation from determining what *is the case* (factual knowledge).
- **Practical reasoning is essential**: Ethical action relies on practical reasonableness (similar to Aristotle's practical wisdom, ***phronesis***), which is the applied skill of making sound, well informed decisions guided by the nine requirements.

Key terms

***sophia*:** philosophical wisdom
***phronesis*:** practical wisdom

Key quotes

A self-evident principle is only self-evident to the subject, in this case Finnis, and then only to the extent that it has become self-evident and not challenged by that subject's experience. It is quite conceivable that different people would come up with entirely different formulations of goods to be attained. Self-evidence provides no real explanation of how each agent generates their own list of basic values corresponding to Finnis's seven.

(White)

Moral virtue comes about as a result of habit, whence also its name (*ethike*) is one that is formed by a slight variation from the word *ethos* (habit).

(Aristotle, *Nichomachean Ethics*)

Finnis' natural law theory heavily depends on the philosophical tradition of Plato and Aristotle, while deliberately distancing itself from the purely theological elements of Aquinas. Finnis avoids Aquinas' divine levels of law and the teleological end goal of the beatific vision (returning to God). Instead, Finnis revisits the Aristotelian premise that the aim of a good life is to flourish or achieve *eudaimonia* (complete well-being). For Finnis, the purpose of natural law is to answer the question, 'What are the basic aspects of my well-being?' and to guide human law to serve the common good for every citizen. Finnis reformulates Aquinas' primary precepts into his basic goods to give them a modern, secular relevance.

For Finnis, law and morality are intricately bound together

The seven basic goods are fundamental to achieving *eudaimonia*. These are the common objectives for any rational person seeking a good life. They are similar to Aristotle's concept of philosophical wisdom, *sophia*. Although one good might be more relevant in a specific situation, this simply reflects a shift in focus, not a permanent priority. The goods do not have a hierarchy. Finnis writes: 'Each is fundamental. None is more fundamental than any of the others, for each can reasonably be focused upon, and each, when focused upon, claims a priority of value. Hence there is no objective priority of value amongst them.' The goal is to participate in all of them throughout life.

The basic goods tell people what is inherently valuable, but they do not tell people *how* to act when pursuing them. Therefore, the good of practical reasonableness must be applied, acting as the key to the healthy and balanced management of the basic goods in the real world.

Key quote

Aquinas asserts as plainly as possible that the first principles of Natural Law, which specify the basic forms of good and evil [...] can be adequately grasped by anyone of the age of reason [...] They are not inferred from speculative principles. They are not inferred from facts.

(Finnis)

A statue of the personification of wisdom (*sophia*)

Key quotes

A first basic value, corresponding to the drive for self-preservation, is the value of life. The term 'life' here signifies every aspect of the vitality (*vita*, life) which puts a human being in good shape for self-determination.

(Finnis)

The principle that truth is worth pursuing, knowledge is worth having, is thus an underived principle. Neither its intelligibility nor its force rests on any further principle.

(Finnis)

[...] friendship involves acting for the sake of one's friend's purposes, one's friend's well-being. To be in a relationship of friendship with at least one other person is a fundamental form of good, is it not?

(Finnis)

The third basic aspect of human well-being is play [...] each one of us can see the point of engaging in performances which have no point beyond the performance itself, enjoyed for its own sake.

(Finnis)

Bodily health – part of Finnis' definition of life

Friendship – a basic good

Key term

aesthetic: related to the concept and appreciation of beauty

These are the seven basic goods:

- **Life**: This covers physical and mental health, self-preservation and the act of procreation (as 'life-in-its-transmission'). Finnis uses it broadly to mean the vitality that puts a human in good shape for self-determination.
- **Knowledge**: This is not instrumental knowledge (for example, finding the cheapest supermarket), but knowledge pursued for its own sake because it is good in itself – the general concept of seeking, revealing and appreciating the truth.
- **Friendship (sociability)**: This goes beyond mere social interaction or co-operation; it is the strongest form of sociability, focused on acting for the sake of a friend's well-being and purposes.
- **Play**: This involves engaging in performances purely for the enjoyment of the activities, ranging from hobbies such as painting to sports, and including a sense of humour while working.
- **Aesthetic experience**: This is the appreciation of beauty in art, nature or performance. It is often related to play but is distinct because it is an inner experience initiated by things outside of one's own immediate actions.
- **Practical reasonableness**: This is the basic good that structures a person's pursuit of all other basic goods. It is the ability to use one's intelligence and reason to make sound decisions, bringing intelligent order into one's actions, habits and life plans. Finnis links it directly to Aristotle's concept of *phronesis*. The pursuit of these goods is not a teleological goal (like reaching a finish line), but an ongoing participation in these fundamental values through the projects and commitments people undertake.

- **Religion**: This is the pursuit of ultimate order and meaning. It is the need to reflect on ultimate questions about the origin of the cosmos, human freedom and reason. Finnis states the questions are important, regardless of whether the answers are religious, agnostic or negative.

Key quotes

Although in modern times, belief in Natural Law is strongly correlated to belief in God [...] Natural Law theorists have consistently asserted that individuals can discover the Natural Law, independent of their particular religious beliefs.

(Greenawalt)

Buddhist mandala (a symbol of cosmic order); Finnis uses the word 'religion' in the sense of awareness of some cosmic order

Specification content

Distinction between theoretical and practical reason

The distinction between theoretical and practical reason

For Finnis, the entire structure of natural law depends on clearly separating two types of reasoning:

- **Theoretical (speculative) reason**: This deals with what *is* the case (matters of fact, explanation and prediction). This includes science, history and instrumental knowledge (for example, *where* the cheapest item is). It aims to discern truth but cannot establish moral obligation.
- **Practical reason (reasonableness)**: This deals with what *ought* to be done (normative – that is, reasoning about rules and standards of behaviour – reasoning, ethics). It is person-oriented, based on the self-evident basic goods, and aims to guide action to achieve well-being.

Finnis argues that past moral philosophers have wrongly tried to deduce moral obligations (what *ought* to be done) from factual observations (what *is* the case):

- **Avoiding the naturalistic fallacy**: By insisting that the basic goods are self-evident ethical starting points (known by practical reason) and are *not* derived from empirical facts or human nature (theoretical reason), Finnis avoids the naturalistic fallacy (the error of deriving ought from is).
- **Agreeing with Hume**: Finnis agrees with David Hume's famous point that you cannot logically deduce moral obligation from empirical observation. Unlike utilitarianism, which Finnis suggests makes this error, natural law's ethical duty originates solely from the reflective principles of practical reasonableness.

In short, theoretical reason informs us about the world, but only practical reason tells a person their moral obligations.

Key quotes

Practical philosophy is a discipline and critical reflection on the goods that can be realised in human action and the requirements of practical reasonableness.

(Finnis)

Now each man judges well the things he knows, and of these he is a good judge. And so the man who has been educated in a subject is a good judge of that subject, and the man who has received an all-round education is a good judge in general.

(Aristotle, *Nichomachean Ethics*)

Theoretical reason aims at knowledge of how things are, and its activity terminates in belief about how things are. Practical reason aims at realising the good, and its activity terminates in action rather than belief.

(Lamont)

Practical reasonableness can be seen as a basic good that serves as the skill set for ethical living. This skill demands that people bring intelligent order to their choices, guiding their commitments and shaping their participation in all the other basic goods (life, knowledge, friendship and the rest).

For Finnis, this process of practical reasoning is the methodology of ethics itself. A person who excels at this is an ethical expert, similar to Aristotle's *phronimos* (one possessing *phronesis*). To live up to this standard – achieving the 'fullness of well-being' – requires a structure.

Specification content

Nine requirements of practical reason (view life as a whole, no arbitrary preference among values, basic goods apply equally to all, do not become obsessed with a particular project, use effort to improve, plan your actions to do the most good, never harm a basic good, foster common good in the community and act in your own conscience and authority)

The good of practical reasonableness structures our pursuit of basic goods

The nine requirements of practical reasonableness

Key quote

Each of these requirements concerns what one must do, or think, or be if one is to participate in the basic value of practical reasonableness.

(Finnis)

This structure is provided by the nine requirements of practical reasonableness. These requirements are fundamental, underived and irreducible. While the basic goods identify what is worth pursuing, the nine requirements detail how an individual must think and act to participate in those goods rationally. By following these requirements, a person ensures that their pursuit of values is consistent, fair, and morally sound. In this way, practical reasonableness is both a basic good to be practised and the essential method for ethical living.

- **Coherent plan of life**: People must view life as a whole and have a consistent life plan that harmonises their goals with the pursuit of all the basic goods. This general vision for life's priorities prevents people from being consumed by immediate whims, short-term goals or simply drifting from moment to moment.

- **Values with no arbitrary preferences**: People must maintain balance and accept that all basic goods are equally important, fundamental and non-hierarchical. People must never neglect or deny the intrinsic value of any good, even if their circumstances require them to focus more intensely on some over others.
- **Equality of basic goods which apply to all with no arbitrary preferences among persons**: People must acknowledge that the basic goods are for the benefit of all people, not just themselves. This requirement critiques selfishness and demands that people foster the good of others, avoiding double standards, even if they retain a reasonable scope for self-preference.
- **Detachment so as not to become obsessed with a particular project**: People must avoid fanaticism by maintaining detachment from specific, limited projects (like a job or hobby). If a particular project fails, a person's life should not be drained of meaning; they must retain perspective on the basic goods as a whole.

Detachment from obsession is a balancing act

- **Commitment in using effort to improve**: This requirement balances detachment. A person must not be apathetic or indifferent, but must make a committed effort to pursue and realise their chosen projects and goals, always looking creatively for new and better ways of carrying out their commitments, and not abandoning them lightly.
- **Efficiency within reason, planning actions to do the most good**: When faced with choices, a person must choose the most efficient action that limits negative consequences and maximises the application of the basic goods through reason. This involves preferring human goods over instrumental goods (like property) and choosing lesser over greater damage when harm is inevitable.
- **Harming a basic good is absolutely prohibited to ensure respect for every basic value in every act**: This is Finnis' most controversial requirement because it creates an absolute rule. It is an absolute prohibition that states one must never directly attack or intentionally harm any basic good (such as life) in any action. This would prohibit abortion and euthanasia as they threaten the basic good of life. This rule is used to avoid the dangers of consequentialism, where the ends might justify harmful means.
- **Foster common good in the community**: A person must act to create and maintain a community environment where everyone has the opportunity to pursue and participate in the basic goods. This co-operative approach validates the need for justice, human rights, authority and law – elements that serve the community's best interests.

Conscience for Finnis is the sign of fullness of being

Specification content

The common good and the need for authority

- **Conscience as an authority to be followed**: Ultimately, a person must act in accordance with their own conscience. Finnis views conscience not as a mere feeling, but as the final internal application of the first eight requirements of practical reasonableness, forming the deep structure of moral thought.

The common good and the need for authority

We have already discussed how Finnis' natural law theory places an emphasis on pursuing the common good. This theme arises implicitly in the basic goods themselves and is made explicit in the requirement to 'foster common good in the community'. However, the common good and the need for authority can be considered as one concept, so it is worth drawing these ideas together.

Finnis conceives of the common good not as what is good for most people, but rather as the conditions that allow each person to access and pursue the basic goods. Society itself must be organised in such a way that allows for human flourishing, which is why there needs to be authority. Without some sort of overarching power to co-ordinate individuals' pursuit of the basic goods, they will inevitably conflict with one another. The authority of law comes from the demands of the common good and should act as an enabling support: the laws of any given society should guide its citizens towards the basic goods and prevent them from error.

Importantly, however, Finnis states that authority is only justified so far as it promotes the common good. A law which only benefits those who are in power is not morally authoritative. So, what about unjust laws? What about the variations in different societies' applications of natural law? Finnis has an answer for this too. He is not talking about individual (and therefore fallible) conceptions of natural law which have been applied to society. Instead he is showing us the principles which should be applied. The various conceptions of natural law which societies have come up with over history are merely evidence of humans trying – not always successfully – to live by these principles. Just because those attempts have failed, it does not mean the theory is invalidated. Natural law, Finnis argues, is not a historical trend that can rise, decline or experience 'eternal returns'. It is a constant set of requirements for human reasoning that exists independently of whether a society chooses to recognise it.

Finnis and sexual ethics

A major area of controversy regarding Finnis' approach is in the area of sex. He argues against all non-marital sexual acts, including those between people of the same sex. His argument is complex and is based on three main points:

- **The 'complete union'**: Finnis argues that marriage between a man and a woman is the only way to fully achieve two basic goods at the same time: life (through having children) and friendship (through a lifelong commitment to each other). This union is naturally open to procreation, which Finnis calls life-in-its-transmission.
- **The 'defective choice'**: Acts of sex which cannot result in procreation (homosexual sex) or which occur outside of a lifelong commitment (casual sex) are, according to Finnis, 'defective' or incomplete. These acts can involve some goods (pleasure, for example) but cannot realise the superior good of life-in-its-transmission with complete lifelong friendship.

- **The 'violation of reason'**: Practical reasonableness requires people to make well-ordered choices, and never to choose a partial good when a complete good is available. Finnis argues that by choosing a non-marital sexual act, a person is unreasonably prioritising a lesser good (sensual pleasure) over the full good of life and lifelong friendship combined. This violates one of the requirements of practical reasonableness: that there should be no arbitrary preferences among basic goods.

However, Finnis makes a clear distinction: although he views these acts as a moral evil (meaning they are contrary to reason and a fundamental human good), he firmly argues that this moral judgement should not translate into legal discrimination or interference with the personal freedom of consenting adults. Finnis is adamant that moral evil is not necessarily the same as a crime.

Despite this, some scholars such as Stephen Buckle argue that Finnis – who is a Catholic – has attempted to justify Catholic moral positions through what might appear to be a neutral and apparently secular philosophical framework. For example, the basic goods he identifies as self-evident have their roots in Catholic morality.

Another scholar, Brigita White argues that the basic goods identified by Finnis are only his 'personal conceptions' based on the society in which he lives. White regards Finnis as being conservative in his outlook: 'His account is not grounded in social realities but in abstractions. The result is a law imbued with a morality that essentially serves the interests of the elite.' In addition, the framework he uses means that with the basic good of life, practices such as euthanasia and principles like the right to die are ruled out and ignored.

Key quotes

Implicitly or explicitly one must have a harmonious set of purposes and orientations, not as the 'plans' or 'blueprints' of a pipe-dream, but as effective commitments.

(Finnis)

It is unreasonable to live merely from moment to moment, following immediate cravings, or just drifting.

(Finnis)

Any commitment to a coherent plan of life is going to involve some degree of concentration on one or some of the basic forms of good, at the expense, temporarily or permanently, of other forms of good.

(Finnis)

One should be looking creatively for new and better ways of carrying out one's commitments, rather than restricting one's horizon and one's effort to the projects, methods, and routines with which one is familiar.

(Finnis)

From one's capacity to grasp intelligently the basic forms of good as 'to-be-pursued', one gets one's ability [...] to sympathetically (though not uncritically) see the point of actions, life-styles, characters and cultures that one would not choose for oneself.

(Finnis)

Summary

- Finnis developed a modern version of natural law using the work of Aristotle and Aquinas to establish a rational basis for moral action which is not based on religious belief.
- Finnis argues that ethical action depends on practical reasonableness – the applied skill of making sound, well informed decisions.
- Seven basic goods are: life, knowledge, friendship, play, aesthetic experience, practical reasonableness and religion; they are all fundamental and there is no hierarchy.
- For Finnis, theoretical reason is based on what is the case – factual observations; practical reasonableness is based on what ought to be done based on the self-evident basic goods.
- The nine requirements of practical reasonableness are:
  - coherent plan of life
  - values with no arbitrary preferences
  - equality of basic goods which apply to all with no arbitrary preferences among persons
  - detachment so as not to become obsessed with a particular project
  - commitment in using effort to improve
  - efficiency within reason, planning actions to do the most good
  - harming a basic good is absolutely prohibited to ensure respect for every basic value in every act
  - foster common good in the community
  - conscience as an authority to be followed.
- The nine requirements are fundamental, irreducible and essential for achieving the fullness of well-being (the maximum potential of life).

AO1 Activity

a Outline the seven basic goods and the nine requirements of practical reasonableness. You may find it helpful to devise a mnemonic (pattern of letters) to help in memorising the concepts. (This task develops the ability to recall key points of the approach taken by Finnis, which is essential for AO1 responses.)

b Draw a flowchart to show how Finnis' version of natural law develops and differs from Aquinas'.

This task helps to demonstrate knowledge and understanding of the relationship between the different forms of natural law.

Here a suggested mnemonic for the nine requirements:

Choose Values Equally. Detach, Commit, Efficiently. Help Foster Conscience.

Letter	Requirement (key word)
C	**C**oherent plan
V	**V**alues
E	**E**quality
D	**D**etachment
C	**C**ommitment
E	**E**fficiency
H	**H**arm
F	**F**oster
C	**C**onscience

When completing these tasks, refer to the AO1 band descriptors. Aim for 'extensive depth and/or breadth' with 'thorough, accurate and relevant' knowledge and understanding that is 'clearly structured'.

Issues for analysis and evaluation

Whether Finnis' natural law is acceptable in contemporary society

This section covers AO2 content and skills

Specification content

Whether Finnis' natural law is acceptable in contemporary society

Possible line of argument	Critical analysis and evaluation
It has universal objectivity and legal strength because Finnis uses universal moral principles and connects them to positive law. This provides a firm basis for jurisprudence.	Finnis' natural law, according to Brigita White, is only based on his own 'personal conceptions' and the norms of his society – it has a conservative bias and 'serves the interests of the elite'.
It is entirely applicable because it is grounded in objective reason – the system is rationally derived from self-evident basic goods which offer the basis for moral action and the formulation of laws.	It is not grounded in objective reason: as Stephen Buckle points out, Finnis uses the practical reasonableness requirements alongside the basic good of life to justify, in a subtle fashion, Catholic moral teachings on non-marital sex, abortion and euthanasia.
Finnis' natural law is acceptable because it is based on positively encouraging the basic goods to achieve human flourishing, which can only serve to develop and make a priority of the common good.	The approach taken by the basic goods and the requirements of practical reasonableness lacks any flexibility as it rejects consequentialism – in the fast-moving contemporary society, a consequentialist approach is essential to ensure humane and practical ethics.
The focus on basic goods such as aesthetic experience, play and friendship is vital in contemporary society and keeps the focus on shared values, lawful human rights, common citizenship and tolerance.	Finnis' natural law might appear clear, coherent and cogent in theory but in practice it is too complex, unwieldy and likely to be misunderstood: his argument that sex between gay and/or lesbian people is a moral evil, but should be accepted and not legislated against, might work in an academic sense but not in common sense.
The basic goods leading to the nine requirements of practical reasonableness provide a clear method for people to move from values to action – this will lead to a rational life plan for all.	The approach taken by Finnish only works within a religious culture, particularly given that religion is one of the basic goods; it is not an approach that works well in a modern secular society.

AO2 Activity

a Analyse three possible conclusions that could be drawn from the critical analysis and evaluation of whether Finnis' natural law is acceptable in contemporary society. Select evidence and examples to support each of the three conclusions. Select one conclusion that you think is the **most convincing** and explain why it is so.

b Now contrast this with the **weakest** conclusion of the three. Justify your argument with clear reasoning and evidence.

When completing these tasks, refer to the AO2 band descriptors. Aim for responses that demonstrate sustained and clear views, either of scholars or from a personal perspective, with extensive detailed argument and a clear conclusion.

Specification content

The strengths and weaknesses of Finnis' natural law

Exam practice

Below is an example of part of an evaluation of the strengths and weaknesses of Finnis' natural law.

Sample answer

Philosopher – The introduction clearly frames the key philosophical tension for the entire argument.

Evaluating Finnis' modern natural law theory shows it builds on classical philosophy but aims for a non-religious foundation based on human flourishing. Its strengths lie in its appeal to universal reason, but weaknesses are found in its strict moral applications and alleged religious bias.

Explorer – The essay successfully maps out the universal territory of the basic goods.

A major strength is the universality of his framework. Finnis identifies seven basic goods (for example, knowledge, life and play) that he claims are self-evident and equally valuable to everyone. This provides an objective, common-sense foundation for all moral rules, regardless of culture.

Detective – The link between the basic goods and moral action is traced effectively through the requirements.

Finnis' system highly values rationality, rejecting emotional ethics. He uses the nine requirements of practical reasonableness as a critical bridge. These guide individuals from recognising the basic goods to forming concrete moral choices and a rational life plan.

Judge – The legal clarity derived from the objective nature of the system is well stated here.

The theory offers the certainty of a deontological system. It judges the intrinsic value of an action, focusing only on whether the act itself is right or wrong, regardless of the consequences. This provides firm moral guidance over situational ethics.

News reporter – The main controversies and core criticisms surrounding the theory are all covered in a concise statement.

A key weakness is the charge of theological bias. Critics argue that despite claiming to be secular, the theory functions as a defence for conservative religious morality, suggesting the nine requirements of practical reasonableness support traditional moral stances. This concern is heightened by the insistence on moral absolutes; the rule never to deliberately act against a basic good makes actions like active euthanasia or abortion always intrinsically wrong, which critics find impractical when facing modern dilemmas.

However, proponents counter that the nine requirements of practical reasonableness offer more flexibility than critics admit. They function as formal, guiding principles (like impartiality and commitment), not rigid rules, meaning Finnis' system does not prescribe a single correct choice but rules out only those that are directly destructive to a basic good, leaving considerable room for individual liberty and judgement.

Tennis player **Philosopher**

That's a strong counter-argument, precisely hitting back at the point about rigidity.

Finnis modernises the tradition by making religion a rationally understandable basic good, defined as a concern for ultimate purpose. This avoids the reliance on faith found in Aquinas' work, providing a philosophical entry point for those who are agnostic.

Explorer

The concept of ultimate purpose is charted as a philosophical destination.

Finnis also clarifies the important link between morality and social law. His concept of the common good dictates that all societal laws must be structured to help citizens achieve the basic goods, offering clear justification for civil authority.

Judge **News reporter**

The essay correctly reports on the essential justification for legal and governmental systems.

In summary, Finnis' natural law provides a sophisticated, rational foundation for ethics with clear principles. While it modernises the tradition and can be defended on grounds of flexibility, its perceived bias and inflexible adherence to moral absolutes remain significant points of debate.

Critical thinker

The conclusion provides a measured and balanced final assessment of the overall argument.

Over to you

a Read through the short evaluation on page 124 in response to a question about the effectiveness of Finnis' natural law in making moral decisions.

b Rewrite the evaluation, bringing in references to scholars, quotations and anything which might improve the points made. Some quotations have been suggested below the evaluation; you do not need to use all of them, and you may find other useful quotations to use instead.

When you are writing you might include:

- a reference to a named scholar
- a complete quotation or partial quotation
- a short paraphrase of what the scholar stated.

Phrases such as these can help to bring in appropriate quotations:

- according to x …
- x argues that …
- an alternative view is suggested by x …
- however, as x states …

Remember that quotations can be shortened and paraphrased – the key thing is that the name of the scholar is included. For example: 'As Einwechter writes, natural law depends on reason and not on 'any supernatural revelation'.

As you are completing the task, note the higher band descriptors for A2 (WJEC) or A Level (Eduqas), one of which states: 'the views of scholars/schools of thought are used extensively, appropriately and in context'.

Question

'Finnis' natural law is not an effective way to make moral decisions.' Evaluate this view.

(Eduqas A Level 2019)

Evaluation

John Finnis' natural law is an effective tool for moral decision-making because it is highly relevant to the contemporary world. As a legal scholar, Finnis updates Aquinas' traditional precepts into modern 'basic goods', moving away from a strictly religious focus towards jurisprudence.

However, its effectiveness is questioned because many advocates are religious, supporting specific Roman Catholic teachings. This leads to criticism that the theory serves as a vehicle for religious social values rather than a universal framework.

Nonetheless, the theory's reliance on reason gives it a common-sense appeal. Finnis argues that the principles of natural law are accessible through practical reason, making them applicable to everyone. By framing his approach as a 'whole life project', he offers a comprehensive method for human flourishing.

Conversely, a major challenge is that the theory may not represent everyone's values. Critics suggest it remains tethered to Roman Catholic morality, raising the question of whether Finnis' version is a truly objective way to make moral decisions or merely a reflection of his own cultural views.

Key quotes

Although in modern times, belief in Natural Law is strongly correlated to belief in God [...] Natural Law theorists have consistently asserted that individuals can discover the Natural Law, independent of their particular religious beliefs.

(Greenawalt)

Although, Finnis indeed posits a place for morality in the law, the type of morality Finnis has in mind is questionable.

(White)

Since Natural Law is part of the nature of things the knowledge of it is accessible to all [...] through reason apart from any supernatural revelation.

(Einwechter)

Even a happy life cannot be without a measure of darkness, and the word happy would lose its meaning if it were not balanced by sadness. It is far better to take things as they come along with patience and equanimity.

(Carl Jung)

One should be looking creatively for new and better ways of carrying out one's commitments, rather than restricting one's horizon and one's effort to the projects, methods, and routines with which one is familiar.

(Finnis)

Scholars such as Stephen Buckle argue that Finnis – who is a Catholic – has attempted to justify Catholic moral positions through what might appear to be a neutral and quasi-secular philosophical framework.

His account is not grounded in social realities but in abstractions. The result is a law imbued with a morality that essentially serves the interests of the elite.

(White)

E: Bernard Hoose's overview of the proportionalist debate

The origins of proportionalism

As has already been seen, from one perspective, natural law is a deontological system. For example, Aquinas had a key precept of doing good and avoiding evil along with the primary precepts such as preservation of life. Obeying these precepts and following them as rules can be understood as a deontological approach.

Finnis' natural law developed the approach taken by Aquinas and added basic goods and requirements of practical reasonableness. Here too, a deontological approach can be seen: Finnis stated as one of the nine requirements that harming a basic good was absolutely prohibited to ensure respect for every basic good in every act.

The deontological perspective of natural law is one that views it as providing a system of rules which cannot be rejected but which need to be followed.

From another perspective, natural law also has within it a teleological aspect. This could be seen in the way in which, for human beings, all the primary precepts have an ultimate divine *telos* of the beatific vision.

In addition, through the DDE, natural law also admits that in extreme situations – such as treating a pregnant person for aggressive cancer to save their life resulting in the death of the unborn fetus – there has to be consideration of the outcome. Therefore, what has to be considered is the nature of the act itself (deontological) along with the goal or consequence of the act (teleological).

Against this background, **proportionalism** developed during the 1960s alongside major changes in society and the Catholic Church, such as the debates over contraception and abortion. Some theologians felt traditional natural law was too inflexible. While they wanted to consider the situation, they rejected **situation ethics** (Joseph Fletcher) for being too vague and lacking rules.

The **magisterium** of the Catholic Church traditionally emphasised the deontological side of natural law, with strict secondary precepts and a view that certain acts are intrinsically evil. This focus was a defence particularly against consequentialist theories such as utilitarianism and, in the 1960s, situation ethics. Those who focus on the deontological side of natural law can be called **traditionalists**.

Revisionists took a different approach. They sought to balance this focus on rules against other factors: the intention behind the action, the unique circumstances of extreme situations and the goal of the action. Taken together, these factors might call into question the concept of any action being intrinsically evil.

The revisionist approach required a different view of Aquinas' natural law as being neither deontological nor teleological but a hybrid – a mixture of distinct elements. It combines obedience to rules with a consideration of the outcomes or 'ends'. In all such cases, a principle of assessing the good against

Specification content

As a hybrid of natural law, a deontological/teleological ethic

Vatican dome of the Saint Peter Basilica in Rome, Italy – the 'home' of the magisterium

Key terms

proportionalism: an approach to natural law that focuses in particular on the fourth condition of the doctrine of double effect (DDE) as outlined by Aquinas

situation ethics: a relativist theory of ethics sometimes referred to as situationism, developed by Fletcher

magisterium: the authority of the Roman Catholic Church in maintaining authentic interpretation of the Bible and sacred Roman Catholic tradition headed by the Pope and bishops and supported by a body of scholars

traditionalists: those scholars who support the magisterium; traditional authority of the Roman Catholic Church

revisionists: those scholars who support proportionalism

the evil, which proportionalists argue is implicit in Aquinas' methodology, and which they call the rule of proportionate reason, should be applied.

The rule of proportionate reason gave rise to the name proportionalism. Since this approach had developed over a number of years and involved the views of many scholars working on their own, a major issue was, and remains, reaching agreement on the use of key terms and concepts. The first major evaluation that brought together the various strands of thought was provided in 1987 by **Bernard Hoose** in his book, *Proportionalism: The American Debate and its European Roots*.

Key person

Bernard Hoose (1945–): A British Italian moral theologian and former member of the Carmelite religious order; he lectured in moral theology at Heythrop College, University of London; his most important work is *Proportionalism: The American Debate and its European Roots* (1987), which was his PhD thesis; instead of advancing his own theory of proportionalism, he compiled and critiqued the important revisionist/traditionalist debates that had taken place over the preceding two decades (1967–87); he synthesised the diverse positions within proportionalism for the first time in an accessible format; his book remains the benchmark by which this debate is understood

Key terms

pre-moral/ontic evil: physical natural evil such as the fact of death, disease, pain and suffering

values and disvalues: a proportionalist way of calculating elements of a moral event

A helpful way of understanding proportionalism is to examine the comments of Charles Curran:

> Proportionalism rests on a distinction between physical or pre-moral evil (e.g. killing) and moral evil (e.g. murder). One can do pre-moral evil if there is a proportionate reason. Thus, every killing is not murder. Proportionalism constitutes a middle position objecting on the one hand to neo-Scholastic Natural Law approaches [...] but also objecting to consequentialism and Utilitarianism.

What Curran explains here is that the physical act of killing is a **pre-moral evil** or **ontic evil** – it is a physical loss or disvalue that is bad, but is not morally sinful. By comparison, murder is an immoral act: it is morally evil because it involves the physical act of killing, a morally bad intention and no justifying proportionate reason. On one side of the ethical debate is the traditionalist Catholic magisterium – here called the neo-scholastic natural law approach – which is rejected for being too rigid and absolute; on the other side is the approach of consequentialism – which includes situation ethics – and secular utilitarianism. As Curran suggests, proportionalism adopts a middle position because it looks backwards to deontology – keeping rules, principles and intentions – and forwards to teleology – allowing for consideration of consequences and weighing **values and disvalues**.

The proportionalist maxim

The proportionalist position can be further understood by considering what can be termed the proportionalist **maxim**: 'It is never right to go against a principle unless there is a **proportionate reason** which would justify it.'

The maxim is often interpreted as meaning 'rules are important but can be broken if there is a good reason'. This was seen by many as the position taken by proportionalists. Pope John Paul II in 1993 in the encyclical ***Veritatis Splendor*** criticised this approach. He stated that 'this [...] characteristic of teleological and proportionalist theories' must be rejected. For traditionalists it seemed that the proportionalist approach ignored what St Paul taught in Romans 3:8 – that one 'could not do evil that good may come'.

Proportionalists reject this description, insisting their definition of proportionate reason is rigorous. James Walter warns that it is not simply a 'serious reason' or an 'intention' added to an act, but a specific structural requirement of moral reasoning. Peter Knauer agrees, arguing that a loose definition leads to 'ethical relativism'.

Therefore, the maxim, 'It is never right to go against a principle unless there is a proportionate reason which would justify it,' retains a strong deontological force: it is never right to go against a principle unless the reason is of sufficient gravity. Richard McCormick summarises this in 'Ambiguity in Moral Choice'. He states that a proportionate reason exists only if:

- the value gained is at least equal to the value sacrificed
- there is no less harmful way of protecting the value here and now
- the action does not undermine the value in the long run.

This requires a complex deliberation of values and disvalues; it is not a simple excuse to break rules. Therefore:

- *value* represents the good effect or value that the moral agent is seeking to achieve (for example, saving a life or maintaining health)
- *disvalue* represents the pre-moral evil or disvalue that is unavoidably caused by the action (for example, pain, injury or loss of life).

For an action to be judged morally right, the value sought must visibly and significantly outweigh the disvalue caused. This successful imbalance is the definition of a proportionate reason, proving the moral act is justified. If the scales are equal or tip towards the disvalue, the act is considered morally wrong. For his part, Hoose argued that 'the need for proportionate reason is one of the deeply rooted elements in the tradition of Catholic moral theology'.

Proportionate reason and the DDE

Proportionalists argue that they are doing no more than developing what Aquinas had already stated in the DDE. According to the DDE, it is permissible to perform a good act that has a secondary, unintended bad effect, provided certain conditions are met. Aquinas identified four key conditions:

- The act itself must be good or indifferent.
- The good effect must be intended; the bad effect must not be intended.
- The bad effect must not be the means to the good effect (evil cannot flow directly from the action).
- There must be a proportionate reason for permitting the bad effect (the good must outweigh the evil).

Key quote

If we are satisfied that proportionalism is what must be taught, we must now ask how it is to be taught.

(Hoose)

Specification content

A proportionalist maxim 'it is never right to go against a principle unless there is a proportionate reason which would justify it'

Key terms

maxim: a general rule

proportionate reason: reasoning that ensures evil that occurs is compensated and subsumed by a greater good

***Veritatis Splendor*:** a papal encyclical published in 1993 by Pope John Paul II

A papal encyclical delivers official doctrine and teachings of the Roman Catholic Church

Aquinas first introduced the ideas behind the DDE

While the focus had always been on the third condition, proportionalists changed the focus to the fourth condition – that of proportionate reasoning. Looking at the issue of self-defence involving deadly force which might result in the death of the attacker helps explain how this might work:

Primary precept (good in itself)	preservation of life
Ontic evil	death
Evil act (the means)	killing (introducing a bad thing into the world)
Intention (the end)	self-defence (saving one's own life)
Effects/outcome	own life saved; death of the attacker
Proportionate reason	the unique circumstances (e.g. an immediate threat to life) where the good achieved outweighs the ontic evil
Possible ethical judgements	• morally wrong if the amount of force is excessive and if death is the direct intention and intended result • morally right if the amount of force is measured and necessary to save life, with death being an unintended and indirect consequence

Aquinas' example of killing in self-defence is crucial for understanding proportionate reasoning

In this scenario, the preservation of one's own life is a good in itself and follows the primary precept. The ontic evil is death, and this could be brought about by the evil act of using deadly force against the attacker. The critical factors to decide whether the response is proportionate are the defender's intention and the amount of force they use. If they intend on ending the life of the attacker and they use excessive force as a result, the self-defence is not proportionate; if they intend to save their own life and only use the minimum force required to stop the attacker, it is proportionate.

Proportionalists might argue that in the second instance the maxim, 'It is never right to go against a principle unless there is a proportionate reason which would justify it,' is being fully observed. However, the issue for traditionalists might remain that whatever the justification, an intrinsically evil act has been carried out – killing another human being. Much depends on how the words of Aquinas himself are applied: 'though proceeding from a good intention, an act may be rendered unlawful if it be out of proportion to the end'. Overall, it is important to note that proportionalists still uphold the need for rules.

Key quotes

The principle of double effect leads a marginal existence in the handbooks of moral theology and appears to be useful only in making possible a species of hairsplitting. It is in reality, the fundamental principle of all morality.

(Knauer)

The proponents of proportionate reason have groped to articulate the essential characteristics of the theory and how they relate to the traditional position on double effect.

(Walter)

The proportionality condition is usually understood to involve determining if the extent of the harm is adequately offset by the magnitude of the proposed benefit.

(McIntyre)

It is not merely tradition but common sense that dictates the need for a proportionate reason.

(Hoose)

The attempt to assess the proportion of good or bad likely to proceed from a proposed action is really a common-sense judgment we all make rather routinely.

(Ratzinger)

Moral evil vs pre-moral/ontic evil

To satisfy the proportionate reason criterion, proportionalists must first define the nature of the harm being weighed. This requires distinguishing between harm that is moral and harm that is physical.

The traditional Roman Catholic view defines an 'evil moral act' as **intrinsic evil** – an act that is always wrong in every instance. Proportionalists, however, argue that an act that causes harm (an evil act) may not always be an immoral act if it is justified by the requisite proportionate reason.

This leads to the definition of pre-moral/ontic evil. Professor Joseph Selling, a contemporary proportionalist, clarifies this by distinguishing between the 'act' (what is physically done, or the ***finis operis***) and the 'event' (the entire complex situation, including the intention, or the ***finis operantis***).

Selling explains:

> Making moral evaluations and decisions is a complex process. This is why I refer to it as an 'event' rather than an 'act'. The component parts of the moral event are distinct. When a moral event is complete, all the parts form an inseparable unity.

Specification content

Distinction between an evil moral act (an immoral act) and pre-moral/ontic evil

Key terms

intrinsic evil: an act that is always evil no matter what the circumstances

finis operis: the act-in-itself

finis operantis: the intention behind the act

Applying proportionalism: the ectopic pregnancy debate

One way of seeing how proportionalism might be applied is through the medical dilemma involved in the treatment of an **ectopic pregnancy**. This medical dilemma highlights how proportionalists calculate ontic evil differently from traditionalists.

- **The traditionalist's preferred (licit) procedure (tube removal):**
  - **Action on the tube**: The entire fallopian tube is removed directly.
  - **Result on the fetus**: The removal of the fetus is indirect. Since the tube itself is deemed a pathological (diseased) organ that endangers the pregnant person's life, the intention is to remove the diseased tissue. The death of the fetus is a foreseen but unintended (indirect) bad effect.
  - **Traditional moral verdict**: It is permitted (licit). This method passes the DDE criteria because the act itself (removing a diseased organ) is considered good or indifferent, and the death of the fetus is not the means or the direct intention. The disadvantage is that it reduces the pregnant person's fertility because the tube is lost.
- **The procedure that traditionalists reject (illicit) (cutting and repairing):**
  - **Action on the tube**: The tube is cut/mutilated, the fetus is removed directly and then the tube is repaired.
  - **Result on the fetus**: The removal of the fetus is direct. The act of cutting the tube to remove the fetus is interpreted as a direct act of abortion.
  - **Traditional moral verdict**: It is not permitted (illicit). This fails the DDE criteria because the direct intention and act is to mutilate the tube to destroy the fetus, violating the requirement that the act itself must be good or indifferent.

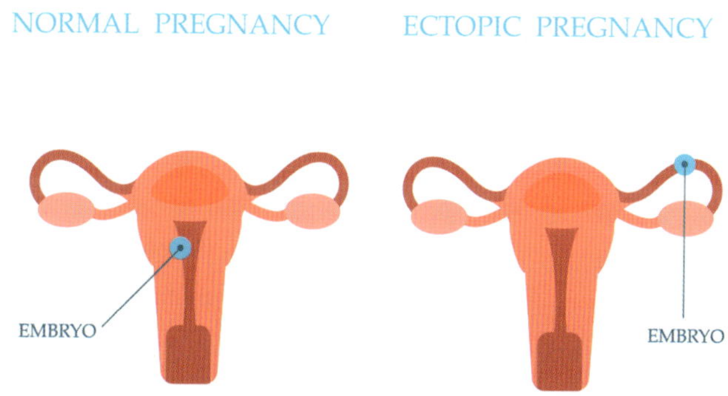

In an ectopic pregnancy the embryo embeds itself in the fallopian tube

Key term

ectopic pregnancy: a pregnancy where the embryo embeds itself 'out of place' (ectopic), most often in the fallopian tube, endangering the life of both fetus and pregnant person

Proportionalists reject the strict distinction between the direct and indirect actions of the ectopic pregnancy treatment options. Peter Knauer observed that the traditional method (tube removal) fails the moral test because it creates 'most evil' by sacrificing the pregnant person's future fertility unnecessarily. As Selling writes, Knauer concluded that the DDE was 'not only being abused in this situation but that the core meaning of the principle itself was being ignored':

- **The proportionalist preference**: They prefer the direct act of removing just the fetus (by cutting the tube).
- **Moral justification**: Proportionalists argue that removing the fetus directly can be the ethically correct decision (right act) because proportionate reason is used. Saving the pregnant person's life *and* preserving their future fertility constitutes a greater good (value) that outweighs the pre-moral evil (disvalue) of directly ending the fetal life.
- **Conclusion**: The act of removing the fetus is not a *good* act (because it causes evil effects/disvalue), but it is the *right* act because the balance of values favours the life and future health of the pregnant person.

As elsewhere the issue for all those involved in the discussion of ethical issues such as this is the distinction to be made between the *finis operis* and the *finis operantis*.

Key quotes

Certain human actions must, by their very nature, be seen as morally unacceptable and may therefore never be performed [...] because they have been found to be evil-in-themselves or 'intrinsically evil'.

(Selling)

Because the human act is a structural unity, no aspect of the act can be morally appraised apart from all the other components. Consideration of the agent's intention, all foreseeable consequences [...] are necessary before making moral judgment.

(Walter)

We may never directly take the life of an innocent human being, though we may sometimes tolerate the indirect and unintended loss of life [...]

(Catholic Education Resource Centre)

Specification content

Distinction between a good act (an act that follows the moral rule) and a right act (an act that is not necessarily a good act but creates the lesser of two evils)

Key terms

aretaic: relating to the moral qualities or virtues of a person or agent; from the Greek *arete* meaning virtue; an *aretaic* question would be 'Is this person good or evil?'

deontic: relating to duty and obligation in moral reasoning; from the Greek *deon* meaning duty; a deontic question would be 'Is this action right or wrong?'

The distinction between a good act and a right act

The distinction between types of evil is important for understanding proportionalism. It allows us to see why moral evil (for example, inflicting pain with the intention to do so) and pre-moral evil (the pain itself) must be evaluated differently than the morally right or morally good.

This moral/pre-moral split borrows heavily from philosopher G.E. Moore's work *Principia Ethica*. Moore states there are two different languages we use when speaking about morality:

- Good/evil is the moral quality of a person or an act. (Philosophers refer to this as **aretaic** language.)
- Right/wrong determines if an act ought to be done or not, depending on circumstance. (Philosophers refer to this as **deontic** language.)

Philosopher William Frankena accused early proportionalists like Richard McCormick of confusing the two. McCormick used aretaic language (calling things good or evil) when he should have been using deontic language (callings things right or wrong).

Philosophical term	Focus	Example terms
aretaic	Agent (character): it focuses more on the person performing the action (their intent and virtue).	good, evil, sinful, virtuous
deontic	Action (duty): it focuses more on whether the action is required or forbidden.	right, wrong, ought, duty

Proportionalists maintain that intention can only help identify what is good in the agent; it cannot, on its own, determine what is right or wrong about the action itself.

The philosophical distinction leads to the final, critical conflict:

Moral term	Proportionalist view	Traditional Catholic view
moral good	Moral good (good intention/ character) is not necessarily moral right (justified action).	Moral good (following the rule) necessarily is moral right.
moral evil	Moral evil (bad intention) is always morally wrong, but pre-moral evil is not necessarily morally wrong.	Moral evil (violating the rule) is always morally wrong.

Hoose suggests that the reason traditional theology rejects this distinction lies in its focus on **soteriology** ('What must I do to be saved?'). For traditional theology, the goal is the beatific vision. Everything is linked to becoming a morally good person (virtue and character). Therefore, the morally right action is inextricably bound up with the morally good action, making the distinction meaningless in a salvific (about the saving of souls) context. Thus, the magisterium holds fast to the idea that rules (deontological norms) are absolute.

Proportionality and *agape*

As we have seen, Aquinas' natural law ethics identifies *agape* (Christian love) as the highest of all virtues. In line with the beatific vision (the ultimate *telos*), Christians aim towards developing a virtuous character grounded in *agape*.

During the mid-to-latter half of the twentieth century, a rejection of purely deontological ethics took place. Joseph Fletcher, in situation ethics, rejected absolutist moral rules, arguing that practical ethics must be based on the single principle of *agape*. This debate primarily occurred within Protestant Christianity.

Crucially, proportionalism was not part of this debate. Roman Catholic moral theologians were united in their traditional rejection of the 'new morality' and consequentialist approaches, defending a purely deontological approach grounded in natural law.

The debate over proportionalism was a distinct, internal discussion within Catholicism, centred around the precise understanding of the DDE and proportionate reasoning.

Key term

soteriology: a quest to discover what the requirements for salvation are

Key quotes

The motive may be important for a decision about moral goodness or badness (sin) but has no part in decisions about the moral rightness or wrongness of acts.

(Hoose)

The conscience cannot mislead one about moral goodness and badness. It always and infallibly calls for moral goodness. However, it can mislead on regarding what is morally right.

(Hoose)

Specification content

Proportionality based on *agape*

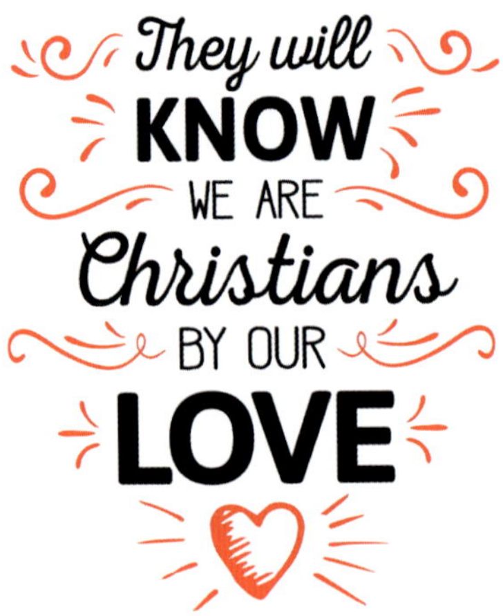

Should love be the only basis of any Christian ethical theory?

While *agape* is a central Christian virtue stressed by both movements, the difference between proportionalism and situation ethics lies in their methodology:

- Proportionalism is not based upon *agape* alone, but on a complex hybrid of rules and consequences assessed by a rigorous calculus (the proportionate reason). The virtue of love is stressed alongside the development of a virtuous character.
- Situation ethics uses *agape* as the single, absolute principle, allowing it to dismiss all moral laws as non-absolute.

This difference in approach led Roman Catholic moral theologians to reject situation ethics outright. As Hoose wrote: 'McCormick accused Fletcher of being ambiguous and of using flamboyant rhetoric as if it were moral reasoning'. Furthermore, the scholar Gustafson criticised Fletcher for using the revealed virtue of love in an evasive way 'that runs through Fletcher's book like a greased pig'. For proportionalists, Fletcher's system lacked the essential academic methodology required for moral decision-making.

Summary

- ★ Proportionalism is a development from natural law which emerged from the 1960s onwards.
- ★ Proportionalism had a different emphasis than that of the magisterium of the Catholic Church and traditionalists who emphasised the deontological aspects of natural law.
- ★ Proportionalists also regarded the teleological aspect of natural law as being important, devising a hybrid ethical approach.
- ★ The DDE, and how it was applied and interpreted in serious ethical issues such as ectopic pregnancy, showed that proportionalists thought that proportionate reason was key.
- ★ Proportionalism balanced the values against the disvalues of an event and questioned the concept of any act being intrinsically evil, recognising that an act might be a pre-moral evil which could be justified by proportionate reason.
- ★ Proportionalism never went as far as situation ethics in stating that all rules could be set aside for a good intention; but the magisterium argued that proportionalism seemed to ignore the rule of St Paul in Romans 3:8 that one 'could not do evil that good may come'.

AO1 Activity

a This scenario is often used in ethical discussion: a person is confronted by a known murderer who wishes to harm an innocent victim, known to the person, who is hiding in the home. The murderer does not know whether the victim is in the home and asks directly if they are there or not. Examine which is the morally correct action by applying the DDE.

i Tell the truth (the victim is inside). This might lead to the murder of an innocent person, but it will mean that truth-telling has been upheld.

ii Tell a lie (the victim is not inside). This might save the life of the innocent person but involves the act of deception through lying.

b Complete the table below. You must judge the specific act of lying (option ii) from both the proportionalist and traditionalist perspectives. Explain which position you think is correct and give reasons for your answer.

Primary precepts involved and values sought	upholding truth; truth-telling is essential for an ordered society; preserving innocent life
Pre-moral evil and disvalues involved	the lie (the deception); lying in itself can undermine an ordered society; the potential death of the victim
Act that is carried out	lying/deception
Intention (*finis operantis*)	saving an innocent life
Proportionalist judgement	
Traditionalist judgement	

To reach the higher bands 4–5, your response should demonstrate accurate and relevant knowledge of both the proportionalist and traditionalist positions. You should make thorough use of specialist language (for example, *finis operis*, *finis operantis*, proportionate reason, intrinsic evil and the DDE) in context and support your answer with evidence such as references to scholars or key quotes. A band 5 response will show extensive depth, answering the specific demands of the question with excellent use of examples.

This section covers AO2 content and skills

Specification content

The extent to which proportionalism promotes immoral behaviour

Issues for analysis and evaluation

The extent to which proportionalism promotes immoral behaviour

Possible line of argument	Critical analysis and evaluation
The magisterium and *Veritatis Splendor* argue proportionalism violates Romans 3:8: 'do not do evil that good may come'. By separating a right act from a good act, the theory justifies using an evil means (e.g. lying) to achieve a desired end, thereby promoting immoral conduct as an acceptable tool.	Proportionalists deny that they are simply consequentialists promoting immoral behaviour. They argue that they do not justify moral evil (sinful intent) but rather recognise the reality of ontic/pre-moral evil (physical loss).
Proportionalism promotes immoral behaviour because it removes absolute moral boundaries by rejecting the view that some physical acts are intrinsically evil (always wrong). This approach undermines what should be absolute rules against, e.g. taking life.	Proportionalists argue that an action in itself cannot be judged to be evil because all values and disvalues have to be weighed and a judgement can only be made through the process of proportionate reasoning; this does not promote immoral behaviour.
With complex ethical issues, proportionalists try to use complex calculations involving values, disvalues and proportionate reason – all this does is encourage sophisticated reasoning to justify immoral behaviour which is against the laws of the Church and of God.	Proportionalists such as Knauer argue that with complex ethical issues, such as an ectopic pregnancy, the focus on a rule simply produces suffering which is immoral – instead morality is upheld by compassionate and proportionate reasoning.
Proportionalism is nothing more than a complex form of consequentialism which can justify any evil act on the basis of the consequences being good for the people involved – this promotes immorality.	Traditionalists have misunderstood what proportionalism attempts to do – it is not consequentialist but is instead a hybrid of teleology and deontology aimed at maintaining morality in the modern age.
Romans 3:8 states explicitly 'do not do evil that good may come', and the DDE as set out by Aquinas' natural law is clear about this – it is not intended to encourage moral flexibility which leads to immoral behaviour.	The whole point of proportionalism has nothing to do with immoral behaviour – the point is to ensure that in exceptional ethical issues that arise, the DDE is interpreted correctly and sufficient room is given for proportionate reasoning to be used in achieving the best possible outcome: that which minimises evil.

AO2 Activity

a Analyse three possible conclusions that could be drawn from the critical analysis and evaluation of the view that proportionalism promotes immoral behaviour. Select evidence and examples to support each of the three conclusions. Select one conclusion that you think is the **most convincing** and explain why it is so.

b Now select the conclusion that you think is the **least convincing** of the three and explain why.

To reach the higher bands 4–5, your response should present sustained, clear and well-supported views with thorough, relevant analysis and detailed evaluation. You should draw on evidence from scholars (for example, Hoose, Knauer and Curran) and key concepts (for example, proportionate reason, intrinsic evil and the DDE). A band 5 response will demonstrate an extensive range of evidence, address the issue comprehensively and arrive at a confident and justified conclusion. Avoid simply listing arguments for and against; instead, weigh up the strength of each line of argument and explain why one is more persuasive than another.

Specification content

The extent to which Finnis' natural law is a better ethic than proportionalism

Exam practice

Below is an example of an evaluation of the extent to which Finnis' natural law is a better ethic than proportionalism.

Sample answer

The main strength of Finnis' natural law is that it is firmly established in the works of Aristotle and Aquinas. Although it works as a religious system, it is designed to be open to everyone, regardless of religion. Finnis, as a legal expert, demonstrates how natural law works practically in society, making it appear more comprehensive than proportionalism.

News reporter: The essay opens with a clear overview of Finnis' strengths and his appeal to a wider audience.

One could argue that Finnis' system has more consistency. Proportionalism is a collection of different approaches within Roman Catholic theology, whereas Finnis' natural law is a systematic theory that can work in any society. It does not depend upon creed, culture or race. In contrast, proportionalism lacks that universal breadth and seems to be entirely focused on the DDE and its interpretation.

Tennis player: A strong serve in favour of Finnis, comparing his consistency against the fragmented and complex nature of proportionalism.

Finnis tends to focus on the common good and his system is less individualistic than proportionalism. His theory encourages active citizens to build a thriving society that achieves well-being through the basic goods. Indeed, Finnis is recognised for contributing to contemporary thought on tolerance and community values.

Explorer: The paragraph opens up the wider territory of Finnis' contribution to society and the common good.

However, critics argue Finnis is using his system to promote a traditional form of Roman Catholicism. Scholars like Stephen Buckle criticise his underlying agenda which upholds basic goods which cannot be contravened, such as life and the value of heterosexual relationships within marriage alone.

Detective: The evidence regarding Finnis' potential bias and controversial stance is examined forensically.

Critical thinker

The essay analyses the technical similarities and the precise point of divergence between the two.

However, one could argue that both theories actually share the same ethic. Both follow Aquinas and are rooted in Catholicism. They promote the same precepts and virtues. The key difference lies in the DDE: Finnis sides with tradition, while proportionalists seek a more flexible application.

Tennis player

The argument rallies back and forth between the flexibility of proportionalism and the objectivity of Finnis.

Proportionalists argue their approach is superior because it offers a modern ethical methodology that is better at handling conflicts. However, Finnis would argue that his system is superior because it applies to all cultures objectively, whereas proportionalism risks becoming inconsistent.

Philosopher

This raises the perceptive point that betterness is subjective and depends on what the individual values in ethics.

Deciding which is better depends on the person evaluating the issue. One person might prefer the flexibility of proportionalism, while another might prefer the rigid clarity of Finnis or even an alternative such as situation ethics.

Critical thinker

A balanced check of how each theory relates to the modern world.

Ultimately, proportionalism fits the postmodern world's desire for flexibility. Yet traditionalists like Finnis would argue that having less in common with changing contemporary values is actually a strength, offering stability in a chaotic world.

Judge

A final, balanced ruling is delivered, acknowledging the validity of both approaches.

In conclusion, both systems have clear strengths and weaknesses. Both genuinely aim for the highest good and the common good. It seems unfair to select one definitively over the other, as both effectively serve the specific ethical goals they set out to achieve.

Over to you

Your next task is to integrate evidence into an evaluation of the effectiveness of proportionalism in dealing with ethical issues.

At present the evaluation below has no references and very few key quotations or key terms to support the arguments presented.

Check again the higher band descriptors for A2 (WJEC) or A Level (Eduqas), one of which states: 'a response that successfully identifies and thoroughly addresses the issues raised by the question set'.

Rewrite the evaluation, integrating the key terms and key quotes provided on page 137 as evidence to address the issues raised by the question set. You might choose other quotations or terms. Integrate the evidence smoothly, ensuring you reference the scholar or text in each instance (for example, 'Hoose argues …' or '*Veritatis Splendor* states …'). Remember that quotations can be shortened to the key elements.

Question

'Proportionalism is not effective in dealing with ethical issues.' Evaluate this view.

(Eduqas A Level 2023)

Evaluation

Proportionalism can be seen as an effective alternative to the strict natural law promoted by the Church because it combines two different ethical approaches. Proportionalists examine the difference between the physical act and the intention. This suggests that proportionalism is effective because it moves away from a rigid system that can cause unnecessary suffering, instead focusing on careful thought and compassion. This arguably reflects the morality of Jesus, who taught that love is the most important principle.

However, critics argue that the theory is not effective because the rules of natural law should be upheld no matter what, a view maintained by the Pope. For these critics, following absolute rules is the only reliable way to achieve moral goodness and the ultimate goal of heaven. They argue that any ethical system supporting flexibility is dangerous to the soul and leads to moral confusion.

Some scholars suggest that proportionalism is an effective expression of the original aims of natural law. By looking at the whole of the act rather than just focusing on things that are evil in themselves, it provides a more balanced and common-sense approach to difficult ethical issues. This allows the theory to remain grounded in traditional values while being flexible enough to respond to specific, complex situations.

Others argue that Church teaching, especially in encyclicals, must always prioritise the development of Christian character and virtue through obedience to fixed laws. From this perspective, proportionalism is not effective because it undermines the authority of the Church and replaces certain duties with subjective calculations. Therefore, for those who believe morality must be based on absolute certainty, proportionalism remains a flawed and ineffective system.

Key terms

hybrid	magisterium	traditionalists	Pope John Paul II
Veritatis Splendor	Hoose	proportionate reasoning	*agape*
intrinsic evil	beatific vision	revisionists	consequentialism
finis operis	*finis operantis*	situation ethics	Fletcher

Key quotes

Proportionalism rests on a distinction between physical or pre-moral evil (e.g. killing) and moral evil (e.g. murder). One can do pre-moral evil if there is a proportionate reason […] Proportionalism constitutes a middle position […]

(Curran)

It is not merely tradition but common sense that dictates the need for a proportionate reason.

(Hoose)

The attempt to assess the proportion of good or bad likely to proceed from a proposed action is really a common-sense judgment we all make rather routinely.

(Ratzinger)

Because the human act is a structural unity, no aspect of the act can be morally appraised apart from all the other components. Consideration of the agent's intention, all foreseeable consequences […] are necessary before making moral judgment.

(Walter)

> **Key term**
>
> **immigration:** the movement of population into a country for residence (short-term or long-term)

F: Finnis' natural law and proportionalism: application of the theories

Immigration

Before discussing the approaches taken by Finnis' natural law and proportionalism to the issue of **immigration**, it is important to first briefly define some core terms and the current legal situation in the UK.

Defining immigration

To begin with, what is the definition of a country or a nation state? The clearest definition comes from the Montevideo Convention on the Rights and Duties of States (1933). This asserted that a state should possess the attributes of a:

- permanent population
- defined territory
- government
- capacity to enter into relations with the other states.

What is implied here is that a state has its own population, exists within a geographical area defined by borders and has a government that is able to interact with other states through trade and political negotiations and through travel. Since a state has its own borders, it has in turn the right to protect its territory and its permanent population.

When people travel from one country their admission into another country often requires some form of documentation. In the case of tourists, for example, travel documentation might be required in the form of passports and visas. In the case of people moving from one country to another, different terms can be noted:

Emigration	The act of leaving one's own native country to settle permanently in another.
Migration	The movement of people – **migrants** – from one place in the world to another, generally for the purpose of establishing a new, permanent or semi-permanent residence.
Immigration	The movement of people – immigrants – *into* a country of which they are not native citizens in order to settle there permanently.

> **Key terms**
>
> **migrant:** a person who moves from one country to another
>
> **refugee:** a person who has sought refuge from a life-threatening situation and been granted asylum

Against this background, different types of migrants need to be distinguished since each type has different legal entitlements. The work of the UN High Commissioner for Refugees helps define the following terms

Refugee	As determined by the UN Refugee Convention (1951), this is a person who has been forced to flee their country because of a well-founded fear of persecution for reasons of race, religion, nationality, political opinion or membership of a particular social group. A refugee is granted specific legal rights by the host country, receiving treatment equal to nationals in areas like elementary education and public assistance. A refugee is granted specific legal rights by the host country and is permitted to remain, with the path to permanent residency governed by national law.

Asylum seeker	This is a person who seeks sanctuary (sometimes referred to as 'international protection') in another country by applying for asylum – the right to be recognised as a refugee and receive legal protection and material assistance.
Undocumented or irregular migrant	This is a person who enters and stays in another country without the legal documentation or authorisation required by that country's government.
Economic migrant	Defined by the UN High Commissioner for Refugees, this is a person who leaves their country of origin purely for economic reasons not in any way related to the refugee definition, or in order to seek material improvements in their livelihood.

In the light of these defined categories, we now turn to the specific legal framework used by the United Kingdom. This is defined by a system introduced in January 2021. It applies to everyone (except Irish citizens) regardless of nationality. There are different systems in place for asylum seekers. Points leading to acceptance are awarded for job offers, salaries, English language skills and shortage occupations. Acceptance may also be based on endorsement or sponsorship from an approved organisation.

- **Skilled worker**: This covers skilled workers with a job offer from an approved sponsor in the UK. This includes the health and care worker visa and the global business mobility routes.
- **Global talent, innovator founder and other high-value routes**: The global talent visa covers leaders in academia, research, arts and technology. The innovator founder visa is for those establishing an innovative business.
- **Seasonal worker**: This allows people to come to the UK for up to six months to do horticulture work (picking fruit and vegetables) or poultry work.
- **Student and temporary work**: The student visa is for those with an unconditional offer from a licensed sponsor. Temporary work visas cover short-term roles for charity workers, creative workers and religious workers.

Finnis' natural law applied to immigration

As we have seen, natural law, as presented by John Finnis, presents a system which is accessible through secular reason and is independent of religious belief. His primary goal shifts from a divine *telos* to achieving human flourishing (*eudaimonia*) and securing the common good within society. The central purpose of Finnis' theory is to inform human law. Governments are justified only in so far as they use the requirements of practical reasonableness to create laws that secure these basic human goods for the common good.

Finnis' natural law is based on seven self-evident basic goods, which are:

- life (and health)
- knowledge
- friendship (sociability)
- play
- aesthetic experience

Key terms

asylum seeker: a person who is seeking refuge from a life-threatening situation

economic migrant: a person who seeks a better standard of life through migration

This section covers AO1 content and skills

Specification content

The application of Finnis' natural law and proportionalism to immigration

- practical reasonableness
- religion.

There are also the nine requirements of practical reasonableness, which are:

- coherent plan of life
- values with no arbitrary preferences
- equality of basic goods which apply to all with no arbitrary preferences among persons
- detachment so as not to become obsessed with a particular project
- commitment in using effort to improve
- efficiency within reason, planning actions to do the most good
- harming a basic good is absolutely prohibited to ensure respect for every basic value in every act
- foster common good in the community
- conscience as an authority to be followed.

When applied to immigration, what has to be considered is the immigrant and the host society in which they wish to live. The first key point to note is that Finnis requires there to be a holistic approach. There is no hierarchy between the seven basic goods since all are equally valuable and they are incommensurable – they cannot be weighed or pitted against each other. As Clare Lloyd notes: 'Finnis requires us to see the goods holistically [...] we do not arbitrarily prioritise one good over another.'

In addition, the seven basic goods are absolute – they do not change. There might be ethical problems, but these are due to particular circumstances – they are not due to the seven basic goods themselves.

The nine requirements of practical reasonableness then provide the methodology for *participating* in the goods and translating them into moral action. They include 'equality of basic goods which apply to all with no arbitrary preferences among persons' and the need to 'foster common good in the community'.

In principle, the approach taken by Finnis' natural law would seem to suggest that controlled immigration is a positive practice. It allows for full participation in the seven basic goods for both the migrant and the host country. For example:

- **Life (and health)**:
    - **The migrant**: For asylum seekers, migration is literally about the preservation of life (escaping death/torture). For economic migrants, it is about sustaining health through better food, shelter and safety.
    - **The host country**: Migrants often fill critical roles in healthcare (for example, the NHS relies heavily on overseas staff) and agriculture (food production), directly supporting the vital functions of the community.
- **Knowledge**:
    - **The migrant**: Many migrate specifically for education (student visas) to seek truth and understanding.
    - **The host country**: Migration brings new skills, scientific collaboration and intellectual perspectives that prevent a society from becoming stagnant or 'echo-chambered'.

- **Friendship (sociability)**:
  - **The migrant**: The migrant seeks to establish new relationships and live in peace and harmony within a new community.
  - **The host country**: This is the most critical good. It challenges people in the host society to extend friendship beyond the immediate group to the 'stranger'. Successful integration fosters social harmony and reduces racism, which is the antithesis of this good.
- **Play**:
  - **The migrant**: For many, migration is a chance to participate in forms of recreation, sports or leisure activities that were restricted in their home country.
  - **The host country**: Migration enriches the world of sport and leisure (for example, in global professional sports leagues). Cultural festivals and shared celebrations allow communities to enjoy recreational activities together, fostering integration.
- **Aesthetic experience**:
  - **The migrant**: The experience of moving allows the migrant to engage with new architecture, landscapes and artistic traditions in their new home.
  - **The host country**: Immigration introduces new forms of music, literature, art, fashion and cuisine (food). This allows the host society to participate in a wider and richer range of beauty than if it remained isolated.
- **Practical reasonableness**:
  - **The migrant**: The act of migrating is often a profound exercise of practical reason – making a difficult, calculated decision to move to pursue a coherent life plan and improve one's circumstances.
  - **The host country**: The government must use practical reason to create fair laws (immigration policy) that balance compassion with order, ensuring the system is not arbitrary and promotes the common good.
- **Religion**:
  - **The migrant**: Migration allows for the freedom to practise one's beliefs if they are persecuted at home. This is a participation in the basic good of religion as it allows the migrant to live in harmony with their conscience, spirituality and understanding of the divine.
  - **The host country**: Migration forces a society to grapple with ultimate questions of human worth, dignity and universal brotherhood, often deepening the spiritual conscience of a nation while fostering interfaith understanding.

It should be noted that the ideal outcome of the seven basic goods above is, for Finnis, linked to what might be termed government-controlled immigration based on a clear legal framework. Here the goal would remain that of maintaining and fostering the common good of the host country.

> **Key quote**
>
> There is no Christian joy when doors are closed; there is no Christian joy when others are made to feel unwanted, when there is no room for them in our midst.
>
> (Pope Francis)

Finnis on uncontrolled mass immigration and the common good

It is the common good which Finnis sees as being challenged and undermined by uncontrolled mass immigration. It is important to remember that Finnis is not opposed to immigration in itself. However, Finnis famously criticised the liberal philosophy of his mentor, H.L.A. Hart, and argued that excessive liberalism has led to negative consequences in Europe. In a controversial 2009 essay, Finnis warned that mass migration could lead to:

> [...] a trajectory of demographic and cultural decay [...] pervasive untruthfulness about equality and diversity; population transfer and replacement by a kind of reverse colonisation [...] and religious inter-communal miseries.

Here Finnis is warning that if a community loses its shared values ('demographic and cultural decay'), the common good is in danger. If a society ignores the rule of law and allows 'reverse colonisation' (where the host country's culture is replaced rather than integrated into), the result is social breakdown. For Finnis, the law has a moral duty to preserve the community's identity to ensure all can flourish.

With regard to government-controlled immigration, Finnis' system of natural law requires distinguishing between migrants based on their circumstances, as this determines the ethical priority.

The acceptance of refugees fleeing situations where their basic good of life is immediately in danger would be an absolute priority. The requirement of no arbitrary preference among persons dictates that safety must be offered to those already in mortal danger. This reflects the universal legal principles of the UN Refugee Convention. An asylum seeker might seek refuge in a host country based on a 'well-founded fear of persecution' in their home country, which includes the risk of death, torture or severe threat to the basic good of life. If they returned, they would be in mortal danger.

What then of economic migrants? Provided that this is again government-controlled, Finnis' approach would seem to accept that such migrants are seeking full participation in the goods of knowledge (self-improvement) and life (better livelihood). Under a managed system, economic migrants could be integrated into the host country.

However, as Pope Francis noted in his sermon on the World Day of Migrants and Refugees in 2018, this integration means that new arrivals should 'welcome, know, and acknowledge', the laws, culture and traditions of their host country. In return, local communities need 'to open themselves without prejudices to their rich diversity, to understand the hopes and potential of the newly arrived as well as their fears and vulnerabilities'. Finnis' approach tries to balance an 'open border' policy, which might fail to foster the common good, against a 'closed border' policy, which would violate the basic good of friendship.

With regard to the UK, the problem from the perspective of Finnis' natural law is that it can appear to be a utilitarian system. Priority is given to high salaries, skills and education in order that, for example, such migrants can maximise national wealth. In this sense they would be being used as tools for economic ends. They would not be respected as persons pursuing the basic goods.

Denying low-skilled economic migrants admission to the UK based on a low points score, in terms of what they might bring with them, goes against Finnis' holistic approach and regards people simply as potential producers of economic output. This approach completely neglects the moral duty of compassion – found in the basic good of friendship. At the same time, it could be argued that practical reasonableness requires that at all times the preservation of the common good of the host country has to be fostered.

Key quotes

Finnis felt that modern society has become so obsessed with individual liberty, or the freedom to pursue any project that we please, that it has taken the existence of our society for granted.

(Lloyd)

It could be argued that the common good may be damaged if it made it impossible for existing indigenous people to participate in all the benefits of the current society as a direct result and it would damage that society's ability to benefit the common good in the rest of the world.

(Lloyd)

In everything do to others as you would have them do to you; for this is the law and the prophets.

(Matthew 7:12)

The cry of the poor is a kind of a prayer; it opens our hearts and teaches us to be attentive.

(Pope Francis)

Proportionalism applied to immigration

Like Finnis' theory, proportionalism is rooted in the natural law tradition of Aquinas. However, whereas Finnis focuses on absolute basic goods, proportionalism offers a more flexible but also more complex middle way between the strict rules of natural law and the unpredictability of situation ethics. There are three proportionalist approaches:

- conflict situation proportionalism (CSP)
- value maximisation proportionalism (VMP)
- revisionist theology proportionalism (RTP).

CSP

CSP is associated with **Richard McCormick**, and suggests that proportionate reason only applies in a genuine conflict situation where some evil is unavoidable.

In CSP, one cannot simply use proportionate reason whenever a rule feels difficult or inconvenient. It can only be used when there is a true conflict situation:

- **A conflict situation**: A scenario where one is forced to choose between two evils, and there is no 'third way' to avoid them. For example, a medical emergency where one must choose between the life of a pregnant person and the life of their unborn child.
- **A non-conflict situation**: A scenario where a third way alternative exists. If one can protect a value *without* breaking a rule, one must do so.

The most important part of CSP is the avoidability test. Before a proportionalist even considers breaking a rule (like 'do not kill'), they must ask: 'Is this harm avoidable?'

If there is a way to achieve the good end without causing the ontic evil (physical harm), then breaking the rule is not proportionate. It would be a moral evil. How might all of this apply to immigration?

In the case of a refugee fleeing for their life, there is an unavoidable conflict between the person's life and the host country's resources. Since the refugee's death is unavoidable without help, the proportionate reason to welcome them is clear. However, CSP also requires looking for a third way through an avoidability test; if a solution exists that avoids the ontic evil while protecting the common good, that path must be followed.

The avoidability test might suggest that if a refugee is at the border, the third way might involve international co-operation. If a host country is already overwhelmed, but a neighbouring safe country has plenty of resources, the 'path to be followed' is to facilitate safe passage or support for that person in the other country. This protects the good of life (the person is safe) while avoiding the ontic evil of social or economic collapse in the first country. However, if no such alternative exists, the only way to avoid the death of the person is to grant them entry. In that specific conflict, welcoming them is the only moral path.

For economic migrants, the third way is often managed migration or targeted aid. If the evil being avoided is poverty in the home country, the state must ask: 'Can we solve this poverty without an open-door policy that might cause social upheaval (another ontic evil)?' The path followed might be a work-visa scheme or investing in the migrant's home country. By following one of these paths, the state avoids the ontic evil of poverty (helping the person) while protecting the common good (maintaining social stability).

> **Key person**
>
> **Richard McCormick (1922–2000):** An American Jesuit priest and moral theologian; he is considered one of the most influential Catholic ethicists of the twentieth century; he created CSP, which asserts that an established moral rule should only be overridden when there is an actual conflict of goods and no amount of effort will avoid the resultant evil; he is known for his focus on the 'avoidability test' as way to prevent abuse of proportionate reasoning

Key person

Garth Hallett (1927–2020): An American Jesuit philosopher and theologian who formulated VMP; in books like *Greater Good* (1995), he proposed that moral choices should be made by objectively balancing values (goods) against disvalues (ontic evils), so that we always choose the action that provides the greatest net good; he expanded proportionalist thinking beyond decisions made in emergency circumstances to regular moral choices

VMP

VMP is often associated with **Garth Hallett**. Where CSP is about necessity – whether the harm is avoidable and whether there is a third way which avoids breaking a precept – VMP is more concerned with weighing up the values involved.

Hallett argued that the use of proportionate reason should not be limited to rare emergencies but should be applied consistently to all relevant ethical decisions, using a method of balancing goods and disvalues. This means that rather than following static rules, the 'whole picture' of an event needs to be considered and a calculation made between:

- the positive values or goods
- the negative disvalues or ontic evils (the inevitable evils that exist, such as pain, financial cost or the loss of resources).

It is important to remember that ontic evil is simply the evil that exists. It is not a moral evil as it does not involve a bad intention and is not intended to cause harm. It is not sinful. Balancing the positive and the negative would then help to determine which action results in the greater good in the long term.

How might this work with regard to immigration? The basic question is whether the act of welcoming migrants creates more value (good) than disvalue (harm).

- **The positive values (goods)**: Welcoming migrants supports the values of justice, compassion and life. It aligns with the Christian concept of *agape* and the teaching of Jesus to 'love your neighbour'.
- **The negative disvalues (ontic evils)**: Immigration – particularly if it is not government-controlled – might cause financial strain on the host country, a temporary lack of resources or social friction.

VMP overall might therefore support immigration. The ontic evil (financial cost/strain) is usually outweighed by the value of saving lives, alleviating poverty and showing compassion. To refuse immigration simply to save money would be a moral evil because there is no proportionate reason to value money over human dignity.

However, the purely objective nature of this calculation presents a challenge when considering state policy. While VMP confirms that controlled migration is morally right, it does not fully address the method by which a government should manage it.

Key person

Joseph Selling (1945–): A Belgian-American Catholic moral theologian and professor emeritus of the Catholic University of Leuven; he pioneered a person-centred version of proportionalist ethics, sometimes referred to as RTP. He wrote *Reframing Catholic Theological Ethics* (2016), arguing that the focus of moral evaluation should be on the character and virtues of the person acting, rather than solely on the act itself, grounding ethics in *agape* and the example of Jesus

RTP

This leads to another approach advanced by **Joseph Selling**: RTP. This can be seen as a person-centred approach. Thus, the focus is not on what people do but on the virtues and character of the persons involved and on how this relates to their 'being a good Christian'.

How might this work with regard to immigration? RTP focuses on these questions:

- Does the immigration policy uphold the dignity and intrinsic worth of the person?
- Does the immigration policy commit a moral evil by using the person merely as a tool for economic gain?

With this approach, RTP would critique policies like the points-based immigration system for prioritising economic contribution (money/skills) over the human dignity and intrinsic worth of the person seeking entry.

Both VMP and RTP would hold that in the case of a refugee who has entered the host country to avoid torture and death, there would be inevitable economic costs to the host country. However, there is no proportionate reason that justifies sending a person back to possible torture or death. The value of life always outweighs the ontic evil of economic cost. Therefore, accepting refugees is a moral obligation.

What then of immigration which is not government-controlled? Here, proportionalism can be seen as realistic. Uncontrolled immigration with an open borders policy might be judged as likely to lead to various forms of social upheaval, severe economic cost and the undermining of the host country's duty to foster the common good of its population. In other words, the ontic evil involved has to be considered and the question asked as to whether or not it is too great.

This brings back into play the issue of proportionate reason. Does a government exercise proportionate reason in placing limits and controls on immigration in order to foster the common good? Is there disproportionate reasoning in granting entry to a hard-working, low-skilled person who simply wants to feed their family through income which could be gained in the host country? Is it proportionate to prioritise the ontic evil of economic cost over the value of the person's survival and dignity?

Capital punishment

Defining capital punishment

Capital punishment has a long history in the UK and was used for certain crimes including treason, murder, robbery, larceny, rape and arson. The usual method was hanging and the Murder Act (1752) stated this was to be done within 48 hours of sentencing. The last executions in the UK were on 13 August 1964, when Peter Allen and Gwynne Evans were hanged for murder.

The death penalty for murder was formally abolished in the UK in 1969, and for all civilian crimes in 1998. The final and complete abolition of the death penalty for all remaining crimes was finalised in 2004, when the UK signed Protocol 13 of the European Convention on Human Rights. This also prohibits the restoration of the death penalty as long as the UK is party to the convention.

At present, the Criminal Justice Act (2003) sets out the purposes behind the whole system of the law and the treatment of criminals as being:

- the punishment of offenders
- the reduction of crime (including its reduction by deterrence)
- the reform and rehabilitation of offenders
- the protection of the public
- the making of reparation by offenders to persons affected by their offences.

Instead of capital punishment in the UK, for the most serious crimes such as murder, a life sentence is imposed with the minimum tariff – the minimum number of years in prison – being set by the judge. Only after the minimum tariff has been served can parole be considered. Even if released, offenders remain on licence for the rest of their lives with various restrictions which, if breached, might result in recall to prison. Of the most serious crimes, some might be seen as being so serious that a whole life order is imposed, which means that the person in prison will never be released except in very rare compassionate circumstances.

Specification content

The application of Finnis' natural law and proportionalism to capital punishment

Hanging was used as capital punishment in the UK up to 1964

Turning to natural law, the traditional position of Aquinas stated that capital punishment was licit (permissible) in certain circumstances. Although there was the commandment in the Bible, 'Thou shalt not kill,' this applied to private individuals who might act out of anger. It did not apply to the state, since the state had to consider first and foremost the common good of society.

Aquinas used the analogy of the human body. If a limb were infected with gangrene, the only way to preserve the body would be to amputate the limb. In the same way, to preserve the common good of society, the state might legitimately carry out capital punishment on a person who was found guilty of the most serious of offences. Public authorities carrying out capital punishment should be seen as acting not out of anger but out of the desire for justice as required by God. The person who had committed the offence might be seen as having committed such a grave sin as to fall away from their human dignity. At the same time, the possibility of such a person repenting and seeking salvation before their execution was always hoped for.

Based on natural law, the *Catechism* issued in the late 1990s stated that capital punishment is acceptable if the gravity of the crime involved is such that it is the only means of protecting the common good. In such a case it is 'a legitimate response to the gravity' of the crime and is to be seen as the 'only possible way of effectively defending human life against the unjust aggressor'. However, the *Catechism* also stated that such cases where capital punishment should be used were 'very rare, if not practically non-existent'.

There is still debate about Aquinas' reasoning with regard to capital punishment

By 2018, approaches to this aspect of Aquinas' natural law had developed, leading to a change in the *Catechism* authorised by Pope Francis. The *Catechism* now states that capital punishment is 'inadmissible because it is an attack on the inviolability and dignity of the human person'. The dignity of the human person remains even after serious crimes. The Catholic Church committed itself to the work 'with determination' for the worldwide abolition of capital punishment.

Key quotes

Therefore if any man is dangerous to the community and is subverting it by some sin, the treatment to be commended is his execution in order to preserve the common good. Therefore to kill a man who retains his natural worthiness is intrinsically evil, although it may be justifiable to kill a sinner just as it is to kill a beast, for, as Aristotle points out, an evil man is worse than a beast and more harmful.

(Aquinas, *Summa Theologica* 2–2, q. 64, a. 2)

Finnis' natural law applied to capital punishment

This rejection of capital punishment by the Catholic Church is strongly underpinned by the ethical reasoning of scholars developing natural law, such as Finnis. His approach is to argue that capital punishment has to be rejected because it goes against the fundamental principles of the seven basic goods and the nine requirements of practical reasonableness.

The most direct argument against capital punishment is that it attacks the basic good of life. For Finnis, the good of life (which encompasses physical and mental health, safety and security) is self-evident and holds intrinsic value. It must never be treated as a mere tool or means to an end.

Once this is accepted, it has to be recognised that capital punishment is a direct, intentional attack on the basic good of life. It completely destroys the possibility of that good for the convicted person, eliminating all future opportunities for them to pursue any other goods (such as knowledge, play or religion).

In this way, Finnis directly rejects the traditional natural law argument of Aquinas which suggests that a person who commits a terrible crime somehow removes or loses their human dignity. Finnis insists that human dignity and the basic goods are inalienable; they can never be lost, even by the worst criminal. The intentional killing of a person, therefore, remains a fundamental violation of Finnis' core principle.

In addition, Finnis argues that capital punishment goes against two of the nine requirements of practical reasonableness, the moral method used to ensure that actions are in accordance with the seven basic goods.

In the first case, practical reasonableness requires that there should be no arbitrary preferences – all the goods are followed together. By intentionally killing a person, the state is acting as if the good of life is less valuable than other goods (such as security or justice). This creates an arbitrary preference for one good over another, which is forbidden.

In the second case, there is the requirement which is an absolute moral rule that one must never intentionally act against or destroy any of the basic goods, even if this is done in pursuit of another basic good. Capital punishment violates this because it is an act which is directly intended to destroy the basic good of life. Against the argument that capital punishment might provide a deterrence, the approach taken by Finnis is to the effect that the act of capital punishment in and of itself is flawed because it violates the integrity of the ethical system by attacking a basic good.

Overall therefore, Finnis' system leads to a firm, uncompromising rejection of capital punishment. He confirms that the state has a duty to uphold the common good (protecting the community), and punishment is necessary. However, the state must not intentionally destroy the basic good of life, especially when alternative punishments, such as a whole life order of imprisonment, are effective in upholding security and justice.

The table below summarises the approach taken by Finnis:

Approach	Finnis' natural law
Key scholar	John Finnis
Central focus	**The seven basic goods and the nine requirements of practical reasonableness**: The goods (like life and sociability) are self-evident and should never be acted against directly.

Key quotes

First, it is important to remember that traditional Catholic teaching never claimed that the state must impose the death penalty [...] St Thomas held that the government has the responsibility to protect the common good by means of just punishments, but he does not specify that one particular crime (e.g. murder) must always and in every case be punished in one particular way (capital punishment).

(Kaczor)

It is seemingly in the best interest of the common good to remove an unrepentant criminal from society to prevent further crime, but capital punishment is not the only way to do this.

(Lloyd)

Capital punishment, since it involves the intent to kill as a means, is 'doing evil that good may come', i.e. the pursuit of a good end (the restoration of the order of justice) by inherently immoral means.

(Finnis)

The criminal is an individual whose good is as good as anyone's, notwithstanding that the criminal ought in fairness to be deprived of some opportunities of realising that good.

(Finnis)

Application to immigration	**Conditional**: It is a matter of practical reasonableness. The state must balance the good of helping others (sociability) with the duty to protect the common good and stability for its own citizens.
Application to capital punishment	**Rejected**: One must not perform any act which 'of itself does nothing but damage a basic good'. Execution is an intentional destruction of the basic good of life.

Proportionalism applied to capital punishment

Applying proportionalism to capital punishment, we return to the three proportionalist approaches: CSP, VMP and RTP.

CSP

In applying the avoidability test to capital punishment, the proportionalist favouring CSP asks: 'Is the execution of this criminal the only way to protect society?' In the modern world, their answer is almost always no. This is because states have secure prison systems – with whole life sentences being available for the most serious of crimes. Such sentences would be a third way to protect the common good without taking a life.

Since the harm (the death of the criminal) is avoidable, there is no true conflict. Therefore, there is no proportionate reason to execute, and doing so would be a moral evil. Richard McCormick argued that life is a basic good that should not be destroyed simply because a prison system is expensive or difficult to manage.

VMP

VMP approaches capital punishment by evaluating whether the good achieved by the state outweighs the ontic evil of the execution. For VMP, the death penalty is not a moral evil in the same sense as murder (as it lacks a malicious intention), but it remains a significant pre-moral or ontic evil because it destroys the basic good of life.

When weighing the values, a proponent of the death penalty might argue that the positive values include retribution (giving the criminal what they deserve) and the protection of society through deterrence. However, Bernard Hoose argues that for a punishment to be proportionate, the values it achieves must be real and substantiated. He points to the frailty of evidence regarding deterrence, noting that murder rates often decrease after abolition of the death penalty. If the value of deterrence is unproven, it may be regarded as an apparent good rather than a real good. Consequently, there is no proportionate reason to commit the certain ontic evil of killing a prisoner for a speculative social gain.

Furthermore, Hallett's VMP suggests that we must consider the whole picture, which includes the disvalues associated with capital punishment. This includes the risk of executing an innocent person – a profound ontic evil that can never be reversed – and the psychological harm to those required to carry out the sentence.

Hoose also argues that societies justifying physical punishments often do so at the expense of investing in 'educational and correctional institutions'. From a VMP perspective, the value of life and the possibility of reform are greater goods than the value of retribution. Therefore, unless it can be proven that execution is the only way to maximise value for the common good, VMP concludes that the death penalty is a disproportionate response.

Key quotes

For a fully objective judgement, the facts are what matter, not our limited, fallible beliefs about the facts.

(Hallett)

If the action is right and is done for the reasons that make it right, right motive or intention is assured.

(Hallett)

RTP

RTP shifts the focus from the calculation of values to a person-centred approach. In the context of capital punishment, RTP asks whether the act of execution upholds the intrinsic dignity of the individual or whether it commits a moral evil by treating the person merely as a tool for social policy. Selling argues that ethics should be grounded in the 'human person, adequately considered', which means looking at the criminal in relation to the whole of reality, including their potential for change.

RTP would critique capital punishment because it is a final, irreversible act that ignores the individual's freedom. If the state executes a criminal to satisfy public anger or to serve as a warning to others, it is using a human life as a means to an end, rather than an end in itself. For Selling, this fails the test of being a 'good Christian' act, as it lacks the quality of *agape* and the recognition of the person as a child of God capable of redemption.

By focusing on the virtues of compassion and forgiveness, RTP concludes that capital punishment is an outdated practice that does not reflect the progress of Catholic social teaching. Because there is no proportionate reason to deny a person the chance for reform and spiritual growth, RTP holds that the death penalty is an illegitimate use of state power.

The table below summarises the three approaches:

Approach	CSP	VMP	RTP
Key scholar	Richard McCormick	Garth Hallett	Joseph Selling
Central focus	**Necessity**: Is this harm truly unavoidable? Is there a third way that avoids breaking the precept?	**Calculation**: Which action produces the most objective value vs ontic evil for the common good?	**The person**: Does this action uphold human dignity and reflect the character/life of Jesus?
Application to immigration	**Conditional**: If the host country is in a state of collapse and cannot support anyone else, a conflict exists. Otherwise, welcoming migrants is possible.	**Supported**: The value of saving a life far outweighs the ontic evil (disvalue) of the financial cost to the host country.	**Supported**: Points systems treat people as economic tools, which is unacceptable. The dignity of the migrant as a person is the focus.
Application to capital punishment	**Rejected**: Because prison is a safe alternative, the conflict is avoidable. There is no necessity to kill.	**Rejected**: The value of deterrence is unproven, while the ontic evil of killing is certain.	**Rejected**: It treats the criminal as a tool for social policy. It leaves no room for *agape* or the person's reform.

Summary

- ★ Immigration is a complex area involving human rights and the duties of a state in relation to the movement of population into the state for residence.
- ★ Based on the seven basic goods and nine requirements of practical reasonableness, Finnis argues that controlled migration can be to the benefit of the migrant and the host country.
- ★ Finnis raises the issue of uncontrolled mass migration being a potential cause of cultural decay and social breakdown in the host country, which would threaten the common good.
- ★ CSP seems to suggest that, provided a third way cannot be found and provided that the host country is not in a state of collapse, welcoming migrants is possible; VMP and RTP both seem to suggest that saving life outweighs any ontic evil and that the dignity of the migrant as a person has to be upheld.
- ★ Finnis rejects capital punishment as, whatever the circumstances, execution is intentional and is the destruction of a basic good – life.
- ★ Proportionalism rejects capital punishment: for CSP because a whole life sentence is a third way, for VMP because the ontic evil of killing is certain but the value of deterrence is unproven, and for RTP because the criminal is not treated as a person with dignity and there is no room for *agape* or reform.

AO1 Activity

a Examine the application of Finnis' natural law and proportionalism to immigration and capital punishment by completing the two tables on page 151. For the first table, revise the passages on Finnis' basic goods and consider which ones you might include. For the second table, revise the passages on the three proportionalist approaches. For each approach, identify the central 'reasoning tool' used to judge capital punishment and determine whether that tool leads to a rejection of the death penalty.

Scenario	Basic goods pursued by the migrant	Basic goods pursued/ protected by the host country
A refugee flees to the UK from a war zone with no legal documents.		
A doctor moves to the UK to work in the NHS.		
A student enrols in a university in the UK for a three-year degree.		
A seasonal worker moves to the UK to pick fruit for six months.		

Proportionalist approach	Key reasoning tool	Application to capital punishment
CSP		
VMP		
RTP		

b Imagine a government wants to introduce capital punishment. It argues that:

- some crimes are so serious that the only punishment should be capital punishment
- life sentences are too expensive and capital punishment would be cheaper overall
- capital punishment would be a powerful deterrent and would therefore definitely save hundreds of lives.

Using the three proportionalist approaches – CSP, VMP and RTP – examine whether the reasoning behind these arguments is sound. In your answer, aim to use specific evidence and examples from this sub-theme to support each point you make.

This checklist might help with your answer:

- **CSP**: Mention the *avoidability test* and the *third way*.
- **VMP**: Contrast *ontic evil* (the death) with the *value* sought (public safety).
- **RTP**: Discuss *agape* and whether the person is being used as a *tool*.

In line with the higher band descriptors, when writing your answer, ask yourself: does my response use a range of accurate evidence and examples – including scholars, key terms and quotations – to build a clear and well-supported argument?

This section covers AO2 content and skills

Specification content

Whether Finnis provides a basis for moral decision-making for believers/non-believers

Issues for analysis and evaluation

Whether Finnis provides a basis for moral decision-making for believers/non-believers

Possible line of argument	Critical analysis and evaluation
Depending on how 'a basis for moral decision-making' is interpreted, Finnis' theory provides a strong foundation for believers by aligning with traditional Catholic theology. His seven basic goods, particularly religion, and the nine requirements mirror the Golden Rule, offering a coherent religious and legal framework for moral life.	Critics like Brigita White argue Finnis' morality is too narrow. By claiming his traditional Roman Catholic interpretations are universal truths, he may alienate believers who hold more liberal or diverse theological perspectives on modern issues and non-believers looking for an entirely secular approach.
For non-believers, the theory is accessible because it is rooted in secular reason and common sense, e.g. the self-evident basic goods. It does not require divine revelation to understand that life, knowledge and friendship are essential for human flourishing and the common good.	However, some argue the basic good of religion or the focus on 'ultimate concerns' feels forced upon atheists. Non-believers might reject the theory as a 'front' for religious dogma, especially regarding his controversial views on sexual ethics and marriage.
The system offers a practical basis for decision-making in a pluralistic society. By distinguishing between public law (fostering the common good) and private morality, it allows citizens to pursue goods without needing constant public approval or religious consensus.	Others suggest that for a secular society, Finnis is 'out of touch'. His rejection of homosexual sex as 'intrinsically unreasonable' is seen by many non-believers as a biological or traditionalist bias rather than a result of pure, objective reason.
Finnis provides clarity on complex issues like capital punishment, arguing that the basic good of life is incommensurable. This provides a clear, rational boundary for both believers and non-believers to protect human dignity within the legal system.	Conversely, his application to immigration is criticised for being less clear. While he supports the common good, his warnings about 'cultural decay' can be interpreted as either a sensible protective measure or a subjective, exclusionary preference.
Ultimately, Finnis offers a universal methodology for ethics. Because his goods are pre-moral and accessible to anyone with practical reasonableness, they provide a shared language for moral debate regardless of an individual's faith or lack thereof.	Nevertheless, believers may find the theory lacks scriptural authority, while non-believers may find it too rigid. Both groups might argue that better bases for decision-making exist, such as direct religious texts for the faithful or utilitarianism for the secular.

AO2 Activity

a Analyse three possible conclusions that could be drawn from the critical analysis and evaluation of the view that Finnis' natural law provides a basis for moral decision-making for both believers and non-believers. Select one conclusion that you think is the **most convincing** and explain why it is so.

b Using your analysis from part a, write a concluding paragraph that presents your own justified viewpoint. Refer to the AO2 band descriptors and ensure your conclusion demonstrates 'a confident and justified conclusion' (band 5). Contrast this with the **weakest** conclusion of the three, justifying your argument with clear reasoning and evidence.

Specification content

The effectiveness of proportionalism in dealing with ethical issues

Exam practice

Below is an example of part of an evaluation of the effectiveness of proportionalism in dealing with ethical issues.

Sample answer

Proportionalism is a middle way between strict rules and total flexibility. A notable case involves a man experiencing homelessness stealing food to survive. While stealing is normally wrong, a court ruled his need for survival was more important. This shows that ethical rules should not be without exception, as the common good can sometimes override a specific law.

News reporter: The essay opens with a clear, real-world example to illustrate the practical impact of the theory.

Aquinas suggested that taking food in extreme need is not 'stealing proper' but it remains stealing, with perhaps less sinfulness involved. Proportionalism builds on this by focusing on the proportion of the act. If the intention is to save a life, the physical act of taking food is seen as a pre-moral evil or ontic evil rather than a sinful moral evil.

Explorer: The paragraph successfully charts the historical links between traditional natural law and modern updates.

Proportionalism is effective because it moves away from a 'one-size-fits-all' approach. It argues that a compassionate Christian ethical system must be flexible. Instead of just following a list of 'don'ts', it encourages believers to look at the unique context of every situation to find the most loving outcome.

Critical thinker: A strong point is made here about the shift from rigid deontology to a more nuanced, person-centred approach.

Richard McCormick's version, CSP, is especially useful for complex issues like ectopic pregnancies. Here, a doctor faces a genuine conflict where they cannot save both the mother and the fetus. Proportionalism provides a logical framework to choose the action that minimises harm when no perfect option exists.

Detective: The essay forensically examines how the theory functions in high-stakes medical dilemmas.

Garth Hallett offers a different version called VMP. This approach argues that we should always aim to produce the most value while minimising ontic evil (physical harm). By using reason to calculate the best result, it prevents people from making decisions based purely on unpredictable emotions.

Philosopher: This section provides a deep look at the logic of balancing values to achieve the greater good.

Critical thinker

The argument identifies a major weakness regarding the lack of consistency in the theory's application.

However, VMP faces a major challenge: there is no universal agreement on how to calculate proportionate reason. Critics argue that if everyone decides for themselves what is proportionate, morality becomes too subjective. Without clear rules, society could fall into moral chaos where any act is justified.

Judge

This paragraph delivers a balanced view of the opposition from official religious authorities.

Traditionalists, including the magisterium of the Catholic Church, as shown in Pope John Paul II's *Veritatis Splendor*, reject proportionalism. They argue that some acts are intrinsically evil and can never be justified, regardless of the intention. For these critics, proportionalism is just a disguised version of consequentialism that ignores absolute moral boundaries.

Explorer

The essay navigates towards a modern solution by integrating virtue ethics with proportional reasoning.

Selling suggests a better way forward is focusing on virtues and the character of the person, rather than just the rules. By following the example of Jesus – who prioritised people over strict law – proportionalism becomes a tool for compassion and *agape* rather than just a complex calculation of consequences.

Judge

A final, balanced ruling is delivered, acknowledging the validity and the practical utility of the approach.

In conclusion, proportionalism is highly effective for those seeking a balance between authority and situation. While it lacks the rigid clarity of absolute rules, it offers a realistic and compassionate framework for the modern world. It ensures that morality serves human flourishing rather than just being an exercise in legalistic obedience.

Over to you

Complete the five points below to write an answer, under timed conditions, to a question requiring an evaluation of the effectiveness of Finnis' natural law in dealing with ethical issues.

1. Make an initial list of arguments or lines of reasoning. It does not need to be in any particular order.
2. Add relevant scholars, quotations and supporting evidence.
3. Consider the order in which you would like to present the information.
4. Use what you have written to make an essay plan.
5. Use the plan to write your essay under timed conditions.

If you can, swap your response with somebody else. Read and mark each other's responses. This collaboration can help you to see alternative perspectives and things you may have missed. It also helps highlight the strengths of your response and of other responses.

When you have completed the task, refer to the band descriptors for AS (WJEC) or A Level (Eduqas) and, in particular, look at the demands described in the higher band descriptors, which you should be aspiring towards. Ask yourself the following questions:

- Is my answer a confident critical analysis and perceptive evaluation of the issue?
- Is my answer a response that successfully identifies and thoroughly addresses the issues the question raises?
- Does my work show an excellent standard of coherence, clarity and organisation?
- Will my work, when developed, contain thorough, sustained and clear views that are supported by extensive, detailed reasoning and/or evidence?

- Have I used the views of scholars/schools of thought extensively, appropriately and in context?
- Does my answer convey a confident and perceptive analysis of the nature of any possible connections with other elements of my course?
- Is my use of specialist language and vocabulary both thorough and accurate?

Question

'Finnis' natural law is effective in dealing with ethical issues.' Evaluate this view.

(Eduqas A Level 2023)

T3 Teleological ethics

This section covers AO1 content and skills

Specification content

Fletcher's rejection of other approaches within ethics: legalism, antinomianism and the role of conscience; Fletcher's rationale for using the religious concept of *agape* (selfless love) as the middle way between the extremes of legalism and antinomianism

Key terms

legalism: an approach to ethics that accepts the absolute nature of established rules or principles

antinomianism: a theory of ethics that does not recognise the authority of established rules or principles – from the ancient Greek words *anti* (against) and *nomos* (law) – lawless

Key quote

The Sabbath was made for the good of human beings, they were not made for the Sabbath.

(Mark 2:27)

A: Joseph Fletcher's situation ethics: his rejection of other forms of ethics and his acceptance of *agape* as the basis of morality

Fletcher's rejection of other approaches within ethics and his rationale for using the religious concept of *agape* (selfless love) as the middle way between the extremes of legalism and antinomianism

In 1966, the American theologian **Joseph Fletcher** published a book entitled *Situation Ethics: The New Morality*. In it, he proposed a new approach that offered a middle ground between two extremes: **legalism** (strict adherence to rules and laws) and **antinomianism** (the rejection of all moral rules and laws).

Situation ethics was part of a trend in Christian ethics that had been growing for decades. It was not something entirely new but, in socio-economic terms, grew out of the more liberal decades after the Second World War leading up to the 1960s. This has been described as a time of developing civil rights, the growth of feminism, teenager and hippy culture, sexual liberation and the gradual rejection of traditional sources of authority and authority role models.

Key person

Joseph Fletcher (1905–91): A professor who was ordained as a priest in the Episcopalian Church of the USA; he became famous for his book *Situation Ethics: The New Morality*; after 1966 he identified himself as an atheist and a humanist and argued in favour of abortion and euthanasia

In the context of Christian ethical thinking, situation ethics was not something completely new. Fletcher argued that what was called the 'new morality' can be found in 'classical' Christianity: it is based on the Christian gospel, in particular in situations where Jesus rejected the religious rules or laws in order to do the right thing. This was exemplified by Jesus stating that the law about not working on the Sabbath should be ignored when necessary in order to put human needs first. The law was a tool and not the master.

Fletcher argued that there are three possible options for making a moral decision:

- **Legalism**: This means applying rules, laws and set principles rigidly and without consideration of context.
- **Antinomianism**: This means championing the complete freedom of the individual without reference to any rules, laws or set principles.

- **Situationism**: This (situation ethics) means using reason in considering each situation before applying the Christian principle of love (*agape*).

Rejection of legalism

Fletcher argued that the moral principles held to by the Christian Church cannot be used as moral absolutes because they do not work in situations where an ethical decision needs to be made. For example, 'Do not kill' is wrong only in given circumstances, not necessarily during war, in self-defence or to provide meat for eating.

Fletcher's conclusion was that applying absolute ethical principles to real-life situations was simply not Christian. It involved too many problems, inconsistencies and contradictions. So-called absolute principles of right and good are not really absolute; there are times when it is inappropriate to apply such principles to the real world. The author Arthur Miller referred to legalism as 'the immorality of morality'.

Fletcher used the example of a conversation about politics with a taxi-driver to illustrate his point. The passenger explained that he and his family had always, on principle, voted for the same political party. The taxi-driver replied: 'There are times when a man has to push his principles aside and do the right thing.'

Fletcher described the legalism followed by the Christian Church as using 'a whole apparatus of prefabricated rules and regulations' as 'directives'. Such an approach was too rigid, according to Fletcher, who wrote that legalism could result in 'a punishing and sadistic use of law to hurt people instead of helping them'.

Rejection of antinomianism

Antinomianism was often linked to secular **existentialism**: the idea that each person creates their own morality without following any established rules or principles.

Fletcher argued that in making moral decisions, antinomians had no strategy as theirs was 'the approach with which one enters into the decision-making situation armed with no principles or maxims whatsoever, to say nothing of rules'.

Critics of Fletcher argued that his approach was more interested in rejecting legalism than in rejecting antinomianism. For Fletcher, freedom to reason was crucial and he rejected outright the constraints of any form of legalism. Overall, critics might argue that his theory does appear to be more in line with the idea of freedom from rules and laws that are seen to be artificial, rather than trying to redefine a flexible legalistic approach.

Situation ethics

Fletcher proposed a middle way between legalism and antinomianism with what he called 'principled relativism'. All revealed established religious rules and principles were rejected. However, they – and the Bible itself – could still be seen as 'illuminators' in any situation *but* they were not to be viewed as 'directors' of moral decision-making. Fletcher argued that there was only

Key quote

The new morality is, of course, none other than the old morality, just as the new commandment is the old, yet ever fresh, commandment of love.

(Robinson)

Key term

existentialism: a philosophy that proposes the individual is free and responsible to determine their own development

Key quote

Even though Fletcher rejects both, he appears to fear the tyranny of legalism more than the anarchy of antinomianism.

(Childress)

Agape: the Greek word for selfless, unconditional love

Key quote

Christian situation ethics has only one norm or principle or law (call it what you will) that is binding and unexceptionable, always good and right regardless of the circumstances. That is 'love' – the *agape* of the summary commandment to love God and the neighbour.

(Fletcher)

one true principle always to be applied through the use of reason in every situation: *agape*.

The roots of new morality can be found in classical Christianity. *Agape* is the word used in the New Testament for pure, unconditional Christian love. It is love which is disinterested and seeks only the benefit of the one who is loved.

Fletcher argued that to make a meaningful ethical decision, the situation needed to be considered first before anything else. Then, when the situation had been considered, deciding to do what is right depended upon the practical application of *agape*. This did not require referring back to set religious moral rules or principles. This approach is situational because the right decision in one situation cannot become the blueprint for all other situations. Each situation had to be considered independently.

In essence, situation ethics is practical and the emphasis is on action and not theory, on doing and not just debating, on being alive and responsive to the context and not just adhering to a set of rules. Since situation ethics does not rely on being told what is good, bad, right or wrong or on what to do in every situation, it has been described as a mature approach to morality. Robinson described it as fit for modern human beings who have 'come of age'.

The role of conscience

Fletcher's understanding of conscience is different from traditional views; he saw it as a 'function, not as a faculty'. He was not so much interested in what it *is* as in *what it does*. He wrote: 'The traditional error lies in thinking about conscience as a noun instead of a verb.'

In other words, conscience is not something that exists inside people or something that directs people. For Fletcher, it was more a description of the way the mind worked in making moral decisions.

Fletcher rejected four traditional ideas about conscience. For him it was not any of the following:

- 'An innate, radar-like, built-in faculty – intuition.'
- 'Inspiration from outside the decision maker – guidance by the Holy Spirit.'
- 'The internalised value system of the culture and society.'
- 'Reason making moral judgments or value choices.'

Instead, he argued:

> There is no conscience; conscience is merely a word for our attempts to make decisions creatively, constructively, fittingly.

Fletcher's understanding of the function of conscience was not one of reviewing past actions or apportioning guilt and shame; according to Fletcher, the way conscience functioned was by looking forwards towards its application, that is, the moral problems to solve.

The Christian Church had in the past – according to Fletcher – derived moral laws, rules and principles from the Bible and traditional teachings. This meant that over time morality had become codified and fixed. In this Church view, to decide what is good, bad, right or wrong in any situation, a person needed only to use their conscience to refer back to the laws, rules and principles and they would then know how to react and what to do. Fletcher saw this as a mistake.

For example, in a situation where abortion was the issue, the law from the Ten Commandments, 'Do not kill,' would be the reference point and this would direct the person's conscience so that they would be guided by the principle of abortion being bad and wrong. For Fletcher this approach was wrong because it was not life-centred or person-centred but was only based on an abstract principle. In contrast, situation ethics called for the practical application of Christian *agape* to a given situation. Laws, rules and principles are put aside because the individual situation and context has to come first.

Fletcher used a variety of references to scripture, but his main focus was on the use of the word *agape*. *Agape* expresses pure, selfless, unconditional love to set it apart from other Greek words describing different aspects of love.

The focus of the word was the use of it in the parable of the Good Samaritan, where the 'strategy of love' was seen to be clearly outlined, and in St Paul's letter to the Corinthians (1 Corinthians 13), where the meaning of *agape* was developed.

Agape in the parable of the Good Samaritan

> On one occasion an expert in the law stood up to test Jesus. 'Teacher,' he asked, 'what must I do to inherit eternal life?'
>
> 'What is written in the Law?' he replied. 'How do you read it?'
>
> He answered, 'Love [αγαπήσεις (*agapeis*)] the Lord your God with all your heart and with all your soul and with all your strength and with all your mind'; and, 'Love your neighbor as yourself.'
>
> 'You have answered correctly,' Jesus replied. 'Do this and you will live.'
>
> But he wanted to justify himself, so he asked Jesus, 'And who is my neighbor?'
>
> In reply Jesus said: 'A man was going down from Jerusalem to Jericho, when he was attacked by robbers. They stripped him of his clothes, beat him and went away, leaving him half dead. A priest happened to be going down the same road, and when he saw the man, he passed by on the other side. So too, a Levite, when he came to the place and saw him, passed by on the other side. But a Samaritan, as he travelled, came where the man was; and when he saw him, he took pity on him. He went to him and bandaged his wounds, pouring on oil and wine. Then he put the man on his own donkey, brought him to an inn and took care of him. The next day he took out two denarii and gave them to the innkeeper. "Look after him," he said, "and when I return, I will reimburse you for any extra expense you may have."'

Jesus then asked which person fulfilled the role of neighbour to the injured man and the reply came that it was the 'one who had mercy'. Jesus then instructed the questioner to 'do likewise'.

Luke used the Greek word αγαπήσεις (*agapeis*) – the future command 'you will love' – from the verb αγαπώ (*agapo*) – 'to love'. This *agape* was to be applied to one's neighbour as to oneself. In being told at the end of the

Key quote

If love is perfect then freedom is a good thing. But if there is no love, or if there is not enough love, then freedom can become licence, freedom can become selfishness and even cruelty.

(Barclay)

Specification content

The biblical evidence used to support this approach: the teachings of Jesus (Luke 10:25–37) and St Paul (1 Corinthians 13)

Jesus told the parable of the Good Samaritan

Key quotes

The moral precepts of Jesus are not intended to be understood legalistically, as prescribing what all Christians must do, whatever the circumstances, and pronouncing certain courses of action universally right and others universally wrong. They are not legislation laying down what love always demands of every one: they are illustrations of what love may at any moment require of anyone.

(Robinson)

There is only one ultimate and invariable duty, and its formula is, 'Thou shalt love thy neighbor as thyself.' How to do this is another question, but this is the whole of moral duty.

(Temple)

parable to 'do likewise' Fletcher argued that the questioner was being told to apply the universal principle of neighbourly love to all as demonstrated by the example of the Good Samaritan.

Agape in 1 Corinthians 13

> If I speak in the tongues of men or of angels, but do not have love, I am only a resounding gong or a clanging cymbal. If I have the gift of prophecy and can fathom all mysteries and all knowledge, and if I have a faith that can move mountains, but do not have love, I am nothing. If I give all I possess to the poor and give over my body to hardship that I may boast, but do not have love, I gain nothing.
>
> Love is patient, love is kind. It does not envy, it does not boast, it is not proud. It does not dishonour others, it is not self-seeking, it is not easily angered, it keeps no record of wrongs. Love does not delight in evil but rejoices with the truth. It always protects, always trusts, always hopes, always perseveres.
>
> Love never fails. But where there are prophecies, they will cease; where there are tongues, they will be stilled; where there is knowledge, it will pass away. For we know in part and we prophesy in part, but when completeness comes, what is in part disappears. When I was a child, I talked like a child, I thought like a child, I reasoned like a child. When I became a man, I put the ways of childhood behind me. For now we see only a reflection as in a mirror; then we shall see face to face. Now I know in part; then I shall know fully, even as I am fully known.
>
> And now these three remain: faith, hope and love. But the greatest of these is love.

Here, the word for love used by St Paul is ἀγάπη (*agape*). The impact of St Paul's words on the development of Christian moral teaching has been very significant, showing throughout that love has the highest value and status.

Specification content

Situation ethics as a form of moral relativism, a consequentialist and teleological theory

Situation ethics as a form of moral relativism,

Fletcher referred to his system of ethics as a 'principled relativism'. Situation ethics is a form of moral relativism because it recognises no universal moral laws, rules or principles and proposes that each situation has to be looked at independently because each situation is different. However, against this relativism Fletcher did have *one* absolute – an *agape* that is binding, always right and always applied in every situation.

For Fletcher, *agape* should be understood as a practical tool that is adapted to, responded to and applied to the needs of each situation; it is not an absolute principle in the sense that it directs each situation in exactly the same way. In other words, the principle of *agape* remains constant but at the same time responds differently according to the needs of each situation. In this sense, according to Fletcher, situation ethics is truly relativist as a moral approach.

Situation ethics is also consequentialist in that the situation is considered with the application of conscience through *agape*, looking forwards to the outcome. In this way, looking towards the consequences, moral decisions can be made 'creatively, constructively, fittingly'. As it is only concerned with the end purpose of bringing about *agape* in the best way possible, situation ethics is also teleological.

Summary

- Situation ethics is a teleological approach to morality developed by Joseph Fletcher in 1966.
- It is a liberal Christian approach based on the idea that religious laws can be ignored in favour of doing the right thing.
- Fletcher placed his ethical theory in the middle between legalism and antinomianism, both of which he rejected.
- According to Fletcher, there is no such thing as a conscience in the traditional sense; the conscience is simply the process of decision-making in a creative and constructive way.
- The parable of the Good Samaritan and St Paul's message in 1 Corinthians 13 show the importance given to *agape*.
- Situation ethics is a form of relativism that is consequentialist: the process of conscience involves using *agape* to work out the result which would produce the most *agape*.

AO1 Activity

a Explain why situation ethics is not a form of legalism and why it is not a form of antinomianism.

b Review your answer to part a. Identify one piece of scholarly or biblical evidence you could add to each part of the explanation to strengthen it. Then check your work against the AO1 band descriptors: does your answer demonstrate 'thorough and accurate use of specialist language and vocabulary in context' (band 5)?

Refer to the AS/A Level AO1 band descriptors. In particular, look at band 5, which requires 'thorough, accurate and relevant knowledge and understanding' with 'excellent use of evidence and examples'.

Key quote

There can be no 'system' of situation ethics, but only a 'method' of situational or contextual decision-making. **(Childress)**

This section covers AO2 content and skills

Specification content

The degree to which *agape* is the only intrinsic good

Issues for analysis and evaluation

The degree to which *agape* is the only intrinsic good

Possible line of argument	Critical analysis and evaluation
Agape is the only intrinsic good because there is nothing negative, harmful, evil or bad about it.	Fletcher argues that *agape* is intrinsically good because it is understood to be wholly positive; however, it is not the *only* good as justice, truth, beauty and courage are also intrinsically good.
Agape is the only intrinsic good from the Christian perspective because it is praised by Jesus in the parable of the Good Samaritan and by St Paul in 1 Corinthians.	Many Christians can understand *agape* as the only intrinsic good given how important it is for Jesus and St Paul, as well as other Christian philosophers; however, other things are also praised as being intrinsically good such as the virtues of peace-making, being humble and pure in heart, having faith, keeping the commandments, being generous.
No concept can be called the only intrinsic good – the Christian understanding of *agape* is no exception to this view.	While there is something simple and attractive about calling *agape* the only intrinsic good, the idea of *agape* is derived from belief in God. In that sense, it would be better to say that God alone is intrinsically good.
Since other goods do not stand alone but are derived from *agape*, it shows that *agape* is the only intrinsic good.	Justice is seen by many as intrinsically good since it implies honesty, fairness, equality and impartiality; however, it could be argued that ultimately justice is derived from *agape* because it is all about loving your neighbour and treating them as you would treat yourself.
Everyone understands the concept of *agape* and from a common-sense point of view it is the only good.	The biblical roots of the concept of *agape* give it continuing authority as the only intrinsic good; however, what exactly *agape* is is unclear as there are different types of love, such as neighbourly love, love of oneself and love of one's family and friends.

AO2 Activity

a Analyse three possible conclusions that could be drawn from the critical analysis and evaluation of the view that *agape* is the only intrinsic good. Select evidence and examples to support each of the three conclusions. Select one conclusion that you think is the **most convincing** and explain why it is so.

b Now contrast this with the **weakest** conclusion of the three. Justify your argument with clear reasoning and evidence.

Refer to the AS/A Level AO2 band descriptors. Band 5 requires 'a confident and insightful critical analysis and perceptive evaluation' with 'a well-substantiated, clear and convincing conclusion'.

Exam practice

Below is an example of part of an evaluation of whether situation ethics promotes immoral behaviour.

Sample answer

Situation ethics has faced accusations of promoting immoral behaviour because it gives individuals too much freedom, a known problem with the philosophy of antinomianism. I would argue that the debate needs to focus on whether people can be trusted to always apply *agape* correctly.

A major argument is that someone could claim to act from *agape* while performing selfish or unjust acts like murder or adultery. Since the theory is relativistic, it grants the individual freedom to redefine 'loving' outcomes based on the situation. For example, murder might be justified as a 'mercy killing' to prevent suffering, or adultery could be excused as a means of seeking emotional fulfilment in an unhappy marriage.

This point is supported by Barclay. He admitted that if love is perfect then freedom is a good thing. However, he recognised that perhaps there might not be the right type of love or not enough of it, which could then result in 'selfishness and even cruelty' – in other words, immoral behaviour.

Against this, Fletcher emphasised that situation ethics promotes individual responsibility by making *agape* alone the ruling principle. Since this is intrinsically good it cannot lead to immoral behaviour.

In addition Fletcher would argue the theory necessarily avoids immorality because it is based on *agape*, which is praised by both Jesus and St Paul as being the greatest principle to follow next to loving God. This is common sense and understood by everyone. It is only the opposite of *agape* which leads to immoral behaviour.

However, situation ethics relies on people being trusted to act in an almost perfect way. Robinson described it as fit for modern human beings who have 'come of age'. That means it requires people to have a level of wisdom and maturity which, in many cases, is lacking. This inevitably allows for immoral behaviour.

Even if someone has the perfect maturity required by situation ethics, nobody has the ability to predict consequences with complete accuracy. There can never be any guarantee that what appears to be the right decision leads to *agape* or to immoral behaviour.

For a religious believer the only guarantee against immoral behaviour is following religious laws such as the Ten Commandments. One of the commandments states clearly that stealing is bad and wrong and should never happen, whereas situation ethics might justify stealing if it produces more *agape*. This shows how it leads to immoral behaviour.

Specification content

Whether situation ethics promotes immoral behaviour

News reporter

Judge

A clear overview of the debate about situation ethics and immoral behaviour. The last sentence already shows a mini-conclusion setting out where the verdict might be heading.

Explorer

Tennis player

Some good points are made which begin the fielding of arguments and which also brings in a new suggestion to answering the question.

Critical thinker

Detective

Here analysis is provided of one of the key issues with situation ethics – the point is also supported by a scholarly view.

Philosopher

This paragraph identifies an underlying issue raised by the question.

Tennis player

This paragraph presents a strong counter-argument, fielding the question being asked and providing flow in the essay.

Philosopher

Some confident and perceptive evaluation is provided here, challenging and questioning the issues raised – the scholarly view is very helpful.

Detective

This provides a good investigation of an important weakness of teleological ethics in general.

Tennis player

During the essay, as here, there is very good back-and-forth of argument and counter-argument.

Judge

Critical thinker

The verdict is now in – it links back to the introduction. The essay offers a clear-cut verdict that situation ethics is likely to lead to immorality.

In conclusion, situation ethics is not intended to promote immoral behaviour but I would argue that it puts too much trust in individuals to be mature enough to understand what *agape* means in every situation. If people cannot be relied upon or trusted then immoral behaviour might be the outcome.

Over to you

Below are listed four basic conclusions drawn from an evaluation of situation ethics. Two are positive and two are negative. Your task is to develop each of these conclusions by identifying the strengths (the evidence or reasoning that makes it a persuasive point) but also the challenges made to it (the counter-arguments or weaknesses that might undermine it). When you have completed the exercise, explain whether your final overall verdict on situation ethics is a positive or negative one and give the key reasons for why you have reached your verdict.

The result should be four very competent paragraphs that could form a final conclusion of any evaluation. Refer to the band descriptors for A2 (WJEC) or A Level (Eduqas) and, in particular, look at the demands described in the higher band descriptors, which you should be aspiring towards. Ask yourself the following questions:

- Is my answer a confident critical analysis and perceptive evaluation of the issue?
- Is my answer a response that successfully identifies and thoroughly addresses the issues the question raises?

Question

'*Agape* should replace religious rules.' Evaluate this view.

Conclusions

- Replacing religious rules with *agape* has the strength of reflecting the heart of the Christian message. It prioritises the 'spirit' of the law over the 'letter' of the law, ensuring that compassion for the individual always comes before strictly following outdated religious laws.
- Replacing religious rules with *agape* recognises the moral maturity of modern believers. It allows for ethical decisions to be made based on the unique context of a situation, providing a flexible alternative to one-size-fits-all religious laws that may no longer be relevant.
- *Agape* should not replace religious rules because it removes the objective framework provided by tradition and scripture. Without fixed rules, *agape* becomes a subjective feeling that lacks the clarity and authority needed to provide moral guidance.
- Replacing religious rules with *agape* is dangerous because it ignores the human tendency towards selfishness. Religious rules represent the 'distilled wisdom' of a faith, providing boundaries that prevent individuals from justifying harmful or immoral actions in the name of *agape*.

B: Fletcher's situation ethics: the principles as a means of assessing morality

This section covers AO1 content and skills

The boss principle of situation ethics (following the concept of *agape*)

Specification content

The boss principle of situation ethics (following the concept of *agape*)

Fletcher quotes St Augustine as saying: *'Dilige et quod vis, fac,'* meaning, 'Love with care and then do what you will.' For St Augustine this was the key part of Christian morality from which everything else flowed.

Developing his ideas, Fletcher placed *agape* at the top of his ethical theory as the concept which controlled everything else. This was why he called it the 'boss' principle.

For St Augustine, love was the foundation of all Christian morality

Fletcher never gave a fully fixed definition of *agape*, but he emphasised its roots in the Bible. In the Old Testament the word used for the loving relationship between God and God's people is ***chesed***. This word describes a love that is faithful, strong, consistently present and kind. It is often translated as 'loving kindness' or 'steadfast love' and includes the ideal of commitment, an already existing bond and a deliberate choice of affection and kindness. The Hebrew people were often reminded to remember this love of God in terms of the action it produced in history when God intervened on their behalf to save them.

However, in Leviticus 19:18 – the verse that is referred to in the parable of the Good Samaritan – the word is ***aheb***. This describes a spontaneous love on behalf of humans towards God and fellow human beings. *Aheb* is universal and not exclusive to God's loving relationship with the Hebrew people. It is outward-looking and embraces all. Arguably, it is this sense of love that provides the origin of *agape*.

Key terms

chesed: Hebrew word that describes an exclusive kind of love in a particular relationship

aheb: Hebrew word for love that is seen to be similar to the idea of *agape*

In the New Testament we have Jesus' recognition of the greatest commandment in Matthew 22:36–40 – to 'love God and your neighbour as yourself'. Jesus quotes this from Leviticus in the Old Testament. The Greek word *agape* is this idea of pure, unconditional, non-reciprocal, neighbour-regarding and sacrificial love that was fully shown in the character and work of Jesus.

Fletcher argued that his understanding of *agape* is biblical because it focuses 'not on what love is but on how to do the most loving thing possible in the situation'. With regard to *agape*, situation ethics is concerned with '*pragma* (doing) and not *dogma* (keeping to a set teaching)'.

Fletcher comments, 'Augustine was right to make love the source principle, the hinge principle upon which all other "virtues" hang.'

All of this explains why for Fletcher, *agape* was the 'boss' principle of situation ethics: 'What a difference it makes when love, understood *agapeically*, is boss; when love is the only norm.'

Key quote

Love alone, because, as it were, it has a built in moral compass, enabling it to [...] be directed completely by the situation.

(Robinson)

One of the major critics of Fletcher and situation ethics was William Barclay (1907–78). He argued in *Ethics in a Permissive Society* that the theory did not give a sufficiently clear definition of *agape* and that it also depended too much on using extreme examples rather than ones taken from ordinary life. For example, Fletcher used the example of a mother hiding from those hunting for her and her family. She had a baby which started crying and was in danger of betraying their whereabouts. Fletcher suggested that the mother could either let the baby cry, thereby leading to the family being caught, or silence the baby by killing it, saving the rest of the family. Fletcher's approach suggested that killing the baby would be the right action because it produced the most *agape*.

Key quote

It is much easier to agree that extraordinary situations need extraordinary measures than to think that there are no laws for ordinary everyday life.

(Barclay)

Specification content

The four working principles (pragmatism, relativism, positivism and personalism)

The four working principles

Fletcher tried to provided clarity to his ethical theory and to demonstrate that situation ethics was not antinomian by giving it a clear structure. He did this by firstly identifying four key working principles to keep in mind when assessing moral decision-making.

Pragmatism

The first working principle of situation ethics is pragmatism: an ethical solution must be practical and actually work in reality.

Influenced by philosopher William James, Fletcher believed the 'good is what works'. It is useless to suggest a solution that sounds good philosophically but fails when applied to a real-life dilemma. The success of an ethical choice is measured by its application, not just its theory. While reason is involved, the pragmatic question of 'what works' is ultimately the guiding priority. The ethical action must be effective and practical.

Key quotes

Love cannot be quantified in such a way that it can produce a clear moral response.

(Barclay)

Thus Christian ethics 'posits' faith in God and *reasons* out what obedience to his commandment to love requires in any situation.

(Bonhoeffer)

A basic maxim is that the disciple is commanded to love people, not principles or laws or objects or any other thing.

(Fletcher)

I think that there are things which can in no circumstances be right.

(Barclay)

Relativism

The second principle, relativism, means avoiding fixed, unconditional words like 'never' or 'always'.

This does not mean morality is random or anarchic. For Fletcher, every moral choice is relative to one absolute measure: *agapeic* love. As Fletcher put it, 'It relativises the absolute, it does not absolute the relative.' Every unique situation is judged not by its own circumstances, but by how best to express unconditional love within it.

Positivism

The third principle, positivism, means that *agape* must be accepted voluntarily, or by an act of faith, rather than being proven by reason.

For Fletcher, faith comes first. You accept the principle of *agape* and then use reason to determine how to apply it within a given situation. As he states, a Christian does not understand God through the concept of love; they understand the concept of love through God as seen in Christ. The unconditional nature of love is affirmed first, then morality is built upon it.

Personalism

The final principle is personalism, which means ethics is fundamentally about people rather than laws, rules or objects.

Situation ethics is a person-centred system: the command is to love people, not to love abstract principles or doctrines. The ultimate ethical concern is the welfare and care of the human subject.

The six fundamental principles

After the four working principles, which provide practical guidelines for applying ethics, Fletcher added six fundamental principles (or propositions) to provide a theological and philosophical justification about the use of *agape*.

Specification content

The six fundamental principles (love is the only good, love is the ruling norm of Christianity, love equals justice, love for all, loving ends justify the means and love decides situationally)

Fundamental principle	Description
Love is the only good	This is the central concept which Fletcher equated with the New Testament's 'law of love'. • **Love is the only intrinsic good**: Everything else (rules, actions and consequences) is good only if it serves or results from love. • **Love is an action, not a thing**: Love is a verb, a 'doing thing', and an active principle – it is something you do, not something you *have* or *are* (except for God, who *is* love). • **Love dictates how we interact with the world**: It is defined as a 'way of relating to persons, and of using things'.
Love is the ruling norm of Christian ethics	Fletcher argued that love is the ultimate ethical standard. • **Love replaces law**: Love (*agape*) is the single ruling norm or 'new covenant' that replaces all former religious and moral laws. • **Laws serve people, not the reverse**: Traditional laws have been given too much authority. Fletcher quoted the saying of Jesus: 'The Sabbath was made for the good of human beings, they were not made for the Sabbath.' (Mark 2:27). The old religious law about the Sabbath had to be given a new spirit of life to show that it was there to serve people. • **Laws are guidelines, not rules**: For the situationist, laws are not disrespected but they are not to be understood as rigid, legalistic commands, rather as a 'distillation' – a helpful summary – of the spirit of love that should only be followed if love is best served by doing so.
Love equals justice	Fletcher explained how *agape* is justice and justice is *agape*. • **Love (*agape*) is giving love**: This means it is unconditional and selfless love, characteristic of Christianity, distinguishing it from other forms of love. • **Justice is love distributed**: In Christian terms, justice is not a separate concept, but love in action. What every person is 'due' or 'entitled' to (which is the definition of justice) is love. • **The two terms are interchangeable**: Therefore, love *is* justice, and justice *is* love – it is the way love is calculated, distributed and applied to the community or the world.
Love for all	In situation ethics, love has a universal quality covering relationships with all people. • **Love is universal and unconditional**: Christian love, *agape*, is not based on emotion, preference or whether the recipient is a friend or foe. It is indiscriminate in its application, meaning it must be given to everyone. • **Love is sacrificial**: Quoting Jesus' command to 'love your enemies', Fletcher defined this love as **kenotic** or self-emptying – it is a deliberate, radical obligation to seek the good of the other, even at personal cost, regardless of how you feel about them.

Fundamental principle	Description
Loving ends justify the means	This principle means that results are the only thing that matters when deciding if an action is right or wrong. • Situation ethics is a teleological system, meaning actions are judged by their consequences rather than by rules. • The only good end is one that creates the most *agape* (unconditional love) in a given situation. • The idea that any action (means) is intrinsically or absolutely wrong is rejected as being a flawed concept. • Fletcher argued that if societies truly believed in absolute rules they would never allow actions like war or capital punishment – the fact that they do shows that they are actually deciding based on the end result they want to achieve. • This proves that the desired end is what actually guides ethical decisions, not a set of unchanging moral laws. When judging an ethical situation, Fletcher suggested considering four main factors: 1 **The desired end**: What are you hoping to achieve? 2 **The means**: How will you achieve it? 3 **The motive**: Why are you doing it? 4 **The consequences**: What will actually happen?
Love decides situationally	This principle means that moral choices must be made in the moment, based on *agape*, and not by blindly following pre-set rules or laws. • **Rejecting rigid laws**: Fletcher argued that people often seek security by following strict moral laws, but this approach fails in real life. • **The problem with prescriptions**: He criticised the practice of paying 'lip service' to moral laws that are constantly ignored or broken because they are too strict or too narrow to handle complex realities. • **Need for freedom**: To make a truly ethical decision, you need freedom and an 'open-ended approach' to the situation, rather than being enslaved to a rule. • **Situation-based choice**: All ethical decisions must be situation-based and guided only by the principle of *agape*. • **Conclusion**: There are no absolute, universal rules that can tell you what to do in every unique circumstance; you must decide what is the most loving action in that moment.

Key term

kenotic: from the Greek *kenosis*, meaning to empty or make oneself completely receptive to something

Key quotes

Disinterested love can only mean impartial love, inclusive love, indiscriminate love, love for Tom, Dick and Harry.

(Fletcher)

Christian situation ethics assert firmly and definitely: value, worth, ethical quality, goodness or badness, right or wrong – these things are only predicates, they are not properties. They are not 'given' or 'objectively' real or self-existent. There is only one thing that is always good and right, intrinsically good regardless of the context, and that one thing is love.

(Fletcher)

Summary

- Fletcher's boss principle is *agape*, from which his approach to morality flows.
- The way that situation ethics uses *agape* can be found in examining the words *chesed* and *aheb* found in the Bible in the Old Testament.
- Fletcher's four working principles give situation ethics a rational and logical structure.
- The four working principles are:
  - pragmatism
  - relativism
  - positivism
  - personalism.
- The six fundamental principles provide situation ethics with a theological and philosophical justification for *agape*.
- The six fundamental principles are:
  - love is the only good
  - love is the ruling norm of Christian ethics
  - love equals justice
  - love for all
  - loving ends justify the means
  - love decides situationally.

AO1 Activity

It is now time to reflect on the information that has been covered so far. It is also important to consider how what you have learned can be focused and used to answer examination-style questions by practising the skills associated with AO1. AO1 involves demonstrating knowledge and understanding. The exercise on page 170 is designed to help you demonstrate knowledge and understanding of the four working principles and the six fundamental principles. This will help you meet what is required by the higher bands: 'Selection of a range of (thorough) accurate and relevant information that is directly related to the specific demands of the question.'

a Outline the four working principles using the mnemonic PRPP to help structure your answer.

b Using your knowledge of the six fundamental principles, choose **one** principle and write a paragraph that fully explains it. Your paragraph should:

  i state the principle clearly

  ii explain what it means in your own words

  iii support your explanation with at least one piece of evidence or an example (for instance, a key quote from Fletcher, a biblical reference or a real-life scenario)

  iv use accurate specialist language throughout.

When writing your paragraph, aim to meet what is required by the higher bands of the AO1 band descriptors. For AS Level, refer to the band 5 descriptor: 'Thorough, accurate and relevant knowledge and understanding with extensive depth and/or breadth [...] excellent use of evidence and examples, including thorough and accurate use of specialist language and vocabulary.' For A Level, use the equivalent A Level band descriptors.

Issues for analysis and evaluation

The extent to which situation ethics promotes justice

Possible line of argument	Critical analysis and evaluation
Situation ethics judges each case separately – unlike systems with strict, unchanging rules – and it can promote justice overall. In this way flexibility leads to fairness and justice.	If there are no fixed moral rules – no overall laws or control – as Fletcher requires, some worry society will disintegrate. When what is right changes all the time, people get confused, which is a sure way to cause unfairness. In this way, situation ethics with no rules can lead to injustice.
The theory encourages people to act with selfless love and think about others first, which makes society kinder and fairer. Fletcher stated this clearly: 'love is justice distributed'.	Despite Fletcher's four working principles and six fundamental principles, the main idea, love, is entirely subjective. What one person thinks is a loving act promoting justice, another might strongly disagree with and see as promoting injustice.
Since situation ethics looks at the results of an action, it makes people think carefully about how their choices affect other people. The careful reasoning required leads to a result which promotes justice.	People can never accurately predict what will happen. What people think will be a just result might cause harm or an unjust outcome. People make incorrect predictions about the consequences of actions, particularly in the long term. This is not a secure way to promote justice.
The principle that 'love wills the good of others' means people should act lovingly towards everyone. This leaves no room for prejudice or bias. People should treat a stranger the same way they treat a family member. The impartiality of the application of *agape* ensures that it promotes justice.	Fletcher is too optimistic in his understanding of human nature. It is unlikely that a stranger would be treated with the exact same amount of *agape* as close family or friends. Strong emotional bonds and duties to family and friends always influence a person's decisions. Therefore, Fletcher's understanding of justice in situation ethics does not work.
Situation ethics can provide a clear and convincing case for justice being achieved in any one specific situation. Since Fletcher defines justice as 'love-distributed' the most loving outcome is by definition the most just one. Therefore, the moral agent can set laws that cause suffering to one side so that the needs of individuals are always prioritised.	The theory lacks safeguards as it relies only on the hope that all humans are good enough to deliver justice through love. A sceptic would say this is not practical, and history shows this hope is often misplaced. Applying situation ethics may promote justice in personal relationships but not in society as a whole.

This section covers AO2 content and skills

Specification content

The extent to which situation ethics promotes justice

AO2 Activity

It is now time to reflect on the information that has been covered so far and consider how it can be used for examination-style answers by practising the skills associated with AO2. AO2 involves 'analysis' and 'evaluation'. The exercise below will help you demonstrate these skills in relation to the extent to which situation ethics promotes justice. This will help you meet what is required by the higher bands: 'Thorough, sustained and clear views are given, supported by extensive, detailed reasoning and/or evidence.' (band 5 AS AO2)

For A Level, refer to the equivalent A Level band descriptors.

a Analyse three possible conclusions that could be drawn from the critical analysis and evaluation of the extent to which situation ethics promotes justice. Select evidence and examples to support each of the three conclusions. Select one conclusion that you think is the **most convincing** and explain why it is so.

b Now contrast this with the **weakest** conclusion of the three. Justify your argument with clear reasoning and evidence.

Specification content

The effectiveness of situation ethics in dealing with ethical issues

Exam practice

Below is an example of part of an evaluation of the effectiveness of situation ethics in dealing with ethical issues.

Sample answer

News reporter

Critical thinker

Situation ethics is summarised well and the technical aspect of the argument is already considered with the focus on relativism.

Situation ethics is a flexible theory because it is relativistic, meaning it judges each situation on its own facts. This is practical as it recognises the complexity of real life. It can help people make difficult choices where all traditional actions seem wrong. It works well by focusing on the unique situation rather than strictly applying a general rule.

Explorer

Tennis player

Good use is made of a scholarly view as a perspective on the question – there is also a sound line of argument.

Robinson argued that situation ethics is for human beings who have 'come of age'. This means that it provides a mature approach, giving people freedom and responsibility when faced with ethical issues. Rather than simply following rules, people can be open-minded and reason out their moral understanding.

Philosopher

A good challenge is identified here to the specific view under discussion.

However, Barclay criticised Fletcher's theory. He argued that the extreme examples Fletcher used – where an immoral act prevents greater harm – were not the only possible solutions. They could not be seen as guaranteeing the intended good result. Barclay felt the theory rested on rare, extraordinary situations, making it ineffective in dealing with everyday ethical issues.

Judge

A mini-conclusion is presented here which provides a clear judgement on the issue.

Against this, Fletcher emphasised that situation ethics promotes the principle of *agape* – selfless love which always puts others first. Arguably this focus on people over laws is key to dealing with ethical issues and it should naturally lead to fairness and justice.

However, Fletcher is very optimistic about human nature in giving so much freedom regarding ethical issues. People are often influenced by self-interest rather than selfless love. Ethical issues require rational thought and should not be based solely on a potentially biased personal viewpoint. In addition, as Barclay stated, 'there are things which can in no circumstances be right'.

Tennis player

This paragraph presents a strong counter-arguments fielding the question being asked and providing flow in the essay.

In my view, this is unfair to situation ethics. After all, Fletcher provided working principles to prompt people to stop and think carefully and rationally about what will happen because of their choices and decisions about ethical issues. This means the best decisions can be made for the best outcome for people.

Critical thinker

Here another new angle is presented by the student using their own suggestion and evidence.

Having said that, I also recognise that since Fletcher rejects any and all absolute moral rules apart from *agape*, there could be a risk of moral issues never being resolved by people. The ideas about right and wrong will constantly change for each situation and this leads to society being unable to share clear common values.

News reporter

This provides perspective on the issue by commenting on the lines of argument put forwards.

Yet Fletcher's approach is a new morality because in addressing ethical issues it recognises that the old ways of simply obeying rules and laws without looking at the situation will no longer work. This is particularly true in fast-changing modern societies. Having one principle of *agape* is therefore simple and very effective.

Explorer

Confident and perceptive analysis is provided here with a fresh insight into the question.

In conclusion, situation ethics is very effective in dealing with ethical issues. Today people need flexibility and freedom with all the various issues they are confronted with. There can be no universal deontological rules and therefore having the positive, personal and teleological principle of *agape* will always work best.

Judge

Critical thinker

The verdict is now in – it links back to the introduction. In this essay it is a clear-cut verdict that the theory's simplicity and flexibility make it effective.

Over to you

Below is a weak answer that a student has written in response to a question requiring evaluation of the extent to which situation ethics does not work. In a group, using the band level descriptors, place this answer in a relevant band that corresponds to the description inside that band. (It is obviously a weak answer and so would not be in bands 3–5.) To do this, it will be useful to consider what is missing from the answer and what is inaccurate. The accompanying analysis will assist you. When analysing the answer's weaknesses, think of five ways you would improve the answer to make it stronger. You may have more than five suggestions but try to negotiate as a group and prioritise the five most important things lacking.

Question

'Situation ethics does not work.' Evaluate this view.

Weak answer

Situation ethics is a moral theory that suggests human behaviour should be guided by the principle of *philia* (1). It argues that because God is love, individuals should follow their own emotional instincts in every situation (2). One of the four working principles is pragmatism, which requires a moral agent to think only about the person or people involved when making moral decisions (3).

Some might argue that a major reason for situation ethics not working is because it is too legalistic and tied to ancient traditions from the Middle Ages (4). However, others might argue that situation ethics does work because all it is based on is just instinctively doing the loving thing in every situation (5). The theory is essentially a form of natural law because it looks for purpose in nature (6). Finally, the Catholic Church endorsed situation ethics as a way to modernise Christian morality (7).

Overall, in some ways situation ethics works because it has the principle that love equals justice. On the other hand it does not work because it is based on religion (8).

Analysis

Point	Corrections needed
1	Identify the specific Greek term for 'sacrificial love' that Fletcher uses.
2	Explain why Fletcher views the theory as a 'reasoned' approach rather than an emotional or instinctive one.
3	There is some confusion here. How would you correct the statement to make it accurate in defining pragmatism?
4	Re-evaluate the historical context. When was the theory written and what was it a reaction *against*?
5	Statements like this are often used about situation ethics. How can you show that the theory does, in fact, have a clear framework to follow in making moral decisions?
6	Correct this statement naming and explaining the theory situation ethics is often linked to in moral decision-making. Think about using accurate vocabulary and specialist language.
7	Check on the information given in the previous sections and explain the position of the Catholic Church towards situation ethics.
8	Correct this statement and then decide on two strong, perceptive statements about why situation ethics works and why it does not. Then make a decision: where do you stand on the issue being evaluated and why?

C: Fletcher's situation ethics: application of the theory

This section covers AO1 content and skills

Specification content

The application of Fletcher's situation ethics to both (1) homosexual relationships and (2) polyamorous relationships

The application of Fletcher's situation ethics to homosexual relationships and polyamorous relationships

Homosexual relationships

During his lifetime, Fletcher wrote critically about law and morality. In 1960, he published an essay 'Sex Offenses: An Ethical View'. In this he argued that the Anglo-American legal approach to sex was inconsistent, hypocritical and unjust. He was especially critical of the Church's long-standing influence on government policy in this area:

- He believed that laws treating people with discrimination or prejudice based on their sexuality were outdated, legally unsound and certainly not Christian. He explicitly argued for legal reform.
- He noted the inconsistency that prostitution, adultery, fornication and sexual activity between women were *not* criminal offences, yet sexual activity between men *was* illegal.

When Fletcher wrote his essay in 1960, English law stated that sexual activity between men – even in private – was a crime of 'gross indecency'. It was under this law that Alan Turing (1912–54) was prosecuted in 1952.

Alan Turing

Alan Turing was a brilliant mathematician and is widely regarded as the father of theoretical computer science and artificial intelligence. During the First World War, he worked at Britain's codebreaking centre, Bletchley Park, where he designed the techniques and machines – most famously the 'bombe' – used to decipher codes from the German enigma machine. His work is estimated to have shortened the war by up to four years, and to have therefore saved countless lives.

While working at Manchester University, Turing was prosecuted for gross indecency with another man and was found guilty. To avoid a prison sentence, he accepted what can be described as chemical castration – a course of hormone injections which was regarded by some as a 'cure' for **homosexuality**. This medical treatment caused severe physical and mental deterioration. Turing died from cyanide poisoning – officially ruled as suicide but some evidence suggests accidental poisoning – in 1954.

In the same year the government set up a committee under Sir John Wolfenden to investigate the law on prostitution and homosexuality and its report was published in 1957. The main conclusion of the **Wolfenden Report** was that the government should decriminalise sexual acts between consenting men in private.

Fletcher supported the distinction made by the Wolfenden Report that the law should not be concerned with private 'immorality':

- The Wolfenden Report stated that the law should 'confine itself to those activities which offend against public order and decency or expose the ordinary citizens to what is offensive or injurious'.
- Fletcher agreed, asserting that any law based on a religious presupposition of sin is unreliable and controversial in a pluralistic culture. He believed the only valid reason for criminal law is the 'common interest, public order, or the collective good'.

Key terms

homosexuality: being sexually attracted to people of one's own sex

Wolfenden Report: a report published by the government in 1957; it recommended the decriminalisation of homosexual acts between consenting men over the age of 21 in private, and the strengthening of laws against prostitution and soliciting; it established a key distinction between private moral conduct and public order under the law

> **Key quote**
>
> We can only see a short distance ahead, but we can see plenty there that needs to be done.
>
> (Turing)

Fletcher tied his legal arguments directly to his ethical theory, using the core belief of situation ethics: concern for neighbour (*agape*/love):

- He stressed that ethics must be linked to social practice, meaning individual freedom can only be limited by the social or public interest.
- Crucially, he argued it was a mistake to let a specific religious view of wrongdoing or sin dictate the law.

Fletcher concluded that sex laws should be legally, not religiously, determined and restricted by only three criteria:

Gay Pride demonstration in London

- the age of consent
- infringement of public decency
- acts involving assault, violence, force or fraud.

This approach ensures the law protects people and public order while leaving the maximum possible scope for personal choice and freedom.

In 1967, the recommendation of the Wolfenden Committee was passed into law with the age of consent between homosexual males set at 21. Since then, various related laws have been passed: in 2000 the age of consent changed to 16, and in 2014 same-sex marriage was recognised by the state.

In 2009, Prime Minister Gordon Brown issued an apology on behalf of the government for the way that Alan Turing had been treated: 'On behalf of the British government, and all those who live freely thanks to Alan's work I am very proud to say: we're sorry, you deserved so much better.' Turing was given a posthumous royal pardon by Queen Elizabeth II in 2013.

> **Key quote**
>
> Society has a right to protect itself from danger within and without, and not to force a monistic and monopoly standard of personal (in the sense of private) conduct.
>
> (Fletcher)

Polyamorous relationships

Polyamory is the practice of having multiple romantic relationships simultaneously with the full knowledge and consent of everyone involved. While not having an exclusive relationship with one partner is not new, the modern concept of polyamory is distinct from practices like polygamy – marrying multiple spouses.

One possible example is the relationship between two famous French philosophers Jean-Paul Sartre and Simone de Beauvoir. They made a 'transparency' pact in 1929 to have a lifelong open relationship in which each would be transparent and honest about their various lovers. De Beauvoir wrote: 'What we have is an essential love; but it is a good idea for us also to experience contingent love affairs.'

> **Key quotes**
>
> The more you love, the more you can love—and the more intensely you love. Nor is there any limit on how many you can love.
>
> (Robert Heinlein)
>
> Those who want to love must want the freedom of the other.
>
> (Sartre)
>
> [...] if all men were angels, situation ethics would be the perfect ethics.
>
> (Barclay)

Polyamory is often misunderstood and there is no single standard model of **polyamorous** relationships. While the definition of the term is still evolving, it is typically defined by what it is, as much as what it is not:

- It requires honesty and consent and does not therefore involve one partner cheating on another.
- It makes love and commitment the priority over sexual encounters and therefore it is not promiscuous.
- It assumes complete equality between those in the relationships and therefore it is not polygamy, which usually involves marriage to multiple spouses (often one man to multiple women).

Despite varying forms (from informal to long-term commitments), ethical polyamorous relationships commonly share these central values:

- **Communication and negotiation**: Because there is no single agreed structure, all parties must continuously negotiate and clearly define the rules and terms of their specific relationship agreements.
- **Fidelity as loyalty – not exclusivity**: Fidelity is redefined as faithfulness to promises and agreements made within the relationship, rather than faithfulness to sexual exclusivity.
- **Trust, honesty and respect**: Full transparency about all relationships is essential to uphold the principle of consent.
- **Non-possessiveness and compersion**: While feelings of jealousy are acknowledged, they are treated as an individual's issue to manage and resolve. Compersion, which is the experience of taking joy in a partner's happiness with another partner, is often the goal.
- **Gender equality**: These relationships often actively challenge and avoid traditional, restrictive gender roles and expectations.

Jean-Paul Sartre and Simone de Beauvoir

Fletcher's situation ethics applied to homosexual and polyamorous relationships

As we have seen, Fletcher's situation ethics rejects legalism and antinomianism in favour of the *agapeic* approach, where *agape* is the boss principle and the only constant norm.

The application of this principle ensures that the moral evaluation of any sexual relationship is identical: a relationship is ethical if it maximises *agape*. This applies in the same way to homosexual and polyamorous relationships.

Fletcher's framework dictates that ethical judgement is based on the four working principles (pragmatism, relativism, positivism and personalism) and the six fundamental principles (for example, love is the only good and love equals justice). When applied, the framework leads to the following conclusions:

- **No predetermined assumptions**: Situation ethics refuses to judge any relationship based on pre-set moral or religious rules or principles. These might rule against homosexuality or sexual relationships between a man and women outside marriage. Situation ethics would ignore the rules and only be concerned with applying *agape* in each situation.
- **The sincerity of love**: The only valid moral assessment of a relationship is whether the love involved is sincere and the ideal of *agape* is upheld. If a relationship is characterised by honesty, consent and genuine love, it is ethically acceptable. In any same-sex relationship or any sexual relationship between two or more people it is possible for their situation to be one in which *agape* is best served.
- **The uniform standard**: Exactly the same standard and judgement of *agape* should be applied to homosexual and polyamorous relationships as to conventional monogamous heterosexual relationships. Any action that infringes on the law or human rights is wrong, but this applies equally to all relationship types.

Consequently, from the perspective of situation ethics, homosexuality and polyamory are not ethically wrong unless they violate the principles of love and justice; the same standard is applied to monogamy. The morality rests not on the structure, but on the presence of *agapeic* concern for the 'neighbour'.

Key terms

polyamorous: having a (loving) sexual relationship with more than one individual with the knowledge and consent of all partners

compersion: taking joy in a partner's happiness with another partner

Key quotes

Whether any form of sex [...] is good or evil depends on whether love is fully served.
(Fletcher)

To discard law is to discard experience.
(Barclay)

What sex probably needs more than anything is a good airing, demythologizing it and getting rid of its mystique-laden and occult accretions, which come from romanticism on the one hand and puritanism on the other.
(Fletcher)

Summary

- Fletcher argued that the laws about sexual offences in 1960 were outdated and inconsistent and needed reform.
- Alan Turing had been convicted under these laws and in 1957 the Wolfenden Report recommended that the government should decriminalise sexual acts between men in private.
- Fletcher agreed with the Wolfenden Report and stated that viewing an action, such as sex between gay people, as sinful in the religious sense could not be a basis for law.
- Fletcher stated that sex laws should be based on *agape* with the restrictions being age of consent, public decency, acts involving assault, violence, force or fraud.
- A polyamorous relationship is a romantic and/or sexual relationship with more than one individual with the knowledge and consent of all partners.
- Under situation ethics, the moral and legal approach for a monogamous heterosexual couple should be the same as that for a homosexual couple or a polyamorous relationship – the only principle should be *agape* with justice.

AO1 Activity

a Outline the key developments in law and attitudes towards homosexuality from 1952 to 2014.

b Write a paragraph explaining clearly what a polyamorous relationship is and the way in which compersion is significant.

For all questions, AO1 involves demonstrating knowledge and understanding. This exercise will help you in developing breadth and depth in these areas.

When completing these tasks, refer to the AO1 band descriptors for AS or A Level. Aim for thorough, accurate and relevant knowledge with depth and/or breadth, excellent use of evidence and examples and accurate use of specialist language in context. At band 5, a response demonstrates 'a very wide range of accurate and relevant information' that is 'clearly structured and well-organised'.

Issues for analysis and evaluation

Whether *agape* should replace religious rules

Possible line of argument	Critical analysis and evaluation
Agape is the core of many religions – Jesus and St Paul both taught that it was the greatest and most important of all religious rules.	Fletcher is partly correct because all religious rules involving human beings are about how they should relate towards each other. However, *agape* was never meant to replace all religious rules such as those involving justice, self-discipline, truth, honesty, faith and practical things like prayer.
By definition, religious rules cannot be replaced because they must come from God and in sacred texts they express God's will.	Situation ethics regards religious rules as being fixed and established in the past. When used as the basis for laws, these rules can cause injustice – such as in the case of Alan Turing; the principles of relativism and personalism state that all rules are entirely conditional in each situation.
Religious rules in all religions have developed over time and reflect the wisdom of the founders and the key figures of religions.	Barclay rightly argued that 'to discard law is to discard experience' – that is why *agape* is too simple a concept to replace religious rules; there is very little experience from the past about how *agape* can be used; however, *agape* as a principle is timeless and constant.
Replacing religious rules with *agape* is a good idea because it distributes the power of religious institutions; each person can understand and apply *agape* in their own way.	Religious institutions such as the Christian Church have many rules, such as that sex should not take place before marriage, which uphold the common good of society. However, there is no evidence today of the effectiveness or truth of these rules – for example, homosexual and polyamorous relationships, which are against the rules, contribute to a healthy, happy, diverse and loving society.
Religious rules, especially on morality, are based on reason, insight and the principles of self-discipline and self-control.	*Agape* remains too subjective, emotive and vague to replace religious rules – it also depends on all people being perfect or, as Barclay argues, being 'angels'; however, *agape* can have an important role, not in replacing religious rules but in guiding how they are interpreted over time in each situation.

This section covers AO2 content and skills

Specification content

Whether *agape* should replace religious rules

AO2 Activity

a Analyse three possible conclusions that could be drawn from the critical analysis and evaluation of the view that *agape* should replace religious rules. Select evidence and examples to support each of the three conclusions. Select one conclusion that you think is the **most convincing** and explain why it is so.

b Now select the conclusion that you think is the **least convincing** and explain why it is so.

When completing these tasks, refer to the AO2 band descriptors for AS or A Level. Aim for responses that demonstrate sustained and clear views, either of scholars or from a personal perspective, with extensive detailed argument and a clear conclusion. At band 5, a response offers 'a confident critical analysis and perceptive evaluation' with 'a well-constructed and reasoned argument leading to a convincing conclusion'.

Specification content

The extent to which situation ethics provides a practical basis for making moral decisions for both religious believers and non-believers

Exam practice

Below is an example of part of an evaluation of the extent to which situation ethics provides a practical basis for making moral decisions.

Sample answer

News reporter – An overview of the basic issue is provided along with a first line of argument being presented.

Situation ethics fits with the ethical approach of Jesus, who broke religious rules and dealt with everyone based on the circumstances. He healed on the Sabbath, which meant breaking the religious rule that stated: 'The Sabbath was made for the good of human beings, they were not made for the Sabbath.'

Tennis player – Here another argument is served and then countered, showing that the essay is beginning to flow.

Relativism makes the theory flexible because it gives believers personal freedom to decide the most loving action, which remains consistent with Jesus' teachings. The spirit of religious laws is also preserved as the theory is not antinomian – it has clear principles.

Philosopher – An interesting and relevant question is raised here which identifies one of the problems with situation ethics.

However, going back to the question, is there any practical element in situation ethics? The principles might seem rational but they are subjective and could provide support for and against any ethical principle.

Critical thinker – An original and creative example is given here, checking how the theory works.

For example, a person has hungry children and no money. Should they steal food from a small shop? Arguably the most *agape* would be generated by the person stealing the food. Yet it could be argued that the owner of the shop needs to receive an *agapeic* and just result, so their property should not be stolen.

Explorer / **Tennis player** – Here an alternative approach of law is introduced to both support and challenge the practical nature of situation ethics.

Barclay argued that 'to discard law is to discard experience'. According to him, laws have lasted because they are practical, which is not true of *agape*. However, following absolute laws can be impractical; they can be wrong and have had to change in the past, as in the case of the laws concerning homosexuality.

An advantage of situation ethics is that non-believers can understand *agape* in a non-religious sense. Fletcher's principles are all modern and democratic. For example, personalism is non-religious: it removes prejudice and focuses on the person and what would produce most *agape* for them.

Detective Here the evidence is examined carefully and a good example is presented as evidence.

Critics who argue there is nothing practical about situation ethics need to remember that the theory is modern and its effects are only gradually being felt. Situation ethics influenced many people to speak up, bringing about changes to the law about homosexuality and achieving equality for women in positions of leadership.

Philosopher Here a problem with situation ethics is raised and successfully challenged.

However, the outstanding problem with situation ethics is that Fletcher uses unusual examples, such as a mother killing her baby so that its cries do not betray where she and her family are hiding from attackers. Examples like this are too extreme, which shows that there is no everyday practical basis for decision-making in situation ethics.

Tennis player

Explorer Confident and perceptive analysis is provided here with a fresh insight into the question.

Situation ethics is a religious form of utilitarianism and it might be practical for Christians. For anybody else, it is not practical because *agape* has no relevance outside of the liberal Christian tradition.

Judge

Tennis player The essay ends with a confident verdict and it introduces a valid new point to end the match, completing the overall flow of the essay.

Over to you

Writing a good evaluation often involves weighing up the arguments and finding a counter-argument with a 'however' objection before providing your personal perspective.

For each of the five arguments below, identify if it is a strength or weakness of situation ethics. Then, write a 'however' objection to challenge the point. At the completion of the exercise, write a conclusion explaining where you stand with regard to situation ethics. In your answer, refer to the material covered in this sub-theme.

Question

'Situation ethics can only lead to immoral behaviour.' Evaluate this view.

Arguments

Argument	Strength or weakness?	Counter-analysis ('However ...')
If *agape* is the only criteria, an individual could justify harmful actions (like theft or lying) by claiming they were done out of love.		
By abandoning fixed moral rules (legalism), the theory removes the traditional safeguards that prevent people from behaving in a selfish or destructive manner.		

Argument	Strength or weakness?	Counter-analysis ('However ...')
Far from leading to immorality, situation ethics ensures that morality is always based on the highest good – love – preventing the immoral cruelty of following a rule when it causes harm.		
Since humans cannot accurately see the future, an action intended to be loving could accidentally result in disastrous and immoral consequences.		
The theory focuses on the needs of the person in the specific context. This prevents the immoral practice of sacrificing a person's well-being for the sake of an abstract religious law.		

D: Utilitarianism – classical utilitarianism by Jeremy Bentham

This section covers AO1 content and skills

Bentham's theory of utility

The term utilitarianism comes from 'utility', meaning 'usefulness'. This teleological ethical theory judges the morality of an action by its consequences (*telos*). Utilitarianism is a secular theory, rejecting religious authority and defining moral actions as those that produce the most utility.

The utility of an action is how much happiness it produces overall. The best moral action is the one that maximises happiness for everyone involved or minimises unhappiness. This is known as the **greatest happiness principle**.

Key person

Jeremy Bentham (1748–1832): An English philosopher, jurist and social reformer; he is best known as the founder of modern utilitarianism; after studying law at Oxford, Bentham went on to work as a lawyer and eventually dedicated his life to legal and social reform; he maintained that the value of legislation should be measured by its utility in increasing happiness or pleasure; his most famous work, *An Introduction to the Principles of Morals and Legislation*, published in 1789, introduced the principle of utility and his hedonic calculus, a method for calculating the greatest happiness

Jeremy Bentham is widely recognised as the founder of modern utilitarianism. As a social reformer and legal expert, Bentham was aware of social injustices in eighteenth-century Britain. His ethical theory was intended to be a practical tool for social and legal reform, promoting actions that would benefit the majority of people.

His guiding principle for public policy was 'the greatest happiness for the greatest number'. Bentham advocated for legal reforms such as reducing criminal penalties and reforming prisons, arguing that punishment should serve as a deterrent rather than inflicting suffering. His views on social issues like censorship and sexual activity reflect the moral standards of his time, but they were guided by the same utilitarian desire to improve public morality and general welfare. Bentham was a radical in his day, rejecting religion in favour of atheism and materialism. It was partly this that led him to put in his will that his preserved body should be publicly displayed in University College London where it still is today.

Bentham's ultimate ethical goal, or 'sovereign good', was happiness. He argued that humans are motivated by the pursuit of pleasure and the avoidance of pain. This view is a form of **hedonism**, the philosophical idea that pleasure is the sole intrinsic good.

While utilitarianism is teleological as it focuses on consequences, it is guided by a core rule known as the **principle of utility**. This principle states that the morally right action is the one that produces the greatest balance of good (pleasure/happiness) over evil (pain) for all affected. Therefore, every action can be measured by its capacity to either increase happiness or decrease pain. This provides a clear rule for assessing the moral value of any action by its consequences.

Specification content

Bentham's theory of 'utility' or 'usefulness'; ultimate aim is to pursue pleasure and avoid pain; principle of utility ('the greatest happiness for the greatest number')

Key term

greatest happiness principle: the utilitarian idea that the happiness and unhappiness each action will cause should be calculated to assess the best course to take

Jeremy Bentham

Key terms

hedonism: an ethical theory that defines what is right in terms of pleasure

principle of utility: an action is right if it promotes and maximises happiness

Key quote

Nature has placed mankind under the governance of two sovereign masters, pain and pleasure. It is for them alone to point out what we ought to do, as well as to determine what we shall do.

(Bentham)

Specification content

The hedonic calculus as a means of measuring pleasure in each unique moral situation; by considering seven factors: intensity, duration, certainty, remoteness, fecundity, purity and extent

The hedonic calculus

Having established that happiness is the ultimate measure of a morally right act, Bentham recognised the need for a way to calculate it. His solution was the hedonic calculus, a method designed to quantify the amount of pleasure and pain an action might produce. The right act was the one that produced the greatest amount of pleasure and the least amount of pain. The hedonic calculus measures how likely it is that the pleasure will actually occur.

Element of pleasure	Meaning
Intensity	How strong or powerful is the pleasure or pain? A more intense pleasure is more valuable than a weaker pleasure. The stronger the feeling, the greater its contribution to overall happiness.
Duration	How long will the pleasure or pain last? A more enduring pleasure is more valuable than a fleeting one. Whether an experience provides happiness over a long or short period is a key factor in its assessment.
Certainty	How likely is it that the pleasure will actually occur? The more certain a pleasure is to follow an action, the more valuable that action is.
Extent	How many people will be affected by the pleasure or pain? This shifts the focus from individual happiness to the well-being of the entire community. In keeping with the greatest happiness principle, an action that produces pleasure for a wider group is considered more morally valuable than one that benefits only a few.
Propinquity (remoteness)	How near in time – propinquity means nearness or proximity – is the pleasure or pain? A pleasure that will be experienced soon is more valuable than one that will be experienced in the distant future. Immediate gratification is weighed more heavily than a pleasure that is a long way off.
Fecundity	How probable is it that a pleasure will lead to further pleasures? An action that is fecund is one that has a high chance of generating more happiness in the future. For example, the pleasure of learning a new skill is fecund because it can lead to many future pleasures, like career success or new hobbies.
Purity	How probable is it that a pleasure will not be followed by pain? A pleasure is pure if it is unlikely to bring about a negative consequence. For example, the pleasure of a healthy meal is purer than the pleasure of eating too much processed food, which might lead to stomach discomfort and ill health later.

Bentham provided a useful verse to assist in remembering the key principles of the hedonic calculus:

Intense, long, certain, speedy, fruitful, pure –
Such marks in pleasure and pains endure.
Such pleasures seek, if private be thy end:
If it be public, wide let them extend.
Such pains avoid, whichever be thy view,
If pains must come, let them extend to a few.

A mnemonic to help you remember the initial letters of the hedonic calculus is: 'In Deep Concentration, Everyone Paints Fences Purple.'

Based on these criteria, Bentham argued that the hedonic calculus could be used to determine the correct course of action in any given situation. By applying the seven factors one could calculate the total amount of pleasure and pain that would result from a specific action. This 'balance' could then be compared against the outcomes of other available choices to identify the action that would produce the greatest overall happiness.

A key feature is the emphasis on the *quantity* of happiness rather than its *quality*. Bentham was not interested in prioritising certain forms of happiness over others, arguing that all pleasures are of equal value. Bentham expressed this idea with these words: '[...] the game of push-pin is of equal value with the arts and sciences of music and poetry'. This means that the simple pleasure of a children's game – push-pin – is, in a purely quantitative sense, just as valuable as the complex pleasure derived from music or poetry. The only thing that matters is the amount of happiness produced, not its source.

Key quote

Create all the happiness you are able to create; remove all the misery you are able to remove. Every day will allow you, will invite you to add something to the pleasure of others, or to diminish something of their pains.

(Bentham)

Act utilitarianism

The term **act utilitarianism** is typically associated with the work of Bentham. Under act utilitarianism, in every specific situation, a person should perform the act that will create the greatest amount of happiness.

Bentham's use of the hedonic calculus makes his theory a form of act utilitarianism. Each moral situation is unique and previous experiences or general rules are not always sufficient to make a moral choice. Therefore, in its strong form, act utilitarianism requires that the hedonic calculus be applied to every single action.

Act utilitarianism is a **relativistic** theory because it holds that there are no universal moral rules that apply to every situation. What is right or wrong is relative to the specific context and consequences of each individual act. It is not accurate to say that act utilitarianism favours the individual over the majority. In fact, it does the opposite – it requires the individual to choose the action that benefits the majority by producing the greatest overall happiness. While Bentham did not insist that the calculus be performed for every single act, the principle of his theory is that the rightness or wrongness of an act is always determined by its specific consequences.

As it considers consequences it is also known as a consequentialist theory. This means that ethical decisions and judgements, whether something is right or wrong, should be based on the outcome or the consequences. Does the action lead to the 'greatest happiness for the greatest number'?

Specification content

Act utilitarianism as a form of moral relativism, a consequentialist and teleological theory

Key terms

act utilitarianism: a form of utilitarianism associated with Bentham that treats each moral situation as unique and applies the hedonic calculus to each act to see if it fulfils the principle of utility – any action is right if it produces the greatest happiness for the greatest number

relativistic: this means there are no universal moral norms or rules and that each situation must be looked at independently because each situation is different

Summary

- ★ Utilitarianism is a secular ethical theory based on utility (usefulness).
- ★ Utility is the measure of happiness/pleasure produced by an action, weighed against the amount of pain or unhappiness it prevents.
- ★ Bentham argued that the utility of pleasure could be quantified using a method of calculation – the hedonic calculus.
- ★ The hedonic calculus measures the intensity, duration, certainty, extent, propinquity, fecundity and purity of every action.
- ★ Utilitarianism is teleological (as it has a goal in mind), relativistic (because there are no rules and everything is relative) and consequentialist (because it is based on the goal and outcome).

AO1 Activity

a Explain Bentham's principle of utility and the role of the hedonic calculus in applying it to moral decisions. This will help to consolidate your learning by developing the skill of applying and focusing on the ethical theory being studied.

b Examine how act utilitarianism might be applied to a decision you face in everyday life, such as whether to revise for examinations or go out with friends. Use the seven factors of the hedonic calculus to structure your answer. This will develop your skill of selecting and organising evidence and examples to support an explanation.

AO1 involves demonstrating knowledge and understanding. It is important to be familiar with how certain skills demonstrate these and how performance is measured (see the generic band descriptors for AS and A Level AO1). Band 5 requires: 'Thorough, accurate and relevant knowledge and understanding of religion and belief [...] coherent, clear and well-organised [...] extensive depth and/or suitable breadth [...] excellent use of evidence and examples.'

Issues for analysis and evaluation

The degree to which pleasure can be seen as the sole intrinsic good

This section covers AO2 content and skills

Specification content

The degree to which pleasure can be seen as the sole intrinsic good

Possible line of argument	Critical analysis and evaluation
Pleasure can be identified as a thing in itself. It is an observable, natural fact and the only thing good in itself – all other actions are only good if they result in pleasure.	Pleasure remains vague and entirely subjective – Bentham himself did not define pleasure – which means that it cannot be identified in any meaningful sense.
Common sense shows that there is general agreement that pleasure is the sole intrinsic good.	There is no universal understanding of what the sole intrinsic good might be (or even if there is such a thing) and some might argue that beauty, truth, justice or love, all of which were rejected by Bentham, have a stronger claim than pleasure.
Pleasure is the sole intrinsic good as it is vital for quality of life and well-being.	The focus on pleasure alone can create a person who is self-indulgent and who has a compulsion or addiction to seek ever new ways of achieving pleasure – one experience of pleasure is never enough.
Every person who is asked would agree that the pursuit of pleasure is their main goal in living their life.	Making pleasure the sole intrinsic good inevitably leads to the fragmentation of the community and society in general as each person has a selfish and self-centred approach to gaining their own particular form of pleasure without regard for other people.
Bentham's hedonic calculus helps to quantify pleasure and to make it a clear and rational sole good for individuals.	Pleasure cannot be quantified or measured according to a calculus; in addition, whether or not something causes pleasure cannot be guaranteed or predicted beforehand as it can only be known after the fact. Despite Bentham's attempts, there is never any guarantee of pleasure being achieved in the long term.

AO2 Activity

a Analyse the view that pleasure is the sole intrinsic good. Select evidence and examples to support your analysis, drawing on the possible lines of argument in the table above.

b Evaluate which conclusion you find most convincing and which you find least convincing. Justify your judgements with clear reasoning and evidence.

AO2 involves analysis and evaluation. It is important to be familiar with how these skills are demonstrated and measured (see the generic band descriptors for AS and A Level AO2). Band 5 requires: 'Thorough, accurate and relevant response to the issues raised [...] a coherent and well-reasoned argument [...] drawing on a range of views [...] with a well-structured and supported conclusion.'

Specification content

Evaluate the extent to which act utilitarianism works in contemporary society

Exam practice

Below is an example of part of an evaluation of the extent to which act utilitarianism works in contemporary society.

Sample answer

News reporter **Detective**

A clear overview of the debate about utilitarianism is provided along with accurate language and vocabulary.

Utilitarianism, as a teleological theory, holds strong appeal. Its goal, happiness, is realistic and widely accepted as the main aim for individuals and society. The pursuit of the greatest happiness for the greatest number underlies modern political democracy, proving its lasting value.

News reporter

Some good development of the opening paragraph is provided here, showing that the question is being thoroughly addressed.

Utilitarianism's aims are attractive: seeking pleasure and avoiding pain are fundamental human goals. The theory is generally easy to apply and aligns with common sense, mainly because it is consequentialist. By focusing on the results of actions rather than just intentions, it offers a crucial, practical basis for social law.

Detective

Here the evidence is provided which supports the deduction made.

The theory is not selfish; it promotes the common good and considers the welfare of everyone affected. Act utilitarianism is highly practical, concentrating on the specific situation and its outcome.

Critical thinker

Some detailed reasoning is given here which helps prepare the ground for challenging other aspects of the argument being made.

A major strength is that it treats everyone equally, giving no individual special treatment – a view consistent with contemporary ideals. Furthermore, act utilitarianism grants individuals autonomy because each act is judged separately; it avoids being overly restrictive. Happiness is the ultimate goal for many, and utilitarianism provides a clear guide for reaching it.

Critical thinker

Some useful critical reflections on the weaknesses of utilitarianism.

Despite its strengths, utilitarianism faces several key weaknesses. While seeking the greatest happiness, its framework can logically justify actions that harm a minority group if, by those actions, *overall* happiness is maximised. For example, torturing one person to force a confession that can be used to prevent a horrific crime against many. This is unacceptable in modern society as it violates basic principles of justice.

Philosopher

Some confident and perceptive evaluation is provided here by challenging utilitarianism's exclusive focus on outcomes.

The theory also tends to ignore motives and intentions. The way the greatest good is achieved becomes less important, implying that an injustice could be deemed the right action based only on the result. This contradicts common sense and the foundational role of justice in society.

Explorer

Connections are made here between the whole concept of morality and whether or not results can be predicted.

Moreover, applying the theory is arguably impossible. Morality relies on the outcome, but outcomes are not predictable (for example, in war or animal testing). To choose the best action, one must predict the results of all possible alternatives, which is a demanding task. Therefore, some argue act utilitarianism fails because we may never choose the action that truly delivers the greatest good.

Utilitarianism also fails to account for inherent duties (like a parent's obligation to protect their child). And it ignores the fact that people are fallible, often misjudging what will truly lead to happiness. Its practical use is further complicated by subjectivity; since happiness and pleasure differ for everyone, the theory lacks consistent social applicability.

Judge

This mini-conclusion provides a verdict by identifying how the personal qualities of moral agents undermine utilitarianism, effectively challenging the theory's focus on outcomes.

In conclusion, although parts of utilitarian theory are useful in society, using it as the sole basis for all ethical decisions remains questionable because of its potential to justify injustice and its impractical demand for perfect prediction.

Judge

This is a fair verdict on the theory. It recognises its good aspects, but makes clear that it faces serious obstacles in application.

Over to you

Below is a brief summary of two different points of view concerning whether or not act utilitarianism leads to immoral behaviour. You want to use these two views and lines of argument to write an evaluation to answer the examination question. However, these views need further reasons and supporting evidence to develop their arguments fully. They also need more use of specialist language and vocabulary along with the views of scholars.

Rewrite these two views in a fully evaluative style by adding further reasons and evidence that link to their arguments. Aim for a further 150 words.

When you have completed the task, refer to the band descriptors for A2 (WJEC) or A Level (Eduqas) and, in particular, look at the demands described in the higher band descriptors, which you should be aspiring towards. Ask yourself the following questions:

- Is my answer a confident critical analysis and perceptive evaluation of the issue?
- Is my answer a response that successfully identifies and thoroughly addresses the issues that the question raises?
- Is my answer a response with thorough, sustained and clear views which are supported by extensive, detailed reasoning and evidence?

Question

'Following act utilitarianism leads to immoral behaviour.' Evaluate this view.

Summary

Act utilitarianism could lead to immoral acts because it only cares about the outcome. If a large group of people gets a lot of pleasure from hurting one person, the theory might say this is the right thing to do. This is often called 'the tyranny of the majority'. It means that basic fairness is ignored. Under this system, an innocent person could be treated badly just because it makes a bigger group of people feel happy.

On the other hand, act utilitarianism is a moral system because it tries to stop pain. By looking at every situation on its own, it stops people from following rules as in other theories that might not work in a specific moment. It is a kind and fair way to make decisions because it wants the greatest good. It is flexible and it makes sure that moral choices are based on what is actually happening.

This section covers AO1 content and skills

Specification content

Mill's idea that not all pleasure is the same: 'higher pleasures' (intellectual) are superior to 'lower pleasures' (basic physical pleasure); the 'harm principle': the actions of individuals should be limited to prevent harm to other individuals

Key person

John Stuart Mill (1806–73): a British philosopher, political economist, civil servant and Member of Parliament; Bentham was his mentor and a close family friend; he was an influential liberal thinker and developed Bentham's utilitarianism; he focused more on the quality of pleasure rather than the quantity; he is often credited with introducing rule utilitarianism

E: Utilitarianism – John Stuart Mill's development

Mill's types of pleasure

John Stuart Mill was raised in the spirit of utilitarianism and was educated almost exclusively by his father, James Mill, a close friend of Bentham's. Mill came to believe that Bentham's theory was too simplistic in its approach to human happiness. He created a more sophisticated version of utilitarianism.

Mill equated happiness with good, and this is a view that can be found in the writings of Aristotle who referred to a life of happiness as *eudaimonia* (flourishing). Aristotle argued that pleasure was not just gratification but rather includes the idea of well-being, living well and being fulfilled. This is much closer to the view taken by Mill.

Higher pleasures

Mill argued that not all pleasures are of equal value.

Higher pleasures engage the mind, intellect and imagination. They are unique to human beings and are superior to physical ones. Mill thought that anyone who experienced both a higher and a lower pleasure would agree that higher pleasures are more satisfying and enduring. Examples include listening to music, reading poetry, engaging in philosophical debate or solving complex scientific problems. These activities enrich an individual's intellectual and emotional life.

Lower pleasures

Lower pleasures are those that are purely physical or sensual. They are shared with other animals and relate to bodily needs. Examples include eating, drinking or engaging in physical activity. While some of these pleasures are necessary for survival, they do not contribute to intellectual or moral development.

Mill stated: 'It is better to be a human being dissatisfied than a pig satisfied; better to be Socrates dissatisfied than a fool satisfied.' This shows his belief that a life rich in intellectual pursuits, even if it is unhappy or lacking, is fundamentally superior to a life of mere physical contentment. Mill was aware that often people do not choose the higher pleasure in preference to the lower pleasure. He felt that this was because they had not experienced both. Had they done so, they would have known that higher pleasures were more satisfying than the lower pleasures.

While Mill acknowledged that people must satisfy basic needs (lower pleasures) he said that the ultimate goal in life is to pursue the higher pleasures.

By making this distinction, Mill shifted utilitarianism away from Bentham's focus on the quantity of pleasure towards its quality. For Mill, the right action was no longer simply the one that produced the most happiness, but the one that produced the highest quality of happiness. This meant that an action resulting in a small amount of intellectual pleasure could be considered more valuable than an action that produced a large amount of purely physical pleasure. This addition made Mill's version of the theory more sophisticated, but also more complex to apply in practice.

The harm principle

Mill promoted the happiness of society as a whole

Mill was deeply involved in social reform and improving the welfare of society. His key contribution was the principle of universalisability, which is an essential part of his utilitarianism. Mill sought to establish that what is right or wrong for one person in a given situation is right or wrong for all. His argument for this principle can be broken down into three steps:

1 **Happiness is desirable**: Happiness is desirable in and of itself because every person desires their own happiness.

2 **Happiness is the only thing desirable as an end**: All other desirable things (such as money, virtue or power) are ultimately desired because they lead to happiness.

3 **The general happiness is the ultimate goal**: If each person's happiness is a good for them, then the general happiness is a good for all people. Therefore, everyone ought to act in a way that aims at the happiness of everyone.

This argument leads to the conclusion that individuals should put the interests of the group before their own. Mill's theory, in contrast to Bentham's act utilitarianism which focused on calculating the consequences of individual actions, aimed to establish a universal ethical framework. Mill's concept of universalisability implies a duty to act in a way that protects the happiness of society as a whole. This is still driven by the principle that the best action is the one that produces the greatest quality of happiness for the greatest number.

It was this thinking that led to Mill developing what has been called the 'harm principle'. In his book *On Liberty* he wrote:

> The only purpose for which power can be rightfully exercised over any member of a civilised community, against his will, is to prevent harm to others [...] The only part of the conduct of anyone, for which he is amenable to society, is that which concerns others. In the part which merely concerns himself, his independence is, of right, absolute. Over himself, over his own body and mind, the individual is sovereign.

Rule utilitarianism

In contrast to Bentham, Mill argued that past experiences can, and should, inform our moral decisions. He believed that humanity has already developed a set of moral rules that, when followed, generally lead to the greatest happiness for the greatest number. In **rule utilitarianism**, the morality of an action is judged not by its direct consequences, but by whether it conforms to a rule that, if followed by everyone, would lead to the best outcome. For example, instead of calculating the utility of every act of giving money to people in poverty, a rule utilitarian would simply follow the rule, 'Give to people in poverty,' because it is a rule that promotes general happiness.

Rule utilitarianism can be understood in two different forms:

- **Strong rule utilitarianism**: This holds that moral rules, once established, must never be broken. An action is right if it follows the rules that maximise happiness. These rules are considered absolute because they are the most effective way to produce the greatest good. The rules are not just guides; they are strict obligations that should be followed without exception.

Key terms

rule utilitarianism: a view associated with John Stuart Mill; rule utilitarians believe that by using the principle of utility (the greatest happiness for the greatest number) one can draw up general rules, based on past experiences, which will help to uphold the principle

strong rule utilitarianism: a strong rule utilitarian believes that any rules formulated and established through the application of the principle of utility should never be broken as they guarantee happiness for society

Specification content

Not all actions need to be morally assessed as actions are morally right if they conform to an historical rule that has demonstrated that it fulfils the principle of utility (now known as 'rule' utilitarianism); Mill's utilitarianism as a teleological/deontological hybrid

Key term

weak rule utilitarianism: a weak rule utilitarian tries to allow for the fact that, in some situations, breaking a rule (originally created because it generally fulfils the principle of utility) may be the right course of action; in a particular situation, breaking a rule (rather than keeping the rule) may make it more likely that the principle of utility is fulfilled

Key quote

All action is for the sake of some end, and rules of action, it seems natural to suppose, must take their whole character and colour from the end to which they are subservient.

(Mill)

- **Weak rule utilitarianism**: This allows for the possibility of breaking a rule in extreme circumstances to achieve a greater overall happiness. The rules are seen as valuable guidelines or 'rules of thumb' that should generally be followed because they are based on past experience and lead to the best outcomes. However, if a specific situation arises where breaking the rule would clearly lead to a significantly greater amount of happiness, the rule can be set aside. Mill is often associated with this weaker form, viewing rules as a way to save time and avoid recalculating utility in every situation, but not as unbreakable laws.

This latter view makes Mill's theory a kind of hybrid. It is deontological because it involves following a set of established rules, but it is also teleological because the ultimate justification for following (or breaking) those rules is the end goal of maximising happiness. The rules are not good in themselves but are valued because they lead to a good outcome.

Summary

- Mill's utilitarianism is qualitative, not quantitative, in looking at consequences.
- Mill does not define pleasure but instead distinguishes two types of pleasure: lower and higher pleasure.
- Mill rejects the use of the hedonic calculus and argues that rules have a place in utilitarianism.
- Strong rule utilitarianism means that the accepted rules of society are never broken, whereas weak rule utilitarianism means that the accepted rules of society can be broken if needed in exceptional circumstances.
- Utilitarianism is universalisable because the happiness of each individual is a good for them and each individual should act so that the greatest happiness of all can be achieved.

AO1 Activity

a Explain how weak and strong rule utilitarianism might work using the example of an ambulance breaking the speed limit – risking a crash involving other vehicles – in order to help someone who is suffering a medical emergency. This will help you to consolidate your learning by developing the skill of applying and focusing on the ethical theory being studied.

b Outline the differences between lower and higher pleasures by drawing a table with lower pleasures on one side and higher pleasures on the other. Examine how easy it is to separate the two. For example, consider whether playing sport at an advanced level is a lower or higher pleasure.

AO1 involves demonstrating knowledge and understanding. It is crucial to be familiar with how the performance of these skills is measured (see generic band descriptors band 5 for AS and A Level AO1):

1. **Knowledge** involves selection of accurate and relevant information directly related to the specific demands of the question.
2. **Understanding** involves explanation that demonstrates depth and/or breadth with excellent use of evidence, examples and specialist language.

Issues for analysis and evaluation

The extent to which rule utilitarianism provides a better basis for making moral decisions than act utilitarianism

Possible line of argument	Critical analysis and evaluation
Act utilitarianism gives the best application of the principle of utility, aiming to maximise happiness in every single action.	Bentham's act utilitarianism asks too much: applying the hedonic calculus each time leads to decision paralysis; act utilitarianism can also justify immoral actions to achieve the greatest overall happiness, leading to the tyranny of the majority.
Rule utilitarianism addresses the major weaknesses of act utilitarianism by establishing general moral rules (e.g. 'Do not lie') that maximise happiness when generally followed.	Rule utilitarianism avoids the demanding nature of act utilitarianism – by removing the need for the hedonic calculus – but the problem of rule utilitarianism being in part deontological presents itself when following a rule in a specific situation can lead to an unhappy/painful consequence (e.g. 'Do not lie', when lying would save a life).
Act utilitarianism is better because through the hedonic calculus it allows the maximum utility to be calculated in every single situation.	Rule utilitarianism maintains established moral practices and social trust – a society where everyone calculates utility case-by-case lacks the predictability and security necessary for the well-being of society as a whole; this means that ultimately rule utilitarianism is better as it leads to greater overall happiness.
Rule utilitarianism can just become act utilitarianism when dealing with exceptions to the rules, often by creating a complex system of sub-rules to cover every situation. Why not save the bother and use act utilitarianism instead?	If weak rule utilitarianism allows a rule to be broken whenever doing so maximises utility, then the rule no longer has any value; if strong rule utilitarianism prohibits breaking the rule even when a better outcome is certain, it sacrifices utility for the sake of the rule.
Rule utilitarianism provides a better framework for making moral decisions because its focus on general rules supports key moral concepts like justice and human rights.	By establishing rules that prohibit immoral actions and promote justice, rule utilitarianism ties in more closely with common-sense morality and protects individual rights from being sacrificed for collective gain – therefore, it is always superior to act utilitarianism.

This section covers AO2 content and skills

Specification content

The extent to which rule utilitarianism provides a better basis for making moral decisions than act utilitarianism

AO2 Activity

a Analyse three possible conclusions that could be drawn from the critical analysis and evaluation of the extent to which rule utilitarianism provides a better basis for making moral decisions than act utilitarianism. Select evidence and examples to support each of the three conclusions. Select one conclusion that you think is the **most convincing** and explain why it is so.

b Now contrast this with the **weakest** conclusion of the three. Justify your argument with clear reasoning and evidence.

AO2 involves the skills of analysis and evaluation. It is crucial to be familiar with how the performance of these skills is measured (see generic band descriptors band 5 for AS and A Level AO2).

Analysis and evaluation involves:

1. an attempt to reach a reasoned judgement
2. the use of scholarly views, evidence and reasoned argument to evaluate and critically analyse the issue
3. a clearly expressed point of view sustained throughout.

Specification content

Whether utilitarianism promotes immoral behaviour

Exam practice

Below is an example of part of an evaluation of whether utilitarianism promotes immoral behaviour.

Sample answer

The key question about utilitarianism is whether its focus on consequences and individual judgement opens the door to immoral behaviour.

Detective: A clear overview of the debate about utilitarianism and immoral behaviour is provided which means we know what is going to be investigated.

Proponents of religious and absolute moral systems argue that morality comes from universal, objective rules, often given by God. They view a secular theory like utilitarianism as in essence unreliable. They believe a system that is applied differently by different people will inevitably lead to wrongdoing.

News reporter / **Tennis player**: Some good points are made here which can be used in the back and forth of the discussion – the paragraph presents the points clearly.

Another criticism is that pleasure/happiness, the goal of utilitarianism, is completely subjective. Since people define the terms differently, two similar moral problems could be solved in opposite ways, resulting in immoral behaviour towards those involved.

Critical thinker: Here analysis is provided of the key issues with utilitarianism and immoral or moral behaviour.

Despite this, utilitarianism – especially Mill's version – is based on a democratic idea: promoting the greatest happiness for the greatest number. Mill's harm principle also acts as a vital defence against misuse and immorality.

Judge The points made here are strong and valid ones which make this paragraph a mini-conclusion.

Arguably, even Bentham's hedonic calculus considers the pleasure and pain of everyone affected by an action. In this sense, the theory itself promotes a broad, fair consideration of consequences, which is a form of justice, not immorality.

Critical thinker **Tennis player** A strong return against the previous paragraph which brings in Bentham. There is also a clear appraisal of the strengths of Bentham's utilitarianism.

Furthermore, act utilitarianism is flexible, taking the details of each situation into account. This makes it more moral than rigid, absolute theories which evaluate, and then forbid or demand, actions without looking at the context of each situation. Absolute systems can promote what Arthur Miller called the 'immorality of morality' – forcing an unhappy/painful outcome just to keep to what seems to be a moral rule.

Tennis player **Philosopher** Some confident and perceptive evaluation is provided here, challenging and questioning the issues raised. The scholarly quote is very helpful.

However, act utilitarianism can also promote immoral behaviour because it has the potential to favour the sacrifice of the welfare of a few for the benefit of the many. It could justify brutal acts, such as the torture of an innocent person, if they somehow led to the greatest happiness for a large majority. This is why many people believe act utilitarianism encourages injustice and immoral behaviour.

Explorer Here an alternative way of looking at the problem of act utilitarianism is provided.

Rule utilitarianism attempts to solve this problem. Weak rule utilitarianism involves following established moral rules, for example, 'Do not lie', that promote overall happiness, but allowing for exceptions when a situation truly demands it. This offers consistency and fairness and avoids the complete inflexibility of absolutism.

Detective Here the paragraph examines the evidence in favour of rule utilitarianism.

In conclusion, no ethical system is designed to *promote* immoral behaviour. Accusations of immorality usually stem from how a theory is carelessly or ruthlessly applied in the real world, rather than from a flaw in the theory itself.

Judge **Critical thinker** The verdict is now in – it is balanced and fair. In this essay it is an open verdict which also challenges the basis of the wording of the question.

Over to you

a Read the response on page 196 carefully. It is about the issue of utilitarianism promoting moral behaviour.

b The response is very one-sided. Your task is to complete the table below with counter-arguments to the claims from the response. When you have completed the task, refer to the band descriptors for A2 (WJEC) or A Level (Eduqas) and, in particular, look at the demands described in the higher band descriptors, which you should be aspiring towards. Ask yourself the following questions:

- Do my counter-arguments help to show a confident critical analysis and perceptive evaluation of the issue?
- Do my counter-arguments help to identify and thoroughly address the issues that are raised?

Claim from the response	Counter-argument
Utilitarianism always promotes moral behaviour. It demands that morality is based on the observable reality of human experience.	

Claim from the response	Counter-argument
[...] utilitarianism recognises the truth that the only intrinsic good is the promotion of pleasure and the prevention of pain.	
This is the only truly moral approach because it is entirely impartial [...]	
By focusing on the consequences of actions, it ensures that morality serves humanity rather than forcing humanity to serve outdated, rigid rules.	
Ultimately, the promotion of the greatest good for the greatest number is the only objective standard we have.	
To reject this is to suggest that there is something more important than the actual pleasure of sentient beings [...]	

Question

'Utilitarianism promotes moral behaviour.' Evaluate this view.

Response

Utilitarianism always promotes moral behaviour. It demands that morality is based on the observable reality of human experience. Other theories hide behind abstract rules or religious traditions, but utilitarianism recognises the truth that the only intrinsic good is the promotion of pleasure and the prevention of pain. This is the only truly moral approach because it is entirely impartial – the stranger is treated as equally as the friend. By focusing on the consequences of actions, it ensures that morality serves humanity rather than forcing humanity to serve outdated, rigid rules. A system that would allow a person to suffer simply because a rule was followed is not a moral system. Ultimately, the promotion of the greatest good for the greatest number is the only objective standard we have. To reject this is to suggest that there is something more important than the actual pleasure of sentient beings, a claim that is logically and ethically indefensible since only utilitarianism promotes moral behaviour.

F: Utilitarianism – applications

This section covers AO1 content and skills

Specification content

The application of Bentham's act utilitarianism and Mill's rule utilitarianism to both animal experimentation for medical research and the use of nuclear weapons as a deterrent

Key terms

dissection: the action of cutting open a body or plant to study its internal parts

vivisection: the practice of performing operations on live animals for the purpose of experimentation or scientific research, generally – but not always – done today with anaesthetised animals

Animal Aid: a charity founded in 1977 that promotes animal welfare through legal and non-violent means, and argues against the use of animals for medical research

Applying utilitarianism to animal experimentation

Animals have been used for medical research through **dissection** and **vivisection** for hundreds of years. In the sixteenth century, for example, William Harvey carried out pioneering work on blood circulation using both vivisection – at that time without any anaesthetic – and dissection on animals such as dogs, deer, sheep, birds, frogs and fish.

William Harvey

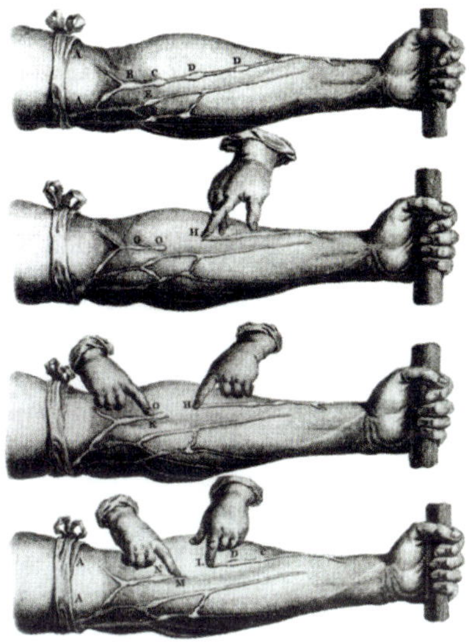

William Harvey's experiments on the valves of the vein of the human arm

Applying ethical theories to the issue of animals and medical research is complicated because the benefits are widely disputed. The key point is the question of whether animal experimentation is genuinely useful:

- **Arguments against usefulness**: Some argue that the practice is ineffective and misleading. The biological differences between humans and other animals mean that a drug or treatment that works on an animal may not work on a human or could even be harmful. Many animal tests are unreliable and alternative research tools, such as cell cultures, computer models and artificial intelligence, and human-based research, are more accurate and ethical.
- **Arguments for usefulness**: Some argue that the practice has been essential for almost every major medical breakthrough in the last century. The development of vaccines, antibiotics and surgical techniques is the direct result of animal testing. Some research into complex diseases, and the effects of new drugs, cannot be done on humans for ethical reasons, making animal models a necessary step before clinical trials can begin.

Arguments against animal experimentation

Pressure groups like **Animal Aid** dispute the usefulness of animal research. A core principle is its rejection of the belief that humans are superior to animals. Animal Aid rejects experiments that involve causing pain or stress to animals, such as those involving electric shocks, starvation or deprivation. They argue that studying animals is often an ineffective way to understand human behaviour.

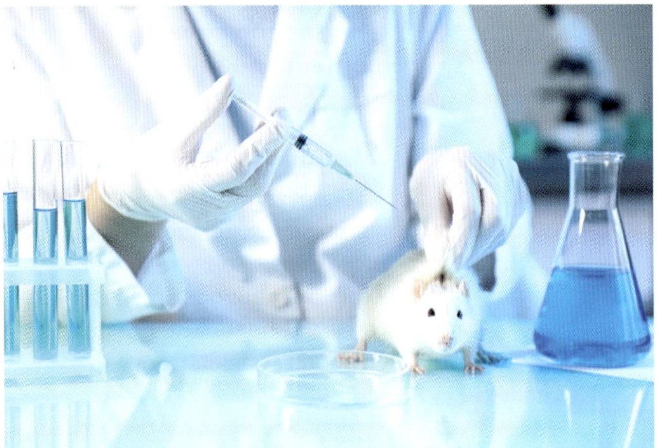

An animal laboratory for experimentation

Animal Aid and other opponents of animal research also highlight cases where animal studies have been misleading. For instance, the link between a damaged pancreas and diabetes was first observed in human autopsies during the eighteenth century. However, because early scientists were unable to replicate the condition in laboratory animals, this theory was not pursued for many years, delaying medical progress. This example serves as evidence that animal models can sometimes hinder, rather than help, scientific discovery.

Animal Aid has much to say about the historical results of medical research using animal experimentation. They argue that:

- much medical research, including into diseases like cancer, is repetitive and pointless
- we have enough drugs – only 200 are necessary to human health and yet there are thousands available through marketing and retail competition
- animal experiments are unreliable; for example, penicillin is useful for humans but kills guinea pigs and hamsters, and chloroform kills dogs but anaesthetises humans
- it has been known for drugs tested and found to be safe on animals to have subsequently caused human deaths
- many cancers are preventable and so we should focus on eliminating causes and not searching for cures.

Gill Langley campaigns against the use of animal experimentation in medical research. She argues that medical history shows that an understanding of health and disease has been set back due to animal research and experimentation. For Langley there are two major uncertainties:

- There are significant species differences in anatomy, metabolism, physiology and pharmacology caused by underlying genetic variations. These variations limit the application of laboratory animal results to humans. For example, mice are the most used species in medical research. Langley observes: 'There are at least 67 known discrepancies in immunological functions between mice and humans – hardly surprising, since our species diverged between 65 and 75 million years ago.'
- Human illnesses are researched in animals because there is a lack of knowledge and the causes and progression of a human condition are unknown. However, an animal model is usually developed based on a narrow range of human symptoms, and upon an ignorance of the distinction between causes and outcomes of illness. Langley compares Parkinson's disease and the contrasting symptoms in humans and marmosets and argues: 'The marmoset model is simplistic compared to the human condition, involving a more limited number and type of brain cells [...] marmosets do not develop the pathological hallmark of Parkinson's disease.'

Arguments for animal experimentation

The counter-argument can be seen in groups such as **Understanding Animal Research (UAR)**. UAR states that it 'supports the humane use of animals in biomedical research, and believes that animal research is a vital part of the scientific process'.

Key quotes

The question is not, can they reason? nor, can they talk? but, can they suffer?

(Bentham)

To discriminate against beings solely on account of their species is a form of prejudice.

(Singer)

Key term

Understanding Animal Research (UAR): a society that explains why animals are used in medical and scientific research

Key quote

That which is morally wrong cannot be scientifically right. To seek one's own advantage regardless of the cost to other sentient beings is to renounce humanity.

(Kingford)

UAR has presented a number of arguments:

- Animal research has played a vital part in nearly every medical breakthrough over the last decade.
- We share 95 per cent of our genes with a mouse, and animals suffer from diseases that are similar to those that humans suffer from, including cancers, tuberculosis, flu and asthma.
- All veterinary research has relied on the use of animal research.
- Non-animal methods cannot replace all use of animals.
- As a result of medical experimentation on animals there have been many breakthroughs, in discovering, developing or perfecting:
  - modern anaesthetics
  - the tetanus vaccine
  - penicillin
  - insulin
  - hip replacement surgery
  - kidney transplants
  - heart transplants
  - blood transfusions
  - herceptin (a humanised mouse protein), which increases the survival rate for breast cancer
  - highly active antiretroviral therapies (HAART), to ensure that acquired immunodeficiency syndrome (AIDS) is no longer terminal
  - asthma inhalers
  - modern vaccines, including those against polio, tuberculosis, meningitis, papillomavirus and smallpox (which has been eradicated from the earth thanks to research in animals).

UAR also argues as follows:

- Dogs, cats and primates altogether account for less than 0.2 per cent of research animals, and 97 per cent of research in the UK is done on mice, rats, fish and birds.
- The UK has some of the highest standards of laboratory animal welfare in the world.
- All research in the UK must be approved by the Home Office, and the researchers and institutions doing the research must be licensed by the Home Office.
- Ethics committees exist to ensure that the potential benefits of research outweigh any suffering to the animals. Animal welfare is underpinned by the 3Rs – there is a legal requirement to **replace** animals with alternatives, **refine** experimental techniques and **reduce** the numbers of animals used in research.

Albert Sabin, who developed the polio vaccine, stated: 'Without animal research, polio would still be claiming thousands of lives each year,' and the former CEO of the Medical Research Council, Professor Colin Blakemore, argued that '[primates] are used only when no other species and no alternative approach can provide the answers to questions about such conditions as Alzheimer's, strokes, Parkinson's, spinal injury, hormone disorders, and vaccines for HIV'.

Bentham and act utilitarianism

Bentham's approach is rooted in the principle that the capacity to suffer, not the ability to reason, is what gives a being moral standing: animal pain is morally relevant and must be included in any ethical calculation.

Key quote

For over 150 years research using animals has advanced scientific understanding of human and animal health and the impact of the environment on wildlife. This research should never be undertaken lightly and animals should only be used when there is no alternative method available.

(UAR)

Key quotes

[...] a full-grown horse or dog, is beyond comparison a more rational, as well as a more conversable animal, than an infant of a day or a week or even a month, old [...] Why should the law refuse its protection to any sensitive being? The time will come when humanity will extend its mantle over everything which breathes [...]

(Bentham)

Even if some individual experiments may be justified, this does not mean that the institutional practice of experimenting on animals is justified. Given the suffering that this routinely inflicts on millions of animals, and that probably very few of the experiments will be of significant benefit to humans or to other animals, it is better to put our resources into other methods of doing research that do not involve harming animals.

(Singer)

Key term

deterrent: a thing that discourages or is intended to discourage someone from doing something

An act utilitarian would apply the hedonic calculus to each individual experiment to weigh the total amount of pleasure against the total amount of pain. This is a difficult calculation. The pain inflicted on animals is certain, intense and often of long duration. The potential benefits for humans are often uncertain and may not be realised for many years. From this perspective, the certain suffering of animals could easily outweigh the uncertain future happiness of humans. Therefore, a strict act utilitarian would likely argue against many forms of animal testing.

Mill and rule utilitarianism

Mill's approach differs significantly due to his distinction between higher and lower pleasures and his adoption of rule utilitarianism:

- **Higher and lower pleasures**: Mill argued that the intellectual and moral pleasures derived from scientific discovery are qualitatively superior to the physical pains experienced by animals. Since animals cannot experience these higher pleasures, their suffering is less valuable in the moral equation. As Julia Driver noted, 'Animals do have moral standing in virtue of their sentience [...] [but] their moral standing is not the same as that of persons.' This distinction would likely lead a utilitarian following Mill to support animal experimentation.
- **Strong rule utilitarianism**: Proponents of this form of rule utilitarianism would not judge each experiment individually. Instead, they would ask whether a moral rule allowing for animal experimentation would lead to the greatest overall happiness if everyone followed it. They would most likely support animal testing, as the rule would lead to new medicines and treatments that bring a great deal of happiness to humanity.
- **Weak rule utilitarianism**: Proponents of this form of rule utilitarianism would view rules about animals as flexible guidelines that can be set aside if a specific situation promises a greater balance of pleasure over pain. While a general rule might permit experimentation for medical progress, the rule could be suspended if a particular experiment is deemed to cause excessive suffering with little benefit. While this offers flexibility, it could be argued that it is nothing more than act utilitarianism as the merits of each case eventually override the rule itself.

Applying utilitarianism to the use of nuclear weapons

The issue of nuclear deterrence is a complex ethical problem for utilitarianism because the theory focuses on consequences. The ethical debate for utilitarianism is not about their use, but about their possession as a **deterrent**. The concept of deterrence is that a nation's possession of a nuclear arsenal prevents other nations from attacking it, thus preventing a catastrophic war. A utilitarian must weigh the risk of a nuclear war against the benefits of preventing conventional warfare.

The use of nuclear weapons marked the end of the Second World War with the bombing of Hiroshima and Nagasaki in August 1945. The ethical justification for this act has been debated using utilitarian principles, but most agree that the consequences of a nuclear war today would be catastrophic, potentially ending human civilisation. For a consequentialist theory like utilitarianism, which judges an action by its results, the use of nuclear weapons is morally indefensible. The immense pain and suffering caused far outweighs any possible benefit; there is no long-term happiness to be gained that could justify their use.

The utilitarian dilemma is whether the peace brought about by deterrence outweighs the risk of a nuclear war and the pain of living under the constant threat of a global catastrophe. A utilitarian must ask whether the world is a happier, safer place with these weapons in existence, even if they are never used. Also, given the financial cost of nuclear deterrents, would the money be better used to address global issues, such as global poverty, famine and disease, or national issues, such as health and education?

Arguments against nuclear deterrence

The **Campaign for Nuclear Disarmament (CND)**, argues for the abolition of nuclear weapons. Their case is based on a series of ethical, legal and practical arguments that challenge the concept of nuclear deterrence:

- **Immoral and illegal**: CND argues that nuclear weapons have no legitimate purpose. Their use would be illegal under international law in almost every circumstance because they are indiscriminate, causing unavoidable civilian casualties. The potential for these weapons to cause widespread death makes them genocidal and completely immoral.
- **Disproportionate power**: A single modern nuclear missile is far more powerful than the bombs dropped on Hiroshima and Nagasaki in 1945, which killed an estimated 240,000 people. The destructive power of these weapons means that their use would not only cause immense loss of life but also inflict long-term suffering and death on immediate survivors through radiation.
- **Global consequences**: The effects of a nuclear detonation would not be confined to a specific area. The radioactive fallout from a weapon like the UK's Trident missile would have no geographical boundaries. Furthermore, recent research suggests that even a so-called 'small exchange' of 50 nuclear weapons could bring about a 'nuclear winter', leading to the most dramatic climate change in recorded human history and potentially causing a global famine that could kill more people than were killed in the entirety of the Second World War.
- **Irrelevance to modern threats**: CND contends that nuclear weapons are irrelevant to today's most pressing security threats. They cannot be used to counter challenges such as terrorism, cyber warfare or climate change, making them an outdated and ineffective tool for genuine national security.
- **Unjustifiable cost**: The UK government estimates that the cost of four new submarines carrying nuclear weapons will be £31–£41 billion. CND estimates that the running costs for the whole lifetime of these submarines will be in the region of £200 billion.

Key term

Campaign for Nuclear Disarmament (CND): a pressure group formed in 1957

CND march in 1983

Key quote

Before nuclear weapons, major powers embarked on two of the most destructive wars imaginable. Many millions died, millions more suffered. Yet, for all the conventional conflicts since, and there have been many of them, there has not been major conflict between nuclear armed states. The devastating possibilities of nuclear war have helped maintain strategic stability.

(Fallon)

Ministry of Defence building in London

Arguments for nuclear deterrence

In 2016, the former UK Defence Secretary Sir Michael Fallon outlined the government's approach to nuclear deterrence. He argued that nuclear deterrence is necessary for three key reasons:

- **Realism**: A realistic view of the current world shows that threats are increasing, not diminishing. Nuclear threats from countries like Russia and North Korea are still present, and other nations are not disarming. Therefore, for the UK to unilaterally disarm would be a naive act of weakness that would not convince other nuclear states to follow suit. The only way to achieve global disarmament is by working multilaterally.
- **Responsibility**: The UK has a moral and political responsibility to protect its own people and its allies. Nuclear weapons are not meant to address threats like terrorism, but rather to deter the most extreme dangers a nation could face. The UK's independent nuclear deterrent also strengthens NATO by providing a third centre of decision-making alongside the USA and France, complicating the calculations of potential adversaries. To abandon this role would be to weaken the alliance and encourage adversaries.
- **Relevance**: Nuclear deterrence is relevant for the foreseeable future. Since no one can predict the geopolitical landscape in the next 30 to 40 years, it would be irresponsible to give up a key form of security insurance. The nuclear deterrent has helped maintain peace between major powers for decades and abandoning it would not make the UK safer. Fallon argued: 'Deterrence means convincing any potential aggressor that the benefits of an attack are far outweighed by its consequences.'

Overall, the official case for the UK's retention of a nuclear deterrent is based on its role in maintaining national security and international stability. It is argued that by having its own nuclear deterrent, the UK can have independent decision-making along with command and control over the use of nuclear force. Only the minimum deterrent is maintained, based on submarines which are intended to be invulnerable and undetectable. Such a deterrence is credible in that it could be used if necessary; this contributes to international security as no country would take the risk of launching a first strike against the UK.

Bentham and act utilitarianism

An act utilitarian, following Bentham's approach, would analyse nuclear deterrence by applying the hedonic calculus to the possession of nuclear weapons. This is an extremely difficult calculation, as it involves weighing a number of potential consequences:

- **The case for deterrence**: The threat of a nuclear attack has prevented large-scale wars between major powers since 1945. The happiness produced by this period of relative peace, avoiding the immense pain and death of conventional warfare, could be seen as outweighing the fear and risk associated with nuclear weapons. The extent and duration of this peace would be considered key factors.
- **The case against deterrence**: The potential for a nuclear war, however remote, represents an almost infinite amount of pain and suffering, as a global nuclear exchange could lead to the end of human civilisation. The low probability of this outcome has to be weighed against the immensity and intensity of the potential pain. Therefore it could be argued that the risk is simply too great to justify the policy, especially given the ongoing cost of maintaining a nuclear arsenal.

Bentham's approach is highly problematic here because the scale of the consequences makes the calculus almost impossible to perform.

Mill and rule utilitarianism

Mill's approach, which distinguishes between higher and lower pleasures and focuses on rule utilitarianism, provides a different perspective:

- **Rule utilitarianism**: A rule utilitarian would not judge the possession of each individual weapon but would ask if a rule that states, 'A nation should possess a nuclear deterrent,' would, if universally followed, lead to the greatest overall happiness.
- **The case for deterrence**: A rule utilitarian would likely support a policy of nuclear deterrence. The higher pleasure of a stable, secure society where people are free to pursue intellectual and moral development is seen as more valuable than the pain and fear associated with the deterrent. Mill's harm principle, which states that the only justification for limiting an individual's liberty is to prevent harm to others, could be extended to the state. The possession of a nuclear deterrent could be seen as a necessary means of preventing the ultimate harm of aggression from adversaries, just as an equipped police force is judged to be necessary to prevent aggressive behaviour within a state's borders.
- **The case against deterrence**: A weak rule utilitarian might argue that in an era of terrorism and cyber warfare, nuclear deterrence is no longer effective and may even increase instability. A rule that creates such a high risk of global devastation may not be justified.

Ultimately, both forms of utilitarianism struggle with the issue. Act utilitarianism is paralysed by the impossibility of the calculation, while rule utilitarianism can justify the deterrent by prioritising the higher pleasures of peace and security, even with the immense risk involved.

Again, regarding the use of the happiness principle (that aims to assess which course of action is the best based upon happiness), and the principle of utility (that 'promotes pleasure and avoids pain'), it would all depend upon how one classifies happiness, pleasure and pain.

Both sides of the debate propose very positive scenarios. On one hand (against deterrence), state money could be better spent; on the other hand (for deterrence), safety and protection is an invaluable investment and insurance.

Summary

- ★ The benefits and costs of medical research on animals are disputed.
- ★ Animal Aid rejects the idea that humans are superior to animals and argues that medical research on animals is ultimately ineffective and unnecessary.
- ★ UAR argues that medical research using animals is essential to medicine and science and has brought about many breakthroughs for the benefit of humankind.
- ★ Based on the animals involved in medical experimentation suffering pain, act utilitarians would tend to oppose this practice, while rule utilitarians would tend to support it because of the greater happiness it can provide for humans.

- If a country has nuclear weapons, it is argued that other countries will then be deterred from launching a nuclear attack against it.
- CND argues that nuclear deterrence increases the risk of nuclear war and that the money spent on nuclear weapons could be better spent in other areas.
- Both act and rule utilitarianism would find nuclear deterrence a problematic issue as the consequences of having or not having deterrence are impossible to calculate – overall does deterrence promote the greatest happiness for society or not?

AO1 Activity

a Examine the arguments for and against animal experimentation and nuclear deterrence. Using clear examples and quoting scholars named in this sub-theme, create a table with three supporting statements and three opposing statements for each issue. This will help to consolidate your learning by developing the skill of using quotations, evidence and examples.

b For both animal experimentation and nuclear deterrence, outline the approach which would be taken to them by:

i act utilitarianism

ii rule utilitarianism (both strong and weak).

This will help to develop further your understanding of the ethical theory and how to apply it in a practical way.

To see how well you are doing, refer to the generic band descriptors for AS/A Level AO1. In order to reach band 5, your work must demonstrate 'thorough, accurate and relevant knowledge and understanding of religion and belief'.

Issues for analysis and evaluation

The extent to which utilitarianism promotes justice

Possible line of argument	Critical analysis and evaluation
Rule utilitarianism promotes justice because it is based on accepted rules of society which maintain and protect collective happiness.	Mill intended rule utilitarianism to be the foundation for a fair and just society – it is not based on individual self-interest but on the idea that promoting each individual's happiness is part of promoting the happiness of all.
Act utilitarianism promotes self-interest as it ignores rules, which are needed for justice, and applies the hedonic calculus to individual acts.	Bentham did not show much interest in the concept of society or community as he believed all that could be measured was an individual's pleasure and pain in response to each individual act – he deliberately avoided rules, principles, duties and the like, which it could be argued are essential in the pursuit of justice.
Rule utilitarianism does not promote justice as it is unable to reconcile the pleasure/happiness of the majority with the pain/unhappiness of the minority.	Mill's form of utilitarianism is intended to be democratic – applying the accepted rules of society, not absolutist principles. This means that, as in any democracy, for justice to be promoted, the will of the majority must take precedence over the will of the minority.
Mill's harm principle is an effective safeguard in promoting justice by asserting that an individual's liberty should only be restricted to prevent harm to others. Individuals are sovereign over themselves but have no right to perform actions that infringe upon the well-being of others.	The harm principle may protect personal freedom, but it fails to guarantee absolute justice. In cases where punishing an innocent person prevents greater social harm, utilitarian logic could still justify injustice to benefit the majority. This risks a 'tyranny of the majority' where individual rights are sacrificed for the general good.
Utilitarianism does promote justice as it is based on a common-sense approach to what pleasure and happiness mean.	There is a fundamental injustice in utilitarianism because an adequate definition of pleasure and happiness is not given – this raises the question of who decides what will cause pleasure and happiness and what their decision is based upon.

This section covers AO2 content and skills

Specification content

The extent to which utilitarianism promotes justice

AO2 Activity

a Evaluate three possible conclusions that could be drawn from the critical analysis and evaluation of the view that utilitarianism promotes justice.

b Select the conclusion you find **most convincing** and analyse the **strongest challenge** that could be made against it. Explain how one might respond to the challenge.

To see how well you are doing, refer to the generic band descriptors for AS/A Level AO2. In order to reach band 5, your work must demonstrate 'thorough, accurate and relevant knowledge and understanding of religion and belief'.

Specification content

The extent to which utilitarianism provides a practical basis for making moral decisions for both religious believers and non-believers

Exam practice

Below is an example of part of an evaluation of the extent to which utilitarianism provides a practical basis for making moral decisions for both religious believers and non-believers.

Sample answer

News reporter

A good overall understanding and overview of the implications of the question is shown here.

Utilitarianism is a secular ethical theory which has no foundation in religious laws or beliefs. This limits its use as a practical basis for making moral decisions for believers. However, it could be practical in a society which has a diverse population including believers of multiple religions and non-believers.

Philosopher

This raises an interesting and relevant point about utilitarianism and clarifies the underlying issues raised by the essay question.

It could be argued that religious believers and non-believers all share common principles such as the Golden Rule: 'Do unto others as you would have them do unto you.' This would be supported by utilitarianism, which has a practical basis in promoting the greatest happiness for the greatest number.

News reporter

Critical thinker

Some very useful extensive and detailed reasoning here in addition to a new angle and perspective on the debate.

Different religions might point to their founders as showing utilitarian ways in which they put their own needs last in favour of helping the greatest number of people. For example, Jesus, the Buddha, Guru Nanak and the Prophet Muhammad all sacrificed themselves in various ways for the good of others. If this point were to stand, utilitarianism could provide a practical basis for decision-making for religious believers.

Judge

The evaluative point made here is a coherent and well-thought out one which make this paragraph a mini-conclusion.

However, utilitarianism only provides a practical basis for moral decision-making for non-believers because it is entirely secular. For example, Islam would uphold rules and teachings as coming from Allah and as being revealed, universal and consistent. What causes pleasure/happiness for the majority would not be important in this view.

Critical thinker

Tennis player

A strong counter-argument against the previous paragraph. There is also good understanding of how utilitarianism works and flows.

On the other hand, many religious believers and non-believers would adopt the position that moral decisions should be taken for the common good and the well-being of individuals and of society in general. In this way, utilitarianism has a place in providing a basis for moral decision-making.

Furthermore, specific practical laws which are based on a utilitarian approach can work equally for religious believers and non-believers. For example, stealing violates the principle of private property and undermines people's sense of security and happiness. Therefore all would agree on the moral conclusion: 'Do not steal.'

Detective **Philosopher**

Some clear substance is added to the discussion through the example of stealing, which also suggests a way of resolving the issue raised by the question.

However, the problem with utilitarianism is that in general it does not accept absolute rules and laws. This might be practical for non-believers, who want each situation to be treated differently, but might not for some religious believers, who want a rule with no exceptions such as: 'Do not commit adultery.'

Tennis player

Explorer

Here a strong counter-argument is presented and other areas of study have been considered in answering the question.

Thinking along the same lines, religious believers cannot look to utilitarianism as providing a practical basis for moral decision-making because most religions have a spiritual goal, whereby acts in this life have a direct impact on life after death. Bentham and Mill are only concerned with pleasure and happiness here and now.

Philosopher

This identifies an interesting and relevant problem and challenge to the issues raised by the question.

In conclusion, utilitarianism is always secular, which means that only non-believers can use it as the basis for moral decision-making. Religious believers would always need a spiritual dimension.

Judge

Critical thinker

The verdict is now in, providing a final opinion which evaluates the wording of the question.

Over to you

Below is an evaluation of the effectiveness of utilitarianism in moral decision-making in the twenty-first century. Think about ways you can improve and develop the analysis by applying your knowledge and understanding of utilitarianism.

This will help you to develop your skills in evaluation and analysis which are required to meet the higher bands in the examination.

Question

'Utilitarianism is an effective way to make moral decisions in the twenty-first century.' Evaluate this view

Evaluation

As used in the twenty-first century, utilitarianism as an ethical theory has many flaws. For example, when you fulfil 'the greatest happiness for the greatest number' principle, a minority are allowed to suffer. Also, this principle allows the justification of any act. However, this goes against religious teachings. Many people would argue that act utilitarianism's lack of rules would lead to moral chaos. In addition to this, many people have different ideas of what happiness is, so how can you make a judgement on this basis? Utilitarianism as a consequential theory asks us to predict consequences, which is impossible.

On the other hand, utilitarianism is fairly successful today as most people want to aim for happiness. Hospitals and medical practices make decisions using the utilitarian principles which are more relevant in the twenty-first century than other ethical theories. Using utilitarianism in the modern world could help to promote a community spirit through the pursuit of the common goal of happiness.

T4 Determinism and free will

This section covers AO1 content and skills

Specification content

Religious concepts of predestination: St Augustine

Key terms

determinism: the doctrine that the past determines a unique future; every event, including human action, is determined by previously existing causes

predestination: the belief that God determines human destiny in advance

indifferent universe: the pagan view that fate is impersonal and the gods are unconcerned with individual human destinies

Platonists: those asserting, in agreement with Plato, that the phenomena of the world are an imperfect and transitory reflection of the eternal reality of the ideal forms

single predestination: God determines only those who will be saved

double predestination: God determines both those who will be saved and those who will be damned

St Augustine

A: Religious concepts of predestination

The difference between determinism and predestination

Determinism is the doctrine that everything that happens, including human action, is the inevitable result of previously existing causes. The past determines a unique future. It is a philosophical concept and does not involve any belief in God. In contrast, **predestination** is a theological doctrine holding that God ordains what happens. In its strongest form, predestination means God determines all actions and events. However, weaker forms accept that humans have limited free will while maintaining that God determines at least some things, including one's eternal destiny.

St Augustine

Aurelius Augustinus was born in 354 CE and lived most of his life in Roman North Africa. He was the first person to develop a doctrine about what he called 'the predestination of the saints', making it a central part of his theology. This offered an alternative to the pagan conceptions of an **indifferent universe**. However, Augustine did not invent the idea of predestination itself; the Apostle Paul used the term and many Jewish scholars already recognised God as an agent acting in the world.

Raised as a Christian by his mother, Augustine initially rejected Christianity. Yet through the writings of the **Platonists**, with their idea of the soul, and the preaching of Ambrose, he was converted to Christianity and baptised by Ambrose at Easter in 387 CE.

From 396 CE until his death in 430 CE, Augustine was bishop of a busy seaport, Hippo, now named Annaba, in Algeria. He was instrumental in merging the Greek philosophical tradition with the Judeo-Christian religious and scriptural traditions. His writings were numerous and reflect his thinking on various theological controversies of the time.

Over the course of his lifetime, Augustine rethought old positions in the light of new situations and demands. In several instances, he changed his mind and admitted in his various letters that he had been in error (for example, he came to see that even faith depends on God's grace). His developing views often require piecing together from a variety of his writings. It is therefore quite difficult to neatly package his views; for instance, whether he believed in **single predestination** or **double predestination** is unclear.

However, what cannot be doubted is the influence he had on later philosophers such as Aquinas, Descartes and Wittgenstein. Probably his most well-known writing is *Confessions* (397–401 CE) which is a spiritual autobiography containing an account of his conversion.

Key person

St Augustine (354–430 CE): Bishop of Hippo in North Africa; his response to the Pelagian controversy shaped Christian teaching on original sin, grace and predestination; his key works were *Confessions* and *City of God*

The Pelagian controversy

As a bishop, Augustine faced various controversies within the Church. The controversy that occupied most of his energies was the **Pelagian controversy** and it reshaped his views on human freedom and predestination. The Pelagian debate engaged him from about 411 CE until his death in 430 CE. You might wonder why this particular debate mattered so much to Augustine.

Pelagius (354–418 CE) was a monk from Britain who taught in Rome from about 380 CE. He was incensed by the lax moral attitude of the Roman Christians and blamed the teaching of grace, especially as taught by Augustine. Pelagius saw this teaching as putting the responsibility on to God – not ourselves. He thought Christians used this as an excuse for any moral failings. This idea of God's grace as the sole necessity for obeying God's commands was rejected by Pelagius. He was not opposed to grace, only to the idea that grace was the only thing necessary for obeying God's commands.

However, Augustine saw this rejection of the absolute nature of God's grace as a **heresy**. It seemed to diminish the power of God and make God something less than an **omnipotent being**. The claim that a person could freely decide to be morally good implied that the person would then be able to claim that salvation from God was on their own merit, so denying the grace of God. Furthermore, it made the sacrificial death of Jesus, intended to provide a path to salvation for human beings, redundant. To Augustine this was an affront to God.

Pelagianism was repudiated by the Council of Carthage (418 CE), mainly through the influence and arguments of Augustine.

Doctrine of original sin

In response to Pelagius' free will theology, Augustine developed the doctrine of **original sin**. This encompassed the nature of Adam's fall, the extent of human corruption, the doctrine of infant baptism, God's grace and the theory of predestination.

The cause of original sin – the Fall

It is important to understand that for Augustine, **the Fall** was not just a story, it explained everything about human nature. In his book *City of God*, he portrays an idyllic picture of the Garden of Eden before the Fall: 'In Paradise, then, man [...] lived in the enjoyment of God, and was good by God's goodness [...] no sadness of any kind was there.'

Key terms

Pelagian controversy: the debate concerning how people obtain righteousness

heresy: a belief that is contrary to orthodox Christian theology/dogma

omnipotent being: a being with unlimited power

original sin: the sin committed by Adam in the Garden of Eden; more particularly, it refers to the doctrine that sin is inherent to human nature because of the original sin by Adam

the Fall: the events of Genesis chapter 3, where Adam and Eve face God's punishment for disobeying his divine command not to eat of the fruit from the tree of knowledge of Good and Evil

Genesis 3 recounts the story of the Fall. The story of Adam and Eve expresses the idea that human nature has fallen from its original pristine state. Augustine believed that Adam and Eve had an original righteousness and were entirely able to avoid sinning. Although mortal by natural constitution, they were immortal by a divine gift that would not have been withdrawn had they not sinned. Therefore, the present state of human nature is not what God intended it to be. The created order has been spoiled – but not irredeemably, since salvation is possible.

Adam and Eve committed the original sin

The question arises: why did Adam sin? Augustine argued that Adam had already turned away from God in his heart which is why the Devil successfully tempted him. Pride was at the heart of Adam's sin – the desire to live by the rule of self.

Augustine argued that creation now exists at a lower level than that intended for it by God. This was in sharp contrast to the views of Pelagius. Pelagius argued that sin only comes about through moral choice, it cannot be passed down from one's ancestors. Individual human beings have the capacity to save themselves since human beings are not tainted with sin from birth. Each person is born as a new, free agent with the same powers of choice and responsibilities as Adam. Pelagius believed that the power of sin, too, was enormous, but that we could strive for holiness through effort and God's grace and forgiveness.

The removal of original sin – baptism

Augustine argued that infants are born with original sin, a guilt and corruption of spirit that they inherit from their parents. He drew a distinction between Adam's sin, which Adam willed, and the sin that newborns contract without any will of their own. Augustine described this inherited sin as 'the guilt from our origin which was contracted by birth'. Each person inherits the effects of Adam's sin through the sexual act of procreation. Hence, Jesus remained sinless, since he was conceived without the sexual act (born of a virgin).

Catholic baptism

However, the guilt remains in us as a stain unless it is forgiven through baptism. Baptism removes original sin and is therefore necessary for salvation, but it does not guarantee it.

Augustine argued that baptism imparts the life of Christ's grace, makes a person a new creature and a member of the body of Christ and turns them back towards God as adopted sons and daughters. Yet baptism does not remove the inclination to sin. This turning back towards God is incomplete, so some who are baptised can be lost unless they receive further grace, including the grace of perseverance.

Infant deaths were very common in Augustine's day. Augustine contended that while infants have no sins of their own, they inherit original sin (this stain of guilt) and therefore they needed baptism. In *Confessions* he quotes from Psalm 51:6 'Surely I was sinful at birth, sinful from the time my mother conceived me.' Augustine believed that this sin must refer to original sin, since it would not be possible for the infant at this age to be guilty of choosing to sin. The *Catechism* (paragraph 1283) states: 'With respect to children who have died without baptism, the liturgy of the Church invites us to trust in God's mercy and to pray for their salvation.'

The consequences of original sin

Concupiscence

Concupiscence refers to humanity's natural pull towards earthly pleasures over spiritual ones. Augustine believed that Adam's sin was so great that it changed not only his nature but also that of the entire human race. Human beings are now born with weakened faculties and subject to death. They have a corrupted orientation, turned away from God and towards lesser goods, which Augustine calls carnal concupiscence. The *Catechism* (405) states: '[...] human nature has not been totally corrupted: it is wounded in the natural powers proper to it, subject to ignorance, suffering and the dominion of death, and inclined to sin – an inclination to evil that is called concupiscence.'

Although concupiscence comes from sin and inclines people towards sin, it is not itself sin. It makes people vulnerable to temptation, but susceptibility to temptation is not the same as sinning. Concupiscence is a deficiency in a person's ability to choose good and resist earthly desires when these conflict with God's laws. The *Catechism* (1264) states: 'since concupiscence is left for us to wrestle with, it cannot harm those who do not consent but wilfully resist it by the grace of Jesus Christ'.

Specification content

Doctrine of original sin: role of concupiscence, humanity as 'a lump of sin' (*massa peccati*)

Key term

concupiscence: strong desire for earthly pleasures; stemming from Adam's first sin, it is not itself a sin but inclines human beings towards sin

Key quotes

It was the position of Pelagius that Adam's sin affected Adam and only Adam. That is to say, as a result of Adam's transgression there was no change wrought in the constituent nature of the human race.

(Sproul)

When the woman saw that the fruit of the tree was good for food and pleasing to the eye, and also desirable for gaining wisdom, she took some and ate it.

(Genesis 3:6)

Augustine's doctrine means that all humans are born moving away from God.

(Rowan Greer)

[...] sin entered the world through one man, and death through sin, and, in this way death came to all men, because all sinned.

(Romans 5:12)

For just as through the disobedience of the one man the many were made sinners, so also through the obedience of the one man the many will be made righteous.

(Romans 5:19)

For as in Adam all die, so in Christ all will be made alive.

(1 Corinthians 15:22)

Humanity as 'a lump of sin' (*massa peccati*)

Augustine believed that, as a result of the Fall, all humanity is born ***massa peccati***. *Massa peccati* is a Latin term meaning a 'lump of sin' or 'mass of sin'. The entire human race was lumped together with Adam when he sinned; as a result, the whole of mankind is a 'condemned lump'. Therefore, for Augustine, humanity's ability to choose freely is infected by sin and incapable of raising itself from spiritual death.

Key term

massa peccati: Latin for 'lump of sin'; humanity as a condemned mass due to Adam's sin

Key quote

All humans were seminally present in the loins of Adam. (Augustine)

Specification content

Doctrine of original sin: an essentially 'free' human nature (*liberium arbitrium*), the loss of human liberty (*libertas*) to our sinful nature

Liberium arbitrium and *libertas*

Here is the key distinction which can be tricky but is essential to grasp: according to Augustine, fallen humanity still has free will (***liberium arbitrium***) in that they can make choices, but they have lost their moral liberty (***libertas***). Sproul (*Willing to Believe* (2002)) explains Augustine's view: 'The state of original sin leaves us in the condition of being unable to refrain from sinning. We still are able to choose what we desire, but our desires are dominated by our evil impulses. Therefore, the freedom that remains in the will always leads to sin.'

It is freedom without liberty, a moral bondage. Although people are still able to choose what they desire, their desires are affected by sin. Baptism was seen to address original sin, but it left untouched concupiscence, the inclination towards sin that original sin had introduced.

Key terms

liberium arbitrium: free will

libertas: the freedom to choose good over evil

St Augustine at prayer

Specification content

Doctrine of original sin: God's grace and atonement for the elect/saints

The need for God's grace

This is perhaps the most important part of Augustine's argument – without understanding grace, none of the rest makes sense. While Pelagius saw freedom as the ability of a person to exercise their free will and make their own decisions, Augustine understood freedom as the ability to fulfil one's nature and to be fulfilled as a person.

As we have seen, Augustine saw the will as enslaved to sin. In *Confessions* he wrote: 'Without exception we all long for happiness [...] All agree that we want to be happy, just as, if they were asked, they would all agree that they desired joy.' But Augustine believed that true happiness is found only in God, and human wills, though free, are not directed to desiring the things of God. Because of this, the role of God's grace in his doctrine is crucial.

For Augustine, true liberty can only come from the work of God on the soul, and people are totally dependent upon grace to liberate the soul from the bondage of sin. Only after the initial divine work of liberation do people co-operate with this grace.

Augustine believed that grace involves God changing the heart's desires so that people can freely obey God and find happiness. This makes sense of Augustine's prayer after his conversion: 'Give me the grace to do as you command, and command me to do what you will.' It was that very prayer that so enraged Pelagius as he saw it causing a lax moral attitude among Christians. Augustine argues that it is by the law that people discover what ought to be done, and by grace that people are enabled to do what the law commands.

Atonement for the elect/saints

Augustine believed that salvation rested totally on God's grace, not on a person's merit. It was God's grace that would maintain a person's faith, enabling them to become holy and obtain final salvation. He drew attention to John 15:16 – 'You did not choose me, but I chose you' – and Ephesians 1:4–5: 'For he chose us in him before the creation of the world to be holy and blameless in his sight. In love he predestined us for adoption to sonship through Jesus Christ.' For Augustine, God must have predestined people before the creation of the world in order that they might become holy (through God's grace), since they could not live holy lives in their own strength.

Those chosen for salvation are also called **the elect** and those receiving God's wrath are called by Augustine **the reprobates**. Two of Augustine's key Bible passages about predestination are Romans 8:29–30 – 'And those he predestined, he also called: those he called, he also justified; those he justified, he also glorified' – and Ephesians 1:11: 'In him we were also chosen, having been predestined according to the plan of him who works out everything'.

John Lennox (*Determined to Believe* (2017)) commented that 'the phrase "the doctrine of predestination" is usually taken as shorthand for the view that some are predestined to salvation'. However, he also argued that the use of the term in the Bible is wider than that as it also applied to the death of Christ and his resurrection.

Single or double predestination?

There is some disagreement as to whether Augustine believed in single predestination (predestined to salvation) or double predestination (predestined also to condemnation). It is not clear whether Augustine taught that God creates some with the express intention of damning them and others with the intention of saving them. Hick (*Evil and the God of Love*) concludes that Augustine's position was 'that people fall freely and culpably and that out of the fallen race God saves some, leaving others to perish; although God knows from the beginning which he intends to save and which to abandon'.

Key quotes

For Thyself Thou hast made us, And restless our hearts until in Thee they find their ease.

(Augustine, *Confessions*)

[Human beings are] so hopelessly corrupted that we are absolutely incapable of doing anything good by our own forces; free choice, if it means a choice between good and evil, has been utterly wasted by sin; our will, insofar as it is ours, and not God's, can merely do evil and desire evil.

(Augustine)

Key quote

For those God foreknew he also predestined to be conformed to the image of his Son

(Romans 8:29)

Key terms

the elect: those people chosen to salvation, by the grace of God

the reprobates: those people, untouched by God's grace, left to be consumed by the defect of concupiscence

Key quotes

By such grace it is effected, not only that we discover what ought to be done, but also that we do what we have discovered – not only that we believe what ought to be loved, but also that we love what we have believed.

(Augustine)

Our wills are ours and it is our will that affects all that we do by willing and which could not have happened if we had not willed [...] the fact that God foreknew that a man would sin does not make a man sin; on the contrary, it cannot be doubted that it is the man himself who sins [...] a man does not sin unless he wills to sin'

(Augustine)

The Last Judgement by Michaelangelo (1536–41)

McGrath (*Christian Theology: An Introduction* (1994)) takes a similar view, arguing 'that the remainder were not, according to Augustine, actively condemned to damnation; they were merely not elected to salvation'. He adds that Augustine treated predestination as active and positive, by which McGrath means a deliberate decision on God's part to redeem rather than a deliberate decision to condemn.

However, there are texts by Augustine that seem to state double predestination clearly. For example, 'As the Supreme Good, he made good use of evil deeds, for the damnation of those whom he had justly predestined to punishment and for the salvation of those whom he had mercifully predestined to grace.' As John Lennox states, 'It is hard to see how one can maintain so-called single predestination without logically affirming double predestination.'

Why are not all people predestined to salvation?

Augustine was only too aware of the problematic nature of his doctrine but saw the resolution in divine knowledge. He believed that the fallen human intellect was incapable of understanding the workings of divine salvation and that grace itself only leads to partial restoration of the intellect. At one point Augustine concluded: '[...] I confess that I can find no answer to make [...] even as His anger is righteous and as His mercy is great, so His judgments are unsearchable'.

Key quotes

[...] God leads some in mercy and repentance and others in just judgement does not lead.

(Augustine)

It is unthinkable that He [Jesus] should deliberately have shed his blood for hell-dwellers-to-be.

(Augustine)

For not only has God given us our ability and helps it, but He even works [brings about] willing and acting in us; not that we do not will or that we do not act, but that without His help we neither will anything good nor do it.

(Augustine)

The problem is that Augustine seems to offer two contradictory explanations as to why some people are not saved. Firstly, damnation demonstrates God's mercy in saving some when all deserve judgement – yet this seems to contradict the view of a loving God who would not want any to be lost.

Secondly, God foresees that some will resist his grace and block his will – yet this suggests that judgement is based on a person's free choice, even though they could not have chosen otherwise.

This whole issue of predestination resurfaced with John Calvin, who featured the doctrine as part of his theological system.

John Calvin's doctrine of election

John Calvin

Key person

John Calvin (1509–64): A French Protestant reformer based in Geneva; he developed the doctrine of election, emphasising God's sovereignty and double predestination; his key work was *Institutes of the Christian Religion* (1536/1559)

Specification content

Religious concepts of predestination: John Calvin

Key term

Protestant Reformation: a sixteenth-century European movement aimed initially at reforming the beliefs and practices of the Roman Catholic Church

John Calvin was born in France in 1509 and became a prominent figure during the **Protestant Reformation**. Having left Roman Catholicism, he joined the Protestant movement and became one of its leaders in Paris. In 1536, while journeying to Basel, he passed through Geneva where he was persuaded to stay and help reform the Church. He remained in Geneva (apart from a short move to Strasbourg 1538–41) until his death in 1564.

During his life, he wrote many books on theology, especially commentaries on the books in the Bible. However, his most famous book was the *Institutes of the Christian Religion* (or *Institutes*), first published in 1536. What began as a short six-chapter work, by its final form (1559) had grown to a hefty four volumes and comprised a thorough systematic theology.

John Calvin

INSTITVTIO CHRI-
ſtianæ religionis, in libros qua-
tuor nunc primùm digeſta, certiſque diſtincta capitibus, ad aptiſſimam methodum: aucta etiam tam magna acceſſione vt propemodum opus nouum haberi poſſit.

IOHANNE CALVINO AVTHORE.

Oliua Roberti Stephani.

GENEVAE.
M. D. LIX.

Calvin's book *Institutes of the Christian Religion*

The parable of the Sower

Key term

Calvinism: a branch of Protestantism based on the theological beliefs promoted by John Calvin; it is also referred to as Reformed Protestantism or the Reformed tradition

Although John Calvin (and **Calvinism**) is often associated with the doctrine of predestination, this doctrine was by no means the central pivot around

Key terms

sovereignty of God: the teaching that all things are under God's rule and control; God is sovereign both in principle and practice

limited atonement: the view that Christ died for the sins of the elect only and no atonement was provided for the reprobate

Key quote

Far from being a central premise of Calvin's thought, predestination is an ancillary doctrine [...]

(McGrath)

which he formulated his other doctrines. Nor was it Calvin's innovation. As we have seen, Augustine and others had already expounded the doctrine of predestination. Perhaps the two central themes for Calvin were:

- the **sovereignty of God**
- the Bible as the revealed word of God.

Some modern scholarship has challenged the extent to which later Calvinism accurately represented Calvin's own views. This has become known as the 'Calvin against the Calvinists' school of thought. For instance, R.T. Kendall (*Calvin and English Calvinism to 1649*) argues that Calvin was not himself a Calvinist on the point of **limited atonement** (see 'Limited atonement' on page 220).

Calvin's beliefs about predestination were derived not only from his ideas about divine omnipotence but also from reflection about human experience, interpreted in the light of scripture. He thought that some people responded to God's grace while others did not. According to Calvin, scripture makes clear that some people respond to the gospel while others do not; for example, the parable of the Sower in Mark 4:1–20. He was also convinced that sin had corrupted both the will and the intellect.

The corrupted nature of human beings

Calvin followed Augustine in his understanding of the fall of humanity. In his *Institutes*, he stated the belief that man was created as an immortal soul in a state of original righteousness. Adam's choice of good and evil was free, but Genesis 3 recounts the Fall. The consequences were that 'the heavenly image was obliterated in him' – and in everyone since. Humanity has lost its original freedom and is now enslaved to sin.

Calvin regarded humanity as 'totally depraved' (morally corrupt) owing to the Fall of Adam and Eve. By *totally depraved* he did not mean completely depraved or as depraved as possible, but tainted or depraved in all areas of the heart, mind and will. Humanity was unable to respond in faithful obedience to the invitation of God through Jesus. In other words, people cannot choose for themselves to repent and believe.

The absolute power of God

Calvin believed strongly in the sovereignty of God – the all-pervasive and over-ruling **providence** of God – and scripture as the source of knowledge of and about God. Nothing happens by chance. The sovereignty of God was essential to Calvin's doctrine of predestination. In his *Institutes,* Calvin stated that scripture functions as a set of 'spectacles' that bring **general revelation** back into proper focus. He thus dismisses all efforts to go beyond scripture as pure speculation, both wrong and sinful. This insistence on scripture rather than philosophy as the central driving force underpins Calvin's doctrine of election.

Key terms

providence: the theological idea that God is closely involved in monitoring and guiding the created world

general revelation: knowledge about God discovered through natural means such as reasoning or observation of the physical universe

Key quotes

[...] all of us, who have descended from impure seed, are born infected with the contagion of sin.

(Calvin, *Institutes of the Christian Religion*)

For we unjustly defraud God of his right, unless each of us lives and dies in dependence on his sovereign pleasure.

(Calvin)

For it is by grace you are saved, through faith, and this is not of yourselves, it is the gift of God.

(Ephesians 2:8)

The elect and the reprobates

Calvin further developed his theory by stating that God divided humanity into two predestined groups: the elect and the reprobates. This view became known as double predestination because God actively chooses some for salvation and eternal life (the elect) and others for damnation (the reprobates). This act of predestination took place before creation, clearly demonstrating that the election had nothing to do with a human's good deeds. The election is unconditional and not based on merit, since it is God who, in eternity past, chose certain individuals for salvation. Since God is active and sovereign in his actions, he chose to redeem or to damn. Eternal life is based solely on God's grace.

The elect

If a person belongs to the elect, they have already been chosen by God to have their sins forgiven, through the **atonement** for sins achieved by the death of Jesus Christ. Calvin believed that while no one can be certain whether they are one of the elect, the elect will persevere to the end. They will persevere because Christ will care for them so that they do not fall away. Therefore, if apparent believers fall away, Calvin concludes they were never part of the elect, as stated in 1 John 2:19: 'They went out from us, but they did not really belong to us. For if they had belonged to us, they would have remained with us; but their going showed that none of them belonged to us.'

Calvin believed that a person can – and should – have the assurance that they are among the elect. In his *Institutes,* he wrote: 'Predestination, rightly understood, brings no shaking of faith but rather its best confirmation.' One indicator of election is what Calvin referred to as 'the calling of God' – a subjective inward certainty. He also expected the elect to show traits of their godly status even though, at times, they might be sinful. There was assurance because 'if we are in communion with Christ, we have proof sufficiently clear and strong that we are written in the Book of Life' (*Institutes*).

The reprobates

Calvin strongly believed that while God elected some for salvation and eternal life, he also barred others from access to salvation and so sentenced them to eternal death. This election took place before creation, making clear that merit is not an explanation for why some are saved and others are not. However, the reprobates sin of their own free choice rather than by divine coercion. They resist grace because they are not chosen. Therefore, in one sense, God did not make them sinners. It was more the case that God left them to their sin.

Calvin appealed to Romans 9:11–13 for scriptural support that all are not created on equal terms: 'Yet, before the twins were born or had done anything good or bad – in order that God's purpose in election might stand: not by works but by him who calls – she was told, [...] Jacob I loved, but Esau I hated.'

Unconditional election

The doctrine of unconditional election derives from Calvin's insistence on the sovereignty of God. If God is sovereign then God must actively choose to redeem or to damn, and this action of God was prior to his creation of the world. Hence, the election is unconditional and unmerited. In *Institutes*, Calvin defined predestination as the 'eternal decree of God, by which he determined what he wished to make of every individual. For he does not

Specification content

John Calvin: doctrine of election: the elect and the reprobates, unconditional election

Key term

atonement: Christian doctrine concerning the reconciliation of God and humankind, accomplished through the life, suffering and death of Christ

Key quotes

I am the good shepherd; I know my sheep and my sheep know me.

(John 10:14)

I am sure He chose me before I was born, or else He never would have chosen me afterwards; and He must have elected me for reasons unknown to me, for I never could find any reason in myself why He should have looked upon me with special love.

(Spurgeon)

[...] a man will be justified by faith when, excluded from righteousness of works, he by faith lays hold of the righteousness of Christ, and clothed in it, appears in the sight of God not as a sinner, but as righteous [...]

(Calvin)

Christ is indeed presented to all, but God opens the eyes of the elect alone, and enables them by faith to seek after him.

(Calvin)

create all in the same condition, but ordains eternal life for some and eternal damnation for others'.

Like Augustine, Calvin believed that there is nothing in humanity to merit any favour or mercy. Each person is worthy of God's wrath and incapable of saving themselves.

Calvin believed that God chose to elect people regardless of their merit. In this, he saw God's graciousness demonstrated, since God redeems individuals irrespective of what they deserve. For Calvin, the elect receive a twofold grace of **justification** and **sanctification**:

> '[...] we principally receive a double grace: namely, that being reconciled to God through Christ's blamelessness, we may have in heaven instead of a Judge a gracious Father; and secondly, that sanctified by Christ's spirit we may cultivate blamelessness and purity of life.'

Justification is a one-time event – being made right with God. Sanctification is a state of living according to God's design and purpose, which involves an ongoing process of growth in holiness and piety through life.

Though justification and sanctification are distinct, they are not separable. Calvin argued that there cannot be justification without sanctification; and there cannot be sanctification without justification. In *Institutes*, he wrote: 'Therefore Christ justifies no one whom he does not at the same time sanctify.'

Key terms

justification: the declaring of a person to be just or righteous

sanctification: the state of proper functioning; living according to God's design and purpose

Key quotes

God preordained, for his own glory and the display of His attributes of mercy and justice, a part of the human race, without any merit of their own, to eternal salvation, and another part, in just punishment of their sin, to eternal damnation.

(Calvin)

For he chose us in him before the creation of the world to be holy and blameless in his sight.

(Ephesians 1:4)

But who are you, a human being, to talk back to God? Shall what is formed say to the one who formed it, 'Why did you make me like this?' Does not the potter have the right to make out of the same lump of clay some pottery for special purposes and some for common use? What if God, although choosing to show his wrath and make his power known, bore with great patience the objects of his wrath – prepared for destruction?

(Romans 9:20–22)

A potter working on some clay

Specification content

John Calvin: doctrine of election: limited atonement, irresistible grace and perseverance of the elect

Limited atonement

Although Calvin used the term reprobate, he did not regard it as a logical deduction from the doctrine of election. Rather, it was an uncompromising affirmation of God's sovereignty over his creation: God excludes the reprobates from the inheritance since he is not under a fixed obligation to call all equally.

Whether Calvin believed in limited atonement is often debated. It is not a phrase he used, even though the L in the TULIP acronym stands for limited atonement (see 'The five points of Calvinism' on pages 219–20). If Calvin did teach it, then he believed that Christ died only for the elect.

Some scholars, such as R.T. Kendall (*Calvin and English Calvinism to 1649*) have argued that Calvin limited who Christ intercedes for, rather than who his death could atone for. In other words, Christ died for all but Christ chose to save only some.

In response, other scholars, such as Paul Helm, pointed to Calvin's own commentary on 1 Timothy 2:5, where he argues that 'the universal term "all" must always be referred to classes of men and not to persons' (*Calvin's Commentaries*, Volume XXI). In other words, 'all' does not mean everyone without exception. Therefore, Calvin *did* teach limited atonement.

A further argument draws on John 10:15, where Jesus laid his life down for the sheep. The following verse notes that Jesus said that people did not believe because they were not his sheep. The implication is that Jesus did not lay down his life for those who are not his sheep. Hence Christ's redeeming work was intended to save the elect only and is therefore limited in its extent.

Greek Orthodox icon of Jesus the good shepherd

Irresistible grace and perseverance of the elect

Calvin also argued that since God has drawn the elect to faith by regenerating their hearts and convincing them of their sins, they will be kept by the same power to the end and so enter heaven. They are eternally saved and kept in faith by God's power and so persevere to the end. But what of those who profess to be believers but later fall away? The doctrine maintains that it only applies to those who have a genuine faith in Christ. Those who appear to profess and then fall away are deemed never to have had genuine faith and are therefore not part of the elect.

Through regeneration, the Holy Spirit changes the believer's heart and remains with them, ensuring they will continue to love Christ. This does not suggest they will be perfect in this life. However, they do not follow God's command to earn or keep their salvation; they follow it out of love and gratitude.

Key quotes

First and last for Calvin, God is not a celestial tyrant but a loving parent who cannot forget her nursing child, and a father who gives good things to his children.

(Lindberg)

This inheritance is kept in heaven for you, who through faith are shielded by God's power until the coming of the salvation [...]

(1 Peter 1:4–5)

They went out from us, but they did not really belong to us. For if they had belonged to us, they would have remained with us; but their going showed that none of them belonged to us.

(1 John 2:19)

The five points of Calvinism

It is helpful to understand where the 'five points of Calvinism' actually came from as they were not Calvin's own summary of his beliefs. After the death of Jacobus Arminius (see 'Arminianism' on page 256) in 1609, 46 of his followers in the Netherlands issued their protest against Calvinist teaching. They summarised their creed under five points concerning predestination, the atonement, faith, grace and perseverance. Unable to reach any agreement

Key terms

synod: an assembly of Church clergy of a particular Church

Arminianism: the doctrinal teachings of Jacobus Arminius and his followers who argued for free will and that Christ died for everyone rather than just the elect

The Synod of Dort

The five points of Calvinism are sometimes summed up with the acronym 'TULIP'

with the Calvinists, a **synod** was convened. The Synod of Dort (1618–19) was an international meeting organised by the Dutch Reformed Church to settle the divisive controversy between Calvinism and **Arminianism**.

The rejection of Arminianism was a foregone conclusion since Arminian delegates were not permitted to vote, although they were allowed to speak and their views were given full hearing.

It is important to note that the famous 'five points of Calvinism' were a direct response to the 'five points of Arminianism' and so in no way represent the sum of Calvinism.

The five points of Calvinism are sometimes summed up with the acronym TULIP.

Total depravity

As a result of Adam and Eve's disobedience to God, sin has extended to every part of a person's being: their thinking, their emotions and their will. Therefore, it is impossible for the ordinary 'natural' human being to understand or respond to God. They are spiritually helpless. As noted in 1 Corinthians 2:14: 'The man without the Spirit does not accept the things that come from the Spirit of God, for they are foolishness to him, and he cannot understand them because they are spiritually discerned.'

Unconditional election

God divided humanity into two groups. One group is the elected. This includes all those whom God has chosen for salvation and eternal life. The rest, the reprobates, remain in sin and eternal condemnation. God alone chooses the elect. Election is not on the basis of any foreseen merit, quality or achievement. God chooses the elect based solely upon his will and he did this before creation. As noted in Romans 9:21: 'Does not the potter have the right to make out of the same lump of clay some pottery for special purposes and some for common use?'

Limited atonement

Christ's death and atonement for the sins of human beings was for the elect only. Calvinists believe that the Bible teaches that Christ died for those whom God gave him to save, the elect. Therefore, Christ died for many people (the elect), but not all (the reprobates). As noted in Matthew 26:28: 'This is my blood of the covenant which is poured out for many for the forgiveness of sins.'

Irresistible grace

The result of God's irresistible grace is the certain response by the elect to the inward call of the gospel. Calvinists believe that the elect cannot resist the call which will result in them being redeemed. As noted in Acts 13:48: '[...] and all who were appointed for eternal life believed'.

Perseverance of the elect

The elect will be kept by God through their earthly life until they are finally glorified in heaven. God will begin and continue a process of sanctification which will continue until they reach heaven. None are lost. It is impossible for them to lose their salvation. The elect will therefore be unable to commit apostasy by giving up their faith. As noted in Philippians 1:6: '[...] being confident of this, that he who began a good work in you will carry it on to completion until the day of Christ Jesus'.

Key quote

Although men are not totally corrupt in the sense that they are incapable of doing any good at all – it would be absurd to say that – the truth is that the best of men and their best accomplishments are tainted or poisoned at the core by their pride or egotism or self-centredness, however far they may look from outside.

(Vidler)

Similarities and differences between Augustine and Calvin on predestination

Larry Sharp ('The Doctrines of Grace in Calvin and Augustine') argues that unlike Calvin, Augustine never made a clear distinction between the grace of God and the Holy Spirit. For Calvin, grace is not some sort of healing power infused in believers, it is primarily about the character of God – benevolent and merciful.

Some scholars conclude that Calvin taught double predestination and Augustine did not. It is argued that Augustine believed that God chose some for eternal life but did not in any direct sense deliberately reject others. Rather he leaves them for rightful judgement. However, as was noted earlier, many feel that this is not as clear a doctrine as is claimed.

Augustine thought that all people are created in an equal condition of being justly condemned but God mercifully decides to save some. In contrast, Calvin does not regard all people as being created in equal condition – human beings have been created for either eternal life or eternal damnation.

Both Augustine and Calvin see justification as a gift from God. For Augustine, justification is something done inside people. It is an infused righteousness whereby people are enabled to live a life pleasing to God and so be saved. However, for Calvin, justification is about the imputed righteousness of Jesus Christ. By this he meant that righteousness was credited or reckoned to people, such that they had a new standing before God. That standing is the same standing as Christ has before God. As can be seen, this is not about a person's ability to live righteously.

Key quote

Augustine is so wholly within me, that if I wished to write a confession of my faith, I could do so with all fulness and satisfaction to myself out of his writings.

(Calvin)

Summary

- ★ Determinism is the doctrine that everything that happens happens because of previously existing causes. It does not involve any belief in God.
- ★ Predestination is the doctrine that at least some things are determined by God, including one's eternal destiny.
- ★ Pelagianism was repudiated by the Council of Carthage (418 CE), mainly through the influence and arguments of Augustine.
- ★ Augustine argued that infants are born with original sin, a guilt and corruption of the spirit that they inherit from their parents.
- ★ Although baptism removes the guilt of original sin, Augustine believed that human beings still have an inclination to sin and so require the grace of perseverance for salvation.
- ★ Therefore, final salvation rests totally on God's grace and not on a person's merit.
- ★ John Calvin, a Protestant reformer, also believed that eternal life was based solely on God's grace.
- ★ The five points of Calvinism are summed up with the acronym TULIP.
- ★ Augustine saw justification as infused righteousness, while for Calvin it was about the imputed righteousness of Jesus Christ.

AO1 Activity

a Explain Augustine's reasons for believing in the grace of perseverance for salvation. This will help you to understand and present Augustine's view of predestination.

b Look at the following list of biblical verses and identify which ones relate to which of the five points of Calvinism:

- **i** John 6:37, 6:39, 6:44, 10:28–9 and 17:9
- **ii** Romans 5:12, 8:14, 8:30 and 9:15
- **iii** Ephesians 4:18
- **iv** 2 Thessalonians 2:13
- **v** Titus 1:15
- **vi** 1 Peter 1:2

This will help you to support your answer about John Calvin's view on predestination by reference to some biblical verses, reflecting Calvin's emphasis on the Bible as the revealed word of God.

In order to achieve the higher bands (bands 4–5), your answer must demonstrate detailed, accurate and relevant knowledge and understanding of the topic. This includes choosing and applying information selectively, using technical terms and language where appropriate and using evidence/examples to support your answer. Answers that are too general will likely be placed in the lower bands.

Issues for analysis and evaluation

A consideration of whether religious believers should accept the doctrine of predestination

Possible line of argument	Critical analysis and evaluation
The Bible is the only source for teachings about predestination.	Teachings about predestination derive from various sources such as Church councils.
God infallibly guided the decisions of the various Church councils.	Part of what people now understand as what the Bible teaches began at the Church councils, then became a focus of discussion, then later gained authority as Church doctrine.
The Bible contains God's revelation to his creation about predestination. It is the authority as it contains the word of God.	The Bible has gone through periods of transmission and change so teachings about predestination must be decided on other criteria.
Predestination has been the doctrine of the Church from its beginnings.	Various religious believers of the Protestant Reformation did not believe in predestination.
The Bible clearly teaches predestination (e.g. Romans 8:2–30).	The Bible clearly teaches the free choice of people to follow God (e.g. Matthew 23:37).
Predestination in the Bible refers to specific individuals.	Predestination in the Bible refers to the plan and goal of salvation itself, rather than to specific individuals.
Augustine accepted the authority of the Bible and accepted predestination of specific individuals.	Various religious believers of the Protestant Reformation accepted the authority of the Bible but did not believe in predestination of specific individuals.
Original sin means that none can be saved without God's intervention through God's grace. This supports predestination.	A person can choose to follow God and be saved by an act of their free will. The doctrine of original sin is a misunderstood added layer of teaching.
If God is omnipotent, there is a logical contradiction between predestination and free will. God's nature cannot be contradictory, therefore there can be no free will.	Free will exists but is limited, so that it cannot ultimately thwart the plans and purposes of God. Some religious believers argue that predestination and free will only appear contradictory because we do not fully understand the nature of God.
If free will exists, it would mean that we have no need of God's grace as we are able to save ourselves.	If we have no free will and God is omnipotent, then surely God could have created beings that always chose to do good.

This section covers AO2 content and skills

Specification content

A consideration of whether religious believers should accept the doctrine of predestination

Possible line of argument	Critical analysis and evaluation
God is benevolent. No person could receive eternal life without God's intervention since all deserve judgement. Predestination shows God's love in that the elect are saved.	God is omnibenevolent and so all could inherit eternal life if he willed it. However, predestination implies that only some are forgiven (the elect) rather than all.
The Bible states that Christ gave his life as a ransom for many (e.g. Matthew 26:28).	The Bible states that Christ died for all rather than just the elect (e.g. Isaiah 53:6).

AO2 Activity

a Analyse three lines of argument from the critical analysis and evaluation of whether religious believers should accept the doctrine of predestination. Research and select three references from scholars, schools of thought or religious and philosophical texts that would support those arguments.

b Evaluate which line of argument you consider **most persuasive** and explain why it is so.

In order to achieve the higher bands (bands 4–5), your answer must be well organised, presenting a logical line of argument. You should critically analyse different perspectives, rather than just describing them, and draw a supported conclusion of your own. Band 1 answers would simply list points.

Specification content

The extent to which God predestines humanity

Exam practice

Below is an example of part of an evaluation of the extent to which God predestines humanity.

Sample answer

Both Augustine and John Calvin supported the view that God predestines humanity, but they held different views as to the extent. Calvin, in the *Institutes*, wrote: 'The will of God is the supreme and first cause of all things, because nothing happens but by his command or permission.' He viewed humanity as having lost its original freedom and it was now enslaved to sin. There was no free will. Calvin was convinced that sin had corrupted both the will and the intellect, and humanity was totally depraved (depraved in all areas of the heart, mind and will), owing to the Fall of Adam and Eve. Since humanity cannot choose for themselves to repent and believe, God chooses certain people to progress to eternal life and some to eternal damnation. Therefore he predestines the whole of humanity. Calvin thought that texts such as Romans 9 supported this view: 'Does not the potter have the right to make out of the same lump of clay some pottery for noble purposes and some for common use?' He argued that this was consistent with the existence of an omnipotent God.

News reporter

Detective

The opening sentence clearly identifies Augustine and Calvin as having different views. A clear and detailed account of Calvin's view is provided, showing good knowledge and understanding. It includes a quote from his writings, as well as references to the Bible used to support his view.

Earlier, Augustine had also argued for predestination. Although both Augustine and Calvin appealed to the authority of the Bible, such as in John 15:16 – 'You did not choose me, but I chose you' – Augustine emphasised texts such as Matthew 26, where Jesus makes clear that his atonement was limited – 'his blood [...] poured out for many' – rather than for all. Calvin instead emphasised texts such as Isaiah 53:6, 'We all like sheep have gone astray, and the Lord has laid on him the iniquity of us all,' indicating that Christ died for all.

Detective

Differences between Calvin's and Augustine's views are explained here by illustrating appeals to different biblical texts.

However, the idea of human beings being created to either eternal life or eternal damnation seems difficult to equate with a God who is omnibenevolent. Even though God is omnipotent, seemingly he chose not to save all. Perhaps the problems posed by the whole concept of predestination are more about philosophical inconsistencies rather than biblical evidence. Augustine did seem aware of this philosophical problem and indicated an attempt to resolve it. He believed that God chose some for eternal life, but he seems not to have argued that God, in any direct sense, deliberately rejected others. Rather, God leaves those not chosen for rightful judgement.

Critical thinker

Philosopher

Challenges are raised here about philosophical difficulties and Augustine's attempt to address them.

Augustine believed in single predestination (predestined to salvation). For him, the emphasis seems to be on God's benevolence in his choosing some to receive mercy and forgiveness even though all deserve judgement. Many might argue that God still seems to predestine all humanity by means of 'not-choosing'. Augustine saw the resolution in divine knowledge. He thought that the fallen human intellect was incapable of understanding the workings of divine salvation and, even when predestined for eternal life through God's grace, there was only partial restoration of the intellect. In contrast, Calvin regarded the authority of scripture as the supreme decider over any philosophical problem and so argued that God created some people for eternal damnation and others for eternal life.

Detective

Judge

Augustine's response to the philosophical problems is further detailed here, contrasted with Calvin's appeals to the authority of the Bible overriding any philosophical issues.

More recent scholars have argued that God does not predestine anyone since the whole concept of predestination is flawed. For instance, Clark Pinnock rejects the notion of a timeless God, since it is questionable whether the God who creates time can be bound by events within time. Many scholars would argue that because human beings have real choices in life there are at least some outcomes that are not predetermined. Predestination seems to rule out free will, yet we are depicted as moral beings – which implies some freedom to make moral choices. For others, modern study of the texts of the Bible has cast doubt on the reliability of those texts, or at the least on the way they can be interpreted. This raises the problem about appealing to the authority of the Bible as the means to decide about the extent of God's predestination of humanity.

Philosopher

Critical thinker

The idea of predestination and the authority of the Bible is strongly criticised.

Finding consistency between biblical texts and philosophy seems impossible. But perhaps that is to be expected given that we are seeking to understand the workings of the Creator.

Philosopher

Judge

A concise judgement is given here, ending with a challenging reflection on the whole issue.

Over to you

On page 226 is a list of indicative content that could be used in response to a question requiring an evaluation of whether all human life is predestined by God. The problem is that it is not a very full list and needs completing.

As a group, consider what is missing from the list. You need to add at least six points (three in support and three against) that you would use to improve the list, and/or add more detail to each point that is already in the list. Remember: it is how you use the point in an evaluation that is the most important factor.

Apply the principles of evaluation by making sure that you:

- identify issues clearly
- present accurate views of others and comment on the views presented
- reach an overall personal judgement.

You may add more of your own suggestions but try to negotiate as a group and prioritise the most important things to add (additional points or additional detail to existing points).

Then, as a group, agree on your final list and write out your new list of indicative content, remembering the principles of explaining with evidence and/or examples. Put this list in the order of how you would present the information in an essay; then you will have your own plan for an ideal answer.

List of indicative content

In support of predestination:

- In Ephesians, Paul wrote to the Christians at Ephesus: 'For it is by grace you are saved, through faith, and this is not of yourselves, it is the gift of God.'
- Because of the Fall, humanity has lost its original freedom and is now enslaved to sin.
- Those chosen for salvation are called the elect and those receiving God's wrath are called by Augustine the reprobates.

Against predestination:

- The Bible clearly teaches the free choice of people to follow God. Every call to repent is a call to choose (for example, Acts 3:19)
- In Matthew 23:37, Jesus says 'how often I have longed to gather your children together, as a hen gathers her chicks under her wings, and you were not willing'.
- God's nature is omnibenevolent and therefore he could not predestine some to destruction.

B: Concepts of determinism

Hard determinism

The idea of determinism is firmly grounded in the principle of causality. The world around us appears to be a 'closed' phenomenon. We can observe causality and it appears that every event appears to result from earlier events, combined with the laws of nature. We therefore look for an explanation for everything, including the way in which we choose to act.

Any decision made must have a cause. If this is the case then **hard determinism**, a term coined by William James in 1884, takes the no-nonsense line that everything that occurs in the universe has a sufficient explanation through causes and conditions. This is what is called the law of cause and effect. Human actions, the ones people actually do, are the *only* ones that they can do. Therefore, human beings are not free to act; free will is no more than an illusion. It is illogical to speak of free choice or free will because it is clear from observing the interactions of phenomena that everything is determined by causality.

Specification content

Hard determinism: philosophical (John Locke – free will is an illusion, man in bedroom illustration)

Key terms

hard determinism: the doctrine that determinism is true and hence no human actions are free

fatalism: the belief that all events are destined to occur regardless of human choices

Hard determinism states that humans have preconditioned, programmed choices over which they have no control. One implication of this idea is that it would make no sense to praise good deeds because the person who did them had no alternative. Neither can a person be blamed for a bad deed. Our behaviour could not have occurred other than it did.

A set of dominoes falling down, showing causality

The idea of determinism is very different from **fatalism**. Fatalism is the theory that all events are destined to occur no matter what people choose. Whereas determinism looks to natural laws and cause-effect relations, fatalism looks to the wills of gods, divine foreknowledge or mystic forces to guarantee events will happen.

Determinism is also very different from the idea of predestination. Predestination is the doctrine that God has foreordained souls to either salvation or damnation. Whereas determinism has no concept of a final goal, predestination is all about final goals foreordained by God.

Key quote

Any other future set of outcomes other than the one fixed from eternity is impossible

(W. James)

Locke's philosophical determinism

Key person

John Locke (1632–1704): An English philosopher; in *An Essay Concerning Human Understanding*, Locke argued that the will is determined by a person's strongest desire and that freedom belongs to persons, not to the will itself; his 'man in the bedroom' illustration is a classic statement of hard determinism

John Locke (1632–1704) was an English philosopher and in his book *An Essay Concerning Human Understanding* (Book 2, Chapter 21), he developed views on the nature of freedom of action and freedom of will.

John Locke

The meaning of 'the will'

First, he distinguished between voluntary and involuntary actions. A voluntary action is one you choose to do: for example, raising your arm to show you want to say something or ask a question. An involuntary action is one that happens without any choice or intention on your part: for example, someone pushing your arm up or a leg-twitch caused by an illness. Locke noted that voluntary actions often feel free and people seem to have the power to choose certain thoughts and actions. He called this power the will, which he then went on to consider. In particular, he considered whether the will is itself free.

In the first edition of his book, he argued that the will was determined. However, in the later editions he qualified this slightly, arguing that although the most pressing desires for the most part determine the will, there are occasions when the will weighs them against other desires which may change their preference. Some regard this later view as moving towards a form of soft determinism (see 'Soft determinism' on page 234).

The meaning of 'freedom'

Locke regarded the idea of freedom as the idea of a power in a person to do any particular action, according to the determination or thought of the mind. Therefore, freedom is not an idea belonging to the will itself, but to the person having the power of action according to whatever their mind chooses.

In this way, Locke regarded the question of free will (whether the will is free) as 'altogether improper'. Both the will *and* freedom are powers, and it is absurd, he argued, to suppose that powers are capable of having powers. As Locke writes: 'A person in respect of willing any action in their power once proposed to their thoughts cannot be free.' For Locke, then, free will was an unintelligible concept; the two terms simply cannot be meaningfully combined.

'Man in the bedroom' illustration of freedom

In the light of Locke's conclusion about the phrase free will, he commented: 'I think the question is not proper, whether the will be free, but whether a man be free.' The proper question concerns whether a person has the power to enact their will, not whether the will itself possesses some mysterious freedom. In Book 2, Chapter 21 of *An Essay Concerning Human Understanding,* Locke illustrated his understanding of freedom in his example of the man in the bedroom:

> Again: suppose a man be carried, whilst fast asleep, into a room where is a person he longs to see and speak with; and be there locked fast in, beyond his power to get out: he awakes, and is glad to find himself in so desirable company, which he stays willingly in, i.e. prefers his stay to going away. I ask, is not this stay voluntary? I think nobody will doubt it: and yet, being locked fast in, it is evident he is not at liberty not to stay, he has not freedom to be gone. So that liberty is not an idea belonging to volition or preferring; but to the person having the power of doing, or forbearing to do, according as the mind shall choose or direct. Our idea of liberty reaches as far as that power, and no farther. For wherever restraint comes to check that power, or compulsion takes away that indifferency of ability to bear acting, their liberty, and our notion of it, presently ceases.

Freedom and the will are two different concepts.

Key quotes

Hard determinists say that our actions are caused in a way that makes us not as free as we might have thought, so that responsibility, if it implies free will, is an illusion.

(Lacey)

It follows [...] about states of the brain as effects, as correlates and as causes, that on every occasion when we decide or choose, we can only decide or choose as in fact we do.

(Honderich)

There is no absolute or free will, the mind is determined to wish this or that by a cause.

(Baruch Spinoza)

Locke considers freedom with respect to actions. The illustration shows that though the man wills to stay in the room (making it a voluntary action), this is not sufficient for freedom. If the man were to will to leave the room, he could not do so; the locked door removes that power. His ignorance of this constraint creates an illusion of freedom, but Locke concludes that the man is not genuinely free. He can only stay in the room, despite believing he chose to do so voluntarily.

Locke also considers freedom with respect to avoiding willing an action. He argues that human beings are not free to do this. Determinism, which Locke believed in, implies that what a person does is what they willed, and it could not be otherwise. Therefore, a person having willed an action cannot but do it. In other words, he is not free to avoid willing the action.

Finally, Locke considers whether a person is free with respect of willing a particular action. Because of determinism, only the willed action is enacted. No alternative action is possible since it is not willed. Therefore, the person is not free with respect to willing a particular action, other than the one they have willed.

In all these ways, Locke shows that no human actions are free. Therefore, he is often seen as a classic example of a hard determinist.

Key quotes

[...] liberty being as little applicable to the will, as swiftness of motion is to sleep, or squareness to virtue.

(Locke)

[...] Liberty, which is but a power belongs only to agents, and cannot be an attribute or modification of the will, which is also but a power.

(Locke)

For how can we think anyone freer, than to have the power to do what he will?

(Locke)

[...] freedom consists in the dependence of the existence, or not existence of any action, upon our volition of it; and not in the dependence of any action, or its contrary, on our preference.

(Locke)

Laplace's scientific determinism

In an introduction to his book *A Philosophical Essay on Probabilities* (1814), Pierre-Simon Laplace postulated a super-intelligence that could know the positions and velocities of, and the forces on all the particles in the universe at one time and therefore know the universe for all times. This view marked the beginning of scientific determinism, including the idea that given the initial state of a system, we can determine any future state of that system by applying the laws of nature and the information about the initial state. In other words, the future occurrence of an event is predictable.

Biological determinism

In more recent times, scientific determinism has gained support from the claim that the development of a person is determined by their genetic inheritance and human behaviour is determined by **genes** and other biological attributes (**biological determinism**). This denies free will since it implies that human beings have no internal control over their behaviour and so are devoid of responsibility for their actions.

Specification content

Hard determinism: scientific (biological determinism – human behaviour is controlled by an individual's genes)

Key terms

genes: the units of heredity in an organism; the region of DNA that influences a particular characteristic of an organism

biological determinism: the view that human behaviour is controlled by genes and other biological factors

DNA and the Human Genome Project

This view was developed considerably by the discovery of **DNA** (deoxyribonucleic acid). The discovery of DNA was a gradual process and had several important contributors including Nikolai Koltsov (1872–1940) and Frederick Griffith (1879–1941). However, it was not until James Watson (1928–2025) and Francis Crick (1916–2004) developed the double-helix model of DNA structure in 1953 after seeing an image captured by Rosalind Franklin (1920–1958) that this theory was widely accepted in the scientific community.

The theory of genetic fixity states that the genes of parents inevitably determine the characteristics of their children. Therefore, some claim that a child's characteristics, health and even future behaviour are determined at the moment of conception. The **Human Genome Project** (1990–2003) attempted to map the genes of the human **genome**. Although the project was not able to sequence all the DNA found in human cells, it did sequence 92 per cent of it. The work on interpretation and analysis of genome data is still ongoing, but some of the findings of research that came after the Human Genome Project are believed to support genetic fixity.

Key terms

DNA: deoxyribonucleic acid, the hereditary material in humans; nearly every cell in a person's body has the same DNA and it carries genetic instructions

Human Genome Project: an international scientific research project with the goal of determining the sequences that make up human DNA, and of identifying and mapping all the genes of the human genome from both a physical and a functional standpoint

genome: the genetic material of an organism; an organism's complete genetic code

Criminality and violent behaviour

According to the United Nations, the global number of people in prison at the end of 2024 was 11.8 million, of which 93 per cent were men. This seems overwhelming evidence that there is a correlation between the Y chromosome (with its unique set of genes) and criminality.

In the X chromosome, the MAOA gene controls the amount of dopamine and serotonin in the brain. This gene is known as the warrior gene because mutations in, or abnormal versions of, the gene often result in aggressive behaviour.

The most recent research has mainly focused on genes that influence how nerve impulses are transmitted and received in the brain. However, the importance of the interplay of genetics with social and environmental factors in influencing a person's propensity to criminality and violent behaviour is now more recognised. For instance, poverty, poor diet, high social inequality levels and low educational attainment are all considered crucial to shaping behaviour; behaviour cannot be solely attributed to biological determinism.

Key quotes

We may regard the present state of the universe as the effect of its past and the cause of its future.

(Laplace)

The law of causation, according to which later events can theoretically be predicted by means of earlier events, has often been held to be *a priori*, a *necessity* of thought, a category without which science would not be possible.

(Russell)

Addiction

In March 2023, *Nature Mental Health* published the results of a research project involving over 150 scientists who combed through genomic data of over a million people and identified genes commonly correlated with addiction disorders, regardless of the addictive substance being used. Their findings reinforce the role of the dopamine system in addiction by showing that the combination of genes underlying addiction disorders was also associated with regulation of dopamine signalling.

However, one difficulty is separating genes and environmental factors as influences on addiction. The director of the National Institute on Drug Abuse in the USA said: 'A better understanding of genetics also brings us one step closer to developing personalized interventions that are tailored to an individual's unique biology, environment, and lived experience in order to provide the most benefits.'

Sexual orientation

In December 2017, *New Scientist* reported that a study comparing DNA from 1077 homosexual men and 1231 heterosexual men had pinpointed two genes whose variants seem to be linked to sexual orientation. One gene is on chromosome 13, which is in the brain region containing the hypothalamus. Interestingly, the neuroscientist Simon LeVay had, as early as 1991, already discovered that the hypothalamus differed in size between gay men and straight men. The other relevant gene identified is found on chromosome 14 and is mainly active in the thyroid.

However, more recent research suggests sexual orientation is more likely a polygenic trait (multiple genes contribute to the characteristic) including prenatal hormone exposure. The environment may also play a role. As a result, many people would see sexual orientation as a spectrum, which would include bisexual people. Little research has been focused on same-sex attraction between women or on people who are asexual.

Scientists are careful not to give the impression that there is any such entity as a 'gene for' a given human trait. Nevertheless, research also makes it clear that genes make a significant contribution to who we are.

Gay Pride has long advocated scientific support for genetic links to sexual orientation, demonstrating that individuals are 'born this way'

Key quotes

Sexuality cannot be pinned down by biology, psychology or life experiences, this study and others show, because human sexual attraction is decided by all these factors.

(*Science* (29 Aug 2019))

In the fertilised egg, the genetic program is complete.

(Christiane Nusslein-Volhard)

Psychological determinism

While biological determinism sees the sources of determinism as being internal – for example, genes – psychological determinism sees the sources as external – for example, **conditioning** or reinforcement. One particular form of psychological determinism is **behaviourism**.

Pavlov's classical conditioning

One branch of behaviourism is classical conditioning, which is learning by association or reflex learning. A Russian psychologist named **Ivan Pavlov** (1849–1936) discovered this by accident while he was conducting experiments on digestion in dogs. He began to study what prompts dogs to salivate. He thought simply that they should produce saliva when presented with food as the saliva helps break down food. However, he noticed that they started drooling when they saw lab coats, even though no food was in sight.

He realised that the dogs made an association between lab coats (the people who fed Pavlov's dogs wore lab coats) and food appearing. So he ran a study in which he rang a bell every time he fed the dogs. Before long, just ringing the bell made the dogs salivate. This was an example of classical conditioning that is learned. The dogs had been conditioned to produce the unconditioned reflex of saliva to the neutral stimulus of the bell.

Specification content

Hard determinism: psychological (Ivan Pavlov – classical conditioning)

Key terms

conditioning: a theory that the reaction to an object or event by a person can be determined by stimuli

behaviourism: a theory of learning based on the idea that all behaviours can be explained without the need to consider internal mental states or consciousness; also known as behavioural psychology

Key person

Ivan Pavlov (1849–1936): A Russian physiologist and psychologist; while researching digestion in dogs, Pavlov accidentally discovered classical conditioning, the process by which a reflex response becomes associated with a new stimulus; his work became foundational to behaviourist psychology and the argument that human behaviour is determined by external stimuli

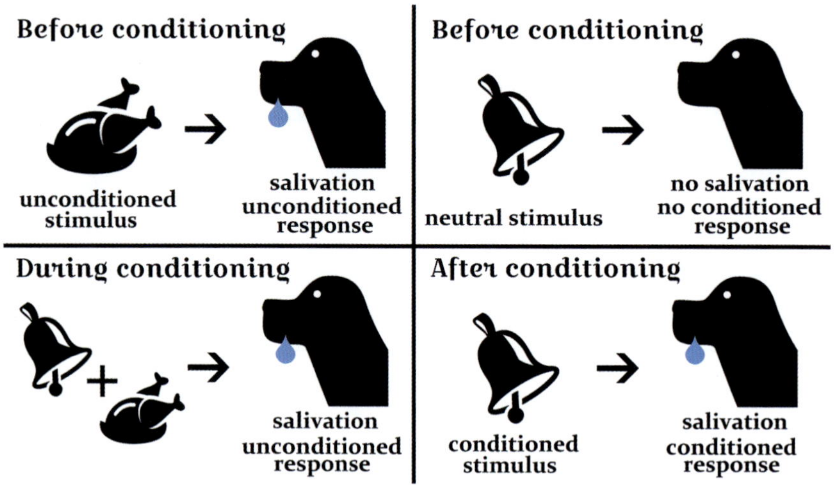

Pavlov's dog experiment

The American psychologist John Watson (1878–1958) and his research assistant Rosalie Rayner (1898–1935), furthered Pavlov's work by attempting to show that the same conditioning also happens in human beings. In a study that would be considered unethical today, they took a baby of nine months, popularly known today as Little Albert, and exposed him to a series of stimuli including a white rat, a rabbit and burning newspapers, and observed his reactions. Albert showed no fear of any of the objects he was presented with.

The next time Albert was shown the rat, Watson made a loud noise by hitting a metal pipe with a hammer. As expected, Albert began to cry. After repeatedly pairing the white rat with the loud noise, Albert began to cry simply at seeing the rat. This demonstrated that emotional responses could be conditioned in human beings.

Watson and Rayner also found that Albert had generalised his fear to other furry objects, including Rayner's fur coat and Watson wearing a Santa Claus beard.

Skinner's operant conditioning

Following Pavlov and Watson, some psychologists of the behaviourist school started to argue that the concept of free will was simply an illusion. They believed that all human action was the direct result of conditioning. One such psychologist was the American B.F. Skinner, who referred to this view as 'radical behaviourism'.

Skinner proposed a further development of classical conditioning, called **operant conditioning**. Here a person is conditioned to always repeat behaviour that is rewarded, but not repeat behaviour that is punished. Through operant conditioning, an individual makes an association between a particular behaviour and a consequence. Reinforcement comes in two forms:

- **Positive reinforcers**: These are favourable events or outcomes given to the individual after the desired result (for example, rewards).
- **Negative reinforcers**: These consist of the removal of an undesired or unpleasant outcome after the desired behaviour.

The behaviourists argued that the mind is not directly observable and so cannot be fully understood, so behaviourism focuses on observable physical reactions of people to stimuli.

Key term

operant conditioning: learning through rewards and punishments

The Libet experiments

However, some neuroscientists argue that we are all just a bundle of electrical impulses and our behaviour is 100 per cent predictable. In the 1980s, a neuroscientist named Benjamin Libet (1916–2007) conducted a series of famous experiments which, it has been claimed since, proved that free will was simply a trick of the mind. The Libet experiments showed that activity occurs in the brain a fraction of time before a person takes an action. According to Libet, our brains decide for us and we act on impulse, only later coming to believe we have chosen an action.

This outcome, while widely regarded for a time as evidence, has now been regarded as just a possible basis for a theory. Many neuro-philosophists are unconvinced that this detectable activity in our brains can actually prove that no level of consciousness is involved in our decisions. Perhaps, they surmise, the formula is more like subconscious activity – the brain is activated, the action is taken and finally post-action reflection (or conscious thought) takes place.

Soft determinism

William James coined the terms hard determinism and soft determinism in an address to Harvard Divinity School in 1884 that was published later that year. Soft determinism is an attempt to combine the opposing theories of hard determinism and libertarianism (the idea that people can be totally free in their moral decision-making). The theory contains the argument that people are determined but nonetheless free. This is because of a particular understanding of what it means to be free.

Being free

To a soft determinist, being free is about being able to do what one wants to do, without external coercion or interference from anyone else. They accept that human actions have causes (background, genetics, education and the rest) but believe that the actions are free if they are caused by our choices rather than by external forces. Soft determinism is sometimes called **compatibilism**. This is not a proposition that determinism is consistent with free will or **origination**. Rather, it sees freedom (which is not the same as free will) and determinism working together. There is a causal story for a person's action.

Indeed, freedom requires determinism in order to make sense; without determinism, all actions would be random and impossible to explain. Freedom involves the empowerment to act and thereby control the desired effect. A.J. Ayer stated this clearly when he wrote: 'If I suffered from a compulsion neurosis, so that I got up and walked across the room, whether I wanted to or not [...] then I should not be acting freely. But if I do it now, I shall be acting freely [...] For it is not when my action has any cause at all, but only when it has a special sort of cause, that it is reckoned not to be free.' This view of people's actions allows for moral responsibility, while hard determinism does not.

Hobbe's classical soft determinism

Classical soft determinism is the claim that determinism is true and that people act freely when they are not constrained or coerced. It redefines free will in terms of a freedom to act.

Key quotes

Men believe themselves to be free, simply because they are conscious of their actions and unconscious of the causes.

(Spinoza)

Man has no will, intention, self-determinism or personal responsibility.

(Skinner)

Responses that produce a satisfying effect in a particular situation become more likely to occur again in that situation, and responses that produce a discomforting effect become less likely to occur again in that situation.

(Thorndike)

Key terms

compatibilism: the theory that freedom and determinism are mutually compatible in the case of some human actions; there is no logical inconsistency in believing in both

origination: the bringing about of decisions and actions in such a way that they are not effects from a chain of cause and effect; the decisions/actions are in the control of the person

Key quotes

Man is free when he chooses what he wants, but he cannot will what he wants.

(Schopenhauer)

Life is like a game of cards. The hand that is dealt you represents determinism; the way you play it is free will.

(Nehru)

Specification content

Soft determinism: Thomas Hobbes (internal and external causes)

Free actions

Thomas Hobbes (1588–1679) was a determinist who believed that everything that happens, including every human action, was the necessary effect of antecedent causes. However, he also argued that there are free actions, but he conceived freedom in such a way that it is consistent with necessity. Hobbes was also a materialist and rejected the idea of a will as a distinct part of the mind. He saw desire as the thing that motivates a person to act.

He therefore denied that choosing or willing are about some special kinds of rational power uniquely possessed by human beings. For Hobbes, there was no such power as the will. He also rejected the idea that a being could determine itself. In his treatise, Hobbes stated 'nothing takes beginning from itself, but from the action of some other immediate agent without itself'.

Internal and external causes

Hobbes defined freedom or liberty as the absence of external impediments (impediments that are not contained in the nature or intrinsic quality of the agent). In this sense a person is as free as an unimpeded river. A river that flows down a hill necessarily follows a channel. However, it is also at liberty to flow *within* the channel. He claimed that the voluntary actions of people are similar. To be at liberty is to be not restrained, which is not the same as to be uncaused. People are free because their actions follow from their will (desires). The actions, however, are necessary in the sense that they originate from a chain of causes and effects. Freedom is all about acting as we will and not being coerced in any way.

An **internal cause** refers to a person's willing to do an act before actually doing it or willing to forbear an act before actually forbearing it. In such cases the action is voluntary. This includes actions that are compelled, if the compulsion works upon the desires of the person and causes the action. As an example of compulsion Hobbes stated: 'A man is said to be compelled when fear makes him willing to do something, as when a man willingly throws his goods into the sea to save himself.'

In contrast, an **external cause** refers to coercion or force and makes an act involuntary, since it is against the agent's will (desire). Hobbes used the example of 'when a man by force, seizing on another man's limbs, moves them as himself, not as the other man pleases […] the action so done is not the action of him that suffers, but of him that uses the force'.

Ayer's soft determinism

Like Hobbes before him, A.J. Ayer supported classical soft determinism. He argued that a person who did action A could be considered to have acted freely if that person could have refrained from doing action A. The fact that an action A can be explained by a cause did not mean that it was not therefore a free action.

Constraint

For Ayer, the key factor involved is constraint. His empirical studies of language showed him that people make a language distinction between hard determinism and soft determinism. He stated that if he walked across a room because someone compelled him to, observers would conclude he was not acting freely and that this 'forced' movement was completely determined. However, if he walked across a room without being compelled by another, observers would still assume it had a cause because all actions must be willed by the person, even if our will is determined. In this case, however,

Key person

Thomas Hobbes (1588–1679): An English philosopher, best known for *Leviathan*; Hobbes was a determinist who believed every human action results from prior causes; he redefined freedom as the absence of external impediments, making him a key figure in the development of soft determinism

Thomas Hobbes

Key terms

internal cause: internalised moral choice (or the person's will to do something) that is completely determined

external cause: when a person's will is stopped from carrying out its predetermined choice

Specification content

Soft determinism: A.J. Ayer (caused acts vs forced acts)

they would not say he was forced. Therefore, for Ayer, it all centred on what is considered as a constraint.

Conditions of constrained actions

He proposed three conditions that identified a person's action as constrained, such that they could not have acted differently:

- **Coercion**: This is when a person is compelled by another to do the action (for example, forced at gunpoint).
- **Habitual ascendancy**: This is when a person does not engage in the deliberative process (for example, a soldier under orders).
- **Internal constraint**: This is when a person's deliberative process is irrelevant (for example, kleptomania).

All actions have causes but it is a special cause that makes the action not free. Therefore, for a person to act freely, it means that they could have acted otherwise; and for this to happen Ayer argued three conditions had to be fulfilled:

- The person could have acted otherwise had they so chosen.
- The person was not compelled by another person.
- The person's action was voluntary and free from internal constraints.

In this way Ayer argued for soft determinism, since it is possible to explain the cause of the action and that the person could have acted otherwise. However, many might argue that it is difficult to identify an internal constraint. In particular, in Ayer's example of kleptomania, it is not clear whether the person could have chosen to stop stealing in a similar way that some alcoholics could stop drinking alcohol. Indeed, it is impossible to show that the person could have chosen to act differently in any given situation, since only one action resulted (that is, the action they actually took).

Modern forms of soft determinism

Some more recent variations of soft determinism have challenged this limited view – that freedom simply means no constraints – and have argued that some of the determining factors can be overcome.

- Peter Vardy (1945–) argues that our intellect is capable of understanding the effects of conditioning and genetics. Being aware of such forces and influences can lead to more freedom and towards a path of self-determination. Vardy admits that true freedom may never be achieved because of the complexity of genetic and environmental influences on us; however, this does not mean that freedom is not possible at all.
- Robert Kane (1938–2024) took a similar view in which he referred to a 'torn decision', in which a person has equally powerful reasons for choosing either way between two alternatives. Whatever way they choose, the person is making a rational decision and Kane claimed that the person is therefore in control of the decision. The decision was caused by the person's efforts. Kane was an example of a philosopher that sees no problems with free will in the face of indeterminism and causal relationships.
- Daniel Dennett (1942–2024) saw intelligence as the key feature. He argued for a concept of freedom that is a highly developed ability, refined in the course of evolution, enabling people to envisage future possibilities and to avoid those we do not like. Dennett saw this as compatible with determinism and that it is all that is required for us to be

Key quotes

We began with the assumption that freedom is contrasted with causality, so that a man cannot be said to be acting freely if his action is causally determined. But this assumption has led us into difficulties and I now wish to suggest that it is mistaken. For it is not, I think, causality that freedom is to be contrasted with, but constraint.

(Ayer)

It may be said of the agent that he would have acted otherwise if the causes of his action had been different, but they being what they were, it seems to follow that he was bound to act as he did.

(Ayer)

regarded as free. In essence, this modern approach is proposing that we can 'step outside' of ourselves to reflect on what we have become and decide whether we want to remain that way. This self-awareness allows us to be free to make new decisions.

Summary

- Determinism is grounded in the principle of causality: natural laws and cause-effect relations.
- Determinism has no concept of a final goal, whereas predestination is all about goals foreordained by God.
- Hard determinism means that our actions are the only ones that we can do because of the causes that precede them, whereas soft determinism means being free to do what one wants to do even though all human actions have a causal story.
- According to John Locke's philosophical determinism, the will and freedom are two different powers. In the example of the man in the bedroom, the man *wills* to stay in a room but he is simultaneously *not free* to leave (the door to the room is locked).
- According to biological determinism (a form of scientific determinism) human behaviour is determined by genes in DNA.
- According to psychological determinism, animal and human behaviour can be determined by external sources, such as conditioning and reinforcement.
- Thomas Hobbes argued that people are free whenever their voluntary actions (which are not uncaused but have internal causes) are not restrained by external causes.
- A.J. Ayer argued that a person acts freely if their behaviour was not forced by either external or internal constraints.

AO1 Activity

a Examine the key terms in this unit by creating a flowchart that links each term to your understanding of determinism. This will help you to develop an ability to present the terms' inter-relatedness, demonstrate extensive depth and/or breadth of knowledge and ensure that you make accurate use of specialist language and vocabulary in context.

b Explain how scientific and psychological deterministic theories might account for the behaviour of a person accused of violent behaviour, as if preparing a defence case for a court hearing. This will help you to select the key relevant information for an answer to a question on deterministic theories.

To assess your work, refer to the band descriptors for AS/A Level. In particular, note the requirements for band 5: 'Thorough, accurate and relevant knowledge and understanding of religion and belief [...] presented with extensive depth and/or breadth [...] excellent use of evidence and examples [...] thorough and accurate use of specialist language and vocabulary.'

Issues for analysis and evaluation

Consideration of the strengths and weaknesses of hard determinism

Possible line of argument	Critical analysis and evaluation
There is clear evidence of causality from biology and psychology.	Some events may be clearly determined, but that does not mean all events are.
Determinative explanations from a variety of social sciences can account for our apparent choices. The cumulative argument is strong.	The cumulativeness of the argument by itself is unconvincing since a failed argument added to another failed argument results in both failing.
There is no explanation as to how free will functions.	Determinism is self-refuting since the ultimate cause of why a person believes that free will is an illusion must also be predetermined.
Newtonian science explains cause and effect and predictability.	Quantum mechanics and indeterminism challenge Newtonian views of causation and predictability.
The unpredictability in the universe is only at quantum levels and does not affect the actions of human beings.	If all actions are the effects of prior actions then determinists fail to explain what is prior to the first ever action. Was it God?
Philosophical determinism suggests that the concept of free will is meaningless and contradictory.	The experience of people is that they do in fact choose freely. They act as though they are exercising a power of self-determination.
Modern therapies for people with mental health disorders have shown some success at controlling human behaviour.	It is impossible to be certain as to the cause of the change to human behaviour from therapies. It neither proves nor disproves determinism.
For an action to be unpredictable only means that its causes cannot be identified, rather than that the causes do not exist.	Determinism is unfalsifiable since it is impossible to show that an action was not the result of some cause.
If events are not causally determined then whether or not they happen is just a matter of chance or luck.	If events are caused by conditions outside my control, I am neither free nor responsible, and there is no way of knowing whether determinism is true or false.
Moral responsibility is to do with control and reason. A person is morally responsible because the action resulted from the person's own reasons.	A person is only regarded as morally responsible for what they have done if they could have done otherwise.

This section covers AO2 content and skills

Specification content

Strengths and weaknesses of hard and/or soft determinism

AO2 Activity

a Analyse three lines of argument from the table on page 237. Research and select three supporting references from scholars or philosophical texts.

b Choose the **strongest** line of argument and identify three key questions that could be asked about it; your questions can be critical, challenging, hypothetical or direct.

To assess your work, refer to the band descriptors for AS/A Level. In particular, note the requirements for band 5: 'Thorough, accurate and relevant knowledge and understanding of religion and belief [...] presented with extensive depth and/or breadth [...] excellent use of evidence and examples [...] thorough and accurate use of specialist language and vocabulary.'

Specification content

The extent to which philosophical, scientific and/or psychological determinism illustrate that humanity has no free will

Exam practice

Below is an evaluation of the extent to which philosophical, scientific and psychological determinism illustrate that humanity has no free will.

Sample answer

Explorer

News reporter

The opening paragraphs set out clear lines of argument to challenge the whole concept of hard determinism and then free will. Reasons to support the various challenges are clearly expressed and assessed.

One approach to this debate would be to challenge the whole idea of hard determinism. Many see hard determinism as self-refuting. If hard determinism is true then there is no way of knowing whether what a person believes is true or false is in fact true or false. What they believe is caused by prior events outside of their control. The problem with such a challenge is that it does not align with our everyday experience.

An alternative argument would be to appeal to modern quantum mechanics and Heisenberg's uncertainty principle to challenge the idea of causality that the arguments for determinism rest on. Modern science is no longer so confident about causation. The problem with this challenge, however, is that randomness is hardly what is envisaged when referring to free will.

Judge

Detective

Clear reference to John Locke is made to support challenges to the whole concept of free will.

Another approach would be to challenge the whole idea of free will. Perhaps the strongest form of determinism that implies that humanity has no free will is that of philosophical determinism, since it argues that free will itself is an illusion. John Locke argued that free will was an unintelligible concept since the concept of freedom cannot be put alongside the concept of the will. Freedom is about whether a person is free to enact their will, which is very different from whether a person's will is somehow free. If this is right, whether or not humanity has free will is a non-question.

Tennis player

Judge

The previous view is then challenged, followed by a counter-argument.

However, such a view seems unpersuasive. It is a common experience that we make choices, and that we could have made alternative choices. Indeed, we are moral beings and morality implies a free choice. In response, it has to be admitted that it is difficult to ever demonstrate that a person could have chosen differently since they only ever enact one choice in each moment.

It is the case that we experience causality in everyday life and the idea of determinism is grounded in the principle of causality. We look for an explanation for everything, including the way in which we choose to act and the decisions we make. Scientific determinism and psychological determinism provide some explanations of the internal and external causes that make us behave in a certain way. The debate between scientific determinism and psychological determinism is essentially a debate between nature and nurture, though most would agree that either one on its own offers a simplistic description of human behaviour. It is more likely there is a complex interaction between genes and conditioning, as well as other factors.

News reporter

Detective

Having dismissed the objections to the ideas of determinism and free will, the argument moves on to consider scientific and psychological determinism.

Today there certainly seems to be strong evidence that genes can influence our behaviour. References to addiction genes and violence genes in modern research are often cited. However, Denis Alexander, in his Gifford lecture, made clear that thousands of genes collaborate together during human development, in interaction with the environment, to generate each individual's character. For instance, having a Y chromosome, with its unique set of genes, does not completely determine a person's tendency to criminality. Therefore, genes may contribute to our personalities, but they do not entirely determine them.

Tennis player

Detective

The evidence for genes affecting our behaviour is debated well here.

Perhaps stronger evidence for determinism, rather than free will, comes from behaviourism. Pavlov argued that all our actions are just conditioned reactions to our environment. Similarly, Skinner argued that people can be conditioned from a young age by a system of rewards and punishments for certain behaviours. However, such evidence has mostly been derived from experiments on animals, and it is not necessarily correct to assume that it applies equally to human behaviour. It is very questionable to assume that general laws governing the behaviour of animals can be applied to complex relations in the human world. If the assumption is false then it undermines the very foundation upon which much of behaviourism rests.

Other criticisms of behaviourism have been voiced by Seligman who argued that it is unable to explain the development of human language and memory. Wyrwicka saw behaviourism as contradicting Darwin's ideas about natural selection. Darwin saw the natural-selection drive as dependent on what is necessary for the survival of the species, whereas behaviourism is more about sensory gratification. What is pleasurable to the senses is not always what is best for survival. It seems that the human brain cannot be fully measured and quantified to the point of predicting behaviour.

Critical thinker

Detective

Behaviourism is discussed to see if it supports determinism rather than free will. Good reference is made to Pavlov and Skinner. This view is then challenged.

The concepts of both determinism and free will seem thwarted with difficulties, and though scientific study has not demonstrated that humanity is determined, it has not explained free will either. It is hard to deny that we deliberate about things, which means we must believe in free will. Yet it is possible that even the decision-making process, including the options considered and the potential influences (both biological and psychological), is determined. Even if it could be demonstrated that humanity is determined at a very basic level of causation, it does not necessarily mean that we have no free will.

Judge

Philosopher

An accurate summing up of the conclusions to the various approaches and arguments considered in the essay. A good, thoughtful conclusion.

Over to you

For this task, you have only instructions with no examples. However, using the skills you have developed by completing the earlier tasks, you should be able to apply what you have learned and complete this successfully.

Your new task is to write a response to the question under timed conditions.

You need to focus for this and apply the skills that you have developed so far:

1. Begin with a list of indicative content. Perhaps discuss this as a group. It does not need to be in any particular order. Remember: this is evaluation, so you need different lines of argument. The easiest way is to use the 'in support' and 'against' headings.
2. Develop the list using examples.
3. Consider the order in which you would like to present the information.
4. Finally, write out your response, under timed conditions, remembering to apply the principles of evaluation by making sure that you:
   - identify issues clearly
   - present accurate views of others and comment on the views presented
   - reach an overall personal judgement.

Use this technique as revision for each of the topic areas that you have studied. The basic technique of planning answers helps even when time is short and you cannot complete every essay.

Question

'Hard determinism is far more convincing than soft determinism.' Evaluate this view. (WJEC 2018)

C: The implications of determinism and predestination

The implications of hard determinism for moral responsibility

The worth of human ideas of rightness, wrongness and moral value

To hold someone morally responsible involves an attitude or feeling. It is an attitude of disapproval or approval with respect to an action. We measure actions against our standards of morality. We blame or praise people accordingly, provided they had a real choice of action. If they could not have pursued any other course of action, then praise or blame seems inappropriate. It would seem that if hard determinism is true then none of us can be held morally responsible since people are unable to act differently from how they actually do.

Such a view has been used as a defence in a court of law. One of the most famous examples of this is in the case of two teenagers, Leopold and Loeb, who, in 1924, admitted to killing a 14-year-old boy. Clarence Darrow was their lawyer at the trial and he claimed that the teenagers 'were decidedly deficient in emotion' since they did not feel revolted by their act. The defence was that they had not made a conscious choice between right and wrong since it had been psychological, physical and environmental influences that had controlled their behaviour. The result was that the judge sentenced them to life imprisonment rather than to death. How much the defence's particular argument swayed the judge is not clear. Darrow also argued that no person under 21 who had pleaded guilty had ever been sentenced to death.

Another approach to moral responsibility is to focus on the idea that morality is about something a person ought to do. But if they *ought* to do an action it must be possible that they are *able* to do it. However, hard determinists claim that it is impossible for them to act differently. Therefore, there is no moral responsibility. Such a view about moral responsibility has implications for the way we view ourselves as moral beings. To what extent can we consider ourselves as being morally responsible?

It is important to understand that even if moral responsibility cannot exist, this does not mean that morality itself cannot exist. Determinism does not affect whether an act is moral or immoral, but it does affect whether a person can be held morally responsible for that act. There is a distinction between morality and moral responsibility.

The value of blaming moral agents for immoral acts

Holding someone morally responsible may involve the desire for retribution and justice. There is a concern for those negatively affected by the immoral act, and a desire that the person who acted immorally is made to know that others disapprove. If hard determinism is true, then how can these attitudes and feelings be addressed?

As has been argued, hard determinism seems to imply that a person is not morally responsible. However, a hard determinist can accept that a person can be changed in the future. Some form of blame and punishment could bring about a change in character, since rewards and punishments have causal effects on people's behaviour. Punishment can reinforce moral acts and discourage immoral ones. The difficulty is deciding what punishment would be the most appropriate to correct a tendency towards immoral acts.

This section covers AO1 content and skills

Specification content

The implications of determinism (hard and soft) on moral responsibility: the worth of human ideas of rightness, wrongness and moral value

Key quotes

Life calls the tune, we dance. **(Galsworthy)**

Any other future set of outcomes than the one fixed from eternity is impossible. **(James)**

Man has no will, intention, self-determinism or personal responsibility. **(Skinner)**

Punishment as punishment is not admissible unless the offender has the free will to select this course. **(Darrow)**

Life is like a game of cards. The hand you are dealt is determinism; the way you play it is free will. **(Nehru)**

In his book *How Free Are You?*, Ted Honderich argues against retributive punishment: 'It cannot be that we should satisfy grievance by imposing great distress on other people. The means of great distress is not justified by the end of satisfaction.'

If no blame is allocated for immoral acts, those acts could serve as contributing causes of future acts and more undesirable outcomes.

The usefulness of normative ethics

Normative ethics examine the sources of, and standards for, moral judgements. They act as a moral guide explaining what people should do and why, and whether their current moral behaviour is reasonable given whatever moral standards are being used in that context. An example of a normative ethic is the divine command theory. This states that an action's status as moral or immoral is based on what God wills and commands. In Christianity, God's commands are claimed to be in the Bible. The Decalogue found in Exodus 20 is an example. Therefore, if this is the normative ethic being followed, then it is morally wrong to murder since a moral command in the Decalogue is: 'You shall not murder.'

Moses receiving the Tablets of Law by Raphael (1518–19)

As with the issue of blame, the statement of the ethic can form part of the causal chain and so influence future actions. Though hard determinists would not agree that a person can freely choose to follow a particular ethic, they do accept that the normative ethic can influence actions.

The implications of soft determinism for moral responsibility

The worth of human ideas of rightness, wrongness and moral value

Soft determinists argue that a free choice or action is one that is voluntary and accords with the person's desires and true nature. This understanding of a free choice can support the view that a person is morally responsible. The fact that a person not only performed, but also wanted to perform, an act, even when influenced by past events, makes the person morally responsible.

Another argument is that if a person had chosen differently, they would have acted differently. Therefore, they are morally responsible. In other words, choice creates moral responsibility.

However, many would argue that for a person to be held morally responsible, the choice they made must be a free and voluntary choice, that is a *genuine* choice. The chooser must be free from mental conditioning caused by either previous behaviour or external influences. Therefore, the idea that a person can be held morally responsible if soft determinism is true is often rejected.

As with hard determinism, soft determinism does not mean we always act immorally. Neither does it mean that morality does not exist. The process of causal determination does not affect whether an act is moral or immoral, but it does affect whether we can be held responsible. Neither hard nor soft determinism invalidates the concept of moral value; determinism of any kind merely addresses the issue of moral accountability rather than the existence of morality itself.

The value in blaming moral agents for immoral acts

The fact that we blame people implies they are responsible agents. We regard people's actions as very different from natural occurrences – for example, an earthquake – in terms of blame. In soft determinism, a responsible person not only performed, but also wanted to perform, an act. They were not forced to act against their desires. Acts are willed actions, however inevitably they might have followed from past events.

As with hard determinism, blame and punishment become part of the causal chain and so can influence future events and actions. The value in blaming is that disapproval is shown, discouraging immoral acts and encouraging moral acts.

> **Key quote**
>
> Without free will, we seem diminished, merely the playthings of external forces. How, then, can we maintain an exalted view of ourselves? Determinism seems to undercut human dignity, it seems to undermine our value.
>
> (Nozick)

The usefulness of normative ethics

Classical soft determinists propose that freedom to act depends on freedom to make a choice, regardless of the causal chain behind that choice. With soft determinism as with hard determinism, normative ethics can influence later actions by being part of the causal chain and encouraging moral actions and discouraging immoral actions.

Implications of predestination for religious belief

> **Specification content**
>
> The implications of predestination for religious belief: the implications for God's omnipotence and omnibenevolence, the use of prayer, the existence of miracles and the link between God and evil

Whereas determinism is a philosophical concept that involves empirical notions of cause and effect, predestination implies that events are specifically directed by God rather than some neutral causal chain. For some, predestination is more about final goals, foreordained by God. It does not necessarily refute free will as such, but it does imply that at no point can human free will thwart the plans and purposes of God. Others see predestination as a predetermination of all actions and events, removing the possibility of free will of any kind. Neither hard determinism nor soft determinism has any concept of a final goal; according to both, the world is a closed phenomenon of universal causation which is neutral with regard to final outcomes.

For God's omnipotence

Although omnipotence is usually defined as unlimited power, many theologians and philosophers would want to qualify that definition. In his book *The Problem of Pain*, C.S. Lewis argued that God's omnipotence means the 'power to do all that is intrinsically possible, not to do the intrinsically impossible [...] not because his power meets an obstacle but because nonsense remains nonsense even when we talk it about God'. Another qualification, often cited, is that God is able to do anything that is in accord with his own nature.

Both Jewish and Christian teachings agree that God is omnipotent. For instance, in Job (42:2), 'I know that you can do all things; no purpose of yours can be thwarted,' and similarly, in Proverbs (19:21), 'Many are the plans in a man's heart, but it is the Lord's purpose that prevails.' Clearly, predestination implies God's omnipotence since he orchestrates the final destiny of every human being.

Jewish and Christian teachings also agree that God creates humans as moral beings who are held responsible for their actions. Augustine opposed the teachings of Pelagius because, according to Augustine, Pelagius' free will theology seemed to diminish the omnipotent nature of God.

Aquinas reconciled freedom with predestination by arguing that not only is everything done that God wills to be done, but it is done in the way God *wants* it to be done. God, in his omnipotence, wants human acts to be done freely. It is because God is all-powerful that human beings are free. God is all-loving, therefore God cannot use that power lovelessly.

Others argue that, by choosing to create human beings with free will, God has chosen to limit his omnipotence. However, the free will is limited in that it cannot ultimately thwart the plans and purposes of God.

Key quote

Give thanks to the Lord, for he is good. His love endures for ever.

(Psalm 136:1)

For God's omnibenevolence

The earliest record of the use of the word omnibenevolence in English is from 1679 and it literally means 'all good will' or 'willing all good'.

Many would argue that because humanity has fallen and inherited Adam's sin, all humans deserve judgement from God, but, because God is omnibenevolent, he predestines some to be saved even though they do not deserve to be saved. The difficulty is that, as both Augustine and Calvin argued, God only predestines *some* people to be forgiven of their sins. It might be argued that if God were omnibenevolent then he would surely have predestined everybody to salvation and forgiveness of their sins. Bertrand Russell stated that God must be 'a monster' because 'a God that punishes or rewards on the basis of God's own eternal decisions is unfair and immoral'.

Bertrand Russell

Some take predestination further and argue that all actions and events are predetermined by God and there is no free will. However, many reject this idea of predestination as it seems to imply God is the author of all sin.

For the use of prayer

If God has predestined all actions and events, it is difficult to see how prayer could have any influence on events. If one purpose of prayer is to change an outcome, but all outcomes are preordained by God and cannot be changed, prayer seems futile.

It might be argued that prayers that are in line with God's plans are the prayers that are answered. However, this would seem to make praying redundant, since those outcomes would have happened regardless as they were part of God's plan.

Muslims at prayer

The Calvinist theory of unconditional election (that it is God alone who chose the elect, based solely upon God's own will, before the world was even created) also seems to undermine the value of prayer. Any attempt to pray to the divine to earnestly ask to become one of the elect would appear to be a complete waste of effort.

However, perhaps prayer does have a use but only for the predestined elect: to build a rapport with God, including seeking forgiveness for sin. Calvin supported this when he stated that the elect could still be sinful, but God predestines them to have faith in the saving atonement of Jesus Christ. Therefore, when the predestined elect sin, they cannot resist the calling on their lives to seek forgiveness, which could be done through prayer.

If God has determined all outcomes, then God has also determined the means by which those outcomes will take place, including prayer. For instance, Elijah prayed for drought and then rain (1 Kings 18–19). If God had already determined that Elijah would pray for those events, then those events would not have taken place if Elijah had not prayed for them.

Key quote

If we are faithless, he [God] remains faithful, for he cannot disown himself.

(2 Timothy 2:13)

Those who believe that predestination is about final outcomes, and feel there is a place for free will within everyday events, have no problem in seeing prayer as an agent of change.

For the existence of miracles

Aquinas defined a miracle as an event beyond the natural power of any created being. It has a 'divine cause' and so is not a normal part of the nature of things.

For religious believers who support predestination, God is active in miracles, and this activity could have been pre-planned by a predestining, omnipotent and omniscient God. God knows the timing of all events, past, present and future, and therefore knows the timing of all miracles that he chooses to do. Predestination, therefore, cannot be an issue here since God alone is involved in the decision about whether to perform a miracle. People having free will or not is irrelevant.

Those who support the view of predestination that accepts free will, in everyday actions and events, accept that God cannot control all earthly affairs, but argue that God can still achieve his goals by judicious intervention. They maintain that God can and frequently does override human freedom or intervene in the natural order (perform miracles) when he deems it necessary.

For the link between God and evil

If God is omnipotent and omnibenevolent then the problem arises as to why there is evil in the world. Both natural and moral evil can cause suffering, and it would seem that God has both the power and the motivation to intervene to prevent it. Predestination implies God is directing individuals to a final outcome. Therefore, one explanation is that the evil experienced is a necessary part of that route to the final outcome. Certainly, Irenaean-type theodicies argue that God is justified in allowing evil since it is part of God's plan for soul-making. This would include natural evils such as earthquakes, since such a world does not suggest that it is one that God would create.

Equally it could be argued that God has not predestined people to be evil but to seek forgiveness. The elect are not without sin: rather, they are predestined to have faith in Jesus Christ and ask for forgiveness and so be forgiven. They may sin but they cannot resist the calling on their lives to seek forgiveness. Predestination sees evil as originating from the Fall and humanity's ongoing rebellion against God. The responsibility for evil, therefore, lies with human beings rather than with God. God predestines what a person does *about* their rebellion and sin.

Those who believe in the form of predestination that allows for free will in everyday actions and events might argue that free will allows for human beings to choose either good or evil. They would argue that God wanted human beings to be free and responsible agents and not to be automatons.

Summary

- ★ There is a difference between moral accountability and the existence of morality itself.
- ★ Determinism implies that people cannot be held morally responsible since they are unable to act differently from how they actually do.
- ★ Rewards/punishments and normative ethics can have causal effects on people's behaviour.
- ★ The fact that we blame people implies they are responsible agents.
- ★ Soft determinists believe that freedom to act depends on freedom to make a choice, regardless of the causal chain behind that choice.
- ★ Predestination implies God's omnipotence, since God orchestrates the final destiny of every human being.
- ★ Predestination raises questions about God's omnibenevolence, since, as stated by Augustine and Calvin, God only saves some (the elect) and condemns everyone else.
- ★ Predestination makes it difficult to see how prayer can change an outcome, but prayer could be an integral part of God's plan to bring about the predestined outcomes.
- ★ Predestination does not exclude miracles, since God can achieve his goals by intervention.

AO1 Activity

a Explain the differences between:

- **i** determinism and predestination
- **ii** hard determinism and soft determinism
- **iii** moral responsibility and morality.

This will help to ensure you make accurate use of specialist language and vocabulary in context.

b Draw a mind map explaining the implications of predestination for religious belief in:

- **i** God's omnipotence
- **ii** God's omnibenevolence
- **iii** prayer.

This will help you to prioritise and select a core set of points to develop an answer and ensure you are making accurate use of specialist language and vocabulary in context.

Issues for analysis and evaluation

A consideration of whether moral responsibility is an illusion

Possible line of argument	Critical analysis and evaluation
The law recognises that people can be held as morally responsible.	The law recognises that the degree of moral responsibility can be challenged, e.g. because of a defendant's age or mental state.
Moral responsibility implies that a person could have acted differently, which free will supports.	If determinism is true then a person could not have acted differently and therefore moral responsibility is an illusion.
Even if determinism is true and there is a causal chain, a person still does what they want to do. The fact they could not have done otherwise is irrelevant.	Is it meaningful to claim a person did what they wanted to do, given they had no other choice? Moral responsibility must involve real choices.
A person can be considered morally responsible if the action results from their own reason (hard determinism). Reasons can be identified as to why a person acted in a particular way.	Moral responsibility requires more than just recognising the reason why a person acted in the way that they did. Moral responsibility is an illusion.
Moral responsibility is embedded in our way of life and our reaction to other people's attitudes and actions in relationships. It is a social judgement, not a theoretical judgement.	Morality is a theoretical judgement. It is about what a person ought to do and assumes they are able to do it and they could have acted differently.
Soft determinism allows for moral responsibility: if a person wanted to act and did act, then it is irrelevant if the person was influenced by past events.	Moral responsibility demands that the choice was free from mental conditioning caused by previous behaviour or external influences.
Even if our decisions are unconsciously prepared, we do not know where the final decision is made, so it is still possible that a free choice is made at a subsequent point in the causal chain.	All moral responsibility is an illusion since recent research suggests that our brains determine what we will do before we become conscious of the decision.
God is moral, and we are made in God's image. God holds us morally accountable.	Belief in the Fall and the moral corruption of human beings suggest that moral responsibility is an illusion.

This section covers AO2 content and skills

Specification content

Whether moral responsibility is an illusion

AO2 Activity

a Evaluate whether moral responsibility is an illusion. From the table on page 247, select three lines of argument and identify three references from scholars, schools of thought or religious and philosophical texts that would support each argument.

b Select the line of argument that you think is the **strongest** and explain why it is so.

To assess the quality of your response, refer to the band descriptors for AS/A Level AO2. In particular, consider whether your response meets the demands of band 5, which requires 'a confident critical analysis and perceptive evaluation of the issue' with 'a response that successfully identifies and thoroughly addresses the issues raised by the question set'.

Specification content

The extent to which predestination influences our understanding of God

Exam practice

Below is an example of part of an evaluation of the extent to which predestination influences our understanding of God.

Sample answer

The doctrine of predestination may reveal attributes of the God of classical theism. One of the most obvious attributes is God's omnipotence. According to Calvin's doctrine of predestination, God determines each action and event with no free will enacted by human beings, resulting in their eternal damnation or eternal salvation. Augustine's doctrine of predestination allowed for limited free will, though it is only through God's grace that people can receive eternal life.

The question arises that if there is a role for free will, does that mean that a person can ultimately thwart God's plans and purposes? One response is to argue that God has willingly, in certain circumstances, given up the exercising of his sovereignty. The claim is that such setting aside of his power is of his own choice, which is not the same as God not having unlimited power. It is just that he chooses not to use it sometimes.

Some would argue that this act of God restraining himself is consistent with his being able to do anything that is in accord with his own nature. One of God's attributes is omnibenevolence. He does not use his power lovelessly. Everything is done that God wills to be done, but it is done in the way that God wants it to be done.

Tennis player

Critical thinker

This extensive opening focuses on God's omnipotence. It identifies a problem with God's omnipotence that is raised by Augustine's doctrine of predestination. Possible responses are then carefully considered.

An alternative criticism would be to question God's omnipotence on the grounds that he was unable to create a species of human beings who always choose good. If he had created such human beings, there would be no need for any to fall from grace and be eternally damned: all would be united with God. However, this can be countered by arguing that it is logically impossible to be both free and controlled at the same time. It is not that God is not all-powerful, it is that the idea of creating a perfectly good and free human species is a logical contradiction and God cannot actualise contradictions.

Judge

Philosopher

A further challenge to God's omnipotence is considered here, and debated with a clever counter-argument.

The doctrine of predestination argues that human beings can do nothing themselves to be forgiven and receive salvation. It is only by means of God's grace, and only an omnipotent deity could execute an eternal predestination plan for all of humanity. This also implies God is omnibenevolent. Given that humanity fell and inherited Adam's sin, all deserve judgement from God. However, God shows his loving nature for humanity by saving some people. He did this by sending his son Jesus to die on the cross, so some can receive atonement for their sins and receive eternal life. 1 John 4:16 states that 'God is love' and Romans 2:11 says that 'God does not show favouritism'.

On the other hand, both Augustine and Calvin agreed that some people do not receive eternal life. This appears to contradict omnibenevolence, since God seems to decide eternal destinies without regard to how people live or their choices. Many see this as the main problem with trying to make predestination consistent with an omnibenevolent God.

The solution is to suggest some element of choice which, as we have argued earlier, then seems to limit God's omnipotence. Understanding why evil exists at all if there is an omnipotent, omnibenevolent God, who has both the means and the motivation to remove evil, has remained a lasting philosophical problem. The doctrine of predestination only reinforces this problem.

Detective

Philosopher

In this in-depth passage, God's omnibenevolence is examined in relation to predestination. The problem is raised that both Augustine and Calvin argued that some people do not receive eternal life. A response is given but it is then seen as contradicting God's omnipotence. The conclusion is that this remains a philosophical problem.

Perhaps the very idea of omnibenevolence is in fact a meaningless concept. If omnibenevolence is defined as an attribute of 'all-loving' then some philosophers have argued that it is a love that has no limits (no intrinsic maximum), which is meaningless.

Explorer

The concept of omnibenevolence is questioned as meaningless, as another approach to the debate.

Another attribute of God is omniscience. However, if some element of free will exists, it is difficult to see how God could know the future, since it has not yet been decided. One solution is to argue that God knows what free choice each person will make in each moment. Though we exist in time, God exists outside of time. Unfortunately, many then object that it would be logically incoherent for the God of the Bible to be outside of time, since a timeless God would be unable to deliberate, remember, do anything or respond to anything. As revealed in the Bible, God is active in time; yet how can the God who created time be himself time-bound?

Perhaps God does know all at once and has always known and foreordains all things simultaneously. Such foreordaining need not exclude logical order. Another explanation could be that God knows everything that can be known but he does not know what is unknowable. Future choices made freely are not knowable since there is nothing yet to be known. Therefore it could be argued that this is not a deficiency in God's omniscience. However, it still leaves unanswered whether God's plans can be thwarted by our free choices.

Judge

Philosopher

The third focus is on the attribute of omniscience and the problem of a timeless God. Worthy attempts are made to resolve the question of whether God's plans can be thwarted by our free choices.

News reporter

Judge

The final area explored is that of prayer in relation to predestination. There is a good conclusion that is consistent with the discussion that runs through the essay.

Finally, predestination may influence our understanding of the role of prayer. If God has predestined all actions and events, it is difficult to see how prayer could produce any effect, since all things are preordained by God and so cannot change.

The doctrine of predestination certainly raises problems with our understanding of God's sovereignty, God's omnibenevolence and God's omniscience. It is also not clear how a person can be considered a moral agent having moral responsibility if predestination is true.

Over to you

This task has only instructions with no examples. However, using the skills you have developed completing the earlier tasks, you should be able to apply what you have learned and complete this successfully.

Your new task is to write another response under timed conditions to a question requiring an evaluation of the view that determinism implies that individuals can never be held morally responsible. You need to do the same as in your last AO2 developing skills task, but with some further development. This time, there is a fifth point to help you improve the quality of your answer.

Guidelines

1. Begin with a list of indicative content. Perhaps discuss this as a group. It does not need to be in any particular order. Remember: this is evaluation, so you need different lines of argument. The easiest way is to use the 'in support' and 'against' headings.
2. Develop the list using examples.
3. Consider the order in which you would like to present the information.
4. Write out your response, under timed conditions, remembering to apply the principles of evaluation by making sure that you:
   - identify issues clearly
   - present accurate views of others and comment on the views presented
   - reach an overall personal judgement.
5. Use the band descriptors to mark your own answer, carefully considering the band descriptors for A2 (WJEC) or A Level (Eduqas). In particular, look at the demands described in the higher band descriptors, which you should be aspiring towards. Ask yourself the following questions:
   - Is my answer a confident critical analysis and perceptive evaluation of the issue?
   - Is my answer a response that successfully identifies and thoroughly addresses the issues raised by the question set?

Then ask someone else to read your answer and see if they can help you improve it in any way.

Use this technique as revision for each of the topic areas that you have studied.

Swap and compare answers to improve your own.

Question

Evaluate the view that determinism implies that individuals can never be morally responsible.

D: Religious concepts of free will

This section covers AO1 content and skills

Specification content

Religious concepts of free will

Free will is one of the most debated issues in human thought. Philosophical and scientific debates on this topic are open-ended. However, religious debates are shaped by the traditional understanding of the God of classical theism, who is omnipotent, omniscient and omnibenevolent. It can be helpful to keep four key points in mind:

- **Determinism vs predestination**: Determinism is a philosophical and scientific concept; predestination is theological. Determinism is about all human actions being caused by prior events, such as the laws of nature and logical causes. Predestination is about the ultimate fate of human beings – whether they are saved or damned in the eyes of God.
- **The nature of control**: In theology, the word 'determined' usually refers to whether or not human behaviour is under the direct control or intervention of the omnipotent God. The debate is not about the laws of physics. Instead, it is about the extent to which human choices can have meaning alongside an all-powerful God, as described in classical theism.
- **Compatibilism and the middle ground**: Although free will and determinism are often treated as opposites, there have also been many attempts to bridge the gap with compatibilism. Compatibilists are theologians and philosophers who believe that free will and determinism are not mutually exclusive and that a middle ground can be found between total freedom and total control.
- **Dialogue across disciplines**: The debate is no longer a simple contest between two sides. Contemporary research in neuroscience and psychology has created a 'dialogue' between science, philosophy and theology. This dialogue shows that there is rarely a single agreed view within any one field. Instead, each offers different perspectives on what it means to be free.

Key term

ascetic: a person who lives a life of strict self-discipline

Pelagianism

Pelagius

Specification content

Pelagius

Key person

Pelagius (c. 354–418 CE): A monk from the British Isles who lived a life of strict self-discipline; he eventually moved to Rome (around 400 CE) where he became quite popular for his writings on moral reform; he gained both followers and critics in Rome and was declared a heretic at the Council of Carthage (418 CE) because of his teachings on original sin and free will; however, his teachings would influence Christianity in the centuries after his death

Pelagius (354–418 CE) was a Christian monk from the British Isles who lived a life of strict self-discipline as an **ascetic**. While some historians view him as a moralist – someone primarily concerned with the practical reform of human conduct and the application of ethical rules rather than a deep theologian focused on the abstract beliefs about God – his ideas fundamentally directed his ethics. He wrote that doctrines and scriptures are human attempts to understand God; therefore, what matters is not what you believe in your head, but how you respond with your heart. To Pelagius, it was not enough to believe in Christ; one had to become like him.

Pelagius promoted the ascetic lifestyle and a life of good works

This perspective placed Pelagius at the heart of the ancient debate over soteriology – the study of salvation. In the New Testament, this tension is

> **Key terms**
>
> **heretic:** a person whose beliefs are against the laws and beliefs of a specific religion
>
> **rationalistic moralism:** the theory that morality is purely accessible through reason and has no need for God

central to St Paul's theology of *sola fide* (faith alone), as expressed in Romans 3:23–24: 'all have sinned and fall short of the glory of God; they are now justified by his grace as a gift, through the redemption that is in Christ Jesus'.

An alternative perspective is found in the letter of James 2:14–24, which argues that 'faith by itself, if it has no works, is dead' and concludes that 'a person is justified by works and not by faith alone'. Pelagius is often associated with this second view, suggesting that salvation requires active human co-operation, an idea that eventually led his critics to label him a **heretic**.

His views were a sharp reaction to the immorality he encountered in Rome. Pelagius blamed the debauchery of the city on a misunderstanding of divine predestination and the doctrine of original sin. He argued that people were using the idea of an inherited, sinful nature as an excuse for moral laziness. If humans were born sinful and unable to control their urges, they felt no responsibility to try. Pelagius insisted that human beings are fully capable of controlling their conduct and that the image of God remains intact within every person.

As a result, Pelagius is often described as supporting religious libertarianism. Unlike philosophical libertarianism, which assumes total autonomy, religious libertarianism suggests we are free within the constraints of being God's creatures. Pelagius argued for a form of moral perfectionism – a view that can be described as **rationalistic moralism**. Pelagius believed that since God is just, he would not command a person to be holy if it were impossible to achieve. He maintained that because human nature is not intrinsically corrupted, individuals have the capacity to use their God-given free will to live a sinless life.

However, this led to significant conflict with St Augustine, who saw Pelagius as an 'enemy of the grace of God'. Augustine argued that by making humans responsible for their own salvation, Pelagius made the sacrificial death of Christ redundant. In Augustine's view, if human beings possessed the natural ability to live sinlessly and earn their way into heaven, then the Crucifixion – Christ's sacrifice to pay the debt for human sin – becomes unnecessary. For the Church, the death of Jesus was a unique and essential act of divine rescue; if salvation is something humans can achieve through their own willpower, then Christ died for a problem that did not actually exist.

This criticism was echoed in the twentieth century by Karl Barth, who insisted that Pelagius substituted a doctrine of 'human self-determination' for the proper theological view of humanity being 'determined by God'. To these critics, the real issue was that Pelagius failed to recognise that an omnipotent God must be the sole author of salvation. While he was officially declared a heretic at the Council of Carthage in 418 CE, Pelagius' insistence on human responsibility continues to challenge traditional views on guilt and depravity.

The role of original sin

While Pelagius' primary motivation was the moral reform of society, he realised that such a reform was impossible so long as the doctrine of original sin remained the dominant perspective through which humans viewed themselves. To Pelagius, the immorality he witnessed in Rome was not just a character flaw; it was the logical result of a theology that taught people they were born with original sin and were therefore incapable of doing good.

Consequently, to empower the individual to take responsibility for their actions, Pelagius had to dismantle the idea that sin was a biological inheritance. This led to a reinterpretation of human nature – not as the location of inherited sin, but as the location of a God-given capacity to develop and change for the better. For Pelagius, the force of sin does not result from a degraded human nature (as it does for Augustine), but from a corruption and ignorance of righteousness that results from a long-term habit of sin. As the Church historian, Robert F. Evans writes, 'Pelagius' theology finds its centre of gravity in the problem of man – his nature, his relation to God and his moral obligation.'

Pelagius argued that human beings were created as rational creatures with the ability to distinguish between good and evil. Crucially, he viewed this ability as a God-given capacity. Natural goodness in humans is 'voluntary goodness' – goodness that is spontaneously willed. This autonomy, albeit granted by the grace of God, is the only way to make virtue meaningful. However, Pelagius insisted that humans cannot take credit for having the freedom to choose; the capacity is a creative act of God. In other words, while a human being performs the act of doing good, they can only do so because God has equipped them with the faculty of will in the first place.

In the biblical book of Genesis, the story of Adam and Eve involves disobedience against the instructions of God. Pelagius' concept of free will is grounded in a specific interpretation of this fall. While he recognised this as the original sin, he argued it was not inherent in humanity. It belonged to Adam and Eve alone. Pelagius was convinced that an omnibenevolent God would never punish someone for another's sin, citing Deuteronomy 24:16: 'Parents are not to be put to death for their children [...] each will die for their own sin.'

Consequently, Pelagius rejected the doctrine of original sin as a 'pre-stain' on human nature. He denied both the idea of a 'fallen tendency' (concupiscence) and the notion that sin is present in a human being from birth. This is the crucial point at which Augustine and Pelagius depart. While both accept free will, Augustine is primarily concerned with upholding God's sovereignty. For Augustine, human will is restricted and must be under the control of God, otherwise:

- human beings would be responsible for achieving their own salvation
- human beings could claim to be as perfect as God
- God's absolute omnipotence would be compromised.

Pelagius argued against this: seeing sin as an inherited 'nature' fell into the trap of the heresy of **Manichaeism** (a dualistic philosophy that viewed matter as inherently evil and determined). He argued instead for the 'ownership' of the individual soul; sin is not a physical substance passed down through biology, but a choice made by the individual. Therefore, a person owns their sin because they chose it; they cannot own something that was forced upon them by their ancestors. To argue that sin is inherited suggests that sin is a necessary element of biology – something a person must do because of their genetic history.

Specification content

The role of original sin

Manichaeism taught that people had a dualistic nature battling within, reflecting an elaborate dualistic cosmological struggle between a spiritual world of light and a material world of darkness

Key term

Manichaeism: a belief in two equally forceful powers of light and darkness in constant battle against each other

For Pelagius, if sin is necessary, then the human will ceases to exist, as the person would be acting out of biological programming rather than choice. As Evans writes, 'To make sin necessary would be to deny the nature of will, whose only necessity lies in its capacity both to sin and not to sin.' In other words, the only thing that must be true about the human will is that it remains unforced; for a choice to be morally meaningful, the individual must always maintain the power to choose the opposite path.

Key quotes

Pelagius is indeed perfectly clear that Adam was in fact the first sinner [...] that sin entered the world through the one man Adam. By this he means simply that men allowed themselves to follow the example set by Adam in disobeying the will of God.

(Evans)

Specification content

Humanity maturing in God's image and accepting the responsibility of free will

Humanity maturing in God's image and accepting the responsibility of free will

Pelagius proposed a radical reinterpretation of the Fall, suggesting that the exercise of autonomous will was essential for humanity to move from a state of 'childlike' innocence to a state of moral health and goodness. He viewed moral health and goodness as the practical habit of choosing to follow God's laws, rather than a mysterious spiritual quality. He argued that humans do not lose the ability to make this choice; instead, through the long-term habit of sin, they simply become ignorant of their own potential to live in such a way. Pelagius wrote:

> If God had simply instructed Adam and Eve to eat from the tree, and they had obeyed, they would have been acting like children. So he forbade them from eating the fruit; this meant that they themselves had to make a free will decision, whether to eat or not to eat. Just as a young person needs to defy his parents in order to grow to maturity, so Adam and Eve needed to defy God in order to grow to maturity in his image.

This perspective argues that the Fall was not a tragedy that destroyed human nature, but a necessary event that allowed the process of maturity to begin. Pelagius reasoned that humans go through a learning process where wisdom is gained by making choices and learning from mistakes. Just as a child must eventually act independently of their parents to become an adult, humanity had to exercise its capacity for defiance to discover its own agency. In this view, the long-term benefits of becoming a responsible, choosing agent outweigh the short-term pitfalls of sin.

By exercising free will, Adam, Eve and all their descendants became fully responsible to God for their own actions. Human beings gained the independence to determine their own moral path. Pelagius developed this further by identifying two clear periods of development in the Old Testament when humanity was reminded of its capacity to follow God's laws:

- **From Adam to Moses**: Pelagius argued that even before the formal laws of Moses, certain individuals lived lives of moral health by being in touch with their own nature. He cited figures such as Abel, Noah, Abraham and Job as examples of people who used their God-given capacity to act uprightly without the need for external instruction.
- **The era of the Mosaic Law**: Pelagius believed that, over time, the habit of sin led to a state of ignorance where humans forgot their natural capacity for goodness. The laws of Moses were therefore introduced not to change human nature, but as a 'remedy for ignorance'. They acted as a reminder of what the human will is capable of achieving.

By constant application of the law, this ignorance is gradually removed. As Evans notes, this reveals the human person's 'newly polished nature', allowing it to 'stand out again in its pristine brilliance'. For Pelagius, the purpose of religious life is to use the responsibility of free will to polish this nature until it reflects the image of God perfectly.

The laws of Moses were there to make human beings aware of their capacity to do good

Free will as used to follow God's laws and the role of grace in salvation

Specification content

Free will as used to follow God's laws and the role of grace in salvation

Pelagius argued an absolute case for free will, based on the logical conclusion that God would not create commandments that were impossible to follow. He wrote: 'No one knows better the true measure of our strength than he who has given it to us [...] this very capacity of ours to be able.'

However, this brings the debate back to the heart of the conflict with Augustine. For Augustine, original sin ensured that human beings could never be worthy of their own salvation; it must be a gift of grace alone. According to Evans, Pelagius was condemned for teaching a doctrine of human achievement 'which appeared to deny the necessity of grace'. Yet Pelagius did not reject grace; instead, he proposed a 'light touch' or 'correlative' doctrine of grace that initiates and stimulates the will without forcibly determining it.

For Pelagius, grace is not a single act of rescue, but a multi-layered system of divine assistance that strengthens human autonomy:

- **The grace of creation (capacity)**: Pelagius viewed the very faculty of free will as a primary grace. God is the 'agent of empowerment' who provides the 'freedom, potential and opportunity' to do good in the first place. This capacity is a creative act of God, not a human achievement.
- **The grace of revelation (instruction)**: God provided external helps, such as the laws of Moses and the teachings of Jesus, to act as a remedy for ignorance. This grace polishes human nature and reminds the individual of their moral potential.
- **The grace of forgiveness (atonement)**: Pelagius accepted that salvation is only possible through the sacrifice of Jesus Christ. However, he maintained that this grace is a divine help for those who choose faith. As Evans writes, 'Faith "merits" grace in the sense that it is the indispensable and freely chosen condition of the effectual working of grace.'

Pelagius understood God's grace as the gentle helping hand of a parent teaching a child to become independent. He argued that the ability to

The cross of Christ was the ultimate source of grace

choose evil is actually a good thing, because it makes the choice to do good meaningful: 'this very capacity to do evil is also good [...] because it makes the good part better by making it voluntary and independent'. Unlike Augustine's 'irresistible grace', Pelagius' grace can be resisted.

For Pelagius, true repentance is not merely a matter of feeling regret or asking for divine forgiveness; it requires a demonstrable aptitude for good works. This means that 'saying sorry' is insufficient on its own. Instead, a person must prove their change of heart through visible actions and a consistent effort to live a moral life. This is where he departs most significantly from Augustine's *sola fide*. While Augustine was concerned that human involvement compromised God's omnipotence, Pelagius was horrified that the doctrine of original sin provided a Manichaean excuse for moral laziness.

In summary, the debate between Augustine and Pelagius reflects two essential sides of the Christian theological tradition. Augustine's focus on human depravity ensures that salvation remains a work of divine mercy, while Pelagius' focus on moral responsibility ensures that the Christian life is one of active striving. Although the Church ruled in favour of Augustine at the Council of Carthage, declaring Pelagius a heretic, his insistence that 'free will is in all good works always assisted by divine help' remains a significant challenge to any theology that suggests humans are merely passive recipients of salvation.

Key quotes

It is also true that Pelagius' understanding of the term 'grace' is a very deficient one when regarded from the point of view of Augustinian theology.

(Evans)

Our most excellent creator wished us to be able to do either (be good or bad) but actually to do only one, that is, good.

(Pelagius)

Specification content

Arminius

Arminianism

Arminius

Jacobus Arminius

Key person

Jacobus Arminius (1559–1609): Born in Oudewater in the Netherlands, Arminius was educated at Leiden and Geneva, where he studied under Theodore Beza, John Calvin's successor; he was initially a High Calvinist but became increasingly dissatisfied with the doctrine of unconditional election; his revised theology of conditional predestination was systematised by his followers, the Remonstrants, after his death in 1609

Jacobus Arminius (1559–1609) was taught by Theodore Beza, the successor of John Calvin. In his early life Arminius identified as a Calvinist and was a supporter of Beza who taught what can be described as High Calvinism.

High Calvinism refers to the most extreme and uncompromising interpretation of Calvinist theology, which emphasises the absolute and unconditional sovereignty of God over all human affairs. Its central feature is supralapsarianism, the belief that God decreed who would be saved and who would be damned before God even created the world or permitted the Fall.

In this framework, God's decisions are entirely independent of human actions, meaning that human beings are seen as passive recipients of an eternal plan that was established without regard for their future choices or faith. To a High Calvinist, any suggestion that human choice or faith could influence God's decision is seen as a challenge to the total omnipotence of the Creator.

Over time, however, Arminius became dissatisfied with High Calvinism and rejected Calvin's predestination for a version of predestination that he developed himself.

Denial of the Calvinist view of predestination

Arminius did not reject the concept of predestination entirely; instead, he sought to distinguish between the High Calvinist view of absolute determinism and what he considered the scriptural reality of divine choice. He wrote: 'The Dogma of predestination [...] is taught and emphasised in the scriptures [...] But it must be seen which and what kind of predestination it is.'

Arminius wrestled with the delicate relationship between human free will and the sovereignty of God, leading to a revised form of **conditional predestination**. This is essentially foreknowledge without determinism; it acknowledges that God knows the future without him being the cause of every specific human action.

This type of predestination is linked closely with the idea of providence. For Arminius, providence is the 'solicitous, continued, and universally present supervision of God' over the created world. He argued that while God is closely involved in monitoring and guiding the universe, this supervision does not involve the pre-programming of human choices.

To explain how God can be both all-knowing and non-deterministic, Arminius utilised the theory of **middle knowledge (MK)**, developed just before his time by the Spanish Jesuit priest, Luis de Molina. MK provides the key to understanding the compatibility between free will and predestination.

According to Arminius and Molina, MK has several specific characteristics:

- It is **prevolitional**: MK is prior to any creative act of God.
- **It is independent of God's will**: God knows what humans will do, but he does not will them to do it.
- **It is contingent**: It is based on the various possible outcomes of free human choices.
- **It is informative**: MK informs God of exactly what humans would do if a certain scenario beset them.

Arminius summarised this logic by stating: 'A thing does not happen because it has been foreknown or predicted, but it is foreknown or predicted because it is about to be.' By using the idea of MK, Arminius was able to argue that God is in full control of the 'overall divine plan' without being the 'author of sin'. Therefore, Arminius denied the Calvinist view of predestination by replacing a God who determines every choice with a God whose sovereign plan is informed by his perfect knowledge of human freedom.

Key quote

Arminius affirms foreknowledge without determinism. In his omniscience, God knows all that exists and he also knows all that will be. Middle knowledge means that God knows the result of any contingent event under any hypothetical set of circumstances without necessarily determining that outcome.

(Skevington Wood)

Specification content

Denial of the Calvinist view of predestination

Key terms

conditional predestination: the complex theological notion based upon the idea that free will and predestination are compatible

middle knowledge (MK): a theory developed by Luis de Molina, a Spanish Jesuit priest, that God is aware of every computation of possible choices

prevolitional: prior to any act of God's will; describing knowledge that God possesses before choosing to act or create

God knows all possible outcomes of any possible choices to be made

Key quotes

Arminius wrestled with divine sovereignty and human freedom without sacrificing either on the altar of the other.

(Stanglin and McCall)

Arminius maintained that God's divine foreknowledge does not result in determinism and, therefore, that, while God's eternal foreknowledge includes knowledge of all those that will be saved as well as those that will be damned, it does not guide, force, or fate any person into either salvation or damnation.

(Brian)

Specification content

The effect of original sin on free will

The effect of original sin on free will

Unlike Pelagius, Arminius believed that original sin had a damaging impact on humankind. He defined original sin as a lack of 'original righteousness' and viewed it as both a spiritual deprivation and a physical punishment. Arminius explored this using two technical concepts:

- **Deprivation**: This is the loss of the original spiritual likeness to God and the 'primeval holiness' that existed prior to the Fall.
- **Depravation**: This is the 'infusion' of a disordered inclination towards sin, making the human heart 'vehement' in its desire for wrong-doing.

Consequently, in a fallen state, human beings are deprived of the righteousness required to seek out the good through their own power. Arminius argued that the human will is naturally inclined towards sin and is incapable of achieving salvation independently. He rejected the idea that humans could 'jump-start' their own recovery; because of the Fall, the soul is effectively imprisoned by its own desires.

However, Arminius maintained that human beings are not necessarily predestined to continually sin. While the human faculty of will is corrupted, it is not destroyed; it remains a faculty that can be 'renewed' and liberated by divine assistance.

Therefore, for Arminius, the primary effect of original sin on free will is not that the will is destroyed, but that it is severely weakened and trapped by sin, remaining unable to choose God until it is set free by his grace.

Key quotes

In this [fallen] state, the free will of man towards the true good is wounded, infirm, bent, and weakened.

(Arminius)

Arminius believed that the culpability of that first sin affected, and continues to affect all people, both biologically and socially.

(Brian)

Arminius is careful to differentiate his understanding of man's free will and ability to do good from that of Pelagius [...] since it always remains dependent upon the work of God's grace in and through man.

(Studebaker)

Providence means God preserves and governs the world throughout time

God's 'prevenient' grace (the Holy Spirit) in allowing humans to exercise free will

Arminius' understanding of original sin means that human beings are not necessarily predestined to continually sin. Although the will is weakened, it is not left without hope; this is because of God's loving grace. For Arminius, this grace is specifically associated with the Holy Spirit. This association is known as **prevenient grace** because it is a grace that precedes (comes before) each human moral decision.

Arminius believed that God has placed the Holy Spirit within all human beings to act as a counter-balance to the inherited impulse to sin. This grace does not just forgive past mistakes; it actively works to restore the human capacity for choice. The Holy Spirit encourages all people to do good works and, as Arminius stated, enables them to 'fight against Satan, sin, the world and their own flesh'. Furthermore, for those who choose to follow God, the Holy Spirit remains ever present to aid and assist believers through various temptations.

The way this grace interacts with the human will is described through the concept of **divine concurrence**. This is the idea that God 'concurs' with human activity by providing the powers and abilities to act, while the human being actually performs the action. Arminius wrote: 'The concurrence of God is [...] an action of God immediately flowing into the effect of the creature.'

In this framework, God is the enabler or agent of empowerment, but God does not perform the act for a person. By providing this divine help, the Holy Spirit restores the freedom of the will without overriding it. As Arminius summarised: 'God has limited his control in correspondence with man's freedom.' God is the enabler (one that empowers) but this is not the same as actually performing or doing the action for the person. This is crucially important for Arminius' idea of free will and his overall theology of how this is compatible with predestination.

Specification content

God's 'prevenient' grace (the Holy Spirit) in allowing humans to exercise free will

Key terms

prevenient grace: God's grace that precedes each human moral decision, associated with the Holy Spirit

divine concurrence: the idea that God participates in every human action by providing the powers and abilities to act, without determining what the person chooses to do

Key quotes

God has limited his control in correspondence with man's freedom.
(Arminius)

God's providence provides the grace to choose freely a righteous path in life

The elect and the possibility of rejecting God's grace

While the Holy Spirit acts as a divine help to empower the weakened will, Arminius was careful to maintain that this assistance does not equate to divine control. This leads to the vital distinction regarding the nature of the elect. Arminius clarified that while God provides the means for salvation through the Holy Spirit, this grace is not irresistible.

This is a point of sharp departure from the Augustinian and Calvinist traditions, which taught that when God decides to save a member of the elect, God's grace is an overwhelming force that the human will cannot refuse. For Augustine and Calvin, if grace could be rejected, it would imply that the

Specification content

The elect and the possibility of rejecting God's grace

human will is more powerful than God's purpose. In their view, the elect are 'carried' to salvation by a divine decree that guarantees their compliance.

Arminius, however, argued that for a choice to be truly moral and good, it must be voluntary rather than forced. He believed that God offers grace to all, but does not impose it. In this framework, the elect are not those who are trapped by a divine decree they cannot escape, but those who choose not to resist the helping hand of God.

Furthermore, Arminius taught that the security provided by the Holy Spirit is conditional on the believer's own will to remain in the faith. Unlike the Calvinist doctrine of the perseverance of the saints (which claims a saved person can never fall away), Arminius argued that believers must continue to co-operate with grace. The Holy Spirit preserves them from falling, provided they 'stand prepared for the battle' and 'be not wanting to themselves'.

Consequently, Arminius established that being among the elect is not a fixed fate, but a status maintained through the persistent choice not to reject God's grace.

Key quotes

God's love is communicated not as an irresistible coercion, but as a tender persuasion that will not finally override the human will.

(Stanglin and McCall)

God's grace is [...] not, however, irresistible, since Arminius sees many scriptural examples of those who do, indeed, 'resist the Holy Spirit and reject the grace that is offered'.

(Studebaker)

[...] provided they (believers) stand prepared for the battle, implore his help, and be not wanting to themselves, the Spirit preserves them from falling.

(Arminius)

Specification content

The election of believers being conditional on faith

The election of believers being conditional on faith

The climax of Arminius' theology is the shift from unconditional election to corporate election. He argued that God's decree of election applies to the whole body of believers as a group and is based on a condition, rather than being an unconditional choice of specific individuals.

To make this distinction clearer, it can be helpful to use the analogy of a ship. In the Calvinist view of individual election, God picks specific passengers to put on a ship; the focus is entirely on the individual person. In the Arminian view of corporate election, God decrees that 'The Ship' (the Church or the body of believers) is going to heaven. Anyone who chooses to stay on the ship through faith becomes part of that group and its destiny. Therefore, according to Arminius, God chooses to save those who are 'foreknown to be penitent believers' and condemns those he knows will be 'impenitent unbelievers'. This distinction is vital: for Calvinists, election is unconditional; for Arminius, it is conditional, based on God's MK of an individual's faith.

Arminius presented his views in his *Declaration of Sentiments* (1608). After his death in 1609, his followers – the Remonstrants – systematised his work into the five articles of the **Remonstrance** (1610), which are often remembered by the acronym FACTS:

- **F – freed by grace to believe**: The human will is renewed by the Holy Spirit, freeing it from its natural bondage to sin so that it can choose the good.
- **A – atonement for all**: Christ died for every person, obtaining redemption for all, though only those who believe actually experience forgiveness.
- **C – conditional election**: God's choice to save is based on the condition of faith; he elects those he foreknows will accept his grace.
- **T – total depravity**: In their fallen state, humans are incapable of doing anything truly good or seeking God without his preceding grace.
- **S – security in Christ**: The Holy Spirit assists believers in all temptations, but this grace is not irresistible; humans can still choose to reject the Holy Spirit.

The official response to these ideas came at the Synod of Dort (1618–19). The Synod of Dort rejected the Arminian articles and established the 'Canons of Dort', which formed the basis of the five points of Calvinism, known by the acronym TULIP:

- **T – total depravity**: Every part of human nature is corrupted by sin, leaving people unable to choose God on their own.
- **U – unconditional election**: God's choice of the elect is based on his own will, not on foreseen faith.
- **L – limited atonement**: Christ's death was intended specifically to achieve the salvation of the elect.
- **I – irresistible grace**: When God calls the elect, the Holy Spirit overcomes all resistance to bring them to faith.
- **P – perseverance of the elect**: The elect can never fall away from grace but are preserved by God until the end.

Despite the rejection at the Synod of Dort, Arminian theology survived and eventually became a central pillar of the Methodist Church under the leadership of John Wesley. Arminius' assertion that the election of believers is conditional on faith fundamentally redefined the relationship between divine decree and human choice.

Key term

Remonstrance: the forceful protest of the Arminians of the Dutch Reformed Church in 1610 to the Staten-Generaal in the Netherlands

Key quotes

It is, moreover, markedly and deliberately Christ-centred and Christ-controlled. Instead of starting off with God's predestination of individuals, Arminius puts first the decree by which God appointed his Son Jesus Christ for a 'Mediator, Redeemer, Saviour, Priest and King'.
(Skevington Wood)

What distinguishes Arminius and Calvinism, in other words, is not that the latter has a doctrine of election or predestination while the former does not. Rather, what distinguishes them is the ground of election or predestination. For Calvinists, election is unconditional. For Arminius, it is conditional, based on God's foreknowledge – middle knowledge, to be precise – of a person's faith.
(Skevington Wood)

It is illogical to argue that it is just a matter of God's choice to redeem because this also implies a rejection of some.
(Lennox)

Jesus Christ is mediator, redeemer, saviour, priest and king

Summary

- Religious concepts of free will attempt to bridge the gap between God's absolute sovereignty (omnipotence/omniscience) and the human necessity for moral responsibility.
- Pelagius argued for religious libertarianism, suggesting that the Fall was a necessary step towards maturity and that humans possess the autonomous capacity to choose a sinless life.
- Pelagius rejected the doctrine of original sin as a biological inheritance, arguing that God would not command holiness if it were impossible for humans to achieve through their own will.
- Arminius sought a middle ground between High Calvinism and free will by utilising the concept of MK; the idea that God foreknows human choices without causing them.
- Arminius argued that while original sin severely weakens the human will, God provides prevenient grace through the Holy Spirit to empower people to co-operate with his divine plan.
- The Arminian view shifts election from an unconditional choice of specific individuals (Calvinism) to a corporate decree, where salvation is promised to the category of all who choose to remain in the faith.

AO1 Activity

Read through these higher band descriptors for AO1 responses, and then ask yourself the following questions:

- Does my work demonstrate thorough, accurate and relevant knowledge and understanding of religion and belief?
- Does my work have extensive depth and/or suitable breadth and have excellent use of evidence and examples?
- Does my response have thorough and accurate reference to sacred texts and sources of wisdom?
- Does my response contain thorough and accurate use of specialist language and vocabulary?

With these points in mind, complete the following exercises.

a Examine Pelagius' view on human responsibility and the role of the law. Use the points below to help structure your response.

- **i** Explain the difference between religious libertarianism and rationalistic moralism in the context of Pelagius' theology.
- **ii** How does Pelagius use Deuteronomy 24:16 to dismantle the traditional doctrine of original sin?
- **iii** In three sentences, explain why Pelagius viewed the Fall as a 'necessary defiance' rather than a tragic corruption of nature.
- **iv** List the three layers of grace Pelagius identified (creation, revelation and forgiveness) and explain why he believed grace must be resistible.

b Read the 'Response' paragraph opposite, which is weak response, explaining the differences between the views of Arminius and High Calvinism. Identify ways in which you could improve the response by correcting errors and by introducing correct specialist language from the vocabulary bank. This will help you in developing AO1 skills and in developing thorough and accurate knowledge and understanding of the topic.

Response

Calvin said that God decides who goes to heaven and who goes to hell at birth, so humans have no say in it. This is his idea of God choosing people randomly and for no reason. Arminius disagreed with this and said that people have the freedom to follow God because human nature remained perfect after the Fall. He argued that humans do not need any spiritual help at all to choose the good. He thought that God just looks into the future to see what people will do and then makes his plan based on what he sees. Arminius said Jesus died for everyone, whereas Calvin said he only died for the lucky ones. Arminius showed how humans are in full control of their own lives because they have the power to save themselves. In the end, Arminius thinks you cannot lose your salvation as long as you continue to be good. Calvin agrees: you are always saved if you perform acts pleasing to God. Arminius' ideas were accepted by the Synod of Dort.

Vocabulary bank

- supralapsarianism: God's decree of election made before the Fall
- unconditional election: choice based on God's sovereign will, not human action
- MK: middle knowledge – God's awareness of all possible outcomes in any scenario
- total depravity: the state of human nature being corrupted by sin
- prevenient grace: divine assistance that precedes and enables human choice
- limited atonement: the belief that Christ died specifically for the elect
- divine concurrence: God providing the power while the human performs the act
- Remonstrants: followers of Arminius who protested against High Calvinism
- Synod of Dort: the council that rejected Arminianism and established TULIP
- perseverance of the elect: the Calvinist belief that the elect cannot fall away

This section covers AO2 content and skills

Specification content

How convincing are religious views on free will?

Issues for analysis and evaluation

How convincing are religious views on free will?

Possible line of argument	Critical analysis and evaluation
The Pelagian view of total responsibility: Pelagius argues that God's justice requires humans to have full capacity for holiness. If God commands it, it must be possible; therefore, the Fall did not destroy human nature.	Critics, like Augustine, argue this is unconvincing as it makes Christ's sacrifice redundant. If humans can achieve salvation through willpower, grace becomes merely an 'optional extra' rather than a necessity.
Arminius and divine concurrence: Arminius suggests that free will and sovereignty are compatible through providence. God is the agent of empowerment who provides the ability to act without determining the specific choice.	This is challenged by Mackie's paradox of omnipotence. Mackie argues that any area outside God's direct control constitutes a compromise of his nature, suggesting that theodicies of free will logically diminish God's power.
Reinterpreting omnipotence: one can argue that God does not 'lose' power by allowing freedom; rather, he exercises his power by choosing when to intervene. This preserves both sovereignty and human agency.	However, this assumes a 'calculated step backwards' (similar to Hick's epistemic distance). Detractors argue this is a semantic trick; a truly omnipotent being cannot 'not know' or 'not control' an outcome without ceasing to be absolute.
Islamic and Jewish perspectives: in Islam, the Mu'tazilites argue for human agency to preserve God's justice, while Jewish Holocaust theologies often posit that God must 'withdraw' to allow for genuine human moral growth.	These views are coherent within their own frameworks but face the same 'convincing' hurdle: they often require a redefinition of traditional divine attributes that many classical theists find difficult to accept.
The distinction between coherence and persuasiveness: religious views on free will are often logically consistent (coherent) once their initial premises – such as MK – are accepted.	Ultimately, their convincing nature depends on the reader's starting point. While they provide a clear basis for moral responsibility, they may fail to satisfy those who hold to a strictly deterministic or High Calvinist view of divine sovereignty.

AO2 Activity

To help you aim for the higher bands in an AO2 response, refer to the AS/A Level band descriptors for AO2. In particular, note that band 5 requires responses to demonstrate 'thorough, accurate and relevant analysis and evaluation of the issue, using evidence and examples; a well-reasoned argument leading to a clear and justified conclusion'.

With these descriptors in mind, complete the following tasks:

a Analyse the issue of how convincing religious views on free will are. Draw three possible conclusions from the critical analysis and evaluation opposite and support each one with evidence and examples. Select one conclusion that you think is the **most convincing** and explain why it is so.

b Now contrast this with the **weakest** conclusion of the three. Justify your argument with clear reasoning and evidence.

Specification content

The degree to which beliefs about free will can be reconciled with beliefs about predestination

Exam practice

Below is an example of part of an evaluation of the degree to which beliefs about free will can be reconciled with beliefs about predestination.

Sample answer

This essay explores whether human liberty can exist alongside a God who has already decided the final destination of every soul. At its heart is a question: if humans are truly responsible for their choices, does this limit God's absolute power? On the other hand, if God is all-powerful and all-knowing, can any human choice be truly independent?

Philosopher

This paragraph establishes the logical boundaries of the debate by highlighting the potential contradiction between divine sovereignty and human agency.

Pelagius provided the most radical support for free will. He argued that God's justice requires humans to have the total capacity for choice; if God were to predestine people, he could not fairly judge them. While Pelagius is often seen as having rejected predestination, he does acknowledge grace as a 'helping hand' that assists the believer in choosing the good life.

Explorer

We are venturing into the territory of moral independence here, where the map of salvation is drawn by human effort.

Augustine countered this by arguing that original sin has 'bent' the human will. A person is still free in a technical sense, but their desires are naturally directed away from God. For Augustine, reconciliation is found in grace: God's grace redirects a person's desires, allowing them to freely choose to obey him. Without this divine intervention, no one would choose the good.

Detective

The evidence suggests a hidden corruption in the human will that only a higher power can solve.

Modern scholars like Alister McGrath argue that predestination is often misunderstood as a cold, deterministic force. McGrath suggests that for Augustine, predestination is single: it is God's positive decision to redeem some, rather than a deliberate choice to damn others. In this light, predestination is an act of mercy that enables freedom rather than destroying it.

News reporter

The latest theological insights suggest that predestination might be a 'rescue mission' rather than a 'prison sentence'.

Critical thinker

We must question the logic here; can you truly choose to save some without simultaneously deciding to leave others behind?

However, the debate remains sharp because some of Augustine's later writings suggest double predestination – the idea that God actively chooses some for punishment. John Lennox argues that choosing to save one group logically implies the rejection of another. This makes the partnership between free will and predestination much harder to defend in ethical terms.

Judge

Philosopher

This provides a robust framework for compatibility, balancing the scales between God's perfect knowledge and man's actual choice.

Arminius offers a sophisticated middle ground through the concept of middle knowledge. He argued that God knew (and knows) exactly how every person will freely respond in any given situation. Crucially, God's foreknowledge does not cause the action. As Arminius explained, 'a thing is foreknown because it is about to happen; it does not happen because it is foreknown'.

Tennis player

The argument is moving back and forth across the court, trying to keep both the power of God and the effort of the person in play.

For theologians, the focus is less on abstract logic and more on the mechanics of salvation. The question is not 'either/or?' but 'how much?'. They seek to understand to what extent a person's ethical actions contribute to their salvation compared to God's sovereign act of grace. The goal is to find a balance where human choice is meaningful without characterising God as a passive observer.

News reporter

There is a growing consensus between secular and religious thinkers that total, unguided autonomy may be a myth.

Philosophers often ask if a person is free at all, but religious thinkers start from the premise that the God of classical theism exists. This 'encased' debate changes the nature of the questions asked. Interestingly, modern philosophy has moved away from 'absolute' free will, mirroring the religious idea that freedom always exists within certain boundaries or 'parameters'.

Judge

Critical thinker

After weighing the arguments, it appears that compatibility is possible, provided we accept that freedom and control can coexist in a carefully balanced system.

In conclusion, free will and predestination are not necessarily polar opposites. Thinkers like Pelagius, Augustine and Arminius actually share significant common ground. The real debate is about the distribution of power: how much control God chooses to exercise and how much freedom he chooses to gift to his creatures.

Over to you

Integrate evidence into the following evaluation of whether religious views on free will are convincing.

At present, the evaluation is basic and lacks the scholarly approach required by the higher bands. It has no specific references and uses very few key terms. Your task is to rewrite the evaluation, integrating the key terms and key quotes provided opposite to support or critique the arguments. You may add other terms and quotations if you feel it is necessary. Make sure that you integrate the evidence smoothly (for example, 'Stanglin and McCall suggest …' or 'The Remonstrance states …'). You may shorten quotations or paraphrase them to maintain a clear flow.

Evaluation

Some people argue that religious views on free will are not convincing because they seem to contradict the view that God is all-powerful. If God knows what is going to happen, it feels like humans are following a fixed plan. Critics argue that any attempt to allow for human freedom must mean that God is not truly in control and so God is not God.

However, other thinkers like Pelagius and Arminius approach the ideas of salvation in a different way. Pelagius argued for freedom, suggesting that sin is just an abuse of freedom rather than a result of people being evil. Arguably, this is a better understanding of what happened when Adam and Eve sinned since their sin is not passed down.

Arminius and his followers developed the idea of a different type of knowledge to explain how God knows all possible choices without being the one who causes sin. They argue that, through a special type of grace and divine action, God helps a person to choose him without forcing them. This is different from full predestination.

Other followers of Calvin at a special meeting took a harsher line. They believed that people are born with evil and, unlike the Arminian focus on a different type of being elected, they argued that God chooses individuals regardless of their future actions.

Question

'Religious views about free will are convincing.' Evaluate this view. (Eduqas A Level 2024)

Key terms

original sin	the Fall	MK/middle knowledge	prevenient grace
divine concurrence	High Calvinists	corporate election	total depravity
conditional predestination	author of sin	corporate election	omnipotent
Synod of Dort	religious libertarianism	the Remonstrants	deterministic
God of classical theism	omnipotence		

Key quotes

Sin is the result of the abuse of the precious gift of freedom that God graciously bestowed upon humanity.

(Stanglin and McCall)

Middle knowledge means that God knows the result of any contingent event [...] without necessarily determining that outcome.

(Skevington Wood)

God has limited His control in correspondence with man's freedom.

(Arminius)

It is not [...] irresistible, since Arminius sees many scriptural examples of those who do, indeed, 'resist the Holy Spirit'.

(Studebaker)

[...] the Fall was a necessary event that allowed the process of maturity to begin.

(Pelagius)

Arminius wrestled with divine sovereignty and human freedom without sacrificing either on the altar of the other.

(Stanglin and McCall)

E: Concepts of libertarianism

Philosophical libertarianism

The religious perspectives of Pelagius and Arminius established a context for human freedom based on the relationship between God and the created human person. However, modern perspectives have moved away from the religious framework and placed the focus on a secular philosophical understanding.

The strict interpretation of philosophical libertarianism from a secular perspective is that the human will is totally free. This is usually referred to as ***causa sui*** (self-caused). (Note that this term reappears later in Galen Strawson's argument against free will, where it is used in a very different way.) This form of libertarianism suggests that our choices are not the inevitable result of:

- prior causes
- external conditions
- biological chains of events.

Instead, the will is independent; it is the self, acting as a free agent, that originates action rather than merely reacting to a series of predetermined influences.

The modern debate about libertarianism explores how freedom might exist within a person's:

- consciousness
- biology
- psychological development.

Libertarianism is opposed to determinism and suggests that free will is a fundamental characteristic of being human. If libertarianism is correct, the human person is not a passive object pushed around by the laws of physics or biological instincts. Instead, they are an active subject with the capacity to initiate their own actions. This has profound implications for ethics. If a person is truly the author of their own choices, then they must accept total responsibility for the consequences. They are then free to shape their own future.

Key term

causa sui: something that is independent of cause

This section covers AO1 content and skills

Jean-Paul Sartre

Jean-Paul Sartre (1905–80) was a leading figure in existentialism and one of the most significant thinkers of the twentieth century. Beyond his work as a philosopher, he was a novelist, playwright and political activist who declined the Nobel Prize in Literature. Alongside his lifelong intellectual and personal partner, the philosopher Simone de Beauvoir, he was central to the cultural and intellectual life of Paris, exploring themes of gender, politics and the radical nature of human liberty.

Jean-Paul Sartre

Key person

Jean-Paul Sartre (1905–80): A leading French philosopher and a central figure in twentieth-century existentialism; he argued that 'existence precedes essence', meaning individuals must create their own purpose through free choice; a prolific playwright and novelist, he declined the Nobel Prize in Literature, maintaining his commitment to political activism

Man is not free not to be free

For Sartre, freedom is not an optional extra added on to human life; it is the fundamental reality of being human. Sartre's atheistic approach moves the debate from a divine plan to the nature of human consciousness. Since there is no God to cause human nature, people must define themselves through their choices.

Sartre's starting point is a well-known philosophical concept – that for human beings, 'existence precedes essence'. In 1945, in his lecture 'Existentialism is a Humanism', he explained this point as follows:

> Atheistic existentialism [...] declares [...] that if God does not exist there is at least one being whose existence comes before its essence, a being which exists before it can be defined by any conception of it. That being is man or [...] the human reality. What do we mean by saying that existence precedes essence? We mean that man first of all exists, encounters himself, surges up in the world – and defines himself afterwards.

To understand this, consider a manufactured object like a smartphone: before the phone is even built, its 'essence' (its purpose, software and design) has already been decided by engineers. It is created to fulfil a specific function.

Sartre argues that humans are not manufactured for a purpose. Human beings 'surge up' in the world first, and only afterwards define who they are through their choices. Because there is no God to provide a blueprint, there is no predetermined essence for a human person. They are entirely self-created.

Consequently, a human being is 'condemned to be free' because they are 'thrown into the world' without a choice in their own existence. In other words, while a human being did not choose to be born, they are still forced to make choices every moment they are alive. For Sartre, even a refusal to choose is still a choice, meaning that freedom is a burden a human being cannot lay down from the moment of the first choice until death. The concept of freedom is inherent to the nature of self-consciousness. Therefore, a human person is not free not to be free. Put simply, no one can escape their own freedom.

Key quote

Man is nothing else but that which he makes of himself. That is the first principle of existentialism [...] Before that projection of the self, nothing exists [...] Man is responsible for what he is.

(Sartre)

To explain this point further, Sartre made a distinction between two types of being:

- Being-in-itself (***être-en-soi***): This refers to inanimate objects – such as a smartphone – that are fixed and lack consciousness. These objects are characterised by **facticity**, the brute, physical facts of existence that cannot be changed. Facticity defines and limits them in the same way that the hardware of a smartphone defines and limits its functions.

Specification content

Concepts of libertarianism: philosophical Jean-Paul Sartre: man is not free not to be free

Key quotes

Everything has been figured out, except how to live.

(Sartre)

Freedom has no essence. It is not subject to any logical necessity.

(Sartre)

Every man must invent his own path.

(Sartre)

Key terms

être-en-soi: inanimate matter and being without consciousness, a being-in-itself

facticity: the brute, unavoidable facts of a person's life (e.g. place of birth, height) that they cannot change, but which do not define their freedom

Key terms

être-pour-soi: the authentic self in the process of becoming, a being-for-itself
néant: the no-thingness of consciousness; because consciousness has no fixed essence, it is free to determine itself.
gap: the distance between a person's consciousness and the physical world that necessitates people to have free will
reflet: the reflection that is self-consciousness
mauvaise foi: bad faith, but better understood as self-deception
être-pour-autrui: Sartre's new dimension in which the self exists as an object for others, a 'being-for-others'

Key quote

We are our choices.
(Sartre)

- Being-for-itself (***être-pour-soi***): This refers to human consciousness, which Sartre described as nothingness (***néant***). Human consciousness is not a fixed 'thing'; it is not being-in-itself and is not restricted by the boundaries of facticity. Being-for-itself creates a **gap** between the person and the world, which allows for reflection and the making of choices.

Through the *process* of reflection (*réflexion*), self-consciousness defines itself as a reflection (***reflet***). In other words, consciousness is like a mirror reflecting the world; the mirror itself has no colour or shape of its own – it is 'no-thing'. This is the form in which the being-for-itself establishes its own nothingness. Because consciousness is empty (a *reflet*), it is not stuck being one thing; it is free to choose what it becomes.

This gap of human consciousness is the key feature of human freedom. It allows the person to reflect on their circumstances and realise that they can make things other than they are. The human person is not restricted by the inanimate nature of the being-in-itself.

According to Sartre, this freedom brings anxiety and insecurity. To escape this, people often fall into what he termed ***mauvaise foi*** (bad faith), which is better understood as self-deception. This is a form of self-deception where the person 'pretends' that they are objects defined by their circumstances or their roles.

Human freedom is further complicated by being-for-others (***être-pour-autrui***). This is the awareness that others look at an individual and try to turn them into an 'object' with a fixed essence or label. Authenticity, the ultimate goal for an existentialist, requires that a person takes full responsibility for their life through their choices, despite the pressure from others or from their own facticity.

As Sartre concluded: '[I am] condemned to exist forever beyond my essence, beyond the causes and motives of my act. I am condemned to be free.'

Key quote

Actually, we are a freedom which chooses, but we do not choose to be free: we are condemned to freedom.
(Sartre)

I build the universal in choosing me, I build it by understanding the project from any other man, whatever time it is.
(Sartre)

Specification content

Concepts of libertarianism: philosophical Jean-Paul Sartre: waiter illustration

The waiter illustration

For Sartre, the establishment of an authentic and free existence can only be achieved through the eradication of *mauvaise foi*. Self-deception is an attitude of fear in which an individual attempts to remain a being-in-itself – an object. This is done because the state of an object is safe from the anxiety of freedom.

An individual might adopt this attitude because an object has a fixed nature; it knows exactly what is expected and what is allowed. With this attitude, the individual seeks the safety of a fixed essence by hiding beneath the expectations of etiquette and social constraints. Even though choosing to hide behind a role is a free decision, it is an act of 'self-negation' because the person is using their freedom to pretend they do not have any. By doing this, they are trying to escape the overwhelming reality of their own complete freedom. Sartre used the illustration of a waiter in a café to demonstrate this concept:

> His movement is quick and forward, a little too precise, a little too rapid. He comes toward the patrons with a step a little too quick. He bends forward a little too eagerly; his voice, his eyes express an interest a little too solicitous for the order of the customer. Finally there he returns, trying to imitate in his walk the inflexible stiffness of some kind of automaton while carrying his tray with the recklessness of a tight-rope walker [...] He is playing, he is amusing himself. But what is he playing? We need not watch long before we can explain it; he is playing at being a waiter in a café.

As a matter of facticity (the physical reality of being-in-itself), the man is indeed a waiter. There is no deception in the physical act of waiting upon tables. However, self-deception arises when the individual identifies their entire self with the role of waiter. The deception occurs when the job is considered the sum of a person's identity, providing a false sense of security. As Professor Vincent Spade writes:

> But of course being a waiter is not the end of the story about this man. It doesn't give him any kind of definition once and for all [...] On the contrary, he is a waiter who is free. Every morning he freely gets up early and sweeps out the café [...] At any time, he could stop doing that. He could just decide to stay in bed some morning. He might get fired, of course, but he is free to get fired. He could quit, he could burn the café to the ground. He could run off and join the Foreign Legion.

In other words, a person's essence cannot be defined by a social role. The role provides the context from which one exercises free will, but the person is always more than a label. Sartre's point is that by trying too hard to be an object (the waiter), the man is engaging in an act of self-negation. This means he is using his freedom to pretend he has no freedom at all. Instead of looking outward at the infinite possibilities of what he could do or become, he turns inward. He tries to act as if he is a fixed, unchanging being-in-itself.

Key quotes

Anxiety is the dizziness of freedom.

(Sartre)

Not choosing is a choice.

(Sartre)

Choice and consciousness are one and the same thing.

(Sartre)

Being-for-others

Sartre suggested that human beings move from an initial state at birth that is fixed (being-in-itself) towards a state of freedom through the development of self-consciousness (being-for-itself). However, this journey is challenging and full of anxiety. To be truly free means to be fully responsible.

This focus on authenticity shares some similarities with the 'uniqueness' described by Max Stirner. While Stirner spoke of being a slave to 'spooks' (social norms), Sartre spoke of bad faith. However, Sartre's freedom has very different implications for ethics. While some critics have viewed Sartre's existentialism as a form of ethical egoism (the view that individuals ought to act in their own self-interest; see 'C: Ethical egoism' on page 32), Sartre identified himself as a Marxist. For Sartre, there was no contradiction between these positions: truly free individuals must work to remove the social and economic structures that prevent others from achieving the same freedom.

He reconciled the radical freedom of the individual with social responsibility through the concept of *être-pour-autrui*. He argued that there is a moral duty to the self to be ethical in dealings with others. If individuals truly appreciate the authenticity of their own freedom, they must recognise the same freedom in others. Therefore, Sartre's understanding of free will inevitably means that the individual is fully and unconditionally responsible for their behaviour and actions.

Specification content

Concepts of libertarianism: scientific (Dr Angela Sirigu's research evidence that the brain allows for free will)

Key terms

cognitive neuroscience: scientific study of the biological processes and neural connections in the brain

parietal cortex: one of the four major lobes of the cerebral cortex in the brain containing grey matter that transforms visual information into motor commands

premotor cortex: a specific region within the frontal lobe of the brain that is involved in planning and initiating movement

Scientific libertarianism

The scientific concept of libertarianism considers evidence from **cognitive neuroscience**. This field of study explores the biological processes that underlie human thought and behaviour. It specifically looks at how the 'hardware' of the brain – its neurons, circuits and chemicals – creates the 'software' of the mind – such as memory, emotion and decision-making. In the context of the free-will debate, cognitive neuroscience focuses on how different brain regions communicate to initiate action.

For a libertarian, the key question is whether there is a physical 'space' in the brain where a choice is made, or whether human actions are simply a chain reaction of biological causes. Researchers have experimented by stimulating the specific areas responsible for initiating choice and initiating movement. By doing so, they aim to see whether the intention to act – the will – and the actions themselves can be explained through biological mechanisms.

In 2009, a team of scientists led by Dr Michel Desmurget and Dr Angela Sirigu, based at the Centre for Cognitive Neuroscience in Lyon, published a significant study in the journal *Science*. They claimed that by electrically stimulating the posterior parietal cortex – an area of the brain that transforms visual information into motor commands – it was possible to produce a conscious intention to act.

The study involved seven patients undergoing awake brain surgery. Because the brain lacks pain receptors, patients remained conscious and could describe their sensations. The findings revealed a distinct difference between the will to move and the act of moving:

- **The parietal cortex (the will)**: Stimulating the parietal regions generated a strong desire or intention to move (such as wanting to move a hand or foot). However, no physical movement actually occurred. When the stimulation was increased, participants became convinced they had moved, even though their muscles remained perfectly still.
- **The premotor cortex (the action)**: In contrast, stimulating the premotor region produced actual physical movements. However, the patients firmly denied that they had moved. They did not experience these movements as a conscious act of will; they were entirely unaware of their own physical actions.

This experiment identified specific cortical circuits associated with the sensation of wanting to initiate an action. Sirigu and Desmurget's team continued this work, and in 2018 they looked at how these intentions could be prevented. They concluded that a specific area in the parietal cortex could also inhibit, or block, a choice.

During these tests, patients were fully aware of their inability to move, reporting: 'I cannot do it; it is hard,' and, 'I cannot move anymore.' This suggests that the parietal cortex is the area where the decision to act, or not to act, is initiated and monitored. As Desmurget concluded:

> Our results indicate that electrical stimulation at focal sites within a restricted area of the dorsoposterior parietal cortex inhibits volitional upper-limb motor responses with high selectivity. Identification of this inhibitory process is of primary importance to understand how intended actions are suppressed [...]

In simpler terms, Desmurget found that stimulating a precise area of the brain could selectively stop a person from carrying out a deliberate movement.

For Professor Christof Koch, these studies represent 'true progress' in the debate over freedom. However, he acknowledges that knowing how the brain processes an intention does not necessarily prove the existence of free will in the traditional sense.

Interpretations of this neurological research can sometimes involve a significant, and sometimes illogical, leap in reasoning. In an article for *National Geographic*, science writer Ed Yong noted that such studies suggest the human feeling of free will originates, at least partially, in the parietal cortex. It is the activity of these neurons that creates the sensation that an individual initiates actions of their own accord.

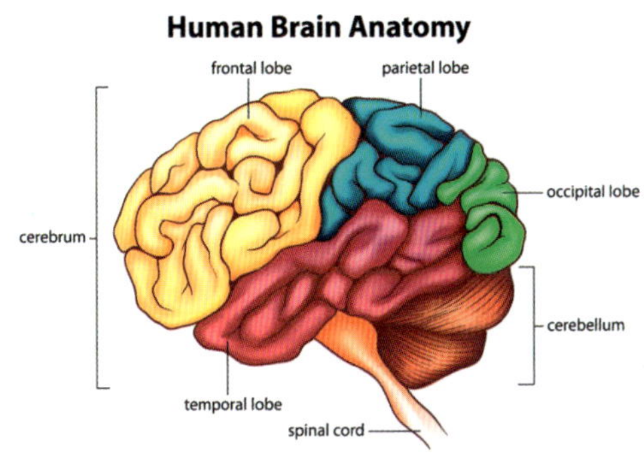

Anatomy of the human brain

However, Yong also quoted Professor Patrick Haggard, a neuroscientist who described these experiments as 'unsatisfactory, even paradoxical'. From Haggard's perspective, asking a participant to will a movement during a trial is as contradictory as commanding someone to 'have free will now!' While it is clear that these experiments produce a sense of ownership over physical movements, a fundamental question remains: who or what is the self that claims that ownership? Yong concluded that traditional dualism and the idea of an independent 'operating agent' are challenged by these neuroscientific studies. They demonstrate that the conscious intention to move emerges from the electrical activity of neurons – tangible, physical objects that are part of the material world.

Key quotes

How can this ghost, made out of some kind of metaphysical ectoplasm, influence brain matter without being detected? What sort of laws does Casper follow? Science has abandoned strong dualistic explanations in favour of natural accounts that assign causes and responsibility to specific actors and mechanisms that can be further studied. And so it is with the notion of the will.

(Koch)

In the debate concerning the meaning of personal freedom, these discoveries represent true progress, beyond the eternal metaphysical question of free will that will never be answered.

(Koch)

Key term

Carl Ransom Rogers (1902–1987): An American psychologist and university professor; his most influential work, *Client-Centered Therapy* (1951), established the foundation of humanistic psychology; he argued that humans possess a drive toward self-actualisation and that personal growth requires unconditional positive regard, empathy, and genuineness; he is regarded as one of the founders of the person-centred approach.

Specification content

Concepts of libertarianism: psychological (Carl Rogers: humanist approach, self-actualisation)

Psychological libertarianism

Carl Ransom Rogers (1902–87) was an American psychologist and is often seen as the founder of the humanistic approach to therapy. His method is known as Rogers client-centred therapy (RCCT), and, throughout his career, Rogers received numerous awards for his contributions to applied psychology.

Key quotes

The only means of healing that psychotherapy has learned to use is itself a human being, the therapist, whose own psychology also must have a decided influence upon the treatment and its outcome.

(Rank)

Psychology does not deal primarily with facts as science does but only with the individual's attitude towards facts.

(Rank)

Key term

fully functioning person (FFP): a congruent individual who participates fully in the richness of life experience

The correct client–therapist relationship was key for Rogers

Key term

actualising tendency: an innate directional tendency in each person to grow and seek new and varied experiences

Rogers advocated humanistic psychology, which focuses on the individual's capacity for self-directed growth. This approach stands in contrast to Sartre's existentialism. While Sartre argued that existence precedes essence, Rogers assumed that 'essence precedes existence'; he believed human beings are born with an innate goodness. Rogers was a professional practitioner, and this clinical background is the context in which his ideas on free will must be understood.

Rogers rejected two major trends in psychotherapy:

- Freud's objective approach, which viewed the client as an object to be analysed rather than a subject to be engaged with.
- The idea that human behaviour is determined solely by external social conditioning or past negativity.

For Rogers, free will is the ability of the individual to grow through conscious change. He was inspired by the work of Otto Rank, who suggested that a therapist should act as an 'assistant I' – an extension of the patient's self – rather than an outside observer.

Although the professional term is RCCT, Rogers' focus was not on the particular *therapy* but on the *person* as a whole. His research explored the relationships humans have with one another and the ability individuals have to help each other emerge as self-empowered people. His work outlines the process of self-development towards becoming a congruent, creative and **fully functioning person (FFP)**.

Rogers held that a therapist must possess three essential characteristics:

- Be congruent – have a balanced and fully functioning personality.
- Accept that the client is a separate individual with their own valid perspectives on life.
- Have genuine empathy and sensitivity towards the client's needs.

Underlying this approach are several principles:

- All people are inherently good and are born with an essence of good character.
- A holistic approach is required to become fully functioning.
- Special attention should be given to creativity, free will and positive human potential.
- The individual is a whole person greater than the sum of their parts, suggesting something beyond mere physicality.
- Self-exploration, rather than studying the behaviour of others, is the key to personal strength.
- Humanistic psychology acknowledges a desire for fulfillment as an integral part of the psyche.

Rogers' theory of self-development assumed that humans are born with an inherent **actualising tendency**. This is a directional urge in all living organisms to develop capacities in ways that maintain or enhance the organism and move it towards autonomy. This tendency requires a belief in free will, as it involves a drive to grow and seek new experiences. Rogers argued that the organism has one basic striving: to actualise and enhance the experiencing self.

Rogers argued that although life's challenges may suppress this actualising tendency, it can never be destroyed without the destruction of the person. He used this idea to develop a therapy based on self-actualisation, focusing on an individual's perspective in the 'here and now'. Two significant terms in this process are the **actual self** (or real self) and the **ideal self**.

Key terms

actual self: the view that an individual has of themselves as a result of life experience

ideal self: an individual's aspiration of who they want to become

congruence: a state of harmony between the real self and the ideal self

Key quotes

This approach lays stress upon the therapeutic relationship itself as a growth experience.

(Rogers)

Real therapy has to be centred around the client, his difficulties, his needs, his activities [...] My technique puts the patient himself as chief actor in the centre of the situation.

(Rank)

Consistency between a person's ideal self and their actual experience in life is not always apparent. When a large gap exists, the person is 'incongruent' and prone to psychological issues. The greater the consistency between these two concepts, the better the **congruence**. While total alignment is rare, the aim of self-actualisation is to bring them as close together as possible. The congruent individual is what Rogers called an FFP. This is not a final destination, but a process of 'becoming' through balanced participation in the changes one experiences.

Rogers' theory is optimistic because it suggests everyone is free to achieve fulfillment. He argued that an FFP is balanced and adjusted, often becoming a high achiever in society. To be an FFP involves a fluidity of experience and understanding in the here and now. There are four areas to be developed:

- **Openness**: This means being increasingly open to all experiences, including those that are threatening. Negative experiences are seen as opportunities for growth.
- **Existential living**: This means living fully in each moment. This involves an acceptance of change and being adaptable rather than being controlled by preconceived ideas.
- **Increasing trust**: This is a form of self-confidence where an individual trusts their own instincts and gut reactions to arrive at satisfying behaviour.
- **Functioning more fully**: This is the integration of the previous three aspects. It involves using internal equipment to sense a situation accurately and trusting one's judgement.

For Rogers, being an FFP was a measure of strong and positive personal development

Key quotes

One aspect of this process which I am naming the 'good life' appears to be a movement away from the role of defensiveness toward the pole of openness to experience.

(Rogers)

If I can provide a certain type of relationship, the other person will discover within himself the capacity to use that relationship for growth and change, and personal development will occur.

(Rogers)

Key quotes

One way of expressing the fluidity which is present in such existential living is to say that the self and personality emerge from experience, rather than experience being translated or twisted to fit preconceived self-structure.

(Rogers)

Individuals are able to trust their organismic reaction to a new situation because they discover [...] doing what 'feels right' proves to be a competent and trustworthy guide to behaviour.

(Rogers)

Rogers was a psychologist rather than a philosopher. His view of free will was deeply integrated into his theory of personal change. However, he also appreciated the scientific evidence for determinism, noting that every thought, feeling and action could be seen as determined by what preceded it.

Rogers faced this challenge by arguing that the dilemma disappears in the light of his theory. He suggested that in the optimum state of therapy, a person experiences 'complete and absolute freedom'. The FFP chooses a course of action that is the most effective response to all internal and external stimuli. While an outside observer might say this action was determined by the factors in the situation, the individual experiences it as a voluntary choice. In contrast, the incongruent person is determined by denial and distortion. Rogers concluded that the FFP experiences as a free choice that which is, from an objective perspective, entirely determined by their situation.

Why might Rogers be seen as having supported psychological libertarianism? The following five points show the libertarian elements in Rogers's approach:

- **The rejection of determinism**: By rejecting the idea that human behaviour is 'determined solely by external social conditioning' or unconscious drives, Rogers took a libertarian stance. He argued that human beings are 'subjects to be engaged with' rather than 'objects to be analysed'. This implies they have an independent agency.
- **The actualising tendency**: This is described as an innate and directional urge to move towards autonomy. For a libertarian, this internal drive is the engine of free will, suggesting an internal power to choose a direction.
- **The FFP and absolute freedom**: Rogers argued that an individual who is congruent and open to experience can experience 'the most complete and absolute freedom'. He described this person as someone who voluntarily chooses and wills their actions.
- **The capacity for change**: Rogers' theory is based on the idea that individuals can grow and change through self-exploration. If human beings were determined by their past, the type of personal transformation Rogers described would be impossible.
- **The resolution of the dilemma**: Rogers acknowledged that while a scientist might see human actions as determined, the individual has a subjective experience of choice that is real and valid. This emphasis on subjective feelings and trusting one's judgement is a hallmark of the libertarian position.

It might appear that Rogers was a compatibilist – accepting deterministic features while acknowledging the reality of experienced freedom. However, Rogers provided the psychological evidence for the libertarian claim that humans are free agents. He suggested that while physical and social factors exist, the individual retains the power to will their own personal evolution.

Summary

- ★ Libertarians argue that human beings are free to choose their actions and are therefore morally responsible; they reject the notion that all events are determined by external or prior causes.
- ★ Jean-Paul Sartre, a philosophical libertarian, argued that existence precedes essence, meaning that humans are not born with a fixed nature or purpose but must create their own identities through a series of free, conscious choices.

- ★ Sartre suggested that to deny this absolute freedom is to live in bad faith, as individuals are condemned to be free and must accept total responsibility for the values and character they project into the world.
- ★ Dr Angela Sirigu provided a biological basis for scientific libertarianism through her research on the parietal cortex, arguing that the brain generates an internal intent to act before any physical movement occurs, suggesting the will is an active agent.
- ★ Carl Rogers adopted a humanistic approach to psychological libertarianism, focusing on the actualising tendency, an innate drive towards autonomy which suggests that each individual possesses the free will to grow, move towards congruence and become an FFP.
- ★ Unlike hard determinism, in which humans are regarded as objects shaped by genes and/or environment, psychological and philosophical libertarianism identify the subjective experience of choice as a reliable and essential guide for personal and moral evolution.

AO1 Activity

a Outline the three main forms of libertarianism studied in this sub-theme, covering the philosophical, scientific and psychological approaches.

b The following summary of the three forms of libertarianism is too brief and lacks technical depth and references to scholars. Develop the summary by integrating the technical terms and concepts listed below. There may be other terms you can bring in as well.

Refer to the band descriptors for A2 (WJEC) or A Level (Eduqas). For band 5, your responses should demonstrate 'thorough and accurate knowledge and understanding' with 'an extensive and relevant response' that makes 'excellent use of evidence and examples'.

Concepts

- **Sartre:** existence precedes essence, *mauvaise foi*, condemned to be free
- **Sirigu:** parietal cortex, internal intent, active agency
- **Rogers:** actualising tendency, congruence, FFP

Summary

Some thinkers using philosophical, scientific and psychological approaches argue that human beings are entirely free. Sartre suggests that people aren't born with a pre-set purpose and they have to make themselves who they are through their choices. If people pretend they aren't free, they are just lying to themselves. Sirigu has looked at the brain and found that people actually intend to move before the body reacts, which might prove free will is real. Finally, Rogers suggests people have an inner drive to grow and improve. This suggests that as they become more balanced, people experience more freedom to choose how they react to the world around them.

This section covers AO2 content and skills

Specification content

The extent to which philosophical, scientific and/or psychological views on libertarianism inevitably lead people to accept libertarianism

Issues for analysis and evaluation

The extent to which philosophical, scientific and/or psychological views on libertarianism inevitably lead people to accept libertarianism

Possible line of argument	Critical analysis and evaluation
Sartre argues that humans move from a fixed state (being-in-itself) to self-consciousness (being-for-itself). This transition allows us to 'nihilate' our physical constraints (facticity).	A paradox arises because the being-for-itself is effectively a nothingness. If there is no substantial agent or self to perform the action, the concept of who actually exercises free will remains problematic.
Rogers suggests that the FFP experiences absolute freedom. By responding to surrounding conditions, a person 'voluntarily chooses that which is absolutely determined'.	It is difficult to categorise Rogers as a pure libertarian. His view that freedom is an adaptive, creative response to stimuli suggests a form of compatibilism rather than libertarianism.
Some argue that because scientific evidence for determinism is not absolute, libertarianism remains a viable possibility. Sirigu's theories suggest the brain chooses the optimum path from various computations.	Just because evidence might suggest the brain choosing, it does not mean libertarianism is inevitable. Scientific scepticism, exemplified by Christof Koch, suggests that the metaphysical question of free will may remain eternally unanswered.
Rogers views the creative, free response as a 'vanguard of human evolution', allowing individuals to adapt and survive under changing environmental conditions.	If our free choices are merely the most efficient biological adaptations for survival, this challenges the libertarian claim that people are truly independent of their environment.
The statement suggests an inevitable acceptance of libertarianism. Given people's lived experiences of making choices, which can sometimes be spontaneous and which sometimes require considerable reflection, it does seem inevitable.	Libertarianism is no longer seen as having one absolute version. Given the variety of inconclusive evidence from philosophy, science and psychology, the claim that libertarianism is inevitable is unconvincing.

AO2 Activity

a Analyse three possible conclusions that could be drawn from the critical analysis and evaluation of the view that philosophical, scientific and/or psychological views on libertarianism inevitably lead people to accept libertarianism. Select evidence and examples to support each of the three conclusions. Select one conclusion that you think is the **most convincing** and explain why it is so.

b Now contrast this with the **weakest** conclusion of the three. Justify your argument with clear reasoning and evidence.

Refer to the band descriptors for A2 (WJEC) or A Level (Eduqas). For band 5, your response should demonstrate 'a confident critical analysis and perceptive evaluation', presenting 'a thorough, sustained and accurate argument' that 'successfully identifies and thoroughly addresses the issues raised'.

Specification content

The extent to which an individual has free choice

Exam practice

Below is an example of part of an evaluation of the extent to which an individual has free choice.

Sample answer

While hard determinists argue that every action results from prior causes, libertarians such as Sartre, Sirigu and Rogers suggest that human agency is real. By examining philosophical, scientific and psychological perspectives, one can evaluate the degree to which individuals are truly the authors of their own lives.

News reporter
The introduction successfully sets the scene, providing a clear overview of the conflicting 'headlines' in the free will debate.

Philosophically, Sartre argues for absolute freedom. He asserts that existence precedes essence, meaning humans are not born with a pre-set purpose. Unlike an object designed for a task, a human being first exists and then defines themselves through conscious choices. For Sartre, the extent of our freedom is total; individuals are condemned to be free because they have no choice but to choose.

Philosopher
This paragraph accurately captures the ontological weight of existentialism and the inescapable nature of human agency.

To deny this level of choice is to live in *mauvaise foi*: a form of self-deception where people pretend they are determined by their environment or social roles. Sartre insists that even in restrictive circumstances, the individual retains the freedom to choose their attitude. Therefore, the extent of free choice is limited only by a willingness to accept the radical responsibility involved.

Detective
The motive behind bad faith is identified here; the essay correctly describes it as an attempt to escape the evidence of our own liberty.

From a scientific perspective, Dr Angela Sirigu offers empirical evidence that the will is an active agent. Her research on the parietal cortex suggests that the brain generates an internal intent to act before any physical movement occurs. This distinguishes voluntary actions from mere reflexes, providing a biological basis for the libertarian claim that choice is a real, internal process rather than a deterministic reaction.

Critical thinker
The use of empirical data here provides a necessary counter-balance to the abstract theory, strengthening the overall case.

Explorer

This section successfully maps out the 'new territory' of the brain, showing how biological discovery can support the concept of the will.

Tennis player

This description of the engine of growth resonates with the internal drive required to improve one's performance on the court.

Judge

The evidence for personal transformation is presented clearly, demonstrating how an individual can move towards a state of total accountability.

Critical thinker

News reporter

The summary provides a robust final verdict while remaining accessible and balanced for a student audience.

The extent of choice in Sirigu's model is significant because it locates the source of action within the mind. If the parietal cortex simulates an action before execution, the person is not merely a biological machine. Instead, they are an active participant in their physical movements, suggesting that the will has a genuine, measurable impact on the material world.

Psychologically, Carl Rogers argues that the extent of freedom is linked to personal growth. He identifies an actualising tendency – an innate drive towards autonomy. While external factors may suppress this drive, they can never destroy it. For Rogers, free choice is the 'engine' that allows an individual to move towards their potential rather than remaining a victim of past conditioning.

The level of choice an individual experiences depends on their state of congruence. An incongruent person may feel determined by social pressures. However, as one becomes an FFP, one experiences 'complete and absolute freedom'. By being open to experience, a person voluntarily chooses the most effective course of action, successfully harmonising their real self with their ideal self.

In conclusion, while individuals are influenced by biological and social factors, the evidence suggests that the extent of free choice is profound. Whether through Sartre's radical responsibility, Sirigu's neurological intent or Rogers' psychological growth, it appears that humans are not mere objects. We possess a unique capacity to will a personal evolution, making the individual the primary architect of their existence.

Over to you

The following five conclusions are drawn from an evaluation of the libertarian concept of psychology. Your task is to develop each of these conclusions by identifying its strengths (the evidence or reasoning that make it a persuasive point) but also the challenges made to it (the counter-arguments or weaknesses that might undermine it). When you have completed the exercise, explain whether your final overall verdict on the libertarian concept of psychology is positive or negative and give the key reasons why you have reached your verdict.

The result should be five very competently written paragraphs that could form a final conclusion of an evaluation. Refer to the band descriptors for A2 (WJEC) or A Level (Eduqas) and, in particular, look at the demands described in the higher band descriptors, which you should be aspiring towards. Ask yourself the following questions:

- Is my answer a confident critical analysis and perceptive evaluation of the issue?
- Is my answer a response that successfully identifies and thoroughly addresses the issues the question raises?

Question

'The libertarian concept of psychology inevitably leads to the belief that we are totally free.' Evaluate this view. (Eduqas A Level 2018)

Conclusions

- Rogers' actualising tendency identifies an innate drive towards autonomy. This suggests humans are not merely products of environment or conditioning but possess the inherent power to self-determine.
- The FFP achieves a state of complete and absolute freedom. By reaching congruence and being open to experience, individuals move beyond defensive reactions to voluntarily will their own actions.
- Sartre contradicts Rogers by viewing freedom as an inescapable burden rather than a psychological goal. Sartre argues people are condemned to be free from birth; Rogers' focus on an innate good essence actually limits the radical, unconditioned freedom Sartre demands.
- From a hard determinist perspective, psychological libertarianism is a delusion. Critics argue the actualising tendency is simply another form of biological programming, and the feeling of choice is merely an illusion that ignores external causes.
- The term 'totally free' may be a misleading description of Rogers' position. He could be viewed as a compatibilist, as he acknowledges that while an individual feels free, a scientist could still see those actions as determined by the stimuli of the here and now.

This section covers AO1 content and skills

Specification content

Implications of libertarianism on moral responsibility

F: The implications of libertarianism and free will

The implications of libertarianism on moral responsibility

If the libertarian position is correct, the consequences reach far beyond philosophy and into:

- the way society is structured
- how the mind is understood
- how religious believers relate to what they understand as God or the divine.

The assertion that human beings are the originating causes of their own actions fundamentally shifts the understanding of responsibility. It suggests that choices are not merely the result of a long chain of physical or social causes, but are instead genuine choices for which the person – the moral agent – is fully accountable.

This creates several significant areas of debate:

- **It raises the nature of moral value**: Are ideas of right and wrong simply evolutionary survival mechanisms, or are they meaningful products of human reasoning?
- **It forces a re-evaluation of praise and blame**: If human beings are truly free, then the legal and social systems that punish and reward are justified. However, if freedom is an illusion, these systems may be fundamentally unfair.
- **It challenges the understanding of the brain and consciousness**: We must ask whether the conscious will is a powerful director of the physical body or if it is merely a bystander to biological processes.

Nelson Mandela was inspired by the poem 'Invictus'

For those with religious convictions, free will impacts on the concept of God. It raises the question of how the all-powerful Creator can exist alongside truly independent creatures, and what this means for the problem of evil and the purpose of prayer. Each of these implications tests the boundary between a strong sense of freedom and the scientific and logical arguments that suggest life might be determined.

The central implication of libertarianism is the belief that human beings are the primary architects of their own existence. This means that each person is a moral agent – they freely make their own moral decisions. This concept has been central for many figures and can be summed up by the poem 'Invictus' by William Henley, which inspired Nelson Mandela (1918–2013) and which was read at his funeral by President Obama.

The final lines of the poem are:

> I am the master of my fate:
> I am the captain of my soul.

If human agency is real, then moral responsibility is not a shared burden or a product of environmental factors; it is an absolute personal reality. Each person can state that they are the 'master of their fate' and 'the captain of their soul'. Under this view, an individual cannot shift the credit for their successes or the blame for their failures onto their biology, their upbringing or any external force.

To be a libertarian is to accept that human decisions are 'up to us', meaning that agents possess the capacity to have acted otherwise in any given situation. This creates a profound sense of accountability that connects philosophy, psychology and neuroscience.

The philosophical approach: Sartre

In terms of philosophy, Sartre presents perhaps the most radical implication of libertarianism. By asserting that 'existence precedes essence' (see 'Man is not free not to be free' on page 269), Sartre removes any pre-set purpose or deterministic excuses. If there is no fixed human nature, then humans are 'condemned to be free'. The implication for moral responsibility is that individuals are entirely responsible for what they are and what they do. Two points can be considered here:

- **Facticity and mauvaise foi**: Sartre argues that any attempt to blame circumstances – what he calls 'facticity' – is an act of *mauvaise foi* (self-deception). Whether facing extreme hardship or in a position of power, the agent retains the freedom to choose their attitude and response. Consequently, libertarianism implies that individuals cannot hide behind social roles or psychological labels; they are always and entirely accountable for the lives they create.
- **Radical freedom and authenticity**: For Sartre, morality is a subjective creation for each person as they create their essence from their existence. Therefore, there is no objective set of moral laws to be discovered. The right moral choice is one which is authentic to the person making it so that they are always turning away from *mauvaise foi*. This represents radical freedom, whereby a person can create themselves during their existence.

Feature	Jean-Paul Sartre
The basis of freedom	Existence precedes essence; there is no pre-set blueprint for human nature.
The nature of the agent	A being is born as 'nothing' and must define themselves through choices.
The role of the will	We have radical freedom to create values; our choices must be authentic to be valid.
Implication for responsibility	We are condemned to be free and entirely accountable for our actions.
The key insight	Denial of freedom is *mauvaise foi* (bad faith); people are the authors of their essence.

The scientific approach: Sirigu

Turning to science, the research of Dr Angela Sirigu provides a neurological framework for the perspective that libertarianism has a biological basis. By identifying the role of the parietal cortex of the human brain in generating an 'internal intent' to act, Sirigu distinguishes voluntary movements from mere reflexes. Two points can be considered here:

- **The reality of internal intent**: Sirigu's work identifies that the will is a distinct neurological event. When the parietal cortex was stimulated, patients reported a desire to move their limbs, even though no movement occurred. In contrast, stimulating the motor cortex caused movement without any prior desire or intent.

  The implication for moral responsibility is profound: it suggests that intent is the primary cause of an action, rather than a mere side effect of biological processes. For the moral agent, this confirms that choices are not simply reflexes; they are initiated by a conscious, internal intent that can be distinguished from involuntary physical reactions.
- **The rejection of automatism**: A common argument in hard determinism is that humans are 'biological machines', automata, reacting to stimuli without any real control. Sirigu's findings challenge this by showing that the brain simulates an action and its consequences in the parietal cortex before it is executed.

  This implies that the individual is the source of their own movements. If the brain is capable of internal simulation, the agent is not just a passenger in a determined body but is an active participant in the decision-making process. This validates the libertarian claim that decisions are up to us.

By identifying the parietal cortex as the seat of intention, Sirigu provides a biological justification for treating humans as free moral agents who are accountable for the actions they take. It should be noted that the advances in neuroscience have been considerable. As brain-imaging technology improves, newer studies often challenge these earlier findings. Furthermore, while science can map the brain's activity, it may not yet be capable of capturing the full complexity of human moral choice.

Feature	Angela Sirigu
The basis of freedom	A neurological framework in the parietal cortex of the brain simulates actions.
The nature of the agent	Each person is a rational architect who simulates actions and consequences before acting.
The role of the will	A person's will serves as an initiator that generates internal intent, distinguishing choice from reflex.
Implication for responsibility	We are responsible because the conscious will is the primary cause of an action.
The key insight	The parietal cortex provides a neurological justification for free moral agency.

The psychological approach: Rogers

Turning to psychology, the research of Carl Rogers provides a humanistic framework for the perspective that libertarianism is rooted in the individual's drive for growth. By identifying the capacity for self-actualisation, Rogers distinguishes self-determined growth from conditioned behaviour. Two points can be considered here:

- **The capacity for self-direction**: Rogers' work proposes that the 'self' is not a static object but an active process of becoming. He argues that every individual possesses an 'actualising tendency', an innate motivation to fully develop their potential. This contrasts with deterministic psychology, which might view a person as a passive recipient of environmental conditioning or biological drives.

The implication for moral responsibility is significant: it suggests that the individual has the power to override past conditioning and social pressures. For the moral agent, this confirms that they are not merely a product of their upbringing; they possess a capacity for self-direction. Consequently, a person can be held responsible for their actions because they have the internal resources to evaluate their situation and choose a path that aligns with their true self, rather than simply reacting to external forces.

- **The FFP and agency**: A central concept in Rogers' theory is the FFP, which describes an individual who is in touch with their own feelings and desires. Rogers argues that a hallmark of psychological health is the recognition of one's own agency. Unlike the deterministic view that humans are 'biomachines', Rogers suggests that as a person moves towards self-actualisation, they become increasingly aware of their power to choose.

  This implies that the individual is the source of their own moral progress. If a person is open to experience and trusts their own internal judgement, they are an active participant in creating their own values. This supports the libertarian claim that decisions are up to us. By achieving a state of congruence – where the ideal self and actual self align – the moral agent accepts the burden of freedom. Under this view, moral responsibility is a mark of psychological maturity: to be fully human is to accept that one is responsible for the choices that shape one's existence.

By identifying the drive for self-actualisation as a core human trait, Rogers provides a psychological justification for treating humans as free moral agents who are accountable for the direction of their lives.

Feature	Carl Rogers
The basis of freedom	The actualising tendency consists of an innate drive towards growth and self-direction.
The nature of the agent	Each person moves towards congruence and maturity with the aim of becoming an FFP.
The role of the will	The will is the power to override past social conditioning and environmental pressures.
Implication for responsibility	Accepting responsibility for one's life is a mark of psychological health.
The key insight	Humans are not biomachines but active participants in creating their own values.

The implications of libertarianism: the worth of human ideas of rightness, wrongness and moral value

If libertarianism is true, human ideas of rightness, wrongness and moral value are elevated from being simple biological accidents or social habits to being significant, individual free decisions. These free decisions are part of a creative process resulting in the consequent acts.

In a deterministic world, it is reasonable to argue that a person's moral values are essentially little more than instincts or reflexes that promote their survival.

Specification content

The implications of libertarianism: the worth of human ideas of rightness, wrongness and moral value, the value in blaming moral agents for immoral acts

However, for the libertarian, these ideas are at the very core of what it means to be a rational, intelligent and free moral agent. Since each individual possesses the power to have acted otherwise in each situation, the values they choose to live by define their character and their contribution to society. This provides a clear distinction between humans and animals; while animals act on instinct and lack moral responsibility, humans have control over their moral attitudes and choices.

This means that humans must take responsibility for their actions and cannot hide from this responsibility using the excuse of some form of determinism, whether biological, philosophical or psychological. Humans can be praised for correct moral decisions and blamed for poor ones. This makes punishment fair, as humans have a choice (even if the choice is a burden or a 'curse' on humanity, as Sartre put it) of how to act.

Accepting that humans have freedom of moral choice has implications for legal systems, as these are used to hold adult humans accountable for the moral decisions they make. It also makes it necessary for each jurisdiction to decide at what age children can be held responsible for their choices under the law and places a responsibility on adults to shape the values and character of children to enable them to make correct moral decisions.

A case study: Eugene Grayson

The libertarian approach is reflected in a significant legal case in 1978: United States v. Grayson. Ross Grayson had escaped from custody and, during his trial, stated under oath that he had escaped because he had been threatened by another prisoner and that several incidents had left him with no other alternative than to escape.

The prosecution was able to prove that everything Grayson had said was fabricated and that he had lied in court, even though under oath to tell the truth. The trial judge imposed a longer sentence as a result, stating that Grayson had made a choice of evil over good by lying in court and by not telling the truth.

The Supreme Court of the United States, whose ruling in United States v. Grayson (1978) affirmed that 'belief in freedom of the human will' is a foundation of the legal system

The defence appealed against this decision by arguing that Grayson's background and the immediate 'pressure of the situation', specifically the threat of a long prison sentence and the desperate circumstances of being a person who had escaped from custody, created an overwhelming external force.

They suggested these conditions essentially 'dictated' Grayson's decision to lie as a survival mechanism. They argued that because these external and internal pressures influenced his testimony, his perjury should not result in a harsher penalty.

Having reviewed the case, the Supreme Court issued a majority verdict ruling against the defence. The court stated that a 'universal and persistent' foundation stone in the legal system is the 'belief in freedom of the human will and a consequent ability and duty of the normal individual to choose between good and evil'. The ruling continued:

> The whole theory of the criminal law is that the human being is a free agent [...] whose actions are the result of choices. A deterministic view of human conduct [...] is inconsistent with the underlying precepts of our criminal justice system.

This judgment serves as a practical confirmation of the libertarian position. It rejects the idea that a person is merely a product of their environment, instead asserting that the law must treat adults as the conscious authors of their own moral and legal decisions.

The philosophical approach: Sartre

For Sartre, the worth of moral value was absolute because it is a human invention in a world that otherwise lacks inherent meaning. As Sartre asserted: since there is no fixed human nature to provide a moral blueprint, humans are the sole source of value. Sartre argued that humans cannot hide from this responsibility with the excuse of determinism, whether biological, philosophical or psychological.

This total freedom can be seen as a burden or a curse, as Sartre put it, because people are entirely responsible for the values they create. Sartre provided a philosophical defence of blame by categorising the denial of responsibility as *mauvaise foi*. Consequently, blaming an agent for an immoral act is an affirmation of their personhood, treating the individual as a free master of their own destiny, as the captain of their soul.

Regarding the Grayson case, Sartre would likely view Grayson's perjury as a clear example of *mauvaise foi*. By claiming that the 'pressure of the situation' and his background dictated his decision to lie, Grayson was attempting to deny his radical freedom and turn himself into a passive object of his circumstances.

For Sartre, the judge's decision to increase the sentence is an affirmation of Grayson's personhood; it treats him as a free agent who is condemned to be free, even in a witness box. By fabricating a story to evade punishment, Grayson was not only deceiving the court but also attempting to evade the absolute responsibility he had for creating his own essence through his choices.

The scientific approach: Sirigu

The work of Sirigu provides a biological explanation for why such worth is placed on these moral ideas. Her research into the parietal cortex suggests that the brain does not just react to external stimuli but actively simulates different outcomes through an internal intent. This implies that ideas of right and wrong are tied to our physical capacity to plan and execute actions. In Sirigu's work, blame is given a neurological justification. There is a physical basis for the idea that a person is the author of their actions; and if an action has caused harm, that harm can be attributed (blamed on) the person's will.

This has significant implications for our legal systems, as they are used to hold adult humans accountable for the choices they make. It also raises questions regarding at what age children can be held responsible under the law, as their neurological capacity for internal intent is still developing.

From Sirigu's neurological perspective, Grayson's perjury represents a sophisticated use of the parietal cortex to simulate a false reality. Her research suggests that the brain calculates consequences before an action is executed; in Grayson's case, his internal intent was to produce a fabricated narrative that would lead to a specific desired outcome. Because the parietal cortex allows for this internal simulation, the perjury cannot be dismissed as a mere reflex or a product of environmental conditioning. Instead, it was a biologically authored event. This provides a possible physical justification for the court's view that Grayson was the conscious architect of his own deception.

The psychological approach: Rogers

This theme of human-centred value is mirrored in the psychology of Rogers. For Rogers, ideas of rightness and wrongness have worth only when they are authentic to the individual's actual experience. He distinguishes between 'conditions of worth' – values forced upon the person by others – and the 'organic' values that emerge from an FFP.

In this context, the value of blame is that it encourages the agent to reflect on their choices and take ownership of their actions. Because humans are seen as free to shape their own values, Rogers implies that adult humans have a responsibility to shape the values and character of children to enable them to make correct moral decisions as they grow towards self-actualisation.

Rogers would likely interpret Grayson's lies as having emerged from a state of incongruence in which he used deception as a defensive mechanism. Rather than acting as an FFP open to the reality of his experience, Grayson attempted to protect himself by shifting the blame onto his past and his environment.

Rogers would argue that true psychological maturity involves accepting one's own agency and the consequences that follow. By blaming his background, Grayson was relying on external conditions of worth rather than his own internal drive for self-direction. From a Rogerian perspective, taking responsibility for the lie would be a necessary step towards achieving congruence and self-actualisation.

Specification content

The implications of libertarianism on moral responsibility: the usefulness of normative ethics

The usefulness of normative ethics

Normative ethics is the branch of ethics focused on determining what constitutes right and wrong actions. Within normative ethics, philosophers aim to establish general principles that can guide individuals as moral agents towards ethical living. They do this by examining the motivations behind, and consequences of, actions through theories such as divine command theory, virtue theory, ethical egoism, natural law, situation ethics and utilitarianism.

In terms of libertarianism, these theories can serve as important guidance for a person's free will. If human beings were determined, normative theories would be irrelevant, as there would be no capacity for an individual to alter their actions based on moral reasoning and decision-making. For the libertarian, because moral agents possess free will, it is useful to have guidance on how to exercise this freedom, and the various normative theories offer different ways of navigating this moral landscape.

Deontological systems, such as natural law and divine command theory, can provide fixed rules that an individual must obey. For a libertarian, these can appear restrictive as they leave limited room for the agent to create values.

By contrast, teleological or character-based systems, such as utilitarianism, situation ethics, ethical egoism and virtue theory, require a greater degree of personal interpretation, evaluation and analysis. Whether calculating the greatest happiness, acting in love, pursuing self-interest or maintaining virtues, these theories demand that the moral agent becomes an active navigator of their ethical life – the captain of their soul. Consequently, the ability to deliberate between these systems is what gives human life its moral weight and justifies the worth that is placed on ideas of rightness and wrongness.

The philosophical approach: Sartre

Jean-Paul Sartre suggests that while various normative ethics provide a structure for society, they must be used carefully. If a person follows a rule simply to avoid the anxiety of making a personal choice, that individual is acting in *mauvaise foi*. However, normative ethics remain useful as the context in which freedom is exercised, as they provide the framework for the choices a moral agent must make. For a libertarian, an ethical system is a tool that requires the moral agent to take total responsibility for their decision to follow it. In this view, every moral choice is a personal assertion of freedom that defines the moral agent's own values and sets an example for how others might act.

Sartre argued that morality is created by the individual's decision in a specific moment. Such an approach would necessarily mean a rejection of systems such as utilitarianism, which tries to evaluate consequences and which might apply a mathematical formula such as the hedonic calculus (see the hedonic calculus on page 184). Radical responsibility has to be entirely free and not reliant on the methods promoted by normative theories.

In Sartre's work *Existentialism is a Humanism* (1946) (based on the lecture), he illustrates his approach with the example of a student forced to choose between staying in France to care for his mother or leaving to join the Free French Forces. Sartre uses this dilemma to demonstrate that no pre-existing value – not even love or duty – can provide a clear answer in advance. For an existentialist, following a pre-calculated blueprint such as the hedonic calculus or the greatest happiness principle would be an act of *mauvaise foi*; instead, the agent must create their own value through an authentic, situational choice.

The scientific approach: Sirigu

The research of Sirigu might imply that normative ethics are useful because they provide the 'data' for the brain to use during the decision-making process. If the parietal cortex carries out simulations of different actions before they are performed, normative ethics could provide the frameworks required to calculate which simulation is the best one to execute. In this way, ethics are not just abstract theories but might be essential components of the biological process of decision-making.

Sirigu's research fits best with teleological systems such as utilitarianism. Her discovery that the parietal cortex simulates an action and its consequences before execution suggests that the brain is biologically designed to calculate outcomes. Utilitarianism, which requires a moral agent to calculate the greatest happiness or best consequence, utilises this exact biological simulation capacity. In this way, Sirigu identifies a physical basis for the internal intent required to navigate a system focused on the results of our actions.

The psychological approach: Rogers

For Rogers, normative ethics are useful only if they help an individual move towards congruence. While Rogers warns against 'introjecting' values – accepting external rules without question – it is acknowledged that an FFP must interact with the environment and consider the needs of others. Normative ethics provide the benchmarks that an individual can use to reflect on organismic experience. By comparing internal feelings with external ethical standards, a person can better understand the existential situation, using ethics as a resource for growth and self-actualisation.

Rogers is most naturally paired with virtue theory. Unlike theories that focus on following external rules, both Rogers and virtue theory are agent-centred, focusing on the growth of the person and who they are becoming. Just as Aristotle's concept of *eudaimonia* describes a state of human flourishing achieved through character development, Rogers' concept of self-actualisation describes a person reaching their full potential through their own internal drive. For Rogers, virtue theory provides a useful framework where morality is not about obedience to laws, but about the maturity and congruence of the individual.

Normative theories compared

Ultimately, the libertarian position offers a view of humanity that is as challenging as it is empowering. Whether through the radical existential freedom of Sartre, the neurological simulations of Sirigu or the actualising tendency of Rogers, the conclusion remains the same: human beings are not merely passengers in a determined universe.

By accepting that choices are the genuine starting causes of actions, the individual moves beyond being a biomachine or a product of their environment. Instead, the person takes on the role of the moral agent – the master of their fate and the captain of their soul.

Specification content

The implications of free will for religious belief

The implications of free will for religious belief

For a religious believer who adopts a libertarian perspective, the existence of free will is not merely a philosophical preference but a theological necessity. If human beings are truly the captains of their souls, the relationship between the Creator and the created is fundamentally altered. This perspective shifts the weight of moral consequence away from divine decree and onto the shoulders of the human agent.

The Buddha was a materialist philosopher

Free will as a practical solution

While the Western tradition focuses on a relationship with a Creator, Eastern perspectives like Buddhism demonstrate how free will operates as a practical tool for liberation to obtain ***nibbana*** (nirvana). Buddhism is often described as a philosophy or way of life in which questions of abstract belief are secondary to the goal of diminishing suffering. This path is not dependent on an external supernatural agency or a creator god; there is no one to reward or punish. It is an empirical process involving a practical solution to the human condition.

The notion of free will in Buddhism springs directly from the idea of ***kamma*** (karma). The Buddhist monk Narada Thera wrote:

> Agents are responsible for their own deeds, happiness and misery. Humans build their own hells and create their own heavens. They are the architects of their own fate. In short, individuals are their own karma.

Key terms

nibbana: the term for enlightenment, ultimately beyond all notions of determinism and free will

kamma: the notion of individual responsibility for our thoughts that lead to actions

Buddhism focuses on the individual gaining control of the will through consciousness. In *The Questions of King Milinda*, the monk Nagasena compares an untrained mind to a 'hungry and excited ox' that is easily agitated and determined by its senses. In contrast, the ***arhat*** possesses a mind that is 'well-tamed [...] obedient and disciplined'. Their thoughts are firmly tied to the 'post of contemplation', remaining steadfast and undisturbed. The *arhat*, therefore, is in full self-control of their **volitions**.

Free will is therefore central to spiritual development and the cultivation of a 'morality from within'. It is closely connected to the idea of rebirth; the free, ethical actions of an individual have consequences that extend beyond a single lifetime towards the ultimate goal of liberation.

Free will as the engine of liberation

The implications of free will extend further in Hinduism and Sikhism, where freedom is the engine behind the cycle of life. Both traditions maintain the existence of a soul (***atman*** in Hinduism, meaning a 'spark', and ***atma*** in Sikhism) which acts as the persistent moral agent, transmigrating through **reincarnation** based on the quality of free choices.

In Hinduism, the exercise of free will determines the accumulation of karma. Moral guidance is provided through the **dharma** (religious and social duties). The religion teaches that human beings possess the free will to either pursue an escape from the cycle of existence (moksha) or remain tied to the material world through the process of reincarnation. Therefore the *atman* uses its agency to seek spiritual knowledge and consciously choose actions aligned with dharma. This conscious decision-making is the essential mechanism that allows the individual to break free from the bondage of **samsara** and achieve eternal union with the divine.

In Sikhism, the exercise of free will to follow the path of the *gurmukh* leads to the ultimate spiritual goal of *mukti* (liberation). The **Rahit Maryada** (code of conduct) provides the moral standards for the believer. By choosing a conscious redirection of the will to align with the divine, the individual breaks the cycle of birth and death. Following the *gurmukh* path means the individual has successfully used their free will to avoid a self-centred life (*manmukh*), resulting in a life of selfless service and unity with God.

In both traditions, the law of karma requires the individual to be the starting cause of their actions. If human conduct were determined, the process of reincarnation would be a mechanical accident rather than a purposeful moral journey towards liberation.

Whether expressed through the internal discipline of the Buddhist *arhat* or the adherence to the dharma and Rahit Maryada, the implication of free will is consistent: it provides the foundation for religious meaning. By establishing the individual as an autonomous moral agent, these traditions maintain a system of personal accountability. Without the capacity for free choice, the core religious tenets of spiritual progress, the accumulation of merit and the eventual attainment of liberation would lose their transformative power.

Free will as a moral partnership: protecting omnibenevolence

While Eastern traditions focus on the individual's use of free will to navigate the laws of karma and achieve liberation, the focus shifts significantly when considering monotheistic religions. In Judaism and Christianity, the exercise of free will is not just a personal spiritual tool, but the defining factor in the relationship between a human agent and the all-powerful Creator. Here, the existence of freedom is used to reconcile the presence of suffering in the world with the character of a God who is both omnipotent and omnibenevolent.

Key terms

***arhat*:** the worthy one who is in the final stage of rebirth and has full control of the will
volitions: mind processes that initiate action – the will
***atman*:** the Hindu term for soul
***atma*:** the Sikh term for soul
reincarnation: transmigration of a metaphysical soul from one body or form to another that takes place at the point of death
dharma: the notion of moral and religious obligation
samsara: the continuous cycle of birth, life, death, and rebirth (reincarnation)
***gurmukh*:** being God-centred and spiritual
Rahit Maryada: the Sikh code of ethical conduct

Specification content

The link between God and evil, the implications for God's omnipotence and omnibenevolence

Key quote

The Lord God took the man and put him in the Garden of Eden to work it and take care of it. And the Lord God commanded the man, 'You are free to eat from any tree in the garden; but you must not eat from the tree of the knowledge of good and evil, for when you eat from it you will certainly die.'

(Genesis 2:15–17)

For both Jewish people and Christians, the compatibility of God's omnipotence and omnibenevolence with free will is directly tied to the relationship between God and humanity and the overall plan for salvation (soteriology). Free will was bestowed upon the first humans, Adam and Eve, who possessed the capacity to choose while being guided by divine wisdom.

In most world religions, God is viewed as the final standard of good. Because God's character exhibits the highest moral perfection, his actions are always consistent with that nature. Consequently, when God granted free choice to humanity – exemplified by the instruction in Genesis to 'freely eat of every tree of the garden' – it is argued that this was an inherently good decision.

God's goodness is a constant that his people can rely on. For instance, in Jeremiah 32:40, God says: 'I will make an everlasting covenant with them: I will never stop doing good to them.' The nature of a covenant is central to the libertarian argument; it is a two-way relationship that presupposes the human party has the freedom to either uphold or break their side of the agreement. Without free will, the covenant would be a mechanical decree rather than a meaningful moral partnership.

Furthermore, it is believed that God's holiness means that God is separated from sin. God's nature is always to be moral and never sin. And Leviticus 19:2 makes clear that God's holiness is the pattern for people to imitate: 'Be holy because I, the Lord your God, am holy.'

The Old Testament prophets particularly recognised that religion and morality go together, speaking out when Israel did not practise what it preached. True religion meant to freely choose obedience to God's teachings and establish moral consistency.

This Judaeo-Christian view suggests that free will and morality are grounded in the nature of God himself. Humans were created as moral creatures *imago dei* (in the image of God), possessing a reflection of the divine capacity for choice. Consequently, scripture is not seen as a set of deterministic commands, but as the practical guidance needed for an autonomous agent to make moral decisions in response to their Creator.

Free will as a logical necessity: the classical defence

Free will is implicit in classical theodicies of Augustine and Irenaeus (arguments for the goodness of God in the face of evil). They argued that the evil in the world is not caused by God, but by humanity's misuse of the gift of freedom. God intended to create a world in which rational agents could freely decide to love and obey him.

The philosopher Richard Swinburne addresses the challenge of the sheer quantity of evil in the world. He argues that for a person to be genuinely free, they must be allowed to harm themselves and others. While God could intervene, Swinburne suggests that allowing individuals to learn from the consequences of their actions is more consistent with moral freedom. Swinburne also argues that death is a good because it limits the human power to do harm. In a finite life, human choices carry far more significance.

Key term

process theology: the argument that the problem of evil is removed by redefining the meaning of God's omnipotence

Free will as a creative constraint: redefining omnipotence

An alternative solution to the problem of evil is found in **process theology**, supported by thinkers such as A.N. Whitehead. This approach removes the problem of evil by redefining omnipotence. It reacts against classical theodicies in which God appears unaffected by suffering.

Process theology depicts God as a 'co-sufferer' who is intimately involved with the world. The different understanding of God's omnipotence derives from process theology's view that creation was not *ex nihilo* (out of nothing), but rather the achievement of order out of a pre-existing chaos. This limits God's power, since this pre-existing, chaotic world was not totally subject to God's will. God is depicted not as a powerful, almighty despot but rather as someone who creates by persuasion and lures things into being. In this view, evil occurs when these goals are not realised; God cannot simply intervene to stop natural evils, such as the growth of cancerous cells.

Some religious believers believe that God suffers when human beings are given free will

Free will as a divine absence: faith after the Holocaust

The Holocaust (1941–45) represents the ultimate challenge for the free will argument. There have been various responses by theologians to the Holocaust to try to make sense of what happened in the light of a belief in God. The Orthodox Jewish theologian Eliezer Berkovitz addressed God's apparent absence during these atrocities in his work, *Faith After the Holocaust* (1973).

Berkovitz argued that God 'had to create the possibility for evil' to allow for the existence of its opposites: goodness and love. In explaining the Holocaust, Berkovitz used the notion of freedom; with freedom is responsibility to act independently of God. However, Berkovitz used the idea of 'the hiding of the face' of God (*hester panim*) found in Isaiah 45:15: 'Truly you are a God who has been hiding himself, the God and Saviour of Israel.'

For Berkovitz, God could be considered 'saviour' as well as 'hiding' from his people. There is no inconsistency because the hiding is not due to cruel indifference to the situation or pure cold-heartedness; rather, the absence of presence is the price to pay for the bestowing of free will upon humanity. For people to have meaningful free will there needs to be a space between themselves and God. People must decide for themselves whether to follow their evil or righteous inclinations. Helen Gwynne-Kinsey summarises Berkovitz's position:

> This particular justification of evil is known as the free will defence, and Berkovitz makes very particular use of it in relation to the experiences of the Jewish people. God must 'absent himself from history' he writes, and not intervene even when this freedom is grossly misused. Hence the Holocaust should be understood as a manifestation of evil; a tragedy inflicted on the Jewish people by the Nazis. Yet divine intervention did not occur because God had bestowed free will on human beings at the time of creation.

In conclusion, the existence of free will necessitates a nuanced understanding of the divine attributes in the face of evil. For classical theodicists and thinkers like Swinburne and Berkovitz, God's omnipotence is expressed through a deliberate, self-imposed restraint; an absence that is required for human agency to be genuine. In this view, God's omnibenevolence remains intact because evil is identified as a human deviation from the divine pattern, rather than a divine creation.

From a different perspective, process theology resolves the link between God and evil by redefining omnipotence entirely, suggesting that God's goodness is found in his role as a co-sufferer who lures the world towards order. Ultimately, whether through the self-limitation of the sovereign Creator or the persuasive influence of a co-sufferer, free will serves as the primary mechanism for reconciling the reality of a fractured world with a God who is both all-powerful and all-loving.

Specification content

The implications of free will on religious belief: the use of prayer

The use of prayer: Christianity

Building upon the reconciliation of God's nature with the existence of evil, the focus shifts from why God allows suffering to how the human agent interacts with the divine. If free will serves as the primary mechanism for a meaningful relationship between the Creator and the created, then the practice of prayer becomes a vital expression of that freedom.

For the libertarian, the use of prayer raises questions regarding the boundaries of human **autonomy of the will**. If God were to intervene directly in response to every petition, the consistency of the natural world and the independence of the human agent could be compromised. Consequently, the theological focus often moves away from prayer as a request for God to change the external world, and towards prayer as a conscious exercise of the free will – a deliberate decision to seek guidance, express gratitude or align one's personal desires with a higher divine purpose.

Key term

autonomy of the will: the idea that the will is independent

Within the Christian tradition, this involves a complex relationship between human agency and divine will. Much of the debate centres on whether prayer is an attempt to bypass human responsibility through divine intervention or a method of internal spiritual transformation. This distinction is clearly reflected in the foundational teachings of Jesus, where the emphasis remains on the believer's choice to co-operate with God's plan.

Free will as moral alignment: the Lord's Prayer

Jesus provided the foundational model for Christian prayer in the Lord's Prayer, found in a shorter form in Luke's Gospel and in the longer form used today by many Christians in Matthew 6:9–13:

> Pray then in this way:
>
> Our Father in heaven,
> hallowed be your name,
> your kingdom come,
> your will be done,
> on earth as it is in heaven.
>
> Give us this day our daily bread.
>
> And forgive us our debts,
> as we also have forgiven our debtors.
>
> And lead us not into temptation
> but deliver us from the evil one.

The prayer is structured to focus on:

- the believer's relationship with God
- God's plans for his kingdom
- the physical and spiritual needs of humanity.

For the libertarian believer, the phrase 'your will be done on earth as it is in heaven' is highly significant. It serves as a clear indication that God's will is separate from human will. By praying these words, the individual uses their free choice to seek a life that aligns with divine purpose, making it an act of voluntary co-operation rather than a forced decree.

The phrase 'Give us this day' is a recognition that God is the provider of the basic human daily needs. It is not necessarily a *request* to provide but more an *acknowledgement* that God does provide. The emphasis is on God meeting the needs that Christians have, rather than the needs they may think they have. It is also a daily request, implying a continuous dependence on God.

From a libertarian perspective, this reinforces human agency: while God provides the essential means of sustenance, the individual remains the captain of how they choose to employ that physical and spiritual energy. The gift of bread empowers the human agent, but it does not determine their subsequent moral choices.

Similarly, the request for forgiveness – 'forgive us our debts, as we also have forgiven our debtors' – implies that humanity has a choice in how to behave. It suggests that a readiness to forgive others is a natural, freely chosen response to receiving God's forgiveness. The line 'lead us not into temptation' further recognises that while humans are free to choose their actions, they possess a weakness that requires divine guidance. Here, guidance is distinguished from intervention; God provides the spiritual strength and direction, but the individual must still freely choose whether or not to follow their righteous inclinations.

Free will as persistent reliance: asking and seeking

In Luke 11:9–13, Jesus teaches that his followers should 'ask, seek and knock', suggesting that God responds to those who show total determination. This is illustrated through the parable of the Friend at Midnight: the friend persists in disturbing his neighbour and not letting the neighbour sleep until he gives him the loaves he needs. The same idea of persistence is found in the parable of the Unjust Judge: the woman persists in her petitioning to the judge until he is worn down and administers justice.

God is contrasted with the sleeping neighbour and the unjust judge. If the neighbour and judge both respond, then how much more will God? God is a willing giver, but the focus is on the total determination of the characters in the two parables. For a libertarian, this persistence is a clear exercise of the human will. It is not that a believer can force God's hand, but rather that God responds when a person is serious about relying on divine goodness and guidance.

Overall, the implication for free will is that prayer does not exist to bypass human responsibility through divine intervention, but to provide the internal spiritual support necessary for the agent to act ethically in the world.

The use of prayer: Islam

In Islam, the relationship between free will and prayer is arguably more direct, focusing on the individual's conscious choice to live in a state of submission to Allah (God). While Christian prayer often grapples with the tension of petitionary intervention, Islamic prayer (salah) is primarily an act of obedience and gratitude. The theological focus is not on persuading God to alter the external world, but on the believer exercising their free will to acknowledge their total dependence on the Creator. Within this framework, prayer is a

Nabawi mosque in Madinah – the tower (minaret) is the point from which the call to prayer is made by a muezzin (or Arabic mu'addin), the 'servant of the mosque'

positive demonstration of the will to remain spiritually awake, using the guidance provided in the Qur'an to navigate the trials of a transitory life.

Free will as absolute submission: salah in Islam

In Islam, prayer (salah) is an act of pure obedience and submission as one of the five pillars of faith. As such, it is a deliberate exercise of free will that distinguishes the believer from the non-believer. It is also an act of gratitude towards Allah, acknowledging total dependence upon Allah and a confirmation of complete and absolute trust. Prayer increases a Muslim's spiritual awareness of Allah's greatness and is also a form of personal spiritual development; however, it is not seen as a connection with Allah but rather as growth for a human being in appreciation of the deeper truth of Islam.

It would seem that prayer is solely directed from created to Creator; prayer is by no means a conversation with Allah, for there can be no such personal relationship with Allah, and prayer serves as a reminder of Allah's greatness. Once again, this reinforces the nature of the act as a positive demonstration of free will to pray. However, a reminder of Allah's greatness is needed since humans are prone to forget this in everyday living and therefore constantly need waking up from their dreamy distractions. It is no coincidence that the call to prayer in the morning often includes the phrase 'it is better to pray than to sleep'.

Key term

ummah: term used to describe the Muslim community, from a local perspective and up to and including the worldwide community of Muslims

Free will as communal identity: the ummah

As an act of collective will, prayer brings the community together both physically and spiritually. The practice of communal prayer on Fridays builds up a (religious) community demonstrating a united will among the **ummah**. Prayer is simultaneously a public demonstration of freely chosen faith but also a private act demonstrating freely chosen devotion. Prayer typifies the action tantamount of being Muslim, that is, submission. Prostration indicates submission. A Muslim is 'one who submits'. This giving of oneself totally and freely over to Allah is, as Colin Turner phrases it, to 'express one's total and utter impotence before One who is omnipotent'.

Prayer in Islam is all about complete submission of the free will to God as an act of obedience

Whether through the persistent seeking found in Christianity or the disciplined submission of Islam, the implication of free will remains a foundation for religious meaning. By establishing the individual as an autonomous moral agent, these traditions ensure that prayer is a meaningful action rather than a programmed response. Without the capacity for free choice, the act of prayer would lose its transformative power, and the relationship between the Creator and the created would be reduced to a mechanical process rather than a purposeful spiritual journey.

The implications of free will

Specification content

The implications of free will: the existence of miracles

If the capacity for free choice ensures that the relationship between the Creator and the created is a purposeful journey rather than a mechanical process, the existence of miracles presents a significant theological challenge to that autonomy. A miracle, by definition, is a divine intervention into the natural order. This raises the same dilemma found in petitionary prayer: if God steps in to alter the course of history, does God override the freedom of human agents or the consistency of the world they inhabit? To address this, scholars must reconcile the concept of an interventionist God with the libertarian requirement for human responsibility.

Free will as a divine self-restraint: Swinburne and protecting human autonomy

Richard Swinburne argues that miracles are not only possible but probable. For Swinburne, if natural theology suggests that a loving and compassionate God exists, it is reasonable to expect that such a God would wish to communicate with, or intervene for, his creation. He suggests that miracles act as a vehicle for revelation, confirming God's presence and authority through historical events.

Crucially, Swinburne maintains that an interventionist God does not necessarily compromise human freedom. He argues that God's restraint is a deliberate choice to preserve the integrity of human agency. Swinburne suggests that if God were constantly performing miracles to stop evil, his presence would be too obvious: 'God could tell them, but that would make His presence so manifest as to impair their freedom.'

By allowing the laws of nature to operate consistently – and only intervening sparingly – God ensures that humans remain the masters of their own moral destiny. Swinburne links this lack of constant miraculous intervention to the high value of human agency, noting: 'The less he allows men to bring about large-scale horrors, the less the freedom and responsibility he gives them.'

For Swinburne, miracles are an occasional response to prayer or a sign of divine compassion that enhances religious meaning without reducing humans to mere puppets of a divine will.

Free will as moral autonomy: Wiles and the case against intervention

A contrasting view is provided by Maurice Wiles, who argues that the concept of an interventionist God is logically inconsistent with God's nature and human freedom. In his work *God's Action in the World* (1986), Wiles adopts a more rationalist approach. He argues that if God has the power to intervene but chooses to do so only sparingly, we are left with a God who is either arbitrary or partisan.

Wiles finds it impossible to reconcile a God of love with a God who performs trivial miracles while ignoring massive human suffering. He wrote:

> If the direct action of God, independent of secondary causation, is an intelligible concept, then it would appear to have been sparingly and strangely used [...] it would seem strange that no miraculous intervention prevented Auschwitz or Hiroshima, while the purposes apparently forwarded by some of the miracles acclaimed in traditional Christian faith seem trivial by comparison.

Wiles concludes that if God intervened in some cases and not others, he would be a God 'not worthy of worship' as his actions would be unfair and suggest a preference for some individuals over others. To protect the integrity of human free will and the internal

How God would choose to save some and not others was a key inconsistency for Maurice Wiles – for example, why allow Moses to part the Red Sea, saving the Hebrews, and yet allow the genocide of the Holocaust?

consistency of the world, Wiles suggests that God's only miracle was the act of creation itself. Like Aristotle's Prime Mover, Wiles' God brings the world into being but does not intervene thereafter, ensuring that the burden of moral responsibility remains entirely with humanity.

The debate between Swinburne and Wiles highlights the central tension within the libertarian position. For Swinburne, miracles are expressions of divine love that, because they are rare, respect human freedom. For Wiles, the only way to safeguard both human autonomy and the character of God is to reject the idea of direct intervention altogether. Ultimately, the existence of miracles forces the religious believer to decide whether God is an active participant in history or the silent architect of a world where human choice is the only remaining power.

Summary

- Libertarianism establishes that human beings are the primary causes of their own actions, meaning individuals are uniquely accountable as moral agents.
- Since humans have the capacity to have acted otherwise, legal and social systems are justified in applying praise and blame to adult choices.
- Scholars such as Sartre, Sirigu and Rogers argue that internal intent and the drive for self-actualisation override external pressures.
- The existence of free will suggests that God's omnipotence is expressed through a self-imposed restraint to allow for genuine human agency.
- Prayer is understood not as a mechanical request for God to bypass natural laws, but as a deliberate exercise of the will to seek guidance or align the self with a divine purpose.
- Miracles represent a tension between divine intervention and human autonomy, with thinkers debating whether God must remain at a distance to ensure that human moral responsibility remains significant.

AO1 Activity

a The following summary attempts to explain the libertarian view on responsibility. You want to include the summary in an essay, but as it stands, the summary is too brief and lacks technical depth. Expand the summary by using the relevant key terms and concepts provided, which are in a random order. There may be other terms and concepts you might wish to add.

b As a group, using your knowledge of the world religion you have studied and your own research, select specific examples which illustrate the implications of free will on religious belief. Add your examples to the table and explain their implications.

Core concept of religious belief	Example (scripture, ritual or practice)	Implication of free will
The origin of suffering and evil		
The nature of ultimate reality/God		
The purpose of spiritual practice (prayer/meditation)		
The possibility of intervention (miracles)		

Refer to the higher band descriptors for A Level (Eduqas/WJEC), which you should be aspiring towards. Aim to make your summary show 'thorough, accurate and relevant knowledge' in addition to 'thorough and accurate reference made to sacred texts and sources of wisdom'.

Key terms and concepts

mauvaise foi	parietal cortex	simulation of consequences
internal intent	facticity	congruence
existence precedes essence	FFP	active agency
actualising tendency	radical freedom	internal simulation

Summary

Libertarians argue that because people are free, they are the only ones responsible for what they do. Sartre says that since there is no God to give us a blueprint, people must create their own meaning. If people blame their past, he says they are being dishonest. From a scientific side, Sirigu found a part of the brain that handles the desire to act, which means people aren't just reacting to things like robots. Rogers adds that people have a natural desire to get better and reach their potential, which means they can choose to move past the way they were raised.

This section covers AO2 content and skills

Specification content

The extent to which free moral agents should follow a normative ethic

Issues for analysis and evaluation

The extent to which free moral agents should follow a normative ethic

Possible line of argument	Critical analysis and evaluation
Libertarians argue that because a person possesses genuine free will, they can adopt a normative ethic as a 'road map'. Sirigu's research into the parietal cortex identifies internal intent, which suggests a person can consciously choose to align their behaviour with a teleological system like utilitarianism.	Sartre rejects the idea that a person should follow pre-set norms like natural law. He argues that existence precedes essence, so there is no objective moral blueprint. If a moral agent follows a fixed ethical system without freely choosing to do so, they are acting in *mauvaise foi*, denying their radical freedom.
From a psychological perspective, Rogers suggests that following a normative ethic, perhaps virtue ethics, can assist the actualising tendency. By providing a stable framework for social interaction, an ethical code helps a moral agent to achieve congruence between their perceived self and their actions.	Rogers warns that if an ethic imposes rigid conditions of worth, it hinders growth. A person following a code like divine command theory only for social or divine acceptance loses their authenticity. A normative ethic should only be followed if it allows each person to continue making free choices.
For a moral agent who accepts that they have radical freedom, a normative ethic provides a framework for the necessary internal simulation of consequences. Given that a person is entirely responsible for their choices, ethical systems act as a safeguard, ensuring that active agency promotes social well-being rather than random impulses.	Sirigu's research confirms the biological capacity for choice but cannot provide a moral 'should'. While science identifies the mechanism of choice, it does not establish ethical obligations. Therefore, an authentic choice must be made by the moral agent rather than being dictated by a predetermined deontological system.
It can be argued that *should* implies *can*; since a moral agent has the free will to choose their path, they have a duty to choose a virtuous one. Natural law might provide the clarity needed to transform raw freedom into purposeful action.	Critics argue that a universal normative ethic is impossible if freedom is radical. If every moral agent is a 'free legislator' – meaning their choices set a moral standard for themselves and others – then any *should* must come from within. Following a system like divine command theory, grasping for security over authenticity, is a failure of responsibility.

Possible line of argument	Critical analysis and evaluation
Ultimately, a normative ethic is a valuable resource for guidance. Whether through Rogers' congruence or Sartre's authenticity, an ethic is only useful in so far as it is freely and consciously chosen by an agent who acknowledges their total responsibility.	The tension remains between social order and radical autonomy. While Sirigu's research and Rogers' psychological libertarianism allow for the possibility of a moral agent choosing to follow an ethic to improve their lives, Sartre points out that when an ethic becomes a compulsion, a moral agent ceases to be truly free.

AO2 Activity

a Analyse three possible conclusions that could be drawn from the critical analysis and evaluation of the extent to which free moral agents should follow a normative ethic. Select evidence and examples to support each of the three conclusions. Select one conclusion that you think is the **most convincing** and explain why it is so.

b Now contrast this with the **weakest** conclusion of the three. Justify your argument with clear reasoning and evidence.

Refer to the band descriptors for A2 (WJEC) or A Level (Eduqas) and in particular the demands described in band 5, which requires 'confident and perceptive critical analysis and thorough, highly effective evaluation of the issue' with a 'well-constructed and sustained argument, fully supported by evidence and examples'.

Exam practice

Below is an example of part of an evaluation of the degree to which free will makes the use of prayer irrelevant.

Sample answer

If humans have free will and autonomy, it seems that interventionist prayer (requesting for God to interfere in history) is redundant. If God intercedes, human agency is compromised. However, Luke's Gospel, in the parable of the Friend at Midnight, encourages persistence in prayer, implying God responds to human seeking. This creates a tension between the requirement for human effort and the hope for divine response.

In Hinduism, the *atman* is a free agent accumulating karma. Prayer is often less about asking for change and more about the choice to achieve moksha. Similarly, in Sikhism, the goal is to use free will to become a *gurmukh* rather than a *manmukh*. Here, prayer aligns the individual's will with the divine will.

For Christians, persistence in prayer can also be understood as seeking the Holy Spirit. The Lord's Prayer focuses on 'Thy will be done,' aligning human intent with the divine. Guidance is therefore distinct from intervention; the believer remains a free agent but seeks spiritual strength to navigate life.

Specification content

The degree to which free will makes the use of prayer irrelevant

Judge

The paragraph identifies the central conflict, weighing the evidence for both autonomy and divine interaction.

Explorer

This section maps how traditions use prayer to transform the agent rather than the environment.

Detective

Evidently, as described here, a believer can retain their freedom of action while using prayer to find guidance and align their life choices with God's will.

News reporter

A different understanding of prayer: submission serves as a positive demonstration of free will.

Islam's salah provides another example of prayer that does not conflict with freedom. It is an exercise of free will used to show obedience, acknowledging dependence on Allah. As Colin Turner notes, it allows the believer to express 'total and utter impotence' before the omnipotent, reinforcing choice through disciplined devotion.

Philosopher

This paragraph balances the claims of Wiles and Swinburne, exposing the logical challenges of an interventionist worldview.

Philosophically, Wiles argues that an interventionist God is logically inconsistent. If God answers trivial prayers but ignores atrocities, God is 'arbitrary'. Conversely, Swinburne suggests intervention demonstrates God's love, arguing that any perception of God's unfairness is merely a result of limited human rationality failing to grasp a complex divine plan.

Critical thinker

This identifies the freedom involved in choosing to engage with God or the path of the Buddha.

With free will, prayer is a choice to engage with the divine rather than a predetermined act. If an agent is truly free, their prayer must be an authentic expression of that freedom. Similarly, a Buddhist exercises 'right effort' – the conscious discipline of the mind – to become the 'architect of their fate', choosing to move towards enlightenment through their own karma.

Judge

The argument identifies that for freedom to be real, the consequences of actions must be permitted to play out without interference.

Miracles, often the sought-after goal of prayer, remain a challenge. If, to allow for moral growth, the world must be a 'predictable environment', frequent interventions in the form of miracles would risk making human choices meaningless. Therefore, many argue God remains at an epistemic distance, allowing humans the space to succeed or fail on their own merits.

News reporter

Prayer is a communal power-move that reinforces a group's collective free will to do good.

Communal prayer also acts as a social reinforcement of free agency. By gathering together, believers remind one another of shared values and collective responsibility. This transforms prayer from a private 'wish list' into a public declaration of intent and a commitment to moral action.

Critical thinker

Tennis player

The conclusion works well, evaluating the purpose of prayer against the reality of autonomy.

Ultimately, prayer's relevance depends on its purpose. If viewed as a request to bypass the laws of nature, it conflicts with radical freedom. However, as an act of alignment or affirmation, it remains a vital expression of human choice. As Gandhi suggested, it is perhaps 'egotistical' to think God plans the day around us.

Over to you

Read the following guidelines and then write an answer, under timed conditions, to the question requiring an evaluation of libertarianism and the importance of ideas about right and wrong.

When you have completed the task, refer to the band descriptors for A2 (WJEC) or A Level (Eduqas) and, in particular, look at the demands described in the higher band descriptors, which you should be aspiring towards. Ask yourself the following questions:

- Is my answer a confident critical analysis and perceptive evaluation of the issue?
- Is my answer a response that successfully identifies and thoroughly addresses the issues the question raises?
- Does my work show an excellent standard of coherence, clarity and organisation?
- Will my work, when developed, contain thorough, sustained and clear views that are supported by extensive, detailed reasoning and/or evidence?

- Have I used the views of scholars/schools of thought extensively, appropriately and in context?
- Does my answer convey a confident and perceptive analysis of the nature of any possible connections with other elements of my course?
- Is the specialist language and vocabulary both thorough and accurate?

Guidelines

1. It is important practice to read the question very carefully and highlight any words the examiner has used which will help to guide your evaluation. Here, think about the words 'clearly shows' and 'are important'. How might those help you to focus your response?
2. Make an initial list of arguments or lines of reasoning. It does not need to be in any particular order.
3. Add relevant scholars, quotations and supporting evidence.
4. Consider the order in which you would like to present the information.
5. Use what you have written to make an essay plan.
6. Use the plan to write your essay under timed conditions.
7. If you can, swap your response with somebody else. Read and mark the response. This collaboration can help you to see alternative perspectives and possibly things you may have missed. It also helps highlight the strengths of your response and of other responses.

Question

'Libertarianism clearly shows that human ideas about right and wrong are important.' Evaluate this view.

Glossary

absolutist: someone who believes in absolutism, a standard of right and wrong that is fully and totally binding on all human beings; describes something connected with absolutism

active euthanasia: a deliberate action taken to end life, such as administering a lethal dose of medication

actual self: the view that an individual has of themselves as a result of life experience

actualising tendency: an innate directional tendency in each person to grow and seek new and varied experiences

act utilitarianism: a form of utilitarianism associated with Bentham that treats each moral situation as unique and applies the hedonic calculus to each act to see if it fulfils the principle of utility – any action is right if it produces the greatest happiness for the greatest number

aesthetic: related to the concept and appreciation of beauty

***agape*:** Greek word for pure, unconditional love

***aheb*:** Hebrew word for love that is seen to be similar to the idea of *agape*

***akrasia*:** incontinent – lacking self-restraint and uncontrolled

***akrates*:** one who is weak-willed and overcome by vices

altruism: selfless concern for the well-being of others

Animal Aid: a charity founded in 1977 that promotes animal welfare through legal and non-violent means, and argues against the use of animals for medical research

anti-abortion: against abortion

antinomianism: a theory of ethics that does not recognise the authority of established rules or principles – from the ancient Greek words *anti* (against) and *nomos* (law) – lawless

apparent goods: actions or objects that the moral agent wrongly reasons are good – they satisfy desires but contradict one or more primary precepts – ultimately leading the agent away from their true purpose *(telos)*

applied ethics: the debates that arise when ethical issues are considered

***a priori*:** from Latin, meaning 'from what comes before'; refers to knowledge or reasoning that is gained without needing experience or observation

aretaic: relating to the moral qualities or virtues of a person or agent; from the Greek *arete* meaning virtue. An aretaic question would be, 'Is this person good or evil?'

aretaic ethics: another term for virtue theory

arete (plural, ***aretai***)**: a** Greek word meaning virtue

argument from queerness: J.L. Mackie's view that Intuitionism is too odd to accept

***arhat*:** the worthy one who is in the final stage of rebirth and has full control of the will

Arminianism: the doctrinal teachings of Jacobus Arminius and his followers who argued for free will and that Christ died for everyone rather than just the elect

ascetic: a person who lives a life of strict self-discipline

asylum seeker: a person who is seeking refuge from a life-threatening situation

***atma*:** the Sikh term for soul

***atman*:** the Hindu term for soul

atonement: Christian doctrine concerning the reconciliation of God and humankind, accomplished through the life, suffering and death of Christ

autonomy of the will: the idea that the will is independent

beatific vision: the teleological end of Natural Law according to Aquinas whereby one is united with God through Christ

Beatitude: blessing given by Jesus for certain personal virtues

behaviourism: a theory of learning based on the idea that all behaviours can be explained without the need to consider internal mental states or consciousness; also known as behavioural psychology

bigotry: intolerance and narrow-mindedness

biological determinism: the view that human behaviour is controlled by genes and other biological factors

blastocyst: a group of multiplying cells

Calvinism: a branch of Protestantism based on the theological beliefs promoted by John Calvin; it is also referred to as Reformed Protestantism or the Reformed tradition

Campaign for Nuclear Disarmament (CND): a pressure group formed in 1957

casuistry: the art of applying key principles to an ethical case

***Catechism*:** a formal summary of Christian beliefs and moral teachings, traditionally used for religious instruction

categorical imperative: Kant's view of an unconditional moral obligation which is binding in all circumstances and is not dependent on a person's inclination or purpose

***causa sui*:** something that is independent of cause

***chesed*:** Hebrew word that describes an exclusive kind of love in a particular relationship

claims: Prichard's term for arguments put together from general reasoning

cognition: the mental action or process of acquiring knowledge and understanding through thought, experience, and the senses

cognitive neuroscience: scientific study of the biological processes and neural connections in the brain

cognitivism: the philosophical view that sentences express meaningful propositions

community ethos: the character or spirit of a community

compatibilism: the theory that freedom and determinism are mutually compatible in the case of some human actions. There is no logical inconsistency in believing in both

compersion: taking joy in a partner's happiness with another partner

concrete universal: Bradley's view that the self is not isolated but is derived from dialectical relations with the world

concupiscence: strong desire for earthly pleasures; stemming from Adam's first sin, it is not itself a sin but inclines human beings towards sin

conditional predestination: the complex theological notion based upon the idea that free will and predestination are compatible

conditioning: a theory that the reaction to an object or event by a person can be determined by stimuli

congruence: a state of harmony between the real self and the ideal self

conscience: traditionally an internal, intuitive guide to good or bad; Joseph Fletcher reinterpreted this notion as a description of ethical action

consequentialist: refers to the theory that the morality of an action is based on the outcomes it produces

courage: a cardinal virtue involving physical, moral or spiritual endurance and strength of character

Decalogue: a term for the Ten Commandments

deontic: relating to duty and obligation in moral reasoning; from the Greek *deon* meaning duty. A deontic question would be, 'Is this action right or wrong?'

deontological: concerned with obligation or duty

Descartes' principle of scepticism: that doubt can be resolved through challenge

descriptive: term used as a criticism of naturalism that it can only describe and not be prescriptive

despotism: Bradley's understanding of absolute power or the ultimate controlling all

determinism: the doctrine that the past determines a unique future; every event, including human action is determined by previously existing causes

deterrent: a thing that discourages or is intended to discourage someone from doing something

dharma: the notion of moral and religious obligation

dialectical synthesis: Hegel's view that two opposite views (hypothesis, antithesis) can be united (synthesis) through philosophical analysis; for example: hypothesis 'the universe began with the Big Bang'; antithesis 'God created the world'; synthesis 'God was the first cause and is compatible with the Big Bang'

dissection: the action of cutting open a body or plant to study its internal parts

divine concurrence: the idea that God participates in every human action by providing the powers and abilities to act, without determining what the person chooses to do

DNA: deoxyribonucleic acid, the hereditary material in humans; nearly every cell in a person's body has the same DNA and it carries genetic instructions

doctrine of double effect: a term to describe an ethical method of interpretation first identified in Aquinas' treatment of killing in self-defence

double predestination: God determines both those who will be saved and those who will be damned

duty: Bradley's view that ethical awareness develops through self-realisation as people interact with society and nature and recognise their station (our role and function within it)

dynamic power: the way in which a word can express or arouse feelings; according to Stevenson, language is best understood by looking at this power to move the listener rather than just its literal definition

dynamic use: Stevenson's view that ethical language is used actively to influence attitudes and behaviour, not just to describe

economic migrant: a person who seeks out a better standard of life through migration

ectopic pregnancy: a pregnancy where the embryo embeds itself 'out of place' (ectopic), most often in the fallopian tube, endangering the life of both fetus and pregnant person

elect, the: those people chosen to salvation, by the grace of God

embryo: an animal in the early stage of development before birth; in humans, the embryo stage is the first two months after conception

emotive meaning: the tendency of a word to produce or express feelings and attitudes rather than to describe facts

emotivism: theory that ethical propositions are simply expressions of approval or disapproval

empirical: based on observation or experience rather than theory or pure logic

empiricism: the idea that people gain knowledge gained through their senses

***enkrates*:** one who is tempted, but strong, and lives in the mean

epistemology: philosophy of knowledge derived from the Greek *episteme* (knowledge) and *logos* (words or discussion)

ethical autonomy: the view that human reason is capable of discovering or creating moral laws independently

ethical egoism: the normative view that holds that all action ought to be motivated by self-interest

ethical naturalism: the view that ethical propositions can be understood by analysing the natural world

ethical non-naturalism: an alternative term for Intuitionism

ethics: from the Greek *ethike* meaning habit or behaviour and closely related to the word *ethos*; a study of the framework of guiding principles that direct an action

***ethos*:** a Greek word meaning the character of a person, as expressed in habits and behaviour

***être-en-soi*:** inanimate matter and being without consciousness, a being-in-itself

***être-pour-autrui*:** Sartre's new dimension in which the self exists as an object for others, a 'being-for-others'

être-pour-soi: the authentic self in the process of becoming, a being-for-itself

eudaimonia: a Greek word used by Aristotle to define the end purpose of human life as happiness, flourishing or fulfilment

euthanasia: literally meaning a gentle or easy death, it is the act of intentionally ending a person's life to relieve their suffering and help them to die with dignity

existentialism: a philosophy that proposes the individual is free and responsible to determine their own development

external act: the physical action itself

external cause: when a person's will is stopped from carrying out its predetermined choice

facticity: the brute, unavoidable facts of a person's life (e.g. place of birth, height) that they cannot change, but which do not define their freedom

Fall, the: the events of Genesis chapter 3, where Adam and Eve face God's punishment for disobeying his divine command not to eat of the fruit from the tree of knowledge of good and evil

fatalism: the belief that all events are destined to occur regardless of human choices

***fides et ratio*:** Latin for faith and reason

fetus: the unborn baby; in humans, the fetus stage lasts from the end of the eighth week after conception (when the major structures have formed) until birth

***finis operantis*:** the intention behind the act

***finis operis*:** the act-in-itself

fortitude: a cardinal virtue involving physical, moral or spiritual endurance, courage and strength of character

fully functioning person (FFP): a congruent individual who participates fully in the richness of life experience

gap: the distance between a person's consciousness and the physical world that necessitates people to have free will

general reasoning: using the empirical evidence around us to present logical argument

general revelation: knowledge about God discovered through natural means such as reasoning or observation of the physical universe

genes: the units of heredity in an organism; the region of DNA that influences a particular characteristic of an organism

genome: the genetic material of an organism; an organism's complete genetic code

God's grace: the love and mercy given to humanity by God because God desires humanity to have it, not because of anything humanity has done to deserve it

greatest happiness principle: the utilitarian idea that the happiness and unhappiness each action will cause should be calculated to assess the best course to take

***gurmukh*:** being God-centred and spiritual

hard determinism: the doctrine that determinism is true and hence no human actions are free

hedonism: an ethical theory that defines what is right in terms of pleasure

heresy: a belief that is contrary to orthodox Christian theology/dogma

heretic: a person whose beliefs are against the laws and beliefs of a specific religion

***hexis*:** a Greek word meaning a person's manner of behaviour

homosexuality: being sexually attracted to people of one's own sex

Human Genome Project: an international scientific research project with the goal of determining the sequences that make up human DNA, and of identifying and mapping all the genes of the human genome from both a physical and a functional standpoint

Hume's fork: the principles of *a priori* knowledge (conceptual and prior to experience) and *a posteriori* knowledge (relating to experience) are completely separate types of knowledge

Hume's law: that an *ought* cannot be derived from an *is*

'hurrah-boo!' theory: another term for the theory of emotivism

ideal self: an individual's aspiration of who they want to become

immigration: the movement of population into a country for residence (short-term or long-term)

indifferent universe: the pagan view that fate is impersonal and the gods are unconcerned with individual human destinies

infallibility: without error

innate: part of, integral to

interest theory: Stevenson's theory of emotivism

internal act: the motive or choice of the will

internal cause: internalised moral choice (or the person's will to do something) that is completely determined

intrinsic evil: an act that is always evil no matter what the circumstances

intrinsic goods: acts that are always good no matter what the circumstances

intrinsic value: the worth something has in itself, for its own sake, rather than as a means to an end

intuition: immediate knowledge or understanding without conscious reasoning or proof.

irreducible: cannot be broken down into further parts

jurisprudence: the philosophy of law as presented by a normative (rule-setting) legal system

justice: a cardinal virtue involving guidance in how people act towards others

justification: the declaring of a person to be just or righteous

***kamma*:** the notion of individual responsibility for our thoughts that lead to actions

kenotic: from the Greek *kenosis*, meaning to empty or make oneself completely receptive to something

legalism: an approach to ethics that accepts the absolute nature of established rules or principles

***liberium arbitrium*:** free will

***libertas*:** the freedom to choose good over evil

limited atonement: the view that Christ died for the sins of the elect only and no atonement was provided for the reprobate

logical positivism: school of Western philosophy that sought to legitimise philosophical discussion by arguing philosophical language should be based on scientific language

logical positivists: philosophers who believe that a statement's truth and meaning must be testable in the real world

magisterium: the authority of the Roman Catholic Church in maintaining authentic interpretation of the Bible and sacred Roman Catholic tradition headed by the Pope and Bishops and supported by a body of scholars

Manichaeism: a belief in two equally forceful powers of light and darkness in constant battle against each other

***massa peccati*:** Latin for 'lump of sin'; humanity as a condemned mass due to Adam's sin

master: the state of being a self-governing moral agent

***mauvaise foi*:** bad faith, but better understood as self-deception

maxim: a general rule

mean: the rationally determined balance between the two extremes of excess and deficiency; also known as the 'golden' mean

medical abortion: abortion by means of the abortion pill

meta-ethics: the debates that arise when the *nature* of ethics is considered

middle knowledge (MK): a theory developed by Luis de Molina, a Spanish Jesuit priest, that God is aware of every computation of possible choices

migrant: a person who moves from one country to another

moral: a term used to describe ethical behaviour

moral agent: an individual who possesses the rational capacity to distinguish between right and wrong and is, therefore, held accountable for their voluntary actions

moral reasoning: application of intuition

naturalistic fallacy: Moore's view that it is a logical error to explain that which is good reductively in terms of natural properties such as 'pleasant' or 'desirable'

***néant*:** the no-thingness of consciousness; because consciousness has no fixed essence, it is free to determine itself

***nibbana*:** the term for enlightenment, ultimately beyond all notions of determinism and free will

non-metaphysical moral realism: an alternative term for intuitionism

non-sensuous moral ideal: Bradley's term for Kant's general theory of duty

non-voluntary euthanasia: the person is unable to express a wish (e.g., in a persistent vegetative state), and the decision is made by others in their best interest.

normative ethics: the debates that arise when ethical theories are considered (normative refers to norms of behaviour – how people should behave)

objective: describes something that is based on evidence rather than personal views

omnibenevolence: being all-loving

omnipotence: the attribute of being all-powerful; in DCT, this implies God is not limited by any external moral law

omnipotent being: a being with unlimited power

ontic evil: physical natural evil such as the fact of death, disease, pain and suffering

operant conditioning: learning through rewards and punishments

original sin: the sin committed by Adam in the Garden of Eden; more particularly, the doctrine that sin is inherent to human nature because of the original sin by Adam

origination: the bringing about of decisions and actions in such a way that they are not effects from a chain of cause and effect; the decisions/actions are in the control of the person

other-regarding: actions, duties, or considerations that concern the welfare, interests or rights of other people rather than oneself

parietal cortex: one of the four major lobes of the cerebral cortex in the brain containing grey matter that transforms visual information into motor commands

passive euthanasia: withdrawing or withholding life-prolonging treatment (e.g., turning off a ventilator), allowing the patient to die from their underlying condition

Pelagian controversy: the debate concerning how people obtain righteousness

***phronesis*:** practical wisdom

platitude: a moral comment that has been used too often to be meaningful; cliché

Platonists: those asserting, in agreement with Plato, that the phenomena of the world are an imperfect and transitory reflection of the eternal reality of the ideal forms

polyamorous: having a (loving) sexual relationship with more than one individual with the knowledge and consent of all partners

potential: the possibility, at conception, of becoming a human person

predestination: the belief that God determines human destiny in advance

preliminaries: gathering of claims

pre-moral evil: physical natural evil such as the fact of death, disease, pain and suffering

premotor cortex: a specific region within the frontal lobe of the brain that is involved in planning and initiating movement

prevenient grace: God's grace that precedes each human moral decision, associated with the Holy Spirit

prevolitional: prior to any act of God's will; describing knowledge that God possesses before choosing to act or create

***prima facie*:** first impression; accepted as correct until proved otherwise

primary precepts: Aquinas' five principles: preserve innocent life, orderly living in society, worship God, educate children, reproduce to continue the species

principle of utility: an action is right if it promotes and maximises happiness

process theology: the argument that the problem of evil is removed by redefining the meaning of God's omnipotence

pro-choice: supporting women's reproductive rights (including the right to have an abortion)

proportionalism: an approach to Natural Law that focuses in particular on the fourth condition of the doctrine of double effect as outlined by Thomas Aquinas

proportionate reason: reasoning that ensures evil that occurs is compensated and subsumed by a greater good

proposition: statement

propositions about attitude: views or value judgements about statements of belief

propositions about belief: statements of fact or verifiable by empirical means

Protestant Reformation: a sixteenth-century European movement aimed initially at reforming the beliefs and practices of the Roman Catholic Church

providence: the theological idea that God is closely involved in monitoring and guiding the created world

prudence: a cardinal virtue involving sound judgement

pseudo-concepts: things that are treated as concepts but can only be mentally apprehended and not empirically verified

psychological egoism: the descriptive view that all human action is motivated by self-interest

Rahit Maryada: the Sikh code of ethical conduct

rationalistic moralism: the theory that morality is purely accessible through reason and has no need for God

real goods: actions that the moral agent correctly reasons will fulfil a natural human inclination (primary precept) and help them move closer to the ultimate perfection in the image of God

realism: the view that an object exists in reality independently of our mind

***reflet*:** the reflection that is self-conscious

refugee: a person who has sought refuge from a life-threatening situation and been granted asylum

reincarnation: transmigration of a metaphysical soul from one body or form to another that takes place at the point of death

relational factors: different interpretations of the same words or terms, depending on the viewpoint of the observer

relativist: someone who believes in relativism, an ethical system that believes there is no absolute right or wrong; describes something connected with relativism

relativistic: this means there are no universal moral norms or rules and that each situation has to be looked at independently because each situation is different

Remonstrance: the forceful protest of the Arminians of the Dutch Reformed Church in 1610 to the Staten-Generaal in the Netherlands

reprobates, the: those people, untouched by God's grace, left to be consumed by the defect of concupiscence

revisionists: those scholars who support Proportionalism

rule utilitarianism: a view associated with John Stuart Mill; rule utilitarians believe that by using the principle of utility (the greatest happiness for the greatest number) one can draw up general rules, based on past experiences, which will help to uphold this principle

samsara: the continuous cycle of birth, life, death, and rebirth (reincarnation)

sanctification: the state of proper functioning; living according to God's design and purpose

sanctity of life: the belief that life is sacred or holy, given by God

secondary precepts: deduced from the primary precepts, these apply to specific situations

self-evident: describes something (e.g. a proposition) that needs no verification and remains a truth independently of whether or not people perceive it as so

self-realisation: Bradley's view that, through a philosophical course of discovery, the self interacts with society and nature, and ends with a realisation of its identity and ethical role within the world

situation ethics: a relativist theory of ethics sometime referred to as situationism developed by Fletcher

single predestination: God determines only those who will be saved

***sophia*:** philosophical wisdom

***sophron*:** one who effortlessly lives according to the mean

soteriology: a quest to discover what the requirements for salvation are

sovereignty: supreme and absolute power

sovereignty of God: the teaching that all things are under God's rule and control; God is sovereign both in principle and practice

station: Bradley's term to acknowledge the location, role and function of a human being in the social and natural world

strong rule utilitarianism: a strong rule utilitarian believes that any rules formulated and established through the application of the principle of utility should never be broken as they guarantee happiness for society

subjective: describes something that is based on a personal view

***sui generis*:** a Latin phrase meaning 'of its own kind'

***summum bonum*:** Latin for the highest good, which for Aquinas is perfect fellowship with God

surgical abortion: abortion by means of the suction method

synod: an assembly of church clergy of a particular church

***tabula rasa*:** Latin for 'a clean slate' and refers to the peripatetic axiom – the idea that we're born with no built-in knowledge and learn everything through experience

tautology: saying the same thing twice over in different words

teleological: concerned with the end purpose or goal of an action

***telos*:** a Greek word meaning 'end', 'goal' or 'purpose'; in ethics, it refers to the ultimate aim or outcome that an action is directed towards

temperance: a cardinal virtue involving balance and restraint

theological voluntarism: an ethical approach whereby morality is based on the will of God

traditionalists: those scholars who support the magisterium, the traditional authority of the Roman Catholic Church

transcendental idealism: Emmanuel Kant's complex philosophy found in the *Critique of Pure Reason* (1781, 1787) that rejects the notion of objective empiricism and argues that our experiences of things are only 'sensible forms of our intuition'

ummah: term used to describe the Muslim community, from a local perspective and up to and including the worldwide community of Muslims

underivative: not dependent on or derived from something else, a simple concept

Understanding Animal Research (UAR): a society that explains why animals are used in medical and scientific research

universalisability: Mill's utilitarian principle that everyone ought to aim at the happiness of everyone, as increasing the general happiness will increase individual happiness

unreflective consciousness: Prichard's explanation that intuition is not determined by philosophical reflection

utilitarianism: theory first outlined by Bentham and then developed by Mill stating that people ought to aim to produce the greatest amount of pleasure/happiness and the least amount of pain

values and disvalues: a proportionalist way of calculating elements of a moral event

verification principle: the claim, made by logical positivists such as A.J. Ayer, that a statement is only meaningful if it is either analytically true (true by definition) or empirically verifiable through sense experience

Veritatis Splendor: a papal encyclical published in 1993 by Pope John Paul II

vivisection: the practice of performing operations on live animals for the purpose of experimentation or scientific research, generally – but not always – done today with anaesthetised animals

volitions: mind processes that initiate action – the will

voluntary euthanasia: The person expresses a competent and conscious wish to die

weak rule utilitarianism: a weak rule utilitarian tries to allow for the fact that, in some situations, breaking a rule (originally created because it generally fulfils the principle of utility) may be the right course of action; in a particular situation, breaking a rule (rather than obeying the rule) may make it more likely that the principle of utility is fulfilled

Wolfenden Report: a report published by the government in 1957; it recommended the decriminalisation of sexual acts between consenting men over the age of 21 in private, and the strengthening of laws against prostitution and soliciting; it established a key distinction between private moral conduct and public order under the law

zygote: a cell formed by the union of a male sex cell (a sperm) and a female sex cell (an ovum), which develops into an embryo according to information encoded in its genetic material

Index

Photo credits

Photos reproduced by permission of: **p.9** © M-image/stock.adobe.com; **p.15** © Zev Radovan/Alamy Stock Photo; **p.21** © Panos/stock.adobe.com; **p.24** © Carlo Bollo/Alamy Stock Photo; **p.25** © Gibon Art/Penta Springs Limited/ Alamy Stock Photo; **p.27** © Pavel Losevsky/stock.adobe.com; **p.44** © Imran Khan's Photography/Shutterstock.com; **p.46** *tl* © Bizoo_n/stock.adobe.com, *bl* © Lebrecht_Lebrecht Music & Arts/ W H Eves/Alamy Stock Photo; **p.47** *tr* © Natata/Shutterstock.com, *br* © Gl0ck/Shutterstock.com; **p.48** © Fizkes/stock.adobe.com; **p.49** Pictorial Press Ltd/Alamy Stock Photo; **p.51** © Ron Ellis/Shutterstock.com; **p.52** © Gorodenkoff/stock.adobe.com; **p.57** © Pictorial Press Ltd/Alamy Stock Photo; **p.59** © Cavan/stock.adobe.com; **p.60** © Boonchok/stock.adobe.com; **p.62** © MarekPhotoDesign.com/stock.adobe.com; **p.63** © Sripfoto/stock.adobe.com; **p.69** © Mario Breda/Shutterstock.com; **p.70** Smith Archive/Alamy Stock Photo; **p.71** © LIGHTFIELD STUDIOS/stock.adobe.com; **p.72** © Monkey Business/stock.adobe.com; **p.73** © Ruansan/peopleimages.com/stock.adobe.com; **p.75** © Joe Gough/stock.adobe.com; **p.82** © Carlo Bollo/Alamy Stock Photo; **p.90** S.D. Cason Catholic Gallery, https://sdcason.com/saint-paul-by-bartolomeo-montagna-16th-century-public-domain-catholic-painting; **p.101** © fogbird/stock.adobe.com; **p.102** © Jimlop collection/Alamy Stock Photo; **p.104** © Delmaine Donson/peopleimages.com/stock.adobe.com; **p.111** *l* © Tupungato/stock.adobe.com, *r* © Marcenko/stock.adobe.com; **p.113** © Inspiring.team/stock.adobe.com; **p.114** *tl* © Lucid_dream/stock.adobe.com, *c* © JackF/stock.adobe.com, *bl* © Monkey Business/stock.adobe.com; **p.115** © Warsi/stock.adobe.com; **p.116** © Anton Shaparenko/stock.adobe.com; **p.117** © Fotogestoeber/stock.adobe.com; **p.118** © Lassedesignen/stock.adobe.com; **p.125** © Arta X/stock.adobe.com; **p.127** *c* © Godong/Alamy Stock Photo, *br* © Zatletic/stock.adobe.com; **p.128** © New Africa/stock.adobe.com; **p.129** © Derenskaya/Shutterstock.com; **p.132** © Kathleen Johnson/Shutterstock.com; **p.145** © Somchaisom/stock.adobe.com; **p.146** © Jorisvo/stock.adobe.com; **p.158** © Artem/stock.adobe.com; **p.159** © De Art/stock.adobe.com; **p.165** © Godong Photo/stock.adobe.com; **p.175** © lenscap/stock.adobe.com; **p.176** © Sampajano/stock.adobe.com; **p.177** © Historic Collection/Alamy Stock Photo; **p.183** © Georgios Kollidas/stock.adobe.com; **p.191** © Fizkes/stock.adobe.com; **p.197** l © piemags/ Alamy Stock Photo, *r* © Juulijs/stock.adobe.com; **p.198** © New Africa/stock.adobe.com; **p.201** © Mirrorpix_Trinity Mirror/Alamy Stock Photo; **p.202** © Alex Segre/stock.adobe.com; **p.208** © zatletic/stock.adobe.com; **p.210** *tl* Adam Ján Figeľ/stock.adobe.com, *bl* © Irina Schmidt/stock.adobe.com; **p.212** © wizdata /stock.adobe.com; **p.214** © ART Collection; **p.215** *l* © Fine Art Images/Heritage Image Partnership/Alamy Stock Photo, *c* © Renáta Sedmáková/ stock.adobe.com, *r* © Everett Collection/Shutterstock.com; **p.218** © Mari1408 /stock.adobe.com; **p.219** © Julian/ stock.adobe.com; **p.220** *t* © Tibbut Archive/Alamy Stock Photo, *b* © Exclusively/Shutterstock.com; **p.227** *c* © BillionPhotos.com/stock.adobe.com, *b* Internet Archive, https://web.archive.org/web/20150915171113/http://www.arthermitage.org/Godfrey-Kneller/Portrait-of-John-Locke.big.html; **p.231** © The Curious Travelers/Shutterstock.com; **p.232** © Desdemona72 /stock.adobe.com; **p.234** © Georgios Kollidas /stock.adobe.com; **p.242** © Eraza Collection/Alamy Stock Photo; **p.244** *c* © History and Art Collection/Alamy Stock Photo, *b* © Hikrcn/Shutterstock.com; **p.251** © Album/Alamy Stock Photo; **p.253** © Anita Ponne/Shutterstock.com; **p.255** © mig5533/stock.adobe.com; **p.256** *t* © mbolina/stock.adobe.com, *b* © Art Collection 2/Alamy Stock Photo; **p.257** © Vlad_Chornley/stock.adobe.com; **p.258** © Ixpert/Shutterstock.com; **p.259** © Chathuporn/stock.adobe.com; **p.261** © dislentev /stock.adobe.com; **p.268** © Natata/Shutterstock.com; **p.273** © BlueRingMedia/Shutterstock.com; **p.274** © Holaillustrations/ stock.adobe.com; **p.275** © Edgars Sermulis/Alamy Stock Photo; **p.282** © Creedline/stock.adobe.com; **p.286** © blvdone/stock.adobe.com; **p.290** © efired/stock.adobe.com; **p.293** © weris7554 /stock.adobe.com; **p.295** © Sony Herdiana/stock.adobe.com; **p.296** © Diy 13/stock.adobe.com; **p.297** © Mashosh/Shutterstock.com